Zur deutschen Bischofs-Konferenz zugegen sein.
Dort werde ich die deutschen Bischöfe treffen
und mit denselben ihre Probleme besprechen. -
Da ich nicht in Fargo zur Konsekration von
Bf. Dworschak sein kann, wäre es wirklich
schön wenn Joe, Anna, und Mary hingehen
könnten. Der apostolische Delegat macht uns
die Ehre nach Fargo zu reisen. - Terry darf
sich wirklich freuen, dass die C. J. so viel
von ihr denkt, dass ohne zu fragen ihr Ge-
halt erhöht wurde. Congratulations! -
Heute machten wir einen Ausflug zum
Wann-See in der Nähe von Berlin. Es war
ein schöner Tag und verbrachten auf einem
grossen Segel-Boat einen schönen Nachmittag. -
In den nächsten Tagen werde ich mit anderen
grossen Herren zusammenkommen, um zu
sehen wie Schwierigkeiten, die die Kirche
hat, überwunden werden können. Es geht
mir wirklich sehr gut. Jedermann sucht es
für mich so angenehm als möglich zu
machen. Es ist jetzt Zeit, dass ich ins
Bett komme. - Herzlichste Grüsse und tausend-
Mal Segen.   Dein Petrus.

AMERICAN NUNCIO

Ex libris:

Newman Center (UMD)

October 1969

AMERICAN NUNCIO

Cardinal Aloisius Muench

Colman Barry, osB

COLMAN J. BARRY O.S.B.

SAINT JOHN'S UNIVERSITY PRESS

Collegeville, Minnesota

1969

Copyright 1969 © By the Order of Saint Benedict, Inc., Collegeville, Minnesota

Library of Congress Catalog Card Number: 71-83090

Printed in Saint Paul, Minnesota by the North Central Publishing Company

COMMENTS ON AMERICAN NUNCIO

This book is a monument to one of America's greatest bishops, to a man whose whole life was one of dedication to humanity in the service of the Church. Father Colman Barry has admirably succeeded in presenting with this biography not only a complete record of Cardinal Muench's life, but one at the same time which is an inspiration as it reflects every facet of his unique personality and outstanding career. The reader must love this bishop who in these pages comes to life so human and so homely. This great book will uphold his memory for generations to come that they may be proud of this first American nuncio in Church history.

Placid Max Jordan, O.S.B.
Author and Journalist, Beuron Archabbey

If I were asked to name the four people I know who have done the most in the last fifteen years to build a firm bridge of understanding between the people of the United States and the people of Germany, I would rank them in the following order: Bishop Muench, General Clay, Conrad Adenauer and Jack McCloy.

J. Anthony Panuch
Special Adviser to General Clay
American Military Governor in Germany

According to Father Barry, Aloisius Cardinal Muench was a classical product of the American Catholic ghetto, a Milwaukee German born in the late nineteenth century with all the limitations that such a background implied. He served as a seminary rector and then bishop of a small prairie diocese. No one would have thought that in the chaos of postwar Germany, with a touchy German hierarchy, an uninformed military government, and suspicious Vatican diplomats, Muench would have emerged as a skillful, vigorous papal nuncio and one of the grand architects of the resurgence of German Catholicism — a resurgence which made its way felt with great force at the Vatican Council. Father Barry asks "How could Muench have possibly done it?" and the response seems obvious enough to the reader of the book, for if Muench had all the weaknesses of the American Catholic ghetto, so too, he had all the strengths — strengths which must not be overlooked as Catholicism strives to create a new style in the post-consiliar United States. Whether the present generation will rise to its challenges as well as men like Muench did to the challenges of his generation, still must remain in doubt. But Father Barry's careful and scholarly study of the prairie prince should offer the students of American Catholicism a good deal of information on the strength of Catholicism in the United States during the first half of the present century.

Andrew M. Greeley, *Program Director,*
National Opinion Research Center, University of Chicago

Once again Father Colman Barry has made a significant contribution to the history of American Catholicism with this biography of an utterly simple yet highly intelligent and attractive churchman. The life of Cardinal Muench shows the same thoroughness of research and grasp of important issues that characterized the learned Benedictine's previous books. It does more. It demonstrates that the presidency of one of the liveliest Catholic universities in the land need be no impediment to the constructive employment of an administrator's scholarly talents and tastes if the latter has the will and energy to make it so.

In an age that has witnessed a sharp decline in the value that men set upon the traditional pomp and ceremony associated with high office in the Church — and was not that part of the explanation behind Pope John's altogether extraordinary hold upon the hearts of men — it is refreshing to read the life of an ecclesiastic whose elevated rank was never allowed to rob him of his taste for the unadorned. For like the aged pontiff who made him a cardinal, Aloisius Muench was a simple man. One can scarcely imagine a more difficult assignment for a bishop from the prairies of North Dakota than to be asked in the disastrous year of 1946 to represent the Holy See among the German people. Yet the Bishop of Fargo brought it off with notable success because, as Cardinal Jaeger, Archbishop of Paderborn, told Father Barry, "He met us with complete openness and honesty." The stricken Church trying to regain her balance in the midst of universal ruin and desolation, the highly sensitive German spokesmen for the civil and ecclesiastical orders, the frequently puzzled and sometimes blundersome representatives of the allied military occupation forces, the dedicated but fretful staff of the nunciature, the anxious pontiff in distant Rome — they are all here. And through this bewildering labyrinth walked the serene figure from one of the conquering powers with a sureness of touch and a sense of security bred of a deep inner tranquillity. Seeing the nuncio's quiet confidence, excited and harassed leaders of both Church and State felt new courage in facing the tremendous problems that beset these post-war years.

John Tracy Ellis, *Professor of Church History*
in the University of San Francisco

ACKNOWLEDGMENT

The manuscript of this book was read and evaluated by several competent critics as well as associates of Cardinal Muench. It is a pleasure to express sincere appreciation for their generous and invaluable assistance to Bishop Leo F. Dworschak of Fargo; Monsignor John Tracy Ellis, professor of Church history, University of San Francisco; Father Placid Max Jordon, O.S.B., author and journalist, Archabbey of Beuron; Fathers Gerald Weber, Joseph Senger and Raymond Lessard, priests of the Diocese of Fargo, former secretaries of Cardinal Muench in Germany and Rome; Larry Boyle, secretary in Fargo; Robert Deubel, Frankfurt, and Sister Ilga Braun, O.S.B., Bad Godesberg, former secretaries in Germany.

It is impossible to thank individually all who assisted in collecting materials across two continents. The author was granted interviews with some eighty persons in ecclesiastical, governmental and diplomatic circles in Germany, Italy and the United States. Monsignor Vincent A. Yzermans, Lawrence Merthan, Fathers Edward Malone, O.S.B., Radbert Kohlhaas, O.S.B., and Placid Jordon, O.S.B., assisted with the lengthy negotiations involved in obtaining these interviews.

Help on the manuscript in its various stages was generously supplied by Larry Boyle, Monica Canning and Gunther Rolfson, O.S.B. Typing of the manuscript was expertly done by Elaine Vogel. Frank Kacmarcik designed the book and guided it through the press. Mary L. Christiansen compiled the index. Alf T. Olsen, Fargo, generously supplied photos.

Materials for this volume were collected over an eight-year period from the first interviews with Cardinal Muench, the Muench family, the Fargo, Milwaukee, German and Roman friends and associates. At every turn the author was met with assistance and hospitality. Monsignor Allan Nilles, vicar general, and Father Albert Binder, chancellor, made the writing of the book in Fargo an unforgettable experience. Confrères and colleagues in Saint John's University with understanding encouraged research by an administrator. Father Abbot Baldwin Dworschak, O.S.B., Saint John's Abbey, generously fostered the undertaking at every stage. Bishop Leo F. Dworschak continued throughout the entire period as the primary inspiration and support which made this work possible. It is a rare privilege for an author to have such corroborators.

TABLE OF CONTENTS

INTRODUCTION

Cardinal Muench had a many-sided career. Priest, scholar, professor, dean or rector of the seminary — which was the real Aloisius Joseph Muench? When was he closest to fulfilling his vocation — as priest, bishop, apostolic visitator, papal nuncio, diplomat, statesman, or as a cardinal in curia?

It seems that his career had a regular rhythm of unexpected assignments to tasks for which he had no special preparation or background of experience — professor of dogmatic theology when his graduate program was in economics; bishop of Fargo when all his interests were centered in St. Francis Seminary; apostolic visitor in Germany when he did not have even a remote preparation for diplomatic work.

But each time when he was given a new task it quickly became evident that he was first and always the pastor of souls.

The rigors of the North Dakota climate are legendary. It seemed as though the weatherman was determined to show off the worst he had in store. For the young bishop's first winter and first summer in his new home, the weatherman provided the coldest and hottest on record!

But the climate did not discourage Bishop Muench; it merely helped to emphasize the material and spiritual needs of his people. The drought had impoverished the parishes and left many of them hopelessly in debt and all of them helpless to finance parish development. His answer was the Catholic Church Expansion Fund of the Diocese of Fargo which has since then provided an avenue of credit for the construction of churches, schools, rectories, and other institutions valued at many millions of dollars.

He saw how the harsh winter weather made attendance at Mass extremely difficult and often impossible for families scattered over wide areas. His answer was the Confraternity of Christian Doctrine for children and adults. For the children in the remote areas he invited the Sisters of Service from Toronto in Canada to conduct a correspondence course in religion.

The first item of new equipment in the chancery office was a wall map and tacks indicating the location of parishes, missions and stations distributed over the 35,000 square miles of the diocese. It was obvious that more priests were needed to serve the vast territory. That meant more seminarians and more financial aid to finance seminary costs. That meant more scholarships; the diocese had only one when he came. Many thought him naive: where can you get money to set up scholarships when you can not pay even the current seminary bills. But Bishop Muench persisted. During his eleven years in residence in Fargo the number of seminary students doubled and the scholarship endowment funds passed the quarter million mark. The number of seminarians and the funds doubled again before his death.

Even before the new bishop was installed in 1935 he accepted the offer of the National Catholic Rural Life Conference to have their convention in Fargo the next year. He had been born in a city and had no experience with life in rural areas except what he may have observed when he indulged in his favorite sports of hunting and fishing. Maybe he could not tell the difference between wheat and barley on the stem or in the bin, but he knew that the tillers of the soil were people. He knew nothing about the science of farming; but he was determined to learn everything he could about the art of living on a farm according to Christian principles and ideals. With characteristic thoroughness he studied rural sociology and economics as a means of bringing a message of faith and courage to his predominantly rural people during the dark days of drought and depression.

Twice he was elected president of the National Catholic Rural Life Conference. He collaborated with Monsignor Vincent J. Ryan and Father William T. Mulloy in editing a *Manifesto on Rural Life*.

In June, 1946, a new era began for Bishop Muench. He was sent to Germany by Pope Pius XII to serve as an apostolic visitator. The Holy Father himself defined the nature of this special mission. ". . . a farsighted representative of the Holy See, standing aside and above the controversies of the day, would be conducive to the general good."

It was a delicate mission. Bishop Muench approached the task with a sympathetic understanding of the tragic situation in which the Church in Germany found itself. And the bishops of that unhappy country received him with a graciousness and understanding which removed all danger of suspicion or pettiness in even the most trying circumstances.

How badly Germany was crushed and broken was quite evident. But underneath it all there was a more serious problem, the problem of a great nation broken in spirit and disillusioned by the ruin which fanatical leaders had brought upon it. The young people who had been formed in the mold of Hitler youth groups were a lost generation. To reclaim that generation was a great challenge upon which the future of Germany in a large measure depended.

But, depressed as Bishop Muench was by the sight of misery, destruction and confusion, he had no time to waste on bewailing the situation. There was work to be done. His was a complicated assignment since he had been called upon to serve in various capacities.

As apostolic visitor his first task was to visit all bishops and to see and talk to as many of the clergy and laity as possible in order to make a complete report to the Holy Father. He carried on the normal functions of a papal nuncio without, however, receiving the title until 6 March 1951. He was also called upon to administer the affairs of the Vatican mission which was already functioning when he came to Germany in 1946. The Vatican mission was an agency of the Vatican for the material and spiritual care of displaced persons. Many thousands of people had been brought by Hitler from occupied countries for forced labor in German munitions plants during the war.

Another task entrusted to Bishop Muench which he discharged until being named papal nuncio was that of vicar delegate for American Catholics connected with our armed forces in Germany. This brought him into frequent contact with the Americans in Germany, especially with our military chaplains.

Besides his mission on behalf of the Holy See, Bishop Muench discharged a function entrusted to him by Robert P. Patterson, secretary of war. He was given the high-sounding title of liaison consultant for religious affairs to the military governor. The importance of this work was commensurate with the sonorous ring of the title. His appointment by the secretary of war was really providential. If he had not been given this official status in the army of occupation he and his staff would have found life in Germany difficult indeed. Without PX privileges, food and other supplies would not have been available.

His task was to advise the military governor on matters where the interests of the Catholic Church in Germany and the army of occupation were involved.

General Lucius B. Clay was the military governor during the critical period of Bishop Muench's mission in Germany. He received Bishop Muench graciously and often. He was most understanding of the problems of the Church and pre-eminently fair and considerate in resolving them. After some months had passed, a working pattern was established with the result that Bishop Muench needed to see General Clay less and less frequently; but they remained fast friends throughout the General's tour of duty in Germany, and the Bishop cherished the warmest feelings towards him so long as he lived.

Again, as we review his work during his years in Germany we are struck by the fact that his many activities had pastoral undertones. Whether he was functioning as the head of the Vatican mission which was concerned with the material and spiritual welfare of displaced persons, or whether he was negotiating with officials of Military Government, his primary concern was always the spiritual welfare of the people of God. His work, of whatever nature it was, for him was an exercise of his pastoral office.

As papal nuncio he worked and moved in the highest circles; he dealt with affairs of greatest importance. But that did not change his attitude one iota; even though he ended his life wearing the red of a prince of the Church, he was a pastor always. His greatness was recognized most clearly in the simplicity, regularity and conscientiousness of his daily living.

† Leo F. Dworschak
Bishop of Fargo

AMERICAN NUNCIO

CHAPTER ONE

MILWAUKEE AND FARGO

In the century between 1820 and 1920 some six million Germans emigrated to the United States seeking a new opportunity for a better life. They came with many people of other nationalities from Europe due to the hard conditions of their lives and drawn by the possibility of owning their own land or bettering their standard of living in the developing American industrial centers. There was a labor shortage in the States and agents crossed Europe promising a bright future for those who had the courage to take a risk and find a better life in the new world.

A considerable number of German emigrants headed for the State of Wisconsin where they heard there was a growing German community and opportunity for work and freedom. Wisconsin, one of the Upper Midwest states of the Union, was a wooded and laked swell of land between the three depressions of the Lake Michigan, Lake Superior and Mississippi River basins. Admitted to the Union in 1849, Wisconsin soon became a mecca of immigrants after the Civil War because of its temperate continental climate, rich soil, cheap land, and rapidly expanding industries in lumber, paper, milling, clothing, iron products and beer. The state also quickly became known for the heterogeneous character of its population as artisans and farmers from northern European countries emigrated to Wisconsin. By 1890 three-fourths of its population of 1,586,880 was foreign-born. Nearly 600,000 were of German extraction, over 100,000 were from the Scandinavian countries and entire communities were made up of immigrants from Poland, Ireland, Switzerland, Holland and Belgium.

Milwaukee, eighty miles north of Chicago on the western shore of Lake Michigan, was the metropolitan center of Wisconsin. It grew rapidly to become by 1890 the fourteenth largest city in the United

3

States with a population of 204,468. Shipping facilities, railroad terminals, low rents and expanding manufacturing plants attracted large numbers of artisans and craftsmen from European towns and villages. The city covered a sprawling area in which private dwellings were especially conspicuous. Employment was available in plants as diversified as the manufacturing of clothing, meat packing, cigar making, milling, leather work, mill work and especially the brewing of a well-known lager beer for which the city became famous. Over a million barrels of beer were soon being produced annually in Milwaukee from the excellent barley and hops of the Wisconsin area. Half of the burghers of Milwaukee were foreign-born and Germans especially predominated in the city's cultural, economic and religious life. The strong German patterns of conflict and tension between Lutherans, Catholics and free-thinkers, such as Masons and Turners, were developing in Milwaukee at the end of the nineteenth century. In Milwaukee, and other midwest cities such as Cincinnati, Chicago, Saint Louis or Saint Paul, immigrants had to learn to live with their ancient European differences in a free and democratic society.

During the decade from 1880 to 1890 some 400,000 German Catholics, the largest number of any decade during the nineteenth century, came to the United States. Two young Catholic Bavarian teenagers, eighteen-year old Joseph Muench and fourteen-year old Theresa Kraus, left with their families in the year 1882 on different steamers headed for Milwaukee, Wisconsin. Joseph Muench's father had come from generations of farmers who spoke a Bavarian dialect in the upper village of Sankt Katerina, Neuern, in the *Boehmer Wald* adjacent to Bavaria. The family owned twenty hektars of land at Ganglhof, a clearing in the woods, but the soil was sandy and full of gravel. The Muenchs left because opportunity beckoned across the sea. The father had died of tuberculosis at the age of forty-nine, and the mother and four children joined an emigrant group that walked 350 miles to Hamburg carrying their clothing and feather beds to board a steamer for New York. They traveled in the primitive conditions of steerage, endured storms and ate soup from a common pot to which all contributed whatever they had in their stock of provisions.

Theresa Kraus' father owned a bakery in Stadt Kemnath fifteen miles from Konnersreuth, Bavaria. The family had been bakers for several hundred years but business was bad because of the generally depressed economic conditions and the widowed father determined to take his five children, of whom Theresa was the youngest, to America.[1] After arrival in New York they boarded a train for Milwaukee where Johann Kraus went to work for a baker. Both the Muench and Kraus families belonged to Saint Mary's parish, and they met at parish social functions which were so integral to national parish life in nineteenth-century American Catholicism. Joseph and Theresa were married on 14 May 1888 and moved across the Milwaukee River to rent a house in Saint John de Nepomuc parish, a Bohemian parish at Eleventh and Cherry Streets.

A year later their first child, Aloisius Joseph, was born on 18 February 1889. Joseph and Theresa Muench had seven other children of whom two died.[2] The family at first lived in a rented frame house in the center of Milwaukee, at Fifth and Locust Streets. As the German immigrants began to move north after the establishment of Saint Boniface Parish in 1888 they, too, moved into a rented house in that new German national parish. A landlord suggested to Joseph that he buy a thirty-foot lot near the ball park on Tenth Street between Chambers and Locust Streets. He and a carpenter friend built a house at 2945 North Tenth Street that became the permanent home of the Muench family. Joseph had obtained a job in the Northwestern Furniture Company upon his arrival in Milwaukee. He at first cleaned the sawdust and shavings from under the machines and gradually advanced to cabinet-maker, foreman of four floors and engineer. He worked faithfully for the same company over a period of fifty-two years. Young Allie Muench remembered going with his father on Sundays and holidays, even Christmas day, to check the valves on the boilers at the factory as though he owned it.

The Muench family lived frugally on Joseph's salary of $26.00 a month. Theresa did the sewing and knitting for the whole family and was called by the neighbors "the night watchman of Tenth Street" as she regularly stayed up working until one o'clock in the morning. She often served *Mehlspeise,* mush, or rice as the staple dish and her friends warned that the children would grow up with bad stomachs. The whole family, however, had good health and Joseph and Theresa repeatedly said that God took care of the family, sparing them doctors' bills, one of the constant fears of struggling immigrants. When the children were sick there was always a home remedy at hand such as goose grease and syrup, honey and boiling water, or herbs. When orders were slow at the furniture factory Joseph would make inlaid floors of white and brown cherry wood and maple for the house, dressers, chairs, a hat rack, or a walnut table to be placed before the window in the front parlor. These craft objects in wood were the one small luxury the family could exhibit. The father was proud of his craft and the Muench family throughout their lives cherished design and art in wood. Theresa was an excellent cook and good pastries such as special Bavarian *Kaffeeku-chen* were always prepared for feast and name days. Her noodles were a family specialty as were the homemade *Bayerische Knoedel*. These dumplings became the favorite dish of Allie throughout his life. In later years as a bishop he was particularly pleased when the German-Russian women at parish gatherings, or on his confirmation tours throughout North Dakota, made the kind of dumplings his mother used to serve.

The family was closely knit and their social life centered around their home, Saint Boniface parish and their relatives and friends among the German immigrants on the north side of the city. It was a quiet, slow-paced and happy life. Everything was homemade. Times were hard and there was no money except the monthly pay check. A neighbor family across the street waited until the day after Christmas to go down town to buy toys for their family. When the Muench children played they had to create their own sporting goods. Allie remembered walking five miles to McKinley Beach inside the breakwater of Lake Michigan near the present art gallery. He went behind the saloons and half filled a flour sack with cork, sewed it, and filled the other half in the same way. Then he had wings to float on while swimming, but on the way home two had to carry the heavy water soaked bag on a broom stick.[3] The youngsters also learned to fish with long sticks for perch off the same breakwater.

Joseph had a good sense of humor, liked to tell stories, smoke cigars, sing and dance in the family circle. Frequently on Sunday afternoons friends from the parish gathered in the Muench yard to play cards (*Schafskopf*) under the arbor and linden tree. All contributed to a keg of beer (*ein Achtel*) and Allie had the responsibility of packing ice on top of the keg and wrapping a carpet around it. Both parents were strong characters without pretense and slow to display emotion. They had a delicate reserve and instilled in their children a dignity and respect for each other and for their neighbors. They were poor, honest and free.

Religion was the dominant force in their family life. They prayed together at home and had a deep faith. The parents spoke German while the children answered them in English. Joseph and Theresa would not allow their children to complain or shirk their share of the family chores. The mother had at hand a German religious saying for every occasion: "Wie Gott will, halt dich still" (subject yourself to the will of God); or "Wer auf Gott vertraut, der hat gut gebaut" (he who trusts in God builds well); or "Nur nicht die Himmelsmutter vergessen" (never forget the Blessed Virgin). In later years the family enjoyed teasing her about the regular question she asked each of them as they prepared for Sunday Mass: "Hast du dein Gebetbuch, dein Taschentuch, und einen 'cent'?" (do you have your prayerbook, a handkerchief and a penny). Nuncio Muench also enjoyed repeating these stories of immigrant life in the United States to bishops and dignitaries in Germany after World War II and they were fascinated by the cultural transfer and continuity that the artisans tried to effect in the new world. The future cardinal's father had a deep faith in the guardian angels. One day he was in an elevator that fell four floors in the factory. At supper that evening he quietly said at table: "Today I had a good guardian angel." Allie remembered with pride the time his father took him on an all night pilgrimage to Holy Hill in Wisconsin, twenty-five miles from Milwaukee. Christmas was the great day of the year and there was much preparation in the Muench household so that the full ceremonial could be carried off as was customary in Bavaria. On Christmas eve all the children had to take a nap while their parents helped the *Christkind* decorate the tree. When everything was ready the children had to line up in the kitchen according to age, with the youngest first, and when the bell rang they came into the front room to sing the old German Christmas carols and to receive their simple gifts. Then everyone prepared for midnight Mass at Saint Boniface.

Allie was shy as a boy and cried when people looked at him. His father would scold him and say: "You just wait until you get among people; it will be very hard." When time came to go to school Allie and Mary would go off hand in hand to Saint Boniface parochial school and the neighbors called them "grandpa and grandma." The Saint Boniface School was under the church on the first floor of the new building which had been constructed in 1888 on Eleventh Street near Clark. The hard-working north side Catholics had sacrificed for their parish and school. School Sisters of Notre Dame taught in the school and instruction was in English with classes in German reading and writing as part of the curriculum. By this time the second generation Germans were moving more into the mainstream of American life and

Allie was raised in an atmosphere of German-Americans midway in the process of Americanization.

There were three classes in each school room and Allie early gave evidence that he was a good student. His boyhood school days were normal and he carried newspapers on a morning route from 5:30 to 7:30 a.m. He delivered the German newspaper, Milwaukee *Herold*, made $8 a month and turned the cash in to the family treasury. Each Sunday he was given ten cents and he walked several blocks to buy some taffee candy. In an interview Cardinal Muench stated that this first paper route of his introduced him to work as education. In this way he had to meet people and he thus learned from the discipline of a daily schedule as well as the difficulty of collecting the monthly bills. Muench observed that he did not think child labor laws were needed any longer and that all young people should work at something while they were going to school. By inversion children were now required to go to school and not to work. This advance was not necessarily, in his opinion, progress in realistic training for adult life.

Sister Vitalia Kappel, S.S.N.D., who taught the eighth grade at Saint Boniface from 1892–1904, had become a legend among her students who loved and respected her. During twelve years she directed twenty boys of the parish to the priesthood. She had them running errands for her, helping in church and preparing for liturgical celebrations. She never talked about vocations, but after Allie graduated from the eighth grade in 1903 she directly asked him if he wanted to study for the priesthood. He said "yes," but he feared to ask his parents because he was the oldest and the income he could bring to the family would help them considerably in the years ahead. She said nothing, but the next Sunday she called Joseph and Theresa to the parish convent and talked with them. They said they could not afford it but she encouraged them not to worry and told them she would ask some priests to cover part of the expenses. They then readily gave their consent.

In 1903–04 Allie Muench with six other German-American boys from Saint Boniface began studying Latin and Greek with Father Henry Niehaus, assistant to the famed Monsignor Peter M. Abbelen, chaplain at the motherhouse of the School Sisters of Notre Dame in Milwaukee. Sister Vitalia had arranged the whole procedure. It was the largest number of students Niehaus had at one time and included two of the five Stehling boys who became priests from one Saint Boniface family. Allie and his inseparable companion and classmate from Saint Boniface, Thomas Schmitz, walked four miles each day for classes which began at two o'clock in the afternoon.[4] After the morning paper route Allie worked at Steinmeyer's grocery store on Third and Prairie Streets. When he received his first check he bought a picture of Our Lady of Perpetual Help for his mother which his father framed. In the evening he studied at home, memorized his lessons and struggled with Schultz's Latin grammar. There was no truant officer and the minor seminary training at that time was, indeed, far more un-structured than it later became. It was a natural transition from his home environment to seminary training. It was an experience that he and the entire family participated in and grew to value. The parents and other children joined in helping him, as they could, in memorizing grammar. They would hold up vocabulary cards for him to repeat and made games of the difficult exercises. In later years, Muench said with pride that the whole family received a certain exposure to the classics in this joint educational undertaking which they never would have had if he had been apart from them at a time when, as the eldest, he was needed at home.

Tom Schmitz and Allie Muench would meet each noon near the tanneries to compare their written assignments and practice Latin and Greek exercises on the way to Father Niehaus' study at the motherhouse. For over fifteen years Niehaus did this tutoring of pre-seminary students without any compensation. Muench considered him to be a saintly and scholarly man and stated that he was a major influence in his development. The boys looked forward to every session with their tutor and enjoyed teasing him. They would sneak into his bathroom and light his large Oshkosh sulphur matches so that the fumes would break up the laborious translation of a Ciceronian oration. The six boys ingeniously learned a deaf mute alphabet to prompt each other in translating exercises. Niehaus was kind and encouraging and took the boys on trips. He would bring them out to Saint Francis Seminary for special events and Muench remembered well the first evening that they attended a performance of Macbeth there. It was a dark November evening, his first exposure to Shakespeare, and he saw witches behind every tree as they went home. Niehaus gave them prizes and gradually prepared them for the entrance examination to Saint Francis which was conducted by Father Charles Becker. The examiner had a Latin book in one hand, a cigar in his mouth and a pencil in the other hand. He moved the pencil up and down on his stomach until one of the boys made a mistake. Then the pencil stopped. Becker asked Muench for the infinitive of "morior" and Allie replied: "moreri." The pencil stopped until he could think of "mori" and then it started moving again. The boys passed the examination and prepared to enter the seminary in the fall of 1904. Father Edward Kersting, assistant at Saint Anne's Church, Milwaukee, at the instigation of Father Niehaus, paid half of Allie's $85 semester tuition and his father paid the other half.

The boys entered as third-year high school students and continued to study classics and humanities for four years. Classes were held in Latin, Greek, English, German, history, science and mathematics. Allie enjoyed his studies and the teachers. He soon felt at home in the seminary routine and placed high in the yearly testimonials. Father Charles Becker was master of discipline and instructor in Latin, Greek, mathematics and music. Young Muench liked Father Leopold E. Drexel, instructor in Latin, history, geology and mineralogy. The students called him "schreck" because he always said "shrecklich" when mistakes were made. Drexel and several Milwaukee priests had a cabin on a lake near Minocqua in northern Wisconsin and during the summer months of these seminary years they asked Allie Muench to come along as cook. His friends Father Kersting, who had tuberculosis, and Father August B. Salick, pastor of Saint Anne's, were also in the party. Allie's mother taught him how to prepare different dishes and he became quite accomplished in camp cuisine. These summers passed rapidly in fishing, hunting and nature study and for the remainder of his life Muench was interested in the outdoors. It became a valuable recreational interest for him in his adult assignments.

Aloisius Muench continued his philosophy and theological studies at Saint Francis Seminary. Bishop Sebastian G. Messmer of Green Bay had been transferred to Milwaukee as archbishop in 1903, the year before Muench began his studies for the priesthood. The Swiss-born Messmer had previously taught at Seton Hall College, New Jersey, and at the Catholic University of America, Washington, D.C. He was one of the leading spokesmen for German-Americans in the controversies of the 1880's and 1890's. These controversies raged around the Americanization of the Catholic immigrant and the polarization of conservatives and liberals on educational, social and religious questions and procedures. Messmer, while identified in the conservative camp, took positions as a bishop which moved the German community away from the high level of ethnic consciousness and organizational activity that characterized their battle against the Americanizing liberal Catholics. He encouraged recognition of the *de facto* Americanization that was developing after the turn of the century and the necessity to introduce the use of English language in church and school. The archbishop strove to move the German-Americans into the mainstream of national life while preserving their religious and social traditions.

Messmer inherited in Milwaukee a strong seminary which had been in operation for fifty years before he became the fourth archbishop of that see. John M. Henni, first archbishop, had worked hard with the assistance of Father Michael Heiss, his successor, and Dr. Joseph Salzmann to establish a seminary where priests could be trained in the United States for missionary and parochial work in the Province of Milwaukee. In this way the future supply of priests for their rapidly developing immigrant parishes could be better assured. Volunteers from European dioceses and religious communities could not be counted on indefinitely for a permanent and stable diocesan clergy in the west. Saint Francis had a dominant German tradition and cultural emphasis from its inception due to the majority position of Germans in the Wisconsin area. There were always present, however, significant and growing Irish, Polish and other minorities in the Milwaukee province. Messmer realized that they must all feel equally at home in the American Church, must produce vocations from their parishes and live together in peace and harmony. He aimed at preserving old world traditions, sentiments and feelings in an American mold. This was the only realistic way in which young German, Irish or Polish Americans could be attracted to priestly and religious vocations.

A solid, highly structured and conservatively traditional spirit of study had been developed at Saint Francis. This tradition was augmented by a number of European-trained professors in the major and basic disciplines. When Muench studied philosophy and theology at Saint Francis the seminary was administered by the much admired Monsignor Joseph Rainer who served in that position during the long period of thirty-three years from 1887 to 1920. Patterns of operation were, accordingly, well established and not characterized by innovation. A regular and unbroken schedule of academic courses and spiritual exercises was maintained for all of the some 260 students of whom eighty-eight were theologians, thirty-eight philosophers and 137 enrolled in classics. There were sixteen professors who taught in all three departments. Muench liked Dr. Boleslaus Góral in Greek, Dr. William Metzdorf in biology, and Father Eugene McCarthy in scholastic philosophy.

McCarthy and Father Charles P. Bruehl, a priest on loan from the Archdiocese of Philadelphia until 1914, introduced him to ethical and moral implications of social problems which he augmented by reading eagerly all issues of *Stimmen aus Maria Laach*, the excellent Rhineland Catholic journal edited by the German Jesuits. Father Bruehl was a native German who had received philosophical and theological doctorates at the Universities of Muenster and Louvain. He was a good lecturer and awakened an interest among the better students in the Church's position on social questions of the day. Bruehl was also one of the few professors who did any research and publishing. His essays and books on social issues awakened an interest in young Muench which was destined to last a lifetime. The general atmosphere at Saint Francis was pastoral and aimed at the professional undergraduate training of diocesan parish priests. But just one professor like Bruehl was enough to open up scholarly horizons to a searching mind.

During his four years of theology Muench had Rector Rainer for Scripture, Father David J. O'Hearn for Church history and canon law; Father Frederick Schultze for moral theology and, fortunately, Father Bruehl again for dogma. Dogma was creatively taught and Muench studied hard under Bruehl's encouragement. During February before ordination Bruehl called Muench to his study and told him he was going to recommend him for graduate studies in theology at Innsbruck with the intention of having him return to the Saint Francis faculty to replace Bruehl when he had to return to Philadelphia. Bruehl asked Muench if he would like to do this and the young deacon was not only pleased to be considered but excited at the possibility of studying at the ancient University of Innsbruck, Austria, where several other faculty members, according to Milwaukee tradition, had been sent for advanced degrees. Bruehl discussed the matter with Rainer, who agreed, and the two men went to Archbishop Messmer about the matter. Messmer considered the move an excellent step in building up the future faculty of the seminary.

Father Muench was ordained a priest on 8 June 1913 and offered his first Mass on June 15 at Saint Boniface Church with his friend Father August B. Salick, pastor of Saint Anne's, as homilist. The silver jubilee of the parish was being observed that same year and the church was redecorated for the occasion. June 15 was such a hot day that the new varnish on the pews came off on the women's dresses and they had to go home and change before the dinner and afternoon festivities.

The happy Muench family were not proud but only thankful, his mother said, that God had given them a priest. In the years ahead, as Muench made each step in his career, his mother repeated the same simple and sincere statement.

World War I cancelled all plans for Father Muench's graduate studies at Innsbruck and the chancery told him to go to Saint Michael's Parish in Milwaukee as a temporary appointment. This was a German parish at Twenty-fourth and Cherry Streets, with Father Sebastian Bernard as pastor and Fathers James Huepper and Felix Sipple as assistants. There followed four halcyon years of parish work for the "boy priest" as the parishioners called him. Father Muench enjoyed parochial work, learned from the older priests and his contacts with the laity, and gained experience in the practical problems of lower class people trying to earn a living and practice their faith. During these years he acquired an abiding interest in and love of the common man which he retained throughout his life. The people responded enthusiastically to Father Muench who related meaningfully to them and who delivered German sermons which they cherished. For Allie these years were especially precious because he was able to visit his parents and family regularly and to assist them financially. During this period he was a close companion of Father James W. Nellen, fellow priest of the Milwaukee archdiocese. This friendship with "Boots" Nellen lasted a lifetime and during Muench's mission to Germany after World War II it was Nellen, by then pastor of Holy Redeemer Church, Milwaukee, who supplied the most help to Allie of all the thousands who joined in that apostolate.

In 1917 Father Henry Hengell, chaplain of Saint Paul's University Chapel, University of Wisconsin, Madison, approached Archbishop Messmer with a request to have Father Muench as his assistant there. Fathers J. F. Conway and Peter Leo Johnson, former assistants, had both gone into the army as chaplains. Muench's reputation as a student had spread throughout the archdiocese and Hengell thought he would be able to relate effectively to the Catholic students and in the general academic atmosphere at Madison. Archbishop Messmer called Muench in and told him to throw himself into the apostolate of working with students at a major state university. There were no formal procedures or tradition for such activity, Messmer stated, and since it was new work it needed support. Muench was anxious to go to Madison and to get back into academic life again. He first asked his pastor, Father Bernard, who did not want Muench to leave Saint Michael's but realized how much the move meant to him. Messmer never sent Muench a formal appointment to Saint Paul's Chapel and before he left Saint Michael's his replacement, Father August F. Gearhard, had already arrived. Muench said: "In these matters Messmer was forgetful."

Muench went by train to Madison as there were no automobiles in general use as yet. He found a tudor gothic chapel and a house at 723 State Street which was used as a working headquarters for the Newman Chapel activity. Father Hengell lived at the Dominican Convent, Edgewood, and Muench was assigned a room at Saint Mary's Hospital in Madison where he received board and room in return for assisting the chaplain in the hospital. Muench found the work among the Catholic students on the campus at Wisconsin most discouraging. Father Hengell enjoyed a controversy and was primarily interested in refuting professors who directly or indirectly attacked the Church or the faith. It was the typical apologetic and defensive stance of the American Church in the ghetto and Muench had no stomach for such games. He tried to build up attendance at Newman Club lectures arranged for the Catholic students (315 men and ten women) enrolled at Wisconsin. Few students came, however, and Muench said they were interested in social affairs, studies and religion in that order. He started a unit of the Saint Vincent de Paul Society and interested a dozen students in going about Madison helping the poor with donations of food and clothing.

Father Muench realized that he was among the pioneers in what at present is called the Newman apostolate on American state university campuses while the major thrust of the Church at the time was parochial and concentrated on church-related schools. In interviews at the end of his life, however, he kept coming back to this Madison experience of 1917–19 and comparing it to what he had witnessed with enthusiasm in Germany from 1946–59. In these interviews of 1961 he evidenced that his ideas were advanced beyond those of his fellow American ecclesiastics of that later period. Muench said that Catholics in Germany were not weighed down with supporting a private system of education from kindergarten through doctoral programs. In higher education, especially, there were no Catholic universities in Germany and yet a remarkably excellent corps of Catholic intellectuals were trained in the state system of higher education. He would have no difficulty in comparing them with any group of educated Catholics anywhere. This development of Catholic intellectuals in Germany was accomplished at the major universities by building centers nearby where religious training was given. German university students naturally want to go where the best professors are lecturing. Among these there are always a number of Catholic professors who themselves had been trained at state universities. The German system was not only cheaper, a pressing consideration for American Catholics, but also economical because state universities could concentrate available funds on specific areas. In the United States, on the other hand, Catholics had spread themselves too thin and were not developing educational centers of high quality and adequate leadership. These realities, Cardinal Muench said, would have to be faced in the years ahead as American Catholics came full circle into the mainstream of their national life as the Catholics in Germany learned to do over a longer period.

Since Father Muench found he was not fully occupied in his Newman Club assignment he decided to pursue a master's degree in economics at the University of Wisconsin. He was moved to obtain competent graduate training in areas of the social sciences that he had heard about from Father Bruehl in the seminary and that he had haphazardly tried to learn on his own through undirected reading in the field such as a study of John A. Ryan's *A Living Wage* and all available secondary literature he could find in journals. Accordingly, he submitted his credits from Saint Francis Seminary to the dean of the Graduate School at the University of Wisconsin. He was accepted for graduate studies, but he was directed to take an undergraduate course in economics from Professor William H. Kiekhofer which he willingly did. The graduate courses he pursued at Wisconsin over the next year and a half were the second stage of his opening to the world and he enjoyed every encounter along the way. The University of Wisconsin was emerging at the time as one of the leading land grant institutions in the United States. The progressive tradition of the LaFollettes had influenced the State's university. Muench wanted to know what was being said about social questions and how to reconcile the Catholic social theory he had been studying with the dynamics of the American democratic process. He was, indeed, emerging as a serious student of social sciences.

Muench took courses in economics and sociology while working toward a master's degree in economics from Wisconsin. He liked the courses of the sociologist, Edward Alsworth Ross, despite the fact that he used his graduate classes to try out chapters of future books on the students. Exposure to a man of this caliber was an education for Muench.

When Ross attacked the Catholic Church in class the young priest would go to his office afterwards to discuss the charges with him. In treating "religion as a means of domination," Ross said that in the Middle Ages bishops would deny baptism or burial to Catholics who refused to comply. Muench in private told Ross that placing these generalizations under the term "superstition" weakened his presentation. Ross asked Muench what he would recommend. The young priest then proceeded to argue the point and came up with a new generic term: "Abuse of religious power for temporal reasons."

Muench was not as successful in preserving public peace with Professor John Lewis Gillen during the latter's lectures on social control. One day Gillen talked about the Council of Nicea, quoted part of its creed, and said: "The rest of its rigamarole we all know." Muench raised his hand and replied: "Professor, I object to that statement." There was a dead silence in the class and Gillen countered: "And what would you say?" Muench replied: "Like our American constitution, religious ideas were abroad at that time and needed definition."

Despite such infrequent incidents, Muench thoroughly enjoyed his time at the University of Wisconsin. The professors were consistently of high caliber and he was moved to turn from dogma to the social sciences as his major field of interest. When it came time to take his oral examination for the master's in economics the famed John R. Commons, professor of economics and historian of American labor developments, whom Muench had appreciated so much in class, appeared with the examining team of professors. Commons monopolized the examination by entering into a friendly dialogue with Muench about the encyclical *Rerum Novarum* of Pope Leo XIII and the social ethics of the Catholic Church. Muench stated: "I lectured like a professor that morning," and before the examiners knew it the time was gone. Muench said it was one of the easiest examinations he ever had, and he received a passing grade.

World War I was now over and Archbishop Messmer as a former academic man himself was pleased that Father Muench had obtained an M.A. from the University of Wisconsin. He remembered that the young priest was to go to Europe for doctoral studies in preparation for a seminary professorship. The University of Innsbruck had been decimated by the war and Messmer recommended that Muench go instead to the University of Fribourg in the archbishop's native Switzerland for doctoral studies with the Dominicans at that international center.

Father Muench was happy and ready to do this but, unfortunately, as so often occurred in his later years, Messmer forgot all about expenses and never directed any money toward this expensive undertaking. Muench was too timid to remind the archbishop of this detail so important to a struggling young priest, and set off for Fribourg wondering how he would possibly pay his way. Several lay friends helped him financially but he had to rely for the most part on his own wits over the long pull to pay for what no one in official ecclesiastical circles in Milwaukee realized the aging archbishop had forgotten to underwrite. In later years Muench continually joked about this experience, but at the time immediately following the war it was a worry that he had to live with daily.

The years from 1919 to 1922 were exciting ones for Father Muench and filled with valuable new experiences and insights. In Fribourg he stayed at the Albertinum, a residence hall for student priests operated by the LaSalette Fathers. Some of the clergy in Milwaukee encouraged him to study dogma and not to take "that stuff" in the field of social science, economics, and moral and ethical principles. But he persevered as the only American studying social sciences there. Muench considered the professors at Fribourg equal to those at Wisconsin, and particularly valued Professor Hans Schorer's seminar in statistics which met in a tavern. Schorer's methodology and inductive procedures were a broadening influence and helpful in forming Muench's classroom techniques for the years ahead. After two years of course work and preparation of a thesis on the development of ideas and programs in compulsory health insurance projects in the United States, Father Muench was granted a doctorate in social sciences, *magna cum laude*, in July of 1921.

While studying for his doctorate Muench supported himself in part by writing articles for *America* magazine. He would take a trip or attend a conference and then send a fifteen-page article to Father Richard H. Tierney, S.J., editor of *America*. Only one article was rejected. Muench had done research on DeValera, McSweeney and the Irish rebels in Paris, but Tierney judged he could not run it because it would cause an uproar among that weekly's Irish-American readers.

Muench took every opportunity to travel around Europe during Christmas, Easter and summer vacations. He collected a basic library in his major field, visited all the countries of Europe and especially concentrated on studying art and architecture, both religious and secular. Muench's later definite ideas on continuity and dependence in the development of art were formed during this period of his education. His natural piety drew him to gothic and baroque as expressions of living faith. The great churches, civic buildings and art museums impressed this son of immigrant parents who had never seen anything like them before. He read art history, audited courses in art and insisted to the end of his life that every art period grew out of former artistic advances. Given the categories he had earlier decided upon he never could understand modern art.

Father Muench was more progressive in opening himself to contemporary developments in social theory and action. He traveled to Paris and Basel for conferences whenever possible and was an interpreter in French, German and English at the first meeting called in 1921 at Basel to reorganize the International Association for Labor. He never missed international meetings in Geneva which had become a center for discussion of postwar problems and self-help. Muench became acquainted with Professor Sainger and learned much from him about norms of social justice. When interviewed years later as a cardinal Muench declared: "The providence of God is a mystery. I was trained after World War I for the work I had to do after World War II. I often said that I was the fair haired boy of divine providence in this regard."

The Americans at Fribourg formed a Columbia Society as a participating organization of the International Catholic Student Association. In the years after the war this association was especially interested in all statements made by the Pope. They noted that the Pope gave a yearly address to the preachers of Rome and the Americans of the Columbia Society, much to the shock of the Europeans, wrote a letter to Benedict XV in which they ventured to suggest that the preachers be encouraged to emphasize charity in their sermons. Pope Benedict answered this petition generously and commended the students for their recognition of the basic virtue needed by the age.

Since Switzerland had become a center of help for the victims of World War I, Fathers Muench and Paul Regan, a LaSalette priest, joined with German and Austrian students at Fribourg to form a committee to help the poor and needy. This move was strikingly similar to Muench's concerns and activity after World War II. Representatives of the committee, including Muench, visited Archbishops Luigi Maglione, Vatican nuncio to Switzerland in Berne, and Eugenio Pacelli, apostolic nuncio to Bavaria in Munich, and later Pope Pius XII. It was Muench's first of many future visits with Pacelli who received the young priests enthusiastically and talked at length with them about the help needed by the Church in Germany. Pacelli wanted relief for war victims organized on an international basis, and Muench told him he would write to the Central Verein in the United States for assistance. When Muench contacted the Central Verein he received an answer, which did not satisfy him at all, that they could not help because Catholic organizations had been asked to participate in the Pershing Drive then in progress in New York.

After completing the academic requirements at Fribourg, Muench was granted by Archbishop Messmer another half year of travel and study at leading European universities. He audited classes at the University of Grenoble, the Sorbonne in Paris, the Collège de France where he heard Alfred Loisy lecture, Louvain, Cambridge, the London School of Economics and Oxford. It was an interesting and unique educational hegira that ended at the Eucharistic Congress in Rome. Father Muench then returned to Milwaukee and Saint Francis Seminary to begin his teaching assignment.

The next seven years, from 1922 to 1929, were, he said, the happiest years of his life. Doctor Muench enjoyed teaching more than anything else he was called to carry out in future years. He had a deep attachment for his alma mater, Saint Francis Seminary, and was doing something for which he had been thoroughly trained. He was appointed to teach social science, catechetics and apologetics. In 1923 he was also assigned the dogma classes of Monsignor Charles Breig who was that year appointed rector of Saint Francis by Archbishop Messmer. Breig had succeeded Bruehl as professor of dogma in 1914 and was the last of the European priests who taught at the seminary. Muench was somewhat taken aback at having the important dogma classes added to his schedule. Though he had originally been recommended for advanced study in dogma, he actually had majored in social science. Now he had to prepare carefully for the dogma lectures while retaining his other class assignments.

The Fribourg alumnus proved to be a successful teacher. He was methodical, demanded that his students work hard and set an example for them. He was a perfectionist here as in other areas and expected his students to keep their average in tests above the mark of 90. When someone received a low mark he would call him in and say: "Didn't I get that across to you?" The students found Muench to be human, fair and just. They particularly enjoyed the practical applications he made in class as he tried to evidence the social application of Catholic doctrine and the sacraments. He made constant comparisons of principles to current events and would even take ten minutes from the class periods to read and discuss the newspapers with the seminarians. The seminarians especially enjoyed this practice since in accordance with the seminary discipline of those years their contact with the world through journalism was definitely limited.

Muench employed the scientific methodology he had learned at Madison and Fribourg. He required consultation of primary sources and used the seminar technique to introduce his students into the requirements of research and original writing. He tried to break away from a slavish following of the text book, memorization and uninterrupted lectures all too common in seminary training. Muench was not always as successful as he wanted to be for he was by nature methodical to an extreme. He employed long and involved sentences and was concerned with elaborating general principles in careful detail. Students soon dubbed him "der metaphysische Doktor." They, however, respected him for his learning and interest in teaching them.

Father Muench became aware all too soon of the scholarly malaise that pervaded student life at Saint Francis as it did at the overriding majority of American seminaries. There was little understanding of and respect for scholarship among American Catholic bishops and priests, and seminarians soon learned that their training was primarily pre-professional, pastoral and disassociated from the norms of university procedures. Muench commented on this situation in an interview:

"There was a lack of interest in scholarly work by professors. They would teach their classes and no more. Their interests were elsewhere. There was no sense of scholarship or dedication and as a result the scholars who come out of our American seminaries are rare, too rare.

"At one National Catholic Educational Association convention in Milwaukee, when I was teaching at Saint Francis Seminary, my classmate, Father Francis Haas and I said that seminarians should study social sciences in the seminary. Bishop Francis W. Howard of Covington answered us: 'If seminarians study De Lugo, that is enough.'

"As bishop of Fargo I started a library for priests but only one or two came for books. They had been trained in seminaries not to exert any scholarly effort as priests but just to get by. This spirit was actually begun in parochial grade schools." [5]

In order to improve this situation Father Muench offered a summer course in sociology in 1923 which was attended by seventy-five priests, laymen and women. He gave addresses at the annual meetings of the Central Verein and contributed articles to its organ *Social Justice Review*. He continued to write for *America* magazine and contributed during these years twenty-two articles to *The Salesianum*, journal of the alumni association of Saint Francis Seminary. He wrote on topics such as the priest and social study, the ethical aspects of wages, methods of teaching, sterilization by law, banking in the United States, sound money or inflation, self-government in industry, strikes and recognition of unions, collective bargaining and a new alignment of capital and labor.[6]

During the years as professor Aloisius Muench retained the interest in dramatics which he had acquired during his student days and as an assistant in Saint Michael's parish. He directed two plays for the Albertus Magnus Society at the seminary: "Zriny" in 1925 and "Elmar" in 1928. He regularly spent Sunday at home with the family and returned to the cabin in northern Wisconsin near Minocqua during the summer for vacation periods with his priest friends. Muench became a close personal friend of Valentine Blatz and his family during this period and continued the relationship throughout his life. Val Blatz, grandson of the founder of the Blatz Brewing Company of Milwaukee, had taken instructions in the Catholic faith from Father Muench when the latter was assistant Newman chaplain at the University of Wisconsin in Madison. Blatz and two of his companions, Walter Knapp and Joseph Tiefenthaler, were students at the university at that time and they decided they wanted to become Catholics. Blatz' grandfather had been a Catholic but his father had fallen away from the Church. Muench went on vacations with the Val Blatz family, visited them often, and in the years ahead his friend Val was a continuing supporter of Muench's charitable projects.

Father Muench also was concerned with a wide variety of extracurricular interests. In addition to his work as a seminary professor he was involved in several charitable, social and educational causes. He was spiritual director of the Missionary Association for Catholic Women and of the Holy Childhood Society in Milwaukee; a member of the legislative committee of the Wisconsin Credit Union; treasurer of the Saint Michael's Priests' Society of which he was one of the organizers; a member of the advisory board and metropolitan council of the Milwaukee Society of Saint Vincent de Paul; vice president of the Catholic Conference on Industrial Problems; a member of the Catholic Action committee of the Catholic Central Verein and of the seminary section in the National Catholic Educational Association.

One of the professor's more unique undertakings as a young priest was his assistance in organizing the Apostolate of Suffering. Clara M. Tiry, an invalid with whom he had become acquainted as an assistant at Saint Michael's parish, was the guiding spirit of this movement to organize a spiritual association of persons who were ill, confined to their homes or victims of prolonged sickness. On 24 August 1926 Father Muench and Clara Tiry formally organized the Apostolate of Suffering, and four years later they established the Good Samaritan Guild, a group of women banded together for the purpose of visiting the sick. During the Milwaukee period of his life Muench guided and encouraged leaders of these organizations as their spiritual director. He spent long hours counseling and helping these noble women in their distinctive apostolate which spread across the United States. They published a quarterly bulletin of information and encouragement called *Our Good Samaritan* which brought comfort and spiritual direction to the infirm. During the next thirty-six years, wherever he was, Muench wrote long letters to Clara Tiry and her associates, suggested programs and activities of organized prayer and good works. Whenever he returned to Milwaukee he would offer Mass in the home of Clara Tiry. He never lost interest in this apostolate which he considered to be, perhaps, the most important work he had participated in since it was directed toward interior prayer, sacrifice and joyful acceptance of God's will. Muench's association with this apostolate was a quiet and unassuming support of suffering and hidden people who were chosen by God to grow in interior grace and to participate joyfully in the needs of the world through their prayers and sacrifices.

In 1929 Archbishop Messmer appointed Father Muench, then dean of the Department of Theology at Saint Francis, as rector of the seminary. Monsignor Breig had resigned due to advancing age and younger leadership was needed. After a long administration of twenty-seven years, Archbishop Messmer died on August 4 of the following year and Archbishop Samuel A. Stritch, formerly bishop of Toledo, was appointed fifth ordinary of Milwaukee on 26 August 1930. Stritch, whose Diocese of Toledo had no seminary, was a strong supporter of Saint Francis Seminary, and he and Muench soon became close friends. Stritch wanted to construct new seminary buildings at Saint Francis but his appointment to Milwaukee in the depth of the depression ruled out such a development.

During the depression period, from 1929 to 1935, Father Muench strove to economize and reorganize at Saint Francis. Much had to be done as Monsignor Breig had been aloof from the actual operation of the seminary and had spent considerable time abroad as a traveling companion with Messmer as he visited his native Switzerland during the last years of his life. Muench continued teaching his classes in dogma and apologetics during his term as rector. The seminary had grown to a total of 319 students with twenty professors. Among them were Fathers Francis Haas, social science; William P. O'Connor, philosophy; and Albert G. Meyer, scripture. These faculty members later became fellow bishops with Muench at Grand Rapids (Haas), Madison (O'Connor) and Superior-Milwaukee-Chicago (Meyer). Muench, Meyer and O'Connor were close friends. Muench and Haas did not always agree, however, on ideas and programs in their common field of the social sciences.

Muench as ninth rector of Saint Francis worked hard at organizing the administration of the seminary. He systematized the office files, installed historical archives and merged the student aid and loan funds. He strove to interest people in establishing burses for students at Saint Francis, a badly needed endowment. He started a sustaining endowment for the library and organized an association of priests and laity, called "Friends of the Seminary," to promote and support Saint Francis. Alumni files were established with a clipping service for each priest-alumnus' file. Improvements were made on the seminary grounds to beautify the setting of the historic old buildings, and facilities of the faculty and student body were up-dated as much as was possible at that time.

Muench opened the Salzmann Library to the student body, an important advance, and established a new mission reading room in the Miller Memorial Gymnasium. He strove to raise the academic standard of the seminary by introducing a series of convocations and discussions that would supply intellectual stimulation and break down the existing in-bred tendency toward self-containment. American Catholic seminaries and colleges in the 1920's were all too frequently bastions of fundamentalism with no tradition of intellectual dissent. However, it was evident that while Muench possessed a liberal approach to social and economic issues, he was thoroughly traditional and conservative on moral and theological questions. In this he was typical of the American bishops and academic personnel of that period. The poor and uneducated immigrant background of American Catholics tended to direct their interests toward improvements in the fields of economics and social affairs. There was little interest in theological and biblical scholarship. These second generation Americans had been raised on the morality of their devout and hard working immigrant parents who had settled centers such as Milwaukee. Muench's strength and acceptance by his peers lay in this reverence for conformity combined with an acceptable openness in social action. On 21 September 1934 he was named a domestic prelate.

Muench brought to Saint Francis a rather diversified series of convocation speakers. Father Edwin V. O'Hara, founder of the National Catholic Rural Life Conference, later bishop of Kansas City, spoke on summer vacation schools in 1930; public debates were held between debating teams of Marquette University, Milwaukee, and the Universities of Pittsburgh and Iowa; Doctor Francis V. Murphy, head of the department of architecture in the Catholic University of America, discussed architectural developments; Justice John D. Wickhem described the work of the Wisconsin supreme court; Abner Thompson read from Hamlet; William Bruce, of the Bruce Publishing Company, explained the art of bookmaking and Richard Hennessey spoke on illustrated manuscripts; Father Stephen Klopfer offered a demonstration of the latest methods in teaching the deaf; and Dr. John A. Sherry offered his opinions as a doctor at Lourdes and introduced the students to the phenomenon of Theresa Neumann's visions as a stigmatic as early as 1932. Outside organizations were brought to the campus such as the 250 members of the Saint Vincent de Paul Society of Milwaukee who held their first meeting in the seminary auditorium in 1931. Issues that became public interest a quarter of a century later were presented to the students during these years. Among them were lectures by Brother Andrew of the Servants of the Most Holy Trinity on the problem of the small number of Negro Catholics in the United States; John J. Kenney discussed juvenile delinquency; and in 1931 George Bruce described the Saint Lawrence Seaway that became a reality twenty-eight years later.

The students generally reacted favorably to Rector Muench. He usually presented a formal appearance and would coldly stand off students requesting too frequent "downtown" visits on Wednesday afternoons. But when problems arose they always found a warm and understanding friend in the rector. Muench listened to the students. He was fair and just and even those former seminarians whom he had dismissed or who left the seminary voluntarily, remained close to him throughout their lives. Muench obtained jobs for several of his former seminarians and followed their careers closely through correspondence and visits. Discipline in previous years had been characterized as police surveillance. Muench had a different philosophy of student life. He told the prefects: "Don't check on the students; doors open out." This was, indeed, a welcome and trusting experience for the seminarians. He played baseball and bowled with them. He encouraged students who wanted to start a mission paper to show initiative in the matter. Muench was proud of the students and encouraged those who indicated they had potential.[7]

The old Wisconsin tensions between Germans, Poles and Irish continued during Muench's years as rector and there were those among the minority groups of Polish and Irish descent who considered him to be too strongly pro-German. When asked about this in interviews at the end of his life Muench stated that such ethnic competitions did exist. He considered that the majority of Germans had better relationships with the Poles than with the Irish. However, there were seminarians of Polish descent who believed that Muench favored their fellow students of German descent. Throughout his life Muench would also find some bishops of Irish descent in the United States, as well as the French in Europe, unsympathetic to the emergence of this American prelate of German descent.

An encounter with Father Charles E. Coughlin, the famed radio priest from Detroit, and founder of the National Union for Social Justice, brought Muench national attention in 1935. Archbishop Stritch came to the seminary for a visit and spoke against Coughlin and his money theories in a talk to the seminarians. Before dinner Father Peter Leo Johnson, professor of Church history in the seminary, remarked that no one had as yet really critically refuted Coughlin. Muench replied that he would prepare a refutation of Coughlin's monetary theory if Johnson would publish it. In April of 1935 Muench's article appeared in *The Salesianum*, publication of Saint Francis Seminary. In this essay Muench disagreed with Coughlin's views, but he conceded that by his broadcasts the Detroit priest had diverted attention from socialistic and communistic agitators, created interest in social problems and made people read for the first time the social encyclicals of Popes Leo XIII and Pius XI. Then Muench proceeded to point out the fallacies in Coughlin's simplistic monetary and banking ideas. He denied that the monetary system was the sole cause of the depression; outlined the unsound basis of bimetallism and the remonetization of silver; showed how Coughlin's prediction did not materialize that trade with China would increase if silver were revalued at the ratio of fourteen-and-a-half to one; pointed out that if the metallic reserve were put into circulation there would be no stable reserve for credit expansion and the rich would be the only ones to profit from Coughlin's redemption recommendation; warned that the latter's proposals for paper currency exceeded all safe experience in the monetary history of the United States; debunked the idea that the Federal Reserve banks manufacture paper money on the basis of two and one-half dollars to every gold dollar; denied that the whole system had not been operated honestly and efficiently; stated that no economist of note endorsed the Nye-Sweeney banking bill that Coughlin was supporting; and warned that the Coughlinite proposal to create a United States bank was full of political and economic dynamite. Muench concluded:

"Father Coughlin is at his best in his role as a prophet denouncing and exposing evil in our economic structure. In this role he is so competent as to have no equal. He makes a serious mistake, however, in venturing into a field for which he has neither the mission nor the equipment. By dragging the Catholic program of social justice into politics he is creating for it more than an unusual peril.

"If it fails in politics, as fail it must with his untenable proposals, people will have their confidence shaken in it to such an extent that the laborious work which Catholic sociologists have done in its behalf in the last five decades will suffer a setback from which it will not recover for years to come." [8]

Muench soon learned the extent and intensity of Coughlin's support. He was immediately deluged with telegrams and letters of protest. Catholics who had suffered poverty and lack of opportunity and who now had a champion from their ranks, cried "traitor" at Muench. Coughlin, a classic depression demagogue, aroused a deep emotional response in millions of Americans and active camps formed in support of and in opposition to the dynamic spellbinder from Royal Oak. Coughlin's supporters considered his economic and social panaceas as a quick way of breaking down the concentration of wealth in the hands of a few and creating a new economic system that would eliminate poverty and protect private property. His opponents pointed out that Coughlin, in blaming all social ills on the monetary situation, was going against the papal encyclicals which placed the cause of inequities in the displacement of the social order. Moreover, they were frightened by the similarities of the Coughlin program with totalitarian theories and anti-Semetic tendencies.

Typical of the emotional reaction which Muench's article aroused was a letter he received from a certain E. J. Thompson of San Francisco, on 1 June 1935:

"Point out, I ask you, the result of the five decades of labor by Catholic sociologists that Father Coughlin is about to destroy. You cannot. Whoever they are, they have done nothing outstanding. We, the Catholic laity, can point to them, the Catholic sociologists, as always well fed and washed clean as befits their noble rank. Boo! Father Coughlin stands out preeminently as a leader, and we of the common herd are for him. Whatever he does, he will never hurt the welfare of the Catholic Church. Because France, Spain and Mexico had none such as he, we have to be listening to you fellows bewailing the fate of Catholics in these countries. Men like Archbishop [John] Hughes of New York, our own Father [Peter C.] York and now Father Coughlin have never thought of themselves and 'nearbishop' robes, but of their Lord and Master Jesus Christ.

"A change is coming in this country, you are not so blind that you do not see it. When it has come to pass, watch your skins. Father [James M.] Gillis [C.S.P.] has told us that Leo XIII got his ideas on social justice from studying Saint Basil. Father Coughlin must have studied Basil well when he belonged to the congregation that honored the name of Saint Basil. You, Muench, are so clever, you know it all and Monsignor [John A.] Ryan also, and [William] Cardinal O'Connell and the dear Wilfrid Parsons, S.J.! Why don't you four unite and hire the same halls Father Coughlin is hiring, and for the sake of the poor tell us how to solve this social question. You are rushing into print but where are your followers? Father Coughlin has them. If his teachings are wrong, why don't you as Christian gentlemen show him how this problem of social justice may be solved. That is what we the men of the street want. You are the Catholic sociologists and your labors of 100 years are being destroyed. From thousands of throats — Boo! Spend your time in the shops getting the correct shade of purple for your robes and in the dressmaking parlors having your cinctures made the exact depth. All we can say, when we look around and see our priests sitting back and taking it easy, Poor Jesus!"

There was a steady stream of letters of this type in the months ahead as well as continued newspaper comment. Favorable responses and requests for copies of the article came from sociologists, economists, businessmen, lay friends and seminary professors of philosophy and social science. For example, Father Virgil Michel, O.S.B., editor of *Orate Fratres* magazine at Saint John's Abbey, Collegeville, Minnesota, congratulated him on his clear thinking in explaining Catholic social principles. Father Francis J. Gilligan, professor at the Saint Paul Seminary, thanked him on 9 May 1935 for not treating Coughlin with personal contempt, as was all too often the case, and for evaluating his theories competently. Gilligan said that Coughlin had hurt the cause of social justice because he had made "many of the American bishops more conservative than ever so that they suppress prudent and cautious utterances." Monsignor John A. Ryan, professor of moral theology in the Catholic University of America, and Father Wilfrid Parsons, S.J., in the columns of *America* magazine, joined Muench in accusing Coughlin of offering quack methods for solving the depression malady.

Despite the fact that he continued to receive letters asking him how much the international bankers were paying him, Muench determined to explain his position in a public lecture. He chose a meeting of the Milwaukee Saint Rose Home and School Association on 7 May 1935 to repeat that Father Coughlin's monetary and banking program was unsound, his radio broadcasts imprudent and that Coughlin was not the spokesman for the Catholic Church. Muench stated:

"Coughlin advocates cheap money by a return to bimetallism. Everyone who has studied the history of finance knows that wherever bimetallism has been tried, even in our own country, it has been a colossal failure.

"His proposals for a government-owned central bank inevitably will develop into a huge bureaucracy, controlled by selfish politicians.

"The very poor whom he would help would become the hapless victims of unsound money systems. The promises he has held out about revaluation of silver have remained unfulfilled.

"It would not be wise to throw away an old shoe until one knows whether the new one will pinch. It is highly important in questions of money and banking that a sound system be established and maintained in this country.

"For this reason it is advisable that a special commission of experts be appointed by congress before radical changes be made in the monetary and banking system." [9]

This talk was covered by Milwaukee and Chicago reporters and was soon receiving editorial comment in newspapers. The Milwaukee *Sentinel* without permission published a full page summary of *The Salesianum* article in its Sunday edition of 18 May 1935 and Muench protested to the editors. Father John W. Chapman, S.J., of Newton College, near Boston, took exception to Muench's arguments and Muench responded to him in *The Sentinel* on May 23. The controversy continued during that summer of 1935 until it was suddenly terminated in August by a development which forced Muench, who had been enjoying this academic exercise, to drop out of the lists.

On the morning of 2 August 1935 Monsignor Muench received a letter from the Apostolic Delegate in Washington, D.C., informing him that Pope Pius XI was considering his appointment as third bishop of Fargo, North Dakota. This see had been vacant since the previous incumbent, Bishop James O'Reilly, had died on 19 December 1934. Muench was asked if he would accept. He looked up the Diocese of Fargo in the *Official Catholic Directory* and found that it was a rural diocese while his entire background had been urban. He had never been there, knew only two or three of its priests whom he had met at conventions, liked the work he was doing and decided not to accept. This decision took him two hours to make and he went over to the Convent of the Third Order Sisters of Saint Francis on the seminary grounds where Archbishop Stritch was presiding at a profession of vows. He met Stritch in the corridor and the archbishop asked Muench to come along to the program the novices were having for him. Muench could not remember one part of that program as he sat through it with his letter burning in his pocket.

After the program was over Muench asked Stritch if he could see him for a few minutes. They went into the archbishop's rooms and Muench told Stritch what he had received and that he intended to refuse the appointment. Stritch had left home that morning before reading his mail and, thus, was not as yet aware of the development. He cut Muench short and told him in no uncertain terms: "When the Holy Father calls we don't refuse. You will disappoint me." It was obvious that Archbishop Stritch had recommended the rector of his seminary for a bishopric. Stritch also was conscious that in thirty years no priest of the Archdiocese of Milwaukee had been named a bishop since Father Augustin F. Schinner was appointed as first bishop of Superior, Wisconsin, in 1905. Archbishop Messmer had not bothered to recommend his priests for advancement as Stritch would do now and in the years ahead. In the end the latter persuaded Muench to accept and he went to the telegraph office to send the designated reply: "I agree with the contents of the letter." He was in a daze for the next two weeks until the official appointment was announced.

The Consistorial Congregation in Rome, responsible for appointments to bishoprics, was informed by the apostolic delegate of Muench's acceptance, and a date was agreed upon for the publication of his nomination as bishop of Fargo. The appointment carried the date of 10 August 1935 and the announcement was released on August 12. Allie went home to his mother as soon as the morning release was announced. His father did not hear the news until lunch time when his friend Joe Bunke said to him: "Joe, dein Sohn ist ein Bischof." He would not believe it until he got home to find the whole family by this time gathered there in great excitement. Bishop-elect Muench was sad, however, for he sincerely wanted to stay in his position as rector of Saint Francis Seminary. As his friends came by during the following days to congratulate him they noted the same reaction. Muench told Aloysius Croft as two tears ran down his cheeks: "I don't want to be a bishop; I want to train priests."

Meanwhile the priests of Milwaukee kept asking: "Where is Fargo?" Most of them had never heard of it. The Coughlinite papers announced with satisfaction that Muench had been sent to the wilds of North Dakota. The Detroit *Free Press*, on the other hand, stated on August 13 that the critic who had called Father Coughlin's theories contrary to Catholic philosophy had been honored by Pope Pius. Muench immediately rushed a letter to Father Coughlin in which he denounced the unfair tactics of the *Free Press* and stated that he did not consider his appointment either as papal approval of his economic theories or a condemnation of Coughlin's. "To disagree with me is your privilege as it is mine to disagree with you. It is my conviction that in matters of this kind we may well remember the pertinent words of Saint Augustine: 'In dubiis libertas'." Father Coughlin replied on September 5, felicitating him on his appointment and promising him a remembrance in the prayers at the Shrine of the Little Flower in Royal Oak. Not once did Coughlin allude to the controversy of the past months.

Bishop Bernard J. Mahoney of Sioux Falls, South Dakota, stated when the appointment of Muench to Fargo was announced: "Now the Hindenburg line of Saint Louis, Dubuque, Saint Cloud and Fargo is safe." He was referring to the appointment of Bishop Christian H. Winkelmann two years previously as auxiliary of Saint Louis; the transferral in 1930 of Bishop Francis J. Beckman from Lincoln to the Archdiocese of Dubuque; and the incumbency of Bishop Joseph F. Busch in the Diocese of Saint Cloud. All of these dioceses had strong German-Catholic populations and all now had bishops of German descent. Muench in later years enjoyed repeating this quip of Mahoney's as indicative of the strong ethnic reactions of the dominant Irish in American Catholicism who diligently watched episcopal appointments. On the other hand, Muench's letters of congratulation following the announcement of his appointment repeatedly revealed how satisfied the Germans were that "one of our own" had been chosen. The nineteenth-century conflicts of European nationalities that were carried on in the American Church had not as yet subsided. Muench, personally, made only one comment on his appointment. He noted that he was to be the only academically trained social scientist in the American hierarchy.

Bishop-elect Muench chose 15 October 1935, his mother's name day, for his consecration. The ceremonies were to be held in the Gesu Church in Milwaukee since the cathedral had burned, as Muench said, after nineteen monsignors had been invested. That much red in one place could only bring about spontaneous combustion. Archbishop Amleto Giovanni Cicognani, apostolic delegate to the United States, consecrated Muench, as the fifth bishop he had consecrated to date, and Archbishop Stritch delivered the sermon. Co-consecrators were Bishops William R. Griffin, auxiliary of LaCrosse and Christian H. Winkelmann, auxiliary of Saint Louis. After the lengthy ceremonies Bishop Muench passed through the church blessing the people for the first time. As the group pictures were being taken in front of the church Muench noticed, to his dismay, that the episcopal ring Val Blatz had given him was gone. He began looking for it and found it at the edge of the walk in the grass. Because his fingers were so small Muench would have trouble keeping a ring on his finger throughout his life.

The festive banquet was held at the Schroeder Hotel. Place cards had a stork carrying a baby with a mitre and the pastry had replicas of Saint Mary's Cathedral, Fargo, and the North Dakota Cass County jail traced in the frosting. Forty priests from Fargo were present for the consecration of their new bishop and Father Edward Geraghty, veteran pastor of Saint James Church, Jamestown, North Dakota, found himself at a table of Milwaukee priests. They proceeded to ask him what kind of a house the bishop had. Geraghty said: "A sod house," and went on to describe at length to the innocent Milwaukee burghers the dimensions of a prairie sod house with its woodshed and the potbellied stoves in every room. When these priests came to visit Muench in Fargo they asked to see the sod house and found instead to their surprise the large brick bishop's house at 608 Broadway with its twenty some rooms.

From October 15 to November 5 Bishop Muench celebrated pontificals at the seminary and in his home parish, and was honored at farewell banquets by the many organizations which he had belonged to or assisted. There were not enough dinner occasions to go around and luncheons and breakfasts had to be scheduled before the Muench party departed on the evening of November 4 in special cars attached to the Milwaukee Railroad train from Milwaukee to Saint Paul. The next morning there was time for Mass at the Saint Paul Cathedral which Archbishop John Gregory Murray, as was his custom, insisted on serving. Then the special Great Northern train departed for Fargo located 250 miles northwest on the Minnesota–North Dakota border. All of the family and many Milwaukee friends were present for the installation ceremonies at Saint Mary's Cathedral on November 6. There were five inches of snow on the ground and the temperature was zero. As the Elks band went up Broadway to the Fargo cathedral their instruments froze in their hands. It was a chilling introduction to North Dakota and worse was to follow. That winter of 1935-36 set new records. From January 15 to February 26 the temperature never rose above zero day or night and sank at one point to −37°. During the following summer the first five days of July were above 100 degrees. Fathers Oscar Ziegler and Albert G. Meyer came from Saint Francis Seminary for a visit and they sat with Muench on the cement driveway of the bishop's house, the coolest place they could find. It was the summer of North Dakota's worst dust storms when lights had to be turned on during the day time. Muench had arrived in his diocese at the height of the worst depression and drought in the history of the State.

The first morning's mail on Bishop Muench's desk that day after his installation as third bishop of the See was from creditors. There was to be no honeymoon for the new ordinary. During the ten months between Bishop O'Reilly's death and Muench's arrival in Fargo the administrator, Father Vincent J. Ryan, had said because of the diocesan debt and depression conditions: "Wait for the new bishop." Now a funded debt of $800,000 faced Muench. Income was decreasing rapidly and monthly payments on outstanding parochial notes and bonds could not be met. The picture was not exceptional among American dioceses in 1936 but conditions in North Dakota made the situation especially critical.

Bishop Muench returned to Milwaukee to ask Neal Gleason of Northwestern Mutual Life Insurance Company for a short term loan. His old friend had to refuse the worried bishop but gave him excellent advice on how to begin reducing outstanding diocesan debts.[10] Gleason showed Muench a large map of the United States in his office with red blotches on it indicating places where he had to refuse requests for institutional loans. The whole State of North Dakota was solid red and Muench got the message. The depression, drought, and North Dakota Governor William Langer's moratorium on mortgage foreclosures had frightened away possible loan companies. Muench came back to Fargo empty-handed and not knowing where to turn. He determined to study thoroughly the background and character of his diocese as a first step in arriving at a solution.

The Diocese of Fargo, established forty-six years earlier on 12 November 1889, embraced 35,786 square miles of the eastern half of North Dakota. Bismarck was the other diocese in North Dakota and included the area of the western half of the State. Bishop John Shanley, former rector of the Saint Paul Cathedral, had come to North Dakota in 1889 during the year that statehood was achieved as first bishop of the entire State with the cathedral at Jamestown. He soon saw that Fargo was potentially the largest center of North Dakota and moved there in 1897. Bismarck was separated as a diocese from Fargo in 1910, the year that Shanley's successor, Father James O'Reilly, pastor of Saint Anthony Church, Minneapolis, and another friend of Archbishop John Ireland of Saint Paul, succeeded to Fargo.

The diocese was over ninety per cent rural in character with a limited number of small sized cities such as Fargo itself (30,600), Grand Forks, Jamestown, Wahpeton, Grafton, Devils Lake and Valley City within its confines. In 1935 there were 69,871 Catholics in the area of the diocese. Of these Catholics, 63,673 were white and 6,198 were Sioux and Chippewa Indians. There were 127 diocesan and eight religious priests caring for 187 churches of which 102 had resident pastors. Among these 102 pastors only eight had received their full salaries of $100 a month since

1929. Only twenty-four parishes had parochial schools and there were eleven high schools staffed by nine religious communities of sisters.

Muench quickly realized that his diocese was missionary and in distressed circumstances, "an impossible burden," as he said. The total income from all parishes reached only $430,000, half of the existing funded debt. There were twenty-six students studying for the diocesan priesthood but vocations were far short of meeting current needs. During previous years a substantial number of Irish missionaries had generously worked in the diocese, but Bishop O'Reilly had decided by 1929 that foreign-born Irish clergy would no longer be solicited for the diocese. If a native diocesan clergy was to be established a strong vocation program was urgently needed. The Catholic population included German-Russian, French-Canadian, Bohemian, German and Irish immigrants and their descendants. Muench quickly faced the reality that his administration at first could be only a holding operation. All plans for expansion and development would have to await the end of the farm depression and full recovery.

The situation was especially frustrating because the Diocese of Fargo embraced some of the most fertile land in the United States. The rich Red River Valley, extending from Wahpeton through Grafton, had dried up from lack of moisture. Top soil was blown against fences like snow as North Dakota became a disaster area of the semiarid "dust bowl" northern plains. Muench remembered seeing a cow in 1936 under a tree near the Sheyenne River in West Fargo stretching up to eat the leaves. In the spring of 1936 the whole area was so short of moisture that the grain which had been planted never germinated, and the grass, even the tough prairie and buffalo grass, never turned green. Many farmers did not take their binders or combines into the fields that year as there was nothing to harvest. The State's population was decreasing yearly as bankrupt people left North Dakota in search of a decent and respectable life elsewhere. Nothing disturbed Muench more in the first years than the outstate migration of families from their farm homes because of debts and substandard living conditions.

It was a traumatic experience for the people of the State of North Dakota who suffered more than the rest of the nation. The drought and depression accentuated long-standing difficulties created by North Dakota's status as a producer of raw materials while having little or no control over the markets where these products were bought and sold. Thousands lost their farms, and more than a third of the population lived on relief. Muench found parishes in his diocese where every family was on relief. Nine of the eleven years from 1929 through 1939 had less than average rainfall. Throughout the 1930's grasshoppers also menaced the whole of the northern plains. State and federal assistance was needed for control programs. Added to the drought and grasshopper disasters were the depressed prices for meager crops. Elwyn B. Robinson, in his excellent *History of North Dakota*, explains conditions:

"At the bottom in 1932, North Dakota farmers sold wheat for 36¢ a bushel, oats for 9¢, barley for 14¢, potatoes for 23¢, flaxseed for 87¢ and beef cattle for $3.30 per hundredweight. Prices recovered somewhat, but were never good in the 1930's: wheat sold for only 53¢ a bushel in 1938.

"Yields were scanty and income small. From 1929 to 1941, North Dakota farmers produced only two wheat crops of more than 100,000,000 bushels — a minimum for a satisfactory yield. In 1936 the crop was a pitiful 19,000,000 bushels . . . Drought and depression deprived the State's farmers of the staggering sum of $1,340,000,000 from 1929 to 1938.

"In 1933, the low year, the per capita personal income in the United States was $375, but in North Dakota it was only $145. By 1938 the figures were $527 in the United States and $278 in North Dakota. From 1932 through 1937 the per capita personal income in North Dakota was only forty-seven per cent of the national average. Plainly, the 1930's brought much greater hardship to North Dakota than they did to the nation as a whole.

"Low income caused a multitude of misfortunes; a decline in land values, delinquent loans and foreclosures on mortgages, unpaid taxes, increasing tenancy, growing public ownership of land, large numbers of people on relief, and a great movement of people out of the State. The average value of farm land per acre fell from $22 in 1930 to $12 in 1940, the average farm from $12,200 to $6,600 . . .

"Thousands fled the stricken State. By 1940 the population was down to less than 642,000, a loss of 5.7 per cent, or nearly 39,000 persons, in a decade. The loss was really much greater. The excess of births over deaths in the 1930's was more than 82,000. That is, if no one left the State, its population would have increased by 82,000 from 1930 to 1940. North Dakota lost not only that number, however, but also 39,000 more, a loss by out-migration of over 121,000, or about double the loss of the 1920's."[11]

Bishop Muench found himself in a situation that was, in many ways, parallel to his position as rector of Saint Francis Seminary and his future assignment as apostolic visitor and nuncio to Germany. At Saint Francis Seminary he had succeeded Monsignor Breig, a German professor who for nine years had been aloof from the actual problems of a seminary in need of up-dating. Now, in Fargo, he succeeded Bishop O'Reilly, an Irish scholarly recluse who was remote from the mounting problems of an American prairie diocese suffering from a severe depression. O'Reilly preferred living alone with his books. In Germany after World War II Muench would be concerned with restoring the prestige of the papal mission there after the long tenure of Archbishop Cesare Orsenigo as nuncio who was not popular with the German people and who had left the impression of being too sympathetic to the Nazi regime. In each major assignment of his life Muench found himself in a position of restoring and renewing conditions that had deteriorated. These jobs as a repair man had their difficult moments and at each stop there were people who did not like the thoroughness which he quickly evidenced.

On the train returning from Milwaukee to Fargo, Bishop Muench took one of his little black notebooks that he always carried with him for memoranda, quotes and figures and began to outline his plans. For some years he had, as an economist and sociologist, been thinking of a possible diocesan co-operative program of financing. He had mentioned the project to Bishop Paul P. Rhode of Green Bay some years earlier, but he had been told it would not work because a bishop would need an iron fist and could not enforce it. But, now, in the crisis atmosphere of the depression, Muench was determined to give it a try in his new diocese.

The plan, which he was to call the Catholic Church Expansion Fund of the Diocese of Fargo, was based on the corporative principles of the encyclicals of Pius XI and the co-operatives and credit unions of Antigonish, Nova Scotia. Individual, small parishes experienced difficulties in obtaining loans from hard-pressed local banks since parish income was voluntary and in depression times people were not able to contribute. Individual schools and hospitals were in an equally disadvantageous position. But a diocese as a whole could present a better picture if a fund was created by pooling the resources of all parishes in the diocese to aid its member organizations with loans. Character would be rated as collateral, the diocese would receive interest on the money invested in the common fund and thrift would be promoted.

Muench received help in organizing the Catholic Church Expansion Fund as an audited, separate corporation from Herbert G. Nilles, lawyer; John C. Heisler, auditor; Fathers Vincent J. Ryan, vicar general, and Leo F. Dworschak, chancellor, all of Fargo and Monsignor John Quillinan of Casselton. Letters were sent to people inviting them to invest in the Diocese of Fargo by loaning money to the Expansion Fund at interest rates of 2% for one year, 2½% for two years, 3% for three years, 3½% for four years, and 4% for five years. Returns were immediately encouraging and one widow brought in $30,000 left by her husband because she wanted to help the Church in this way and to have a safe medium of investment. The diocese invested its own scholarship money and Priests' Mutual Aid Fund in the Expansion Fund. At first these funds were minimal but they soon developed. The scholarship fund for priesthood students, for example, totaled only $5,300 when Muench first came to the diocese. The new bishop also directed those parishes with surplus funds to invest them in the Expansion Fund. All assets of the diocese and parishes were pooled and individual parishes and institutions of the diocese then borrowed from the separately incorporated Fund.

There was co-operation on all fronts and by the second year of operation the Expansion Fund had a credit line of $100,000 where at the beginning Muench could not even obtain one loan in Milwaukee. After two years $188,000 was refinanced at a saving of $20,000 in interest. When Muench resigned as bishop of Fargo there were eighty parishes with no debt that had invested in the Fund, that had helped others in the diocese, and that could borrow from the Fund whenever they needed assistance. During the years 1936 to 1945 over a million dollars in loans was distributed by the Fund. It was repeatedly said throughout the diocese that this program which Muench initiated was his major material contribution to his people of Fargo. There would have been no possibility of expansion without it. Fargo was one of the first dioceses in the United States to inaugurate such a successful and well-managed fund. Several variations of the same program were soon in operation in other American dioceses. Muench was particularly pleased that the character of those involved in this co-operative venture had proved to be the best collateral. During the entire period of his administration there was no one who failed to meet obligations or whose payment had to be deferred.

Muench realized that he quickly had to acquaint himself with his far-flung diocese and during the first year he visited every parish within its confines. Father Dworschak warned him that he would be eating chicken constantly on these trips and Muench soon found this to be the case. In the days before deep freezers were common in homes the only fresh meat available was chicken. Muench had much to learn about rural problems, wheat farming and row crops on the prairie, as well as the outlooks of clergy and laity in a rural diocese. He admitted that he scarcely knew what a cow looked like, to the delight of his listeners, who quickly warmed to this open, friendly, learned and yet simple bishop who was deeply interested in their problems and who would listen to them. Muench was personally "astounded" at their favorable reaction to him. From the beginning he experienced co-operation from the priests as he began to develop his plans for an extensive renewal of Catholic life. Muench soon became attached to the hard-working and generous people of the prairie. They were independent, conservative and honest. He said: "I liked the diocese, the priests, the people. I found myself entering into their problems with enthusiasm. There were terrific problems then but I liked the fresh air of North Dakota even if I was a burgher." Doctor Richard J. Purcell, professor of American history in the Catholic University of America, visited him in Fargo during that first summer of 1936, and said: "I think he's going to do all right. He's already interested in crops, grain, rainfall, and harvest quotas and is getting over his city background."

The people of the diocese enjoyed Muench's sense of humor and facility in telling stories. He frequently quoted Bishop Shanley's definition of North Dakota as "the state where the Red River runs north and the Irish vote Republican." Muench liked to recall that his birthday was the same as Martin Luther's and that he was born the same year that North Dakota became a state of the union, but he was still trying to see the significance of these relations.

The new bishop quickly became attached to the wide, flat prairie lands of his diocese. The winters were long and bitterly cold and the wind howled almost constantly. But in the spring when the first prairie grass blazed up, the wild crocus and prairie rose appeared, and the meadow larks were singing, the vast land was beautiful. In the late summer the prairie was a sea of waving golden wheat and to watch the sun setting on the far horizon was one of the unique experiences of life. After the harvest the bishop enjoyed the duck and pheasant hunting season as well as shooting deer in Canada. Muench was a good shot and enjoyed hiking over the rough country in the crisp autumn weather with a party of priests and laymen.

Bishop Muench's arrival in Fargo brought a transformation in the style and activity of the Catholic Church in the city and the diocese. He was young, forty-six years old, articulate and active. He surrounded himself with young men, initiated new programs and brought in national figures for meetings. The dominant civic and religious groups in the cities and State began to pay attention to the Church. Young people took notice and there was soon a growth in vocations to the priesthood and religious life in the diocese.[12] In the first year Bishop Muench ordained one priest, Father Thomas Hendrickson. From that day forward he determined to work unceasingly for vocations. There was not a confirmation ceremony at which he did not speak about and ask the people to pray for vocations. From 1935 to 1945 forty-one priests were ordained for the diocese and in 1945 sixty-five seminarians were studying for Fargo.

Bishop Muench strongly encouraged the establishment of burses for priesthood scholarships. Each of these scholarships totaled $5,000 or more and was invested for income to help defray the expenses of training future priests. He was instrumental in establishing eighty-eight of these scholarships. Muench realized that in a diocese without a minor or major seminary he would have to make a special effort to establish a tradition of native vocations. He also established a Priests' Mutual Aid Fund for retired priests in 1937 which would supply monthly benefits to those clergy who had devoted their lives to the spiritual needs of the people of Fargo. The active priests contributed annual dues to this Fund, as did each parish of the diocese. Starting with a monthly benefit check of $50 to retired priests, he was able after two years to increase these monthly checks to $100 and to make increases as the cost of living rose. The bishop also encouraged membership of the clergy in Blue Cross health insurance coverage and became a charter member of the organization in North Dakota along with Fathers Leo F. Dworschak and Anthony R. Peschel.

Muench set a personal example of taking no definite salary during his tenure as bishop of Fargo. The people of the diocese furnished his house, expenses and automobile from the *cathedraticum* collection, but expenses were scarcely met from this annual donation. During the years he was active in Fargo he never took more than $1,000 a year for his own personal needs; and during his years in Germany he took only $500 annually from the diocese.

After his first tour of the diocese, which is 210 miles in length and 198 miles wide, Bishop Muench realized that he would have to employ further means of remaining in contact with his priests and people. The number of priests was small and the parishes were dispersed and often isolated. The diocese could not afford a weekly paper or radio programs. Muench saw that his contacts with the diocese through speaking engagements would be mostly confined to confirmation tours. The only other possible means of contact was through the written word. It was at this point that the new bishop remembered how impressed he was when he was studying in Fribourg that Swiss and German bishops issued annual pastoral letters to the clergy and laity of their dioceses. Muench determined to prepare annual pastorals for his diocese which would be read in the churches in five sections during the Sundays of Lent through First Passion Sunday. For the next twenty-four years he faithfully continued this practice. He wrote on basic topics such as charity, marriage, family life, education, the priesthood and peace. He tried, not always with success, to use simple language and uncomplicated sentences. Priests sometimes complained that the pastorals were too heavy and over the heads of the people. Muench had a tendency to use involved sentences and ponderous comparisons. He was conscious of this and admired the style of his neighbor, Bishop William O. Brady of Sioux Falls, South Dakota, who wrote a light and interesting column in his diocesan paper.

Muench did his own research for these pastorals over a year's time, purchased and consulted journals and current documents on the topic at hand. He was unique among American bishops in this pastoral practice. He was determined not to be a remote administrator. Muench brought to diocesan life through these pastorals a spiritual teaching dimension that was not only an ancient episcopal tradition that was being neglected in the United States but, unfortunately, an example that was not followed by his peers. The primary pastoral and teaching office of a bishop was effectively evidenced in Fargo during these years through pastoral letters.

The reception by clergy and laity was generally favorable. Some 8,000 copies of each pastoral were printed; 6,000 copies were sent to the parishes of the diocese at a charge of five cents a copy. The remaining copies were distributed among bishops, friends, senators and congressmen, newspaper editors and an international mailing list of people who reacted enthusiastically to these pastoral statements by a diaspora bishop from the American prairie. There was an annual deficit of around $200 resulting from the publishing of the pastorals and Muench personally paid this bill.[13]

Another release from the chancery, *Folia Cleri*, was prepared each month by Bishop Muench for the clergy. In this house organ the priests were reminded of pastoral procedures at hand such as liturgical observances, Roman directives, reports that were due and current events of general concern. In 1939 a monthly diocesan newspaper, *Catholic Action News*, was initiated for the people of the diocese.[14] A weekly paper would have cost twice as much as the annual *cathedraticum* collection and Muench preferred to encourage the people to read existing national Catholic publications. *Catholic Action News*, attractively designed and written by young priests and laity of the diocese, concentrated on local news items and soon had a circulation of 15,000. It continues in unbroken publication to the present. During his years in Fargo and Germany Bishop Muench never failed to write a column for each issue. He viewed this publication as primarily a historical record and binding force among his scattered flock.

The choice of the name *Catholic Action News* for his diocesan paper dated Bishop Muench in the Pius XI period. Catholic Action was ever a reality to Muench who had studied in Europe at the time that it was being formulated as a program of Catholic lay participation with the hierarchy in the sanctification of souls through prayer, study and sacrifice. The political vagaries that developed in Italian Catholic Action circles were foreign to Muench's outlook on this apostolate. He considered Catholic Action as a parish co-operative effort by pastor and people to deepen liturgical life, discuss Catholic social principles and work together for the advancement of the common good.

To that end Bishop Muench inaugurated a series of annual Catholic Action Days throughout the Fargo diocesan deaneries. They were modeled on the *Katholikentage* of Germany, the famed annual liturgical and discussion gatherings of Catholics. Begun in 1936 these Catholic Action Days were popular and well-attended for eight years and then slowly died out over the next four years primarily because the restrictions and gas rationing of World War II made it impossible for people to gather in large numbers for meetings. Each Catholic Action Day had a general theme which was developed at an opening general session at two o'clock on a Sunday afternoon in the fall of the year. Sectional meetings then followed and were divided into general youth conferences, adult discussions of religious topics and lively sessions on co-operatives and farm problems that Farmers Union and Farm Bureau representatives attended.

Muench was also an enthusiastic supporter of discussion clubs which he found were more viable in rural than in urban parishes. People took an interest in reading according to an outlined program and talking about religious, social and economic matters. Father M. M. Coady, professor in the extension department of Saint Francis Xavier's University, Antigonish, Nova Scotia, came to the diocese the month after Muench was installed and traveled through its deaneries explaining the nature and procedures of discussion clubs. He convinced Bishop Muench and his consultors to undertake an extensive program of sponsoring discussion clubs throughout the diocese. Coady explained that people would never understand the principles of co-operatives unless there was previous discussion. Discussion clubs could be the threshold to Christian co-operative social action according to this theory which grew out of the depression atmosphere of the 1930's. The program was highly successful in Fargo during the period of the 1930's before the outbreak of World War II. At one time there were some 11,000 Catholic people actively participating in the undertaking. Muench brought in nationally known speakers to stimulate and sustain the discussion clubs such as Father Daniel J. Lord, Jesuit youth leader; Father George Johnson, professor in the department of Education of the Catholic University of America; and Monsignor Luigi Ligutti, DesMoines, Iowa, executive secretary and director of the National Catholic Rural Life Conference.

The National Catholic Rural Life Conference was another organization that Muench become actively engaged in supporting during his Fargo years. Father Vincent J. Ryan asked him in 1935 before he arrived in Fargo if the national convention of that organization could meet in Fargo in 1936 and Muench readily consented. The fourteenth annual convention of October, 1936, was held at the North Dakota Agricultural College in Fargo with some 5,000 persons attending. Father William T. Mulloy, pastor of Saint John the Evangelist Church, Grafton, North Dakota, was also an active supporter of the organization along with Ryan. Muench was not a founder of the conference but he studied rural problems carefully, and as an economist and sociologist was soon engrossed in the discussion and program of the organization. Ryan, Mulloy and Muench all became national presidents of the NCRLC during these years.

The National Catholic Rural Life Conference was a midwestern phenomenon that developed in American Catholic circles during this period of the 1930's. Catholics were predominantly urban in numbers and the so-called leaders of the Church in the United States were centered in the large eastern cities and along the industrial belt of the Great Lakes. But the large majority of American Catholic dioceses embraced the great land areas of the continent where Catholics lived as minorities and in need of special attention which they were not receiving from the "eastern establishment." Midwestern and western Catholics, accordingly, organized among themselves to advance a movement which Muench always considered did much good at the time in emphasizing the spiritual and human benefits of life on the land. Much money was spent on publications which did not convert as many as was hoped but an inroad was made. Bishop Edwin V. O'Hara of Great Falls, Montana, helped in emphasizing the religious education thrust of the NCRLC during its formative years, but he gradually veered away toward the work of the Confraternity of Christian Doctrine. The adult religious educational effort was then concentrated in the Confraternity, and the NCRLC stressed economic and social aspects of rural living.

A *Manifesto on Rural Life* was prepared by Ryan, Mulloy and Muench in 1939 as a publication of the NCRLC. They had consulted a wide variety of authorities including Bishop O'Hara and Father Virgil Michel, O.S.B., who involved students at Saint John's University, Collegeville, in doing research for the publication. The authors considered it necessary, Muench said, to state fundamental principles and policies of Christian rural life just as the Communists were doing for socialistic doctrine at the same time. Father Ryan made the final textual revision and the Bruce Publishing Company of Milwaukee published the volume. A Spanish edition was soon in circulation and the New York *Times* reviewed the volume favorably on 8 October 1939. The book was called "one of the most complete statements on concrete problems of economic and social problems to be issued by a representative agency of the Roman Catholic Church in America. Under present conditions," the *Times* review continued, "serious disadvantages prevent the farm family from realizing a full and satisfying life and these can and should be removed. Vanishing ownership is a major problem in American agriculture today . . . An economic system to be equitable must provide opportunity for the masses to become owners."

The NCRLC flourished for a time in such Midwest dioceses as Green Bay, Winona and Fargo where the farmers themselves were involved in the programs of the organization. In Fargo, Muench strove to emphasize pastoral problems in rural life panels and discussions as well as thorough adult education programs for the people of his diocese. Farmers' retreats, Grail schools and rural life institutes for priests were conducted. The family farm was advanced as an ideal by proponents of the NCRLC but year after year the reality of the American mechanized and industrialized large farm bore in upon them. It became obviously more economically efficient for farmers to own and operate larger units of production. Smaller farmers were not producing equal quotas and they soon began to drift toward the towns where they obtained part- or full-time construction and industrial employment. Two-thirds of the rural parishes in the Diocese of Fargo declined during the war period and its aftermath. Bishop Muench in the years after the war realized this fact economically, but persisted to the end in opposing the whole trend and saying that it should not be encouraged. His vital reactions had been developed in the depression years of the 1930's and he did not understand, after his prolonged absence in Germany, that the principles of Catholic social action that he advanced in the 1930's did not apply to the new phenomenon of industrial agriculture in the postwar world.

Another national Catholic organization in which the bishop of Fargo retained a lasting interest was the Catholic Central Verein of America. As a seminarian he had attended its annual sessions on a student scholarship, and as a professor at Saint Francis Seminary he regularly gave addresses at the conventions. During the years Muench was in Fargo he continued attending the meetings and when he went to Germany he always sent a message to the annual convention of the societies. Muench was, in many ways, "the man" of the Central Verein among American bishops. He was a close friend of Frederick P. Kenkel, director of the federation's Central Bureau in Saint Louis and maintained that it was Kenkel who had inspired him to study economics at the University of Wisconsin after Father Muench had attended summer schools in social action directed by Kenkel before and during World

War I at Spring Bank, Wisconsin. It was also at the Central Bureau that the groundwork of the National Catholic Rural Life Conference was laid in 1923 in collaboration with Father Edwin V. O'Hara. Muench and Kenkel carried on an extensive correspondence throughout their lives on procedural problems of the Verein, and moral and social principles of national and international life.[15]

Muench greatly admired and respected the record of the Central Verein in developing the lay apostolate among German Catholics in the United States, in supporting the family in need, in social charity among its members, in advancing the growth of the Catholic parochial school, in its national and international charitable works, and in its pacemaking statements in social study and action. The Central Verein, dating back to 1854, was among the first national organizations established for Catholics in the United States and when Muench gave the main address at the organization's 1939 annual meeting in San Francisco there were 90,000 affiliated members in 1,280 societies in twenty states. When the Central Verein observed the centennial of its founding, Archbishop Muench flew back from Germany to give the sermon at the opening Mass in Rochester, New York, on 13 August 1955. On that occasion Muench said:

"The social philosophy of the Central Verein reveals due regard for the state and its powers of intervention for the removal of grave social evils and the enactment of appropriate social legislation, but draws at the same time sharp lines demarcating the field of its competence. The Verein has always looked with distrust on the expanding powers of the so-called welfare state, knowing from history that all too easily they are unduly exercised in the end at the expense of the rights and freedoms of its citizens. The Verein has consistently advocated and fostered the spirit of self-help and self-reliance, mutual help and co-operative action. This may be seen from the bold steps it took in respect to consumers' and producers' co-operatives in the rural field and in the pioneering of parish credit unions. These are growing in numbers, strength and influence.

"In other words, in condemning the individualism of the liberal school, which exploited child and woman labor and took advantage in its greed of the unorganized worker, it did not condemn individualism based on the dignity of the human person with its consequent rights and freedom. In truth, it advocated this Christian individualism against the grasping powers of the modern state. Bound by the dictates of social justice and the obligations of social charity, it may well be called social individualism. It recognizes the rights and freedoms of the individual, but at the same time reminds him of his social duties toward others in human society." [16]

Muench was conscious that other Catholic organizations had entered the field of Catholic social action, that the Verein was accused of not having relevant programs, of projecting an image of nineteenth-century horse and buggy sentimentalism, of laboriously preparing ponderous statements of principle, of devoting too much of its energies to establishing a library at the Central Bureau as the special hobby of Kenkel, and especially of not developing meaningful youth programs. He strove year after year to encourage the Verein's leaders to formulate new objectives that would attract a fully and enlarged Americanized membership. In this vein he recommended that the federation support a strong Catholic press and with considerable vision stated:

"With regard to forming social action groups certainly nothing could be more desirable. However, we have to face the fact that they are hard to form and once formed are hard to hold together. People generally are no longer interested in social questions as was the case some decades ago . . .

"As to new objectives, they should be taken, I am sure, from the wide field of the lay apostolate. The century ahead, in my opinion, will be one of great lay activity . . .

"In the field of lay activity we shall have to give special attention to sound adult religious education because of the encroachments of secularism. In other words, the CCVA will have to put forth its best efforts toward good religious education along lines, of course, different from those when it encouraged and promoted our parochial school system in the decades of the past." [17]

Besides his participation in the national activities of the NCRLC and the CCVA Bishop Muench also served as one of the three-member Bishops' Committee on the Pope's Peace Points in 1942 and was named in 1945 as a member of the Pontifical Commission for Sacred Sciences at the Catholic University of America. Muench was also a charter member of *Pax Romana*, international Catholic organization promoting peace.

Bishop Muench was happy to have three priests of the Fargo Diocese appointed bishops during these years. Bishop Vincent Wehrle, O.S.B., Dakota pioneer and first bishop of Bismarck, retired in 1940 and Monsignor Vincent J. Ryan, pastor of Saint Anthony's Parish, Fargo, and vicar general of Fargo was appointed to Bismarck on 19 March 1940. Muench realized the importance of the State's two dioceses cooperating in close harmony and Ryan's appointment contributed to continued good relations. On 10 January 1945 Monsignor William T. Mulloy, pastor of Saint Mary's Cathedral, Fargo, was appointed sixth bishop of Covington, Kentucky, and Muench noted that it was the first time, to his knowledge, that a western priest was appointed to an eastern see. It was also significant that two of the Fargo priests whom Muench had recommended for consideration as bishops were of Irish descent. Throughout his life Muench had a strong aversion to nationalistic bias in political, social or religious relations. Despite this fact he was repeatedly labeled both in America and Europe as being pro-German in attitude. He learned gradually to live with this unfounded assertion, although he was hurt by such charges since his whole life was devoted to healing and building up relations between people separated by exaggerated nationalistic outlooks. His vicar general, Monsignor Leo F. Dworschak, was to be the third bishop chosen from the Fargo Diocese. On 22 June 1946 Dworschak was named coadjutor bishop of Rapid City, South Dakota.

During his first ten years as bishop of Fargo, Muench saw thirteen new parishes established. The Catholic Church Extension Society, based in Chicago, as a supporting organization for missionary dioceses, was a major source of financial aid in the establishment of these parishes. Bishop William D. O'Brien, auxiliary of Chicago and president of Extension, remained throughout these years a close friend and strong supporter of Bishop Muench's needs. During the years from 1935 through 1959, the Catholic Church Extension Society gave $195,228 to the Fargo Diocese. There were also established during these years seven new missions, seven hospitals, three catechetical centers, three homes for the aged and two parochial schools. In addition, large reserves began to build up for a postwar building program in the diocese which, unknown to Muench as he made long-range plans, he would not actively direct. Parish finances were organized on a uniform basis in 1939 when a systematic record of accounts was drawn up and copies of the account books sent to all parishes. All articles of incorporation and bylaws of the parish corporations were revised and approved by the Secretary of State of North Dakota in April of 1942. A diocesan synod, the first in the history of the diocese, was held in Fargo on

29–30 September 1941 and a diocesan synodal book was published. Considerable work went into the planning for this synod. Specialists in liturgy, moral theology, canon and civil law and Latin were consulted. Five preparatory commissions of the priests of the diocese helped prepare the proposed 608 Latin and 395 English statutes. The resulting statutes attracted interest and favorable comment in journals and reviews. In Germany after the war bishops continually were surprised, when Muench proudly showed them his synodal statutes from Fargo, that such a comprehensive approach could come from an American diocese. This reaction delighted Muench as he made it a point to see that Germans became acquainted with American practices.

The bishop of Fargo supported a strong Confraternity of Christian Doctrine program in the diocese and 862 discussion clubs were organized for some 11,000 participants. In 1944 there were 134 vacation schools for 6,462 students. The work of the Confraternity of Christian Doctrine was coordinated by a Catholic Action Bureau which also organized the activity of the Diocesan Rural Life Conference, the Confraternities of the Blessed Sacrament and the Holy Spirit, the Catholic Charities Bureau, the Diocesan Youth Council and the Catholic Boy Scouts.

A Catholic Educational Association of the diocese was organized in 1939 as was the Catholic Hospital Conference during the same year. Catholic nurses were organized in 1943 and affiliated the next year with the National Council of Catholic Nurses. A Laywomen's Retreat League was organized in 1941 and retreats were held in Grand Forks and Devils Lake as well as in Fargo. One of the most effective arms of the new activity that was evident on all sides in the diocese was the opening of a convent of Sisters of Service in Fargo on 21 August 1939. Four sisters from Toronto took census, made parish and hospital visits, conducted vacation schools and established a religious correspondence school that brought religious instruction to thousands who otherwise would never have been contacted.

When Bishop Muench observed the tenth anniversary of his arrival in Fargo during November of 1945 he wrote in his monthly column in *Catholic Action News*:

"As we review the achievements of the past ten years we are reminded that God gave the increase. We were but his laborers who planted and watered the seed in his vineyard.

"The ten years that now have become a part of history were burdened for us with many problems. They tell of drought and depression, lean crops and low prices. They record the most terrible war in all history. For us, no less than for others elsewhere, it hindered the normal growth of religion. Many fruitful activities had to be stopped.

"Our priests were put to a crucial test during the terrible thirties. Parishes were loaded down with debts; principal payments went into default, and in some cases, despite the utmost sacrifice and the greatest efforts, even interest could no longer be paid. The morale of the people was low; with one blow they had lost their savings; banks were closed, and, once proud possessors of homes, farms and businesses, our people saw them slip away from under their hands.

"In these black years our pastors stood by their flocks; at the cost of many personal sacrifices they carried on. Not a single parish was closed. On the contrary, new parishes were started during the past decade, proof once more that the hardy, pioneering spirit of their forebears still burned within the souls of priests and people. Defeatism did not extinguish its flame. Nor were any schools closed in this period . . .

"The past is gone. The future with its promise of better things lies ahead. For those who are alert to the opportunities of the newer day, for those who are thrifty, courageous, and industrious, the future comes with abundant gifts in its hands . . .

"Our program is simple: to live our life with God, to pattern it after the life of his Divine Son, to strengthen our Catholic sense, to work wholeheartedly with our leaders in the Church, to defend our faith against attacks, in short, to be Catholics in every thought, word, and deed of our lives.

"This program is not impossible to carry out. We will easily do so if, consecrating ourselves anew to God, we pray and work with steadfast purpose, conscious ever that every breath we draw brings us closer to the real goal of our lives."

Parish church in Stadt Kemnath,

Bavaria, birthplace of Theresa

Kraus Muench.

1908 Football Team at St. Francis

Seminary, Milwaukee; Aloisius Muench

standing, third from left.

Father Muench with his

mother at home on

Tenth Street, Milwaukee.

With deer in northern Wisconsin.

With first car.

Canoeing on Lake Minocqua.

Father Thomas Schmitz, classmate
and good friend, who died
suddenly of leukemia,
6 January 1930.

Bishop Muench with his
parents following the first
pontifical Mass at their home
parish, St. Boniface Church,
Milwaukee, 16 October
1935.

St. Mary's Cathedral and
Bishop's House, Fargo; not
a sod house after all.

Installation of Bishop Muench as third Bishop of Fargo in

St. Mary's Cathedral, 6 November 1935.

Chapel in Bishop's House, Fargo; woodcarving by August Schmidt

of Cologne, Germany, in 1938.

The Muench family on the grounds of the Bishop's House in Fargo for his silver jubilee

of ordination, 21 June 1938: l to r: Dorothy (Mrs. Ray E. Ott), his sister; Albert Muench,

nephew; Teresa E. Muench, sister; Frank J. Muench, brother; Mrs. Theresa Muench, mother;

Robert Herrick, nephew; Joseph T. Muench, brother; Marla Muench, niece; Bishop

Muench; Ray E. Ott, brother-in-law; Frank Herrick, brother-in-law; Mary (Mrs. Frank

Herrick), sister; Herbert Herrick, nephew; Mrs. Joe Muench, sister-in-law (Anne);

Mrs. Frank Muench, sister-in-law (Doris).

"Chief Northern Light," third from left, at fiftieth anniversary of Sioux Indian Congresses, Saint Michael, North Dakota, 25 June 1940.

Bishop Muench with Fargo ordination class on 7 June 1941: l to r: Fathers James A. Wehlitz, George F. Krile, John W. Roth, Joseph L. Hylden, Jerome E. Filteau, and Howard Smith.

Young priests were encouraged to study for advanced degrees.
First to earn doctorates were Fathers Thomas Hendrickson (left),
Ph.D. in Education, and David J. Boyle, J.C.D. in Canon Law.

A Rural Life School at the North Dakota Agricultural College, Fargo, 1945.

Central Verein Meeting with Mr. and Mrs. Ben
A. Schwegmann and children, New Ulm, Minnesota.

The sixtieth anniversary of ordination and thirty-fifth anniversary of consecration of Bishop John J. Lawler. Black Hills monument to presidents, Rapid City, South Dakota, 16 May 1945: l to r: Bishops Peter W. Bartholome, Aloisius J. Muench, Archbishop John G. Murray, Bishops John J. Lawler, Joseph F. Busch, William T. Mulloy and Vincent J. Ryan.

CHAPTER TWO

THE CALL TO GERMANY

During the long years of the war Pope Pius XII as a sign of mourning had not appointed new members to the College of Cardinals. At the first opportunity after the war, his consistory of 23 December 1945, Pius XII announced that thirty-two prelates from nineteen nations would receive red hats in a unique demonstration of international unity based on Christian charity. During five days of traditional ceremonies in February, 1946, representatives from all six continents would gather in Saint Peter's Basilica as a living testimony to the Church's unity surmounting barriers of race and nationality which had been so bitterly contested during the previous tragic decade.

Among the cardinals-elect were four American archbishops: Saint Louis' John J. Glennon, Detroit's Edward A. Mooney, New York's Francis J. Spellman, and Chicago's Samuel A. Stritch. Archbishop Stritch planned a party of fifteen to accompany him to Rome for the occasion, and among his invited guests was his close friend, the former rector of Saint Francis Seminary when Stritch was an archbishop in Milwaukee, Bishop Muench of Fargo. On February 12 the party left Chicago aboard a four motored TWA constellation, stopped for nine hours in Detroit for Cardinal-elect Mooney and his party, and arrived in Rome forty-six hours later after stops in Gander, Shannon and Paris.

Bishop Muench enjoyed every aspect of the triumphal ceremonies in Rome and also thriftily used the occasion to make his *ad limina* visit required every five years from the world's bishops to report to the pope and the Roman curia on the state of their dioceses. Commenting on the colorful pageantry of the public consistory of February 22 when the cardinals received their red hats, the bishop of Fargo wrote to his diocesan monthly *Catholic Action News*:

"Statesmen have been wrestling with the problem of forming a United

Nations Organization. They feel the need of united common action among the nations of the earth. But their laborious efforts will be in vain because in their building they have rejected Christ, the cornerstone. They spurn his means for saving the world, grasping instead the sword of force and power, forgetful of Christ's words: 'All those who take up the sword shall perish by the sword.' Armies and navies, tanks and atomic bombs are powerless to create a United Nations Organization because material forces never yet have stopped, and never will stop, the forces that destroy peace — envy, jealousy, hatred, greed, and lust for power. No atomic bomb will ever be made that can destroy these war-makers.

"The ceremonies in Saint Peter's proclaimed once more to all the world that the Catholic Church is a united nations organization which has the vitality to endure. Against enemies from within and without it has existed for nineteen hundred years, more vigorous and strong today than in many centuries. Christ is still with his Church. He can die no more. He is the life of his Church . . .

"The lesson is clear. Unity must be built on the rock of Peter. Unity must be sought in the sheepfold of Christ, whose shepherd is Peter and his present-day successor, Pius XII."

Muench little realized how quickly he would be called upon to apply these observations in the most important work of his life. While he was composing this column of "The Bishop Writes" in his Roman hotel room, Cardinal Stritch was paying his first courtesy call on Pope Pius XII following the ceremonies. Pius quickly directed the conversation to a major problem which disturbed him deeply, the postwar reconstruction of the German nation. The Pope informed Stritch that the Holy See had been following with growing concern the events that led to the end of the Nazi Reich the previous May and the first faltering steps in Germany toward law and order.

Pope Pius had a personal involvement in German affairs that extended back to his own tenure as apostolic nuncio in Munich and Berlin following World War I, during the period of the Weimar Republic, and his major part as Vatican secretary of state in negotiations effecting the concordat between the Holy See and Germany in 1933. Pius' succession to the papacy in 1939 preceded by only months the beginning of World War II. During the past seven years he had worked unceasingly but without success for the termination of hostilities as well as for better relations with Germany where the Nazi regime steadily increased its determined program of extermination of religion and pluralistic co-existence on every level of society.

The Pope was now worried over the fate of the German people and considered the Allied formula of "unconditional surrender" an unwise decision. He realized and agreed that stern conditions must be imposed on Germany following the long-awaited defeat of the Nazi regime. But he judged that the war had been unnecessarily extended by that policy of unconditional surrender. The highly injudicious Morgenthau Plan of reducing Germany to a burnt-out agrarian fiefdom, without future industrial potential, was to his mind not only short-sighted and vengeful but wrought through with disaster signals for peaceful rehabil-itation of central Europe.

Pope Pius had a special affection for the German people whom he knew so well. He was determined to do his best in assisting them to restore the Catholic Church in Germany to its previous admirable organizational and spiritual strength.

As early as May, 1945, a first apostolic mission to Germany was dis-patched by Pius XII to make initial contacts with the German bishops and to study immediate ways of relieving the sub-human conditions of displaced persons and prisoners of war interned throughout Ger-many. Monsignor Walter Carroll, priest of the Diocese of Pittsburgh, head of the English-language desk of the Secretariat of State, was placed in charge of this first papal mission to Germany. Carroll made contact with the Allies in Algiers and at Caserta and obtained permission from the American Army of Occupation to travel through Germany for two weeks during those first chaotic days following the capitulation. He travelled by automobile with three priests who represented exiled peo-ples from former occupied territories, displaced persons and prisoners of war. They first viewed the horror of Dachau and then drove across Germany to Frankfurt while making as many contacts as they could in that wide area of destruction.

Monsignor Carroll reported to Pope Pius that disaster conditions pre-vailed both in the camps and major urban centers of Germany. The Pope immediately ordered a second apostolic mission to return to Germany in August of 1945. Preparations for the mission were made by the Secre-tariat of State's Commission for Assisting People. This commission included eight former nuncios expelled from occupied nations by the Nazis and their staff of four monsignors. Monsignor Mario Brini, head of the commission, joined Monsignor Carroll on this second mission to

Germany, and Pius XII asked Carroll to obtain permission from the American Army of Occupation for Father Ivo Zeiger, S.J., to accompany him. Zeiger, who was to play such an important role in Muench's future activities in Germany, was then rector of the German and Hungarian College in Rome and professor of canon law at the Gregorian University. The Pope wanted Zeiger to contact the German bishops while Carroll and Brini made further investigations of possible ways to help the thousands of interned people.

Father Zeiger went first to Cardinal Michael Faulhaber in Munich, old Bishop Matthias Ehrenfried of Wuerzburg, Archbishop Josef Otto Kolb of Bamberg and then on to Eichstaett where the papal nuncio to Germany, Archbishop Cesare Orsenigo, was staying in the rooms of Bishop Michael Rackl. Nuncio Orsenigo, who had been in Germany following Archbishop Eugenio Pacelli since 1929, had fled to Eichstaett from Berlin during the bombings of 1945. Pope Pius had no direct contact with Orsenigo or the German bishops since that time and he wanted first-hand information which Zeiger was capable of collecting. The Berlin nunciature had been a gathering place during the war for secretaries from the apostolic nunciatures of occupied countries. While the Germans had returned the Italian nuncios to Rome, their secretaries at least had been able to move to Berlin and do what they could from there for people in such occupied countries as Poland, Belgium, Holland and the former nations of central Europe. But during 1944 they, too, were sent back to Rome, and now only Nuncio Orsenigo, Monsignor Carlo Colli the counselor, and Monsignor Luigi Borettini remained in forced isolation at Eichstaett without the means of contacting churchmen throughout the defeated country.

Brini and Carroll found even worse conditions in the camps than Zeiger had found in the German dioceses. Millions of prisoners of war, among whom were over a million Italians, had no means of returning home from such wretched camps as Mittenwald, Garmisch and Brenner. The condition of the displaced persons was the most pathetic and tragic of all. Twelve million Germans from such areas as East Prussia, Silesia and the Sudetenland had been forced back into Germany by the advancing Russians. These victims of the greatest forced migration of history were living in abject poverty, wanted neither in their former homelands nor among the hostile German population who viewed them as an insoluble economic drain on their prostrate nation.

The United Nations, International Red Cross, Sécours Catholique of France, as well as English, Dutch and American charitable organizations were making preliminary plans to aid these peoples if permission could be obtained from the occupying armies. When Pius XII received the grim reports of his second mission he, too, wished to speed up the Holy See's charitable activity at once and with as much effectiveness as possible into the mainstream of international aid to Germany. The possibility of such action was the only slight hope he had following the two pessimistic reports he had received to date.

Accordingly, extensive planning was begun at once for a third apostolic mission to Germany to leave in October, 1945. Archbishop Carlo Chiarlo of the Secretariat of State's Commission for Assisting People headed this major effort to visit all prisoner and displaced persons' camps in Germany and establish permanent organizational structures of spiritual and material aid. Father Zeiger again went along in an unofficial capacity with the assignment of continued contact with the German hierarchy. Monsignor Alberto Giovannetti of the commission was appointed secretary. Eight nationalities were represented among the expellees in Germany and priests were to be chosen to head relief work among Poles, Lithuanians, Latvians, Romanians, Slovaks, Hungarians, Ukrainians and Yugoslavs.

Eight American ambulances were obtained by the Vatican and they were filled with medical supplies, sugar, coffee, prayer books in all needed languages, and essential religious articles. The Brazilian Embassy in Rome donated a large number of strong Brazilian cigarettes which were invaluable as a sort of currency exchange. Each expelled nationality group in Germany was also to receive $3,000. Max Brzezinski, M.D., from Chicago joined the expedition as interpreter and medical aide. Monsignor Carroll was to meet the mission in Frankfurt, but he was unable to join them as planned.

From the very beginning the convoy which was sent forth with high hopes encountered difficulty at every turn. The roads in Italy were unpoliced and almost impassable; the Italian drivers, recommended by Vatican relatives and friends, proved to be unreliable and participated in the expedition for whatever monetary gain they could obtain. Up through Pisa, Milan, Trent, Bressanone to the Brenner Pass the convoy moved, losing valuable supplies to looters and encountering daily problems such as where to find gasoline, lodging for the night and most of all, cards for basic purchases from the American PX. Dr. Brzezinski was a godsend in this regard. He had been a member of Catholic War

Relief Services in Egypt, Palestine, and Italy, and was chosen personally by Monsignor Carroll for this expedition.

The fact that Dr. Max was the only American present to contact United States military personnel along the hazardous route pointed up the main deficiency of the mission. Daily it became more obvious that an American ecclesiastic would be needed if any progress was to be made in occupied areas. Monsignor Giovannetti called the experience "a daily adventure, this wagon train of ours, like the caravans of the East exposed to every hazard of a medieval trade route."[1]

En route to Germany through Austria the mission stopped first at the former large barracks of the *Alpenjaeger* at Mittenwald. Here they saw at first-hand suffering and misery beyond human assistance. Across Germany the heartbreaking crescendo of man's inhumanity to man bore in on the little group. When they arrived at Frankfurt they found the city seventy-eight per cent destroyed. Dr. Max located quarters in the half-destroyed Carlton Hotel and Archbishop Chiarlo made plans to request an audience with General Dwight D. Eisenhower, commander of the occupation forces in Germany, whose headquarters were in the huge, former IG Farben chemical offices which strangely had not been destroyed in the bombings.

Archbishop Joseph Gawlina, named by Pope Pius to serve as bishop of Polish people deported to Germany during the war, was in Frankfurt at the time the papal mission arrived. Archbishop Chiarlo had formerly served as nuncio in Warsaw, knew Gawlina from prewar days, and asked him to prepare for the interview with Eisenhower. Gawlina was the only official of the party who knew English and it was fortunate that he was present or the ensuing comedy of errors would have been even worse than it was.

Archbishop Chiarlo had always been keenly conscious of his official prerogatives. In Frankfurt he went first to the chief chaplain in the area and, after waiting to be received for two hours, informed the chaplain of his status as apostolic delegate, complaining that nothing was prepared for him and the mission. In a critical time of occupation such procedure was not well received, particularly since it was understood that an American was to head the mission, and everyone concerned was asking where Monsignor Carroll was. Archbishop Gawlina commented that "Chiarlo swore revenge, but it didn't come to anything because the steering wheel was in the hands of the American army."

Archbishop Gawlina, who was present for the encounter with General Eisenhower two days later, best explains the course of events:

"The meeting took place on 10 November 1945 at the American headquarters. Since Eisenhower did not speak Italian, nor Chiarlo English, I gladly acted at interpreter. Eisenhower was very serene, he smiled, he had a quiet military elegance, while Chiarlo was completely Italian, full of fluster and Italian gestures, dressed up in a way that amazed the Americans: with all possible purple, with the *ferraiuolo*, but not only that, no. On top of the *ferraiuolo* he wore a big red coat with two huge cockades, one with papal colors, the other I don't remember. On his head the Roman hat with the green tassels. The American soldiers watched him like an unusual creature; even Eisenhower smiled. Then we started our talk.

"Eisenhower ignored somewhat Chiarlo's points of argument; Chiarlo kept repeating and referring to 'Santo Padre, Santo Padre.' I doubt that this impressed Eisenhower very much because he interrupted Chiarlo, telling him that in his eyes all who are baptized are Christians, not only the Roman Catholics; all baptized persons had to be regarded as Christians. I would say that Eisenhower had the ecumenical viewpoint that was emphasized so much in the discourses of Pope John XXIII."

"The discussions were conducted with military precision. General Eisenhower gave his consent to the following points:

"1. The mission of Archbishop Chiarlo, papal delegate, is of a strictly religious and moral character.

"To this Eisenhower declared that it was his conviction that the world can only be reconstructed with the help and by reason of Christian principles. He asked me repeatedly to tell Chiarlo that he also considered the heretics to be Christians because they also proclaim Christian principles.

"2. The priests of the mission may move to their respective D.P. camps.

"3. His staff will be informed of the execution of the administrative directives.

"He had asked the chief of staff, General Bedell Smith, a Catholic, to attend the conference. When he arrived, he kissed Chiarlo's ring, which caused some consternation. For the rest, he kept quiet, for, of course, he was there only to receive orders. After the visit with Eisenhower, Smith asked to talk to me. It turned out to be an unpleasant encounter.

"4. The papal mission will be given a villa.

"5. Chiarlo will be permitted to keep in touch with the Vatican by telephone.

"Fine. So now Bedell Smith, who as chief of staff accepted all these regulations, made the remark that he wished Monsignor Carroll to head this papal mission. For he, Bedell Smith, had not been informed of the arrival of the mission without Monsignor Carroll who was to be its head.

"Then he added that he did not think it in order that the mission to which so far eight priests had been attached should suddenly include thirteen priests. This meant that some unexpected priests were taking advantage of the mission for their individual local groups or for their own interests. The staff of Chiarlo must be kept small, and the rest of the priests would have to leave or stay at the respective camps.

"The Italian chauffeurs were to be replaced by D.P.'s because the former had tried to sell goods and gas already at Milan and that was not permitted. Also the staff of Chiarlo was to consist of D.P.'s. A villa at Kronberg near Frankfurt had been selected to serve as residence and office for Chiarlo and the members of the mission.

"Smith then asked me for a confidential talk in the course of which he poured out on me his anger and wrath for having given assistance to the papal mission. Those Italians, he said, don't understand a thing about their position in the world. The chief of the mission can only be an American, or (this he said probably out of politeness toward me) a Pole; but never an Italian or a German. The chief definitely cannot act as head of a mission for all denominations. The Soviets are already watching this development, the United States is not a Catholic country either, and you are helping those people instead of aiding us Allies.

"I replied that I would assist the one and the others in order to get this matter settled." [2]

During the autumn months of 1945 the members of the papal mission moved into the Villa Grosch at Kronberg, ten miles north of Frankfurt in the wooded Taunus hills. The Villa Grosch was a three-story villa formerly owned by a German tea merchant. Dr. Brzezinski was at hand to help with American contacts while the priest members of the mission travelled to the camps in the American zone of occupation.

When Pius XII announced the names of the new cardinals-designate in December among them was Archbishop Benedetto Aloisi Masella, nuncio to Brazil. Archbishop Chiarlo in Kronberg knew he was in the running to succeed to the Brazilian post where he wanted to go, and he hastened to end the third mission to Germany. Priest representatives for each nationality in the camps were appointed, Chiarlo and his staff returned to Rome on 18 January 1946, leaving behind only Monsignor Giovannetti as *chargé d'affaires* and Father Zeiger.

Such was the background of Pope Pius' discussion of the needs of the Church in Germany with Cardinal Stritch. An American was needed to head the papal mission to Germany and the Pope asked Stritch's advice in the matter. Stritch replied that he had with him in his party at Rome a most suitable candidate and he went on to explain the credentials of Bishop Muench. Pius said he would discuss the matter with officials in the Secretariat of State. After the interview was over, and Stritch was looking for Muench to inform him of what had transpired, the bishop of Fargo was finally located at a sidewalk cafe on the Via della Conciliazione talking with American journalists who had come to Rome for the consistory.

Bishop Muench received official notification from Pope Pius on the following day during an audience that he was considering appointing him as his personal representative to Germany with the title of apostolic visitator. Monsignor Giovanni Battista Montini, substitute secretary of state, later Pope Paul VI, followed through with details. Montini informed Muench that he would be asked as apostolic visitor to Germany to head the papal mission at Kronberg, take charge of the Papal Commission for Displaced Persons and in that capacity direct the extensive relief activities of the Vatican in occupied Germany. He would also represent the Holy Father in his relations with the authorities of the German Catholic Church. Muench was stunned as he had not seriously considered that the conversation between Pius XII and Stritch would in any way affect him. Archbishop Joseph F. Rummel of New Orleans had also been considered for the position, but he was German-born and an American-born visitator was preferable. Muench asked Montini how long the assignment would extend and the latter encouraged him by suggesting that it would take no less than six months and no more than eighteen months. Muench was relieved as he genuinely wanted to return to his beloved diocese of Fargo and he was at pains to ask if he could retain his position as bishop there. Montini told him there would be no difficulty in the matter, that he should return to Fargo and await the formal appointment after the Vatican had an opportunity to prepare fully for the move.

Bishop Muench returned to Chicago with Cardinal Stritch's party and then went on to Fargo in early March. He was not permitted to discuss the pending appointment with anyone but behind his usual calm exterior he was agitated and apprehensive. He did not consider himself capable of such a serious responsibility. Bishop Joseph P. Hurley of Saint Augustine, Florida, who was assigned as regent of the apostolic delegation in Belgrade, Yugoslavia, and Muench were the first Americans after World War II to be assigned to major posts abroad in the diplomatic service of the Holy See.

In the meantime another important development took place during those spring months of 1946 which affected Bishop Muench's work in Germany in a major way. In December, 1945, a committee of American Protestant clergymen headed by Methodist Bishop G. Bromley Oxnam, president of the Federal Council of the Churches of Christ in America, toured Germany to study the conditions of the Protestant churches there. Upon their return Bishop Oxnam wrote President Harry S. Truman on 18 January 1946 requesting that an American civilian be appointed as a liaison representative in Germany between the Allied Military Government and the Protestant churches of the United States. This move was recommended as a way of easing the difficulties German Evangelical leaders were experiencing with lower officials of the division of internal affairs of American Military Government. Misunderstandings and delays in granting legitimate requests were alienating German Christians and the potential of their co-operation with American aims was being dissipated.

President Truman asked the advice of Generals Dwight Eisenhower and Lucius Clay in the matter and both concurred in the recommendation if similar arrangements were made for representatives of the Catholic and Jewish faiths. Secretary of War Robert P. Patterson also stated that Catholic and Jewish representatives should be included in such a plan especially since there were more Catholics than people of other faiths in the American zone of Germany. Accordingly, Truman endorsed the idea with the stipulation that Catholics and Jews be included, and Oxnam approached the National Catholic Welfare Conference and the Synagogue Council of America on 20 February 1946 in the matter.

Monsignor Howard J. Carroll, general secretary of the National Catholic Welfare Conference, asked the episcopal members of that board by telephone for a vote and requested that a capable American Catholic be nominated for the position. Cardinals Stritch and Spellman;

Archbishops Cushing, Mitty, Rummel, Ryan and Murray; Bishops Alter, Noll and Gannon all concurred in the proposal. The majority judged that Monsignor Anthony Strauss of Saint Louis, well-known in *Central Verein* circles, should be invited to accept the post; Cardinal Spellman thought Monsignor James H. Griffiths of the Diocese of Brooklyn would be the proper person. All of the American bishops preferred that a priest be sent rather than a layman.

When Monsignor Strauss was approached to accept the position he declined because of reasons of health. Cardinal Stritch then encouraged Bishop Muench to accept this second appointment and by April 9 he had convinced Muench of the advantages of such a dual role. While serving as liaison consultant for religious affairs to the military governor in Germany, he could serve the German Catholics more completely in protecting his mission from the difficulties experienced during the first apostolic missions there. He would not only have clearance from the American authorities but an official position in the structure of the occupation. However, Muench always made it clear that he was not an employee of the United States Government and that in his position of liaison consultant he was representing the American hierarchy. Such an independent position would produce confidence in the authorities of the Church in Germany. The Bishops' War Emergency and Relief Committee on 1 May 1946 granted Muench $5,000 to cover his expenses in the discharge of his duties as intermediary between the Catholic authorities and the Office of Military Government in Germany.

On 16 May 1946 a telegram arrived in Fargo from Archbishop Amleto Giovanni Cicognani, apostolic delegate to the United States, announcing that Pope Pius XII had appointed Bishop Muench as his personal representative, the apostolic visitator to Germany *ad interim*. Muench flew to Washington on May 20 to discuss plans with Cicognani, Carroll and American military personnel. Secretary of War Patterson talked with him on May 22 and gave him a letter of official appointment on June 7 that helped considerably in eliminating red tape in preparations for the trip to Germany. His orders included air priority and proved invaluable in the years ahead in his travels throughout Germany. Patterson wrote to Muench on June 7:

"As you know, one of the most important objectives of Military Government in Germany is the development of democratic ideas in that country. It is recognized that the church must play a leading role in the re-education of Germany and in the building of the spiritual basis upon which a free society can be constructed . . .

"It is exceedingly gratifying to the War Department that you have accepted this assignment. I feel that yours will be a noteworthy contribution to Military Government in its program to strengthen the German churches."

In turn the Federal Council of the Churches of Christ appointed as their first temporary representative Dr. Samuel McCrea Calvert, general secretary of the Council, who was in Germany for two months. He was succeeded by Dr. Julius Bodensieck, president of Wartburg Theological Seminary, Dubuque, Iowa. The Synagogue Council of America assigned Rabbi Jacob Bernstein as their representative under the tripartite arrangement.

Bishop Muench, who continued in Germany long after military occupation was terminated, often stated that this liaison arrangement was a major step in obtaining amicable working arrangements between the occupation forces and German church authorities. It also helped to make the task of the American armed forces of occupation considerably easier and gained some respect for American justice in this area. The lot of German priests, ministers and the few remaining rabbis was made more livable. The one insoluble problem was that the occupation forces continually wanted to limit the liaison representatives strictly to religious affairs and could not understand why they were interested in the religious implications of decisions affecting the areas of press or education. The on-going conflicts in these areas, as will be seen, became a constant concern of Muench in the years ahead.

In the midst of hectic preparations for leaving Fargo; answering letters and messages of congratulations and best wishes from bishops and friends; securing a Plymouth to be shipped to Paris from the Chrysler Corporation through the instrumentality of his old friend, Joseph Fields of Saint Clair, Michigan; obtaining passport and medical clearance; arranging for the services of Father Stanley J. Bertke as his secretary in Germany from his old friend, Archbishop John T. McNicholas, O.P., of Cincinnati; flying back and forth from Fargo to Chicago to Washington; Muench received a shock that struck him like the proverbial bolt out of the blue sky of North Dakota.

The Bishop of Fargo had one consolation during the past months of uncertainty and apprehension: the diocese would be safely and without alteration administered by the vicar general, Monsignor Leo F. Dworschak. Then, on 22 June 1946, while Bishop Muench was in Washington just prior to flying to Paris and Rome two days later, word was received from the Vatican that Monsignor Dworschak was appointed coadjutor bishop of Rapid City, South Dakota, to assist the ailing incumbent, Bishop John J. Lawler. While he rejoiced in the advancement of his friend, Muench worried about the administration of Fargo. Accordingly, he determined to leave Father Howard Smith, chancellor of the diocese, behind as administrator rather than take him to Germany as his personal secretary as originally planned.

Muench was sad that he could not be present to consecrate his vicar general a bishop. But Archbishop Cicognani came from Washington for the occasion and he was joined by the two former Fargo priests, Bishops Ryan and Mulloy, on the happy occasion of Bishop Dworschak's consecration in the Fargo cathedral on August 22. Bishop Muench wrote to the priests of his diocese:

"Our Holy Father looks with great favor on the clergy of the Diocese of Fargo. Once more he has taken one of their number and has raised him to the high dignity of the episcopal office. For this we are profoundly grateful. To have three consecrations in a diocese within the space of six years is something notable for even the largest diocese, and certainly it is that for our diocese. . . . We express to our new Coadjutor Bishop Leo Dworschak warmest felicitations. His genial disposition will win him many friends in his new field of labor, and his fine administrative talents, coupled with his priestly zeal, will be productive of greatest good."

Travel orders came unexpectedly late in the afternoon of June 27 for Bishop Muench and Father Bertke, and that evening at nine o'clock they were air-borne in a bucket-seated army plane, the Diplomat, for Rome with stops at Bermuda, the Azores, Paris and Marseilles. From Santa Maria Island in the Azores Muench wrote to his chancery family at 608 Broadway, Fargo: "We took our supper in the mess hall of the soldiers, and while the plane was made ready for the flight to Paris we watched the sun setting far on the western horizon of the Atlantic Ocean. My thoughts went back to the prairies of the diocese, where some six hours later the same sun would be seen in all its glory going down over the golden crops of our State."

A busy week followed, filled with receiving instructions and information from the various Roman congregations regarding the mission to Germany. Muench saw Monsignor Montini several times and then was received in audience by Pope Pius who officially appointed him apostolic visitor and went on to encourage him in his assignment while stressing the deep desire that filled the heart of the former nuncio in Germany for peace and justice among his beloved German people. Then Pius said: "Now, let's talk in German" perhaps, Muench thought, to test the new visitor's linguistic skill in that language.

To relieve the suffering a little, Pius supplied another convoy, this time headed by Muench with American military drivers. The trip north was hazardous and brought a series of startling revelations to Muench who thought he had somewhat understood the extent of destruction and suffering on every side. The shock of that initial experience was still vivid to Muench when, sick and confused, he was interviewed at the end of his life. The misery and overcrowding in the camps, the lean-to housing on the outskirts of the destroyed cities, separated families, less than subsistence food and scraps of clothing, but especially the pall of despair and the hopeless eyes of women, children and old people were something he would never forget.

When the convoy arrived at Villa Grosch in Kronberg on 28 July 1946, Monsignor Giovannetti and Father Zeiger were waiting for Bishop Muench and Father Bertke. During the six previous months Giovannetti had been preparing reports for Rome on the work of the eight priests representing the displaced nationality groups in the camps as well as expediting requests to the occupation authorities for supplies and permissions to re-settle. Father Zeiger had served as best he could the pressing requests from German bishops and people who were under strict occupation laws and quite unable to make contact with Rome or Allied authorities.

Bishop Muench made an immediate impression upon Giovannetti and Zeiger of gentle, pastoral sympathy. His straightforward manner, clear mind, scholarly habits, simple and orderly customs of daily piety put the household at ease. He told them he did not ask for this job, that the Holy Father wished it. He felt entirely unprepared for the overwhelming problems ahead and most humbly asked constant questions. Giovannetti and Zeiger hastened to assure him: the former would help with contacts between the Secretariat of State and the mission; Father Zeiger would be on hand to assist with German contacts. Muench impressed everyone the very first day by setting up a schedule with Giovannetti for studying Italian. During that spring in Fargo he had begun preliminary study as best he could with an Italian-English dictionary. Now he asked for a nightly Italian session with the generous and out-going monsignor and the two soon became fast friends. He was as studious and serious as if he were a student again at Saint Francis Seminary.

The scholarly approach of Muench to every encounter also quickly impressed Father Zeiger who was a true academic person in his own right. This German Jesuit was well-known in German and Roman circles as a professor, adviser to Cardinal Pacelli on the concordat of 1933, jurist who had written a history of ecclesiastical law, and who yet paradoxically possessed, like Muench, a real pastoral soul. During the war years in Rome, while carrying on his administrative and teaching responsibilities, Zeiger had served on a papal commission to aid German war and civilian victims in Italy. He knew intimately the mind of Pius XII in regard to Germany and was sent as permanent member of the papal mission to insure in this time of need that the terms of the concordat of 1933 were fulfilled, and that Germany would begin anew its authentic spiritual and cultural approaches to the world.[3]

Muench respected Zeiger from the beginning and leaned on him for advice and direction in contacts with German Catholics as well as for analysis of political and religious developments. Ivo Zeiger penned many articles in journals in the years ahead which he and Muench had discussed fully beforehand. The influence of the Jesuit Zeiger was not, however, so highly valued in several German and Roman circles, in the same way as the contribution of Father Robert Leiber, S.J., personal adviser to Pius XII, was resented during the years of Pacelli's pontificate. Pius relied on these two Jesuits, Leiber and Zeiger, for information on German affairs as was his custom in exercising personal control of diplomatic procedures. Muench learned very quickly where the lines of communication were laid. In fact, Muench was accused of being controlled by this Leiber-Zeiger Jesuit team who were said to by-pass him, the Secretariat of State and ordinary channels to communicate directly with Pius XII.

The apostolic visitor, however, did not resent this procedure and actually benefited by the competent assistance of both men. He once again evidenced his ability to direct all tides for the common good. Muench often stated that no one was better able to diagnose objectively the true situation of German Catholicism than Zeiger. He told the latter on one occasion: "I value more than I can say our study of complex questions with four eyes. More than you know I depend on your invaluable service and balanced advice in problems." Zeiger worked regularly into the night despite bad health; his charming humor, warm, self-effacing personality and zeal were an inspiration to the majority of the household. Plagued by poor health, Zeiger died prematurely 24 December 1952, but not before he had contributed seven fruitful years to the rehabilitation of religion and the consolidation of the Church in his homeland. In fact, Zeiger's thesis of the *diaspora* character of postwar German Catholicism, as will be seen, was the major creative thrust of the entire period.

Strangely, in the midst of seemingly insoluble problems on every side, the quality of Bishop Muench that drew first attention day by day was the quite obvious fact that he could speak German. True, his German was of another vintage, filled with inherited nineteenth century emigrant vocabulary and out-of-date periodic sentences, yet it was authentic German. Wherever he moved, to his surprise, his free and natural if somewhat nasal and Americanized accent brought instant smiles and expressions of gratitude from a beleaguered people. They had not heard their native language spoken by officials of previous papal missions, and astonishingly, not one of the top-ranking American officers in the Office of Military Government of the United States, OMGUS, could speak German. One of the results of the tragic downplaying of German in American educational and cultural life during and following World War I was this lack of mature, capable American leadership with linguistic expertise in German. It was, as Robert Murphy, representative of the Department of State in Germany declared, no mean feat to govern a country whose language you do not know. Muench, on his part and despite the system, brought a dimension that was basic and effective at every turn. It was another example of the value of preserving immigrant language and cultural values which were far too often abandoned in the nineteenth century by hasty and short-sighted "Americanizing" idealists and the nationalistic Anglo-American bigots of the World War I period.

After the members of the household at Kronberg became acquainted and a daily routine was established, Muench assembled Zeiger, Giovannetti and Bertke to decide on a priority list of problems to be tackled. In reality, the problems tumbled in one upon another, each more important than the other under the headings of Muench's functions: apostolic visitator, head of the Vatican mission, military liaison consultant and military vicar delegate. But a work schedule had to be established if anything was to be accomplished. Muench pleased all concerned by at once engaging, in typical American fashion, two secretaries to expedite the work rather than continuing the time-wasting procedure of everyone typing his own reports and correspondence.

The first confusion to be resolved was the relationship of the papal mission at Kronberg to the existing apostolic nunciature at Eichstaett. After the war the only member of the diplomatic corps still living on German soil was Archbishop Orsenigo, the papal nuncio. A certain shadow hung over his name because he was accused of having been too tolerant and permissive in relations with the Nazis. He had also been unpopular among German Catholics because of his high-handed mode of operation. However he was the Pope's representative, and when the Board of Control in Berlin met to decide whether Orsenigo, the papal nuncio, alone could remain in Germany, the decision was in the affirmative. The next question was: accredited to whom, where, since Germany no longer existed as a nation. The French deputy answered: "He is accredited to Her Majesty, the human misery." In spite of the veto of the Russian deputy, naturally expected, this regulation remained in force.

When Nuncio Orsenigo died on 23 March 1946, Monsignor Carlo Colli continued as *chargé d'affaires* at Eichstaett for relations with the German bishops in order to preserve, according to the wish of Pius XII, the continuity of the nunciature in Germany. Muench had received detailed orders in this regard while he was in Rome: the flag was to be kept flying at Eichstaett as a symbol of the Vatican's diplomatic presence in all of Germany, despite the division of the country, the absence of a legitimate German government, and the refusal of the occupying powers to recognize any official diplomatic ties with the defeated nation. Monsignor Colli then suddenly died at Eichstaett in January, 1947, leaving Monsignor Bernhard Hack, priest of the Diocese of Berlin, and assistant at the nunciature alone on the scene. Hack had been asked by Orsenigo to join his staff in June, 1945, after the capitulation, and this talented and knowledgeable Prussian priest remained at Eichstaett until Zeiger suffered his most serious heart attack in 1950, at which time Hack came to assist Muench. In the meantime Hack received ordinary petitions for faculties from German bishops, processed marriage cases, and each week travelled from Eichstaett to Kronberg with the documents and correspondence to be signed and approved by Muench. Routine ecclesiastical affairs were in this way handled by the apostolic visitator during the first years. He acted in private and *de facto* as nuncio until the time when normal diplomatic relations could again be publicly and *de jure* established. Hack took the diplomatic pouches from Kronberg for Rome via Eichstaett and Munich and was like Zeiger an invaluable assistant for German affairs.

Muench had been instructed by Pius XII that his first assignment was to contact all of the German bishops at their annual conference at Fulda, present himself as well as a message from the Pope which he had brought with him from Rome. Since 1867 the German bishops had met annually for episcopal discussions at the tomb of Saint Boniface, patron of Christianity in Germany. Muench prepared himself carefully for this meeting during the summer months of 1946 by studying with the assistance of Father Zeiger the background of Germany's dioceses and bishops.

There were twenty-two residential bishops in Germany with fifteen auxiliaries. The Sees of Breslau and Ermland were vacant and could not be filled because they were in the Polish zone of administration and part of Ermland had already been incorporated into the Soviet Union. The Prelature of Schneidemuehl was also under Polish administration. Five archdioceses were located in Munich, Freiburg im Breisgau, Cologne, Paderborn, and Bamberg. Germany was partitioned as a result of the Potsdam Agreement by the line of the Oder-Neisse Rivers and further westward by the Elbe River line, the one forming the eastern and the other the western border of the Soviet zone. The area of West Germany, about as large as the combined states of New York and Pennsylvania, formed but fifty-two per cent of the Reich of 1937. Nine states or *Laender* existed in West Germany with seventy-six per cent of the population in an area that before the war held fifty-seven per cent of the total population. Seventy million people lived in West Germany, of whom about twenty-two million were Catholic. Added to these numbers were over eight million expellees who poured into West Germany from the countries east of its prewar borders. They were augmented by over a million displaced persons who did not want to return to Soviet-occupied nations, as well as the refugees who began fleeing from the Soviet zone of Germany and from territories under Polish and Soviet administration until their numbers totaled over two million people.

Germany was divided into four zones of military occupation: French, British, Russian and American. Of the twenty-two dioceses, nine were in the American zone, five in the French zone, six in the British zone and two in the Russian zone. Grave problems existed for the bishops in bringing spiritual care and administering temporalities across four zones arbitrarily imposed without consideration for their history, traditions and deep regional associations in each of the *Laender*. Each of the occupying powers had rules and regulations of its own for the separate zones. Overlapping ecclesiastical jurisdiction of dioceses in several zones created serious complications. For example, Cologne was placed in the British zone with part of the archdiocese in the French zone; Fulda and Wuerzburg were in the American zone with part of their jurisdiction in the Russian zone; Freiburg, Rottenburg and Mainz were in the French zone while overlapping into the American zone; Limburg and Augsburg in the American zone had areas in the French zone. The most flagrant case was the Diocese of Osnabrueck, located in the State of Westphalia, which embraced the City State of Bremen in the American zone, the City State of Hamburg and Land Schleswig-Holstein subject to British authorities, and the State of Mecklenburg under Russian control.

Bishop Muench acquainted himself with the personal histories of the German hierarchy. There was, of course, outstanding in reputation and tenure the scholarly and courageous Cardinal Michael Faulhaber in Munich; Cologne's austere and determined Cardinal Josef Frings, chairman of the Fulda Conference of Bishops; and Berlin's new cardinal, the Nazi opponent Konrad Count von Preysing. The majority of the German bishops were advanced in years although still active. Since 1933 they had to fight a constant battle with the Nazis to protect as best they could the rights of souls and the Church. The majority of them had a satisfactory record of resistance which was recognized by both the German people and the British, French and American occupying powers. It was not until years later that the tortuous process of post-factum evaluation of the German Christians' record under siege was questioned. The record is still not complete. It did, however, become evident that both German Catholic and Lutheran leadership too often placed the survival of their institutional churches first in emphasis, and that less attention was directed toward defending individual and personal consciences. While opposing Nazi terror, ecclesiastical leaders, as in every other country at the time including the Orthodox in Russia as well as in the free countries of the Western Alliance, did support their country's war effort as a duty of citizenship. The moral weakness of this position was not confined to Germany but exists today as a catholic problem for all Christians involved in living during an age dominated by nationalism with all its political, cultural and social implications.

Father Zeiger accompanied Muench to Fulda for that first meeting with the German bishops on 20 August 1946. A meager dinner was served the evening before the opening session at which Muench was introduced to all present. He sat beside Cardinal Faulhaber during the meal and the two at once discovered a mutual compatibility. A friendship began that evening which was to become the main consolation of Muench in Germany until Faulhaber's death six years later. They spoke of Muench's Bavarian ancestry and his parents' birthplaces at St. Katharina in the Bohemian Forest and Stadt Kemnath in the Diocese of Regensburg. When the meal was completed Muench brought out a box of American cigars and passed them among the bishops. This typically American touch made a good impression on those bishops who had waited for years for a good cigar. Faulhaber with Bavarian humor announced that Muench had introduced an innovation into the seventy-eight year old tradition of the Fulda Conference. "What is the innovation?" Muench asked. "Well, never before have the assembled bishops been seen to smoke as you see them this evening. It is a joy to witness."

Faulhaber himself did not smoke, but he asked if he could take his cigar back to Munich for his vicar general. Muench was moved to tell Faulhaber he would like to present some American cigarettes to him which Muench had brought in the convoy. After the dinner he astounded the cardinal by presenting him with nineteen cartons of cigarettes. With tears in his eyes, Faulhaber accepted, and used these precious exchange items to assist in restoring the bombed windows of the *Liebfrauenkirche*, the cathedral in Munich. Such were some of the simple and unforgettable experiences of those first contacts between German and American Catholics whom war had separated for the last years and who now began tentatively to approach each other again with openness and charity. Years later, in telling of this incident, Cardinal Muench mentioned that he had brought twenty cartons of cigarettes with him to Germany. When questioned why he said he had given only nineteen cartons to Cardinal Faulhaber, Muench, in spite of his illness which resulted in periodic loss of memory, promptly replied: "Because one carton had been stolen along the way."

The next morning Muench waited until he was called into the first session of the Fulda Conference to present himself formally to the German hierarchy. The German bishops preserved a sound and healthy independence in their national meetings which precluded by tradition the attendance of nuncios or apostolic visitators. Muench explained the nature of his mission to Germany, brought greetings to the bishops from Pius XII and from members of the American hierarchy, expressed the Holy Father's paternal love and solicitude for the German people, and then proceeded to outline for them the nature of his mission.[4]

All in all Muench made a good first impression. Cardinal Frings of Cologne was chairman of the German Bishops' Conference. As he was being driven to Fulda for the meeting, his car had a blowout at the junction of Frankfurt and Kronberg. As Frings was standing on the road in his house cassock and red socks — he later stated with a smile that he wore them purposely because the Allies showed more respect — another car swung out from Kronberg, stopped and Muench got out, introduced himself and invited the cardinal back to his house that he had just left. But the tire was soon fixed and both cars went on their way. Frings recalled this story years later as his first meeting with Muench. At first the Cardinal of Cologne was skeptical of Muench's presence and mission. He stated to other German bishops during the Fulda Conference that while Muench appeared to be cordial and tactful, it should not be forgotten that he was an American. "What is that bishop from the prairies doing here? I do not understand what the mission at Kronberg is good for." Frings, however, soon changed his mind and was the first to tell Muench so himself. He went out of his way to make up for his initial question by publicly in the presence of Muench and other German bishops speaking in a warm and convincing manner of his honest and high esteem for the apostolic visitator and his contribution.[5]

Before returning to Kronberg, Muench went from Fulda to his beloved Fribourg in Switzerland where he had spent happy years as a graduate student. The twenty-fifth anniversary of *Pax Romana*, an international organization of university students for the promotion of peace, was being observed and Muench celebrated the opening Mass with students from forty-one nations. In his address the bishop rejoiced in the survival of *Pax Romana* which had always held special appeal for him and of which he was a charter member. In his opinion it held out considerable hope for the future: "Once more the spirit of Christian peace triumphed. The enmities of the world were forgotten. The spirit of Christ dwelled in the hearts of these young men and women, and their lips spoke sincerely of brotherly love." In the growing number of international organizations and contacts of the postwar world Muench hoped that educated lay Catholic men and women would be represented. Catholic or nationalistic isolation would be fatal in the years ahead. The battles of the day would be fought in the field of ideas. Christ could be brought to the conference rooms of the world by such young people trained and prepared through *Pax Romana* contacts.

Bishop Muench's first activities as head of the papal mission in Germany did not go unnoticed by the Russians. A Reuters report of 8 September 1946 quoted Moscow Radio's commentator Miranov as calling Muench "an agent of the United States war department" by virtue of the fact that he was chaplain to the American forces in Germany. Moscow Radio also went on to attack the Vatican that Muench was representing as "one of the largest, if not the largest capitalist enterprise. The Vatican has long since ceased to be only the spiritual center of Catholicism. It is rightly classed among the most powerful world monopolies and is constantly expanding and strengthening its ties with the big American monopolies with which it is united by common interest in conquering ever new positions." Muench was destined to come under continued attack from the Russians, but this first blast was a sober eye-opener to him of the realities of Germany's occupation.

When Muench returned to Kronberg he began carrying through Pius XII's second request. He was, as soon as possible, to visit the German bishops in their dioceses, study conditions at first-hand, and report to the Holy See. Muench and Zeiger planned an itinerary that would take them in the next months to all the bishoprics except that of Meissen in the Russian zone. The Bishop estimated that his work in Germany would be completed after this visitation tour and he could return to Fargo. The visits took six months to complete and their termination coincided with Monsignor Montini's minimum time limit on his assignment.

It was this visitation tour, perhaps, more than any other single factor that moved Pius XII to conclude swiftly that the right man was in the right place at the right time. Muench prepared a preliminary report which Giovannetti translated into Italian and forwarded to the Secretariat of State by February of 1947, less than six months after Muench's arrival on the scene. This report, a classic in its own right, was not only a catalogue of statistics. It was a sober, exact analysis in the best academic tradition. Forty-six pages in all, it detailed the visits to each diocese and then in eleven sections presented a thorough critique of the economic, political, moral, educational, social and administrative problems that needed first attention. A final series of observations and proposals for future action revealed that Muench was not presenting only a narrow ecclesiastical overview. His graduate training in economics, sociology and political science enabled him to relate religious phenomena to the complex realities of a society in transition. The tragedy of a prostrate Germany was not an occasion only to warn, prophesy doom or attempt to protect former patterns of ecclesiastical procedure. The possibility was present for a new relation between religion and society which challenged the best potential dormant for too long in Christian tradition. Father Bertke at the same time had helped Muench prepare a second report of seventeen pages on displaced persons which was forwarded to Rome with that on the German dioceses.

Pope Pius was immediately alert to the quality of the work before him. The whole tone of the document coincided encouragingly with the Pope's own hopes for a new relationship between religion and a possible democratic society. The letters and reactions which the German bishops themselves sent to Rome, or discussed with the curia as they began again to come to the Vatican, became a growing crescendo of praise for the apostolic visitator.[6] He was tactful, he was competent, he was sympathetic, and most important he was a pastor like themselves. They were dealing with a brother bishop who understood at once the nature of pastoral problems. He was not a bureaucrat, bound by protocol and diplomatic procedure, who came with the title of bishop but with no actual pastoral experience to balance his presuppositions.

Years later one bishop after another when interviewed at once made the point, and repeatedly, that a breath of fresh air, of kindness, humility and understanding came to them with Aloisius Muench that gave them confidence and hope. Cardinal Frings summarized their reactions as follows:

"Muench helped us to overcome the difficulties of the first years after the war. He came over from the States as our friend; from the very first day of his stay with us he proved to be a friend. This can be explained by the fact that his parents were German, that he had a very good command of the German language, and, above all, that his heart was full of kindness. He arrived in Germany with the conviction that the Germans were not as bad as their reputation and he spoke up against the accusation of a collective guilt for all Germans. We always felt that he took our side, that he was honestly willing to help us. . . .

"He always respected our freedom, never interfered. In general I would say that he acted more like a bishop than a nuncio. Just take the example of anonymous letters against priests or bishops. He would become terribly angry about such informing, and he never forwarded such letters to Rome. And so a very cordial relationship developed between him and the German bishops. . . .

"We were deeply impressed by his heartfelt kindness and his tact; he had a most delicate sense of tact. And he was a person of high intelligence, he had a quick mind."[7]

Muench, on his part, enjoyed these first contacts with the German bishops in their dioceses. Despite the sad evidences of war and destruction on every side, the bishop was back again in the pastoral milieu which he relished so thoroughly. From September 27 to October 5 he was in Fulda, Muenster, Osnabrueck and Hildesheim; from October 14 to 26 in Augsburg and Munich; from October 29 to November 3 in Berlin; from November 6 to 14 in Paderborn, Cologne and Aachen; from November 14 to 21 in Speyer, Freiburg and Rottenburg; November 25–26 in Trier; at Limburg on November 30; in Mainz on December 2; and back to Munich from December 3 to 6. Many difficulties were encountered in covering over 5,000 miles across three zones of Germany but his American travel permit proved to be a godsend.

The apostolic visitator was impressed by the fraternal charity evidenced on every side. He noted that several of the bishops were living frugally in simple rooms since their former homes had been bombed. He was likewise impressed with the scholarly backgrounds of the German bishops, and observed that they were facing realities as they existed. They were equally intent on holding to the sound traditions of their German Catholic past that had been built up so laboriously during the last century. But entirely new problems had now arisen and it was evident that an adjustment must be made in solving them with new methods. In order to make any headway the bishops realized that they would have to enlist the aid of the laity in the various fields of Catholic Action. Reporters and visitors to Germany in that first period after the war, for the most part ignorant of the language, accused the hierarchy of living in the past with no plan for the future. Muench was adamant in insisting that the bishops were facing as best they could the new situation before them and attacking problems with energy and vision. The burden of work before them was overwhelming. Criticism came largely from those pursuing pet panaceas who wanted the bishops to devote the major part of their time and interest to these special programs.

Bishop Muench interrupted his first visitation tour of German dioceses for a flying trip to Paris during the first week of October to make contacts which might help him in his work in the French zone of occupation in Germany. The French inevitably made more difficulties in their zone, due to the long history of German and French differences, than did the English or Americans in their zones. Muench attended the consecration of a French army bishop for French chaplains in Germany and Austria on October 9 and tried to explain his own work as apostolic visitor to French ecclesiastics and army officials. While he was a guest of Archbishop Angelo Giuseppe Roncalli, later Pope John XXIII, at the Paris nunciature, Muench also had time to write a long letter to Bishop Dworschak in Rapid City. In this letter of 7 October 1946 Muench described his reactions to German conditions as experienced on the first visitation tour:

"I'm seeing Germany as no one could see it better, and learning a lot about the work of the Church — religious life in general, education, youth, men and women's organizations, press, charity works, vocations, seminaries, temporalities, problems such as the destruction of churches, poor housing conditions, poverty on a mass scale, *Ostfluechtlinge*, etc. It's a rare experience, sad, encouraging, profitable. The courage with which the bishops and priests are tackling their problems is amazing and edifying. Once again, as in times past, people are coming to their bishops for help. When the record of these times is written it will form a glorious part in the annals of the Church. Youth, particularly, is taking hold of things with energy and enthusiasm. The fear is that conditions may worsen, and that youth will become the prey of agitators.

"The Church is doing marvelous work in the field of charity. We have a lot to learn from the Church in Germany. In the midst of ruins the Church is arising to new strength. On our trips we saw a number of good churches built with cement — modern style. A few are horrible examples of what ought not to be built, but the rest are really beautiful. It is really too bad that Bishop Ryan [Bismarck] could not wait. He would have built differently.

"Right now there is a lack of bread and coal in the Ruhr area, largely the effect of incompetent socialistic bureaucrats. If ever planning has failed, it has happened right here.

"Right now Communism is making a poor showing in Germany, but the trend is leftward, and strongly so. The socialist parties have quite a following. Socialists and Communists fight each other, but in their assault on the confessional school they unite their forces. Russia is feared. Everywhere one hears that only armed might can break the strength of Russia. Displaced persons, refugees and Germans would grasp the gun at once if the U. S. and England would start war against the Soviets. They are looking for liberation. To what extent war is being prepared no one knows. Near Frankfurt the U. S. Army is building the largest airfield in Europe. In the British zone, England has Polish soldiers in English uniforms. The Russians, too, are not idle. A refugee from East Prussia told me that in a little town 6,000 Russian flyers are being drilled. In the U.S., army preparations are under way to strengthen paratroop forces. If all this does not mean war, at least it is an indication of the fear that grips Europe.

"We hope that Germany will get a good peace. Sensible men are agreed that if Germany is laid prostrate with unbearable burdens the whole economy of Europe will suffer. Why men in their senses should fear a new armed Germany is inexplicable to anyone who sees how demolished Germany is. Fear politics have made even statesmen hysterical. French politics are considered to be stupid because France seeks security through might which it cannot maintain. Well, so goes a bad world that does not take its counsels from good common sense enlightened by the teachings of Christ.

"De-nazification is getting to be an ugly mess: men held without trial for fifteen months and longer, severe penalties, ruining of livelihoods, permanent stigma, etc. The result is bitterness, contempt for 'democracy,' and among youth a resurgence of nationalism. German emigrees, now naturalized Americans and back in Germany, are the worst enemies of a better, peaceful Germany. I hope that Congress will start an investigation of the situation that has been created by ill will, revenge and sheer stupidity."

On this first visitation tour Muench interviewed not only the bishops but also obtained first-hand information from sessions with cathedral chapters and conferences with diocesan directors and secretaries of different societies. As a result a composite picture was obtained which supplied a valuable index of basic data for the work ahead. These first two reports to Rome as well as the others which followed with consistent regularity and thoroughness; the extensive annual reports to the American hierarchy on the Church in Germany; the monthly column "The

Bishop Writes From Europe" in the Fargo diocesan paper *Catholic Action News*; the addresses, talks and sermons all meticulously prepared and numbering in the hundreds; the Fargo pastorals which Muench carefully researched and wrote each year over a period of eleven months — all combined would make up a series of volumes which would be invaluable primary source materials in the history of Catholicism during the critical postwar years of midcentury. Muench stood out as unique among the American bishops of that period for the quantity and quality of his writings on a variety of subjects which were as catholic as his interests. Added to this could be volumes including sequences of letters with leaders of Church and State on the pressing problems of the day. When Muench's papers, covering the years 1946–62, were returned from Rome to his diocesan archives their express weight was 2,500 pounds. Nothing like this had ever taken place in the development of American Catholicism. In the midst of this impressive quantitative accomplishment Muench stands forth in his quiet, unassuming manner as a student for all seasons. No tribute could please him more personally. His habits of work, *immer Arbeit*, astounded his staff unaccustomed to a sixteen-hour day, seven days a week. Europeans could never quite believe that an American could work like this. But work he did. His writings resulted in extensive sentences, detailed reasoning, and too often left an impression of dry and drawn-out statements. But his writings were read and they left their mark.

An important case in point was his 1946 pastoral letter, *One World in Charity*. As Muench moved across Germany during his first visitation tour he was time after time surprised to find that the message of this Fargo pastoral had gone before him. This pastoral had been prepared by the bishop of Fargo before he left for Germany to be read in the parishes of his diocese during Lent of 1946. Its message was forthright and fearless: official regulations of powerful governments were making the exercise of Christian charity impossible in Europe and Asia. Individuals and organizations of good will were practically being told that it was wrong to love one's enemy or to do good to those who have done them evil. Christians cannot remain silent, Muench stated; they must raise their voices bravely in behalf of mercy, compassion and charity toward Japan and Germany. The architects who were blue-printing the structure of peace issued no specifications for charity in the one world they wanted to build. Charity had not even been mentioned in any of their statements on the future peace, despite the fact that charity had been civilization's most successful builder.

Muench then detailed the well-known brutalities and atrocities which took place on both sides during and after the conflict. Would a cold, calculated policy of revenge, suffering and death now be inflicted on persons who were for the most part not responsible for the outbreak of the war or its horrors? Such a policy of an eye for an eye, if carried out by hatemongers, would be the same as Hitler's plans. The bishop then exhaustively referred to narrow and prohibitive official regulations such as the refusal of the War Relief Control Board to allow the United Nations' Relief and Rehabilitation Administration to ship supplies to either Japan or Germany; the limiting of food rations in terms of minimum calories rather than contributing food supplies from American surpluses; silence on the part of too large a segment of the press in not exposing this planned conspiracy of revenge by persons who had infiltrated Washington and the military occupation in Germany; the necessity of comparing American action with Britain's or Denmark's governments which had organized help as had the fearless American Friends Service Committee. Individual citizens must speak up, inform their congressmen, and organize for a more humane world. Otherwise, what did we fight for, Muench pointedly asked.

A large section of the pastoral was devoted to refuting the thesis that the German and Japanese people shared collective responsibility for the war. Muench pointed up the economic, political and social implications for the future of the Morgenthau Plan and Bernard Baruch's attempt to make Germany a nation of goat-herders and foresters. The London *Economist* editorially summarized the reaction of all men of good will: "Unfortunately, very few voices have been raised to state the simple fact that Mr. Baruch's plan is immoral, uneconomic, and unworkable." The sad story of the years after World War I should have been a lesson to all who could read. The propaganda charge of war guilt must be revised, reparations must be scaled down to reasonable levels, pledges given to nations large and small, by both conquerors and conquered, must be scrupulously kept, humility must replace pharisaical righteousness, full employment must be guaranteed. If statesmen do not create one world in charity they will fail mankind.

The impact of this pastoral soon spread beyond the Diocese of Fargo. German language papers in the States such as Dickinson's *Nord Dakota Herold*, *Saint Josefsblatt*, Mount Angel, Oregon, and Saint Paul's *Der*

Wanderer soon had it translated into German. A Dutch version appeared in Holland, as did a French version in Belgium and France. William H. Regnery, sr., Chicago industrialist and publisher, distributed 30,000 copies of the pastoral, and soon German papers were running summaries and commentaries on the startling statements which the German people had waited to hear from someone, somewhere. Cardinal Frings told Muench that his pastoral preceded him in Germany as a ghost across the land. Father Bertke heard a group of people talking on a train to Berlin: *"Endlich hat einer den Mut, es zu sagen wie es wirklich ist. Dieser Bericht hat Hand und Fuss und ist mit vielen Menschenliebe geschrieben. Wer ist eigentlich Bischof Muench?"* [8]

There was adverse reaction from Washington circles, American military personnel in Germany, the office of the political adviser, and from the French Military Government in Baden-Baden. Muench was branded as anti-French and reports against him were sent to France, questions were asked of ranking American ecclesiastics and occupation officials about this "pro-German" bishop, and Monsignor Domenico Tardini, substitute secretary for external affairs at the Vatican, received a protest from the French ambassador, Jacques Maritain. Muench was soon informed of all these negative responses but was not moved to retract a single sentence or to buckle under the pressure. He calmly pointed out that the pastoral had been written for the people of his own diocese before he came to Germany, that he had nothing to do with its dissemination abroad, and that he willingly and publicly acknowledged every step taken by the Allied authorities to mitigate the initial "hard peace" directives.

But in Germany, as Muench moved from diocese to diocese, clergy and laity were thanking him for his pastoral letter on their behalf. Monsignor Hack explained the reactions of those first days:

"The nomination of Muench as papal visitator to Germany had an indescribable psychological effect on the Germans. With him an American arrived who, shortly before, had taken a firm pro-German stand in his Pastoral Letter of 1946, and at a time when neither he nor anyone else could in the least suspect his being delegated on such a mission by the Pope. Like Pius XII, Muench also distinguished very sharply between Nazis and Germans in those early days. He clearly saw that National Socialism, as witnessed by the world, was a pestilence, a disastrous germ that could spread to all peoples under proper dispositions. Muench acted accordingly. An American bishop, out of the heart of the victorious occupying powers so to speak, walks as apostolic visitor through the ruins of Germany, perceiving the deep spiritual wounds in the body of the nation, stooping down to its people, consoling them, encouraging them. He possessed the ability to instill joy and hope, to encourage faith.

"It is impossible to imagine the condition Germany was in, and what Muench's attitude meant in those days. This response to his coming, to his activities during the first years in office found no reaction in the news because the press was still greatly dependent. The problems of de-nazification had not even been tackled.

"The appearance of Muench was providential. Nothing was more remote from his mind than to behave as a prince of the Church. He conducted the affairs of his office in utmost, sincere modesty. The 'good people of the protocol' never had an easy time with him. He was, and always remained, an unassuming, simple man and the German people were very quick to discover that. He was not a man of words; his power of attraction had its roots in his heart and in his priestly piety. His manner of action was always fast, efficient help and prayer. Only after that was done would he turn to other fundamentally important subjects, above all, to seeing that true justice was established and enforced." [9]

The written reports of the visitor and the laudatory letters written about him by German bishops to the Pope and the Secretariat of State impressed Pius XII so deeply that on 18 January 1947 he sent the German bishops the following rare letter in praise of Bishop Muench and his work:

"Our decision to send a special apostolic visitor to Germany, as well as the choice of the person fitted for this work, were determined by the conviction that the lack of a clear view of the first postwar years and of the real and juridical complications springing from it would lead to a situation in the religious field in which the presence of a far-sighted representative of the Holy See, standing aside and above the controversies of the day, would be conducive to the general good.

"With satisfaction we learn from your letters that the office itself as well as the person charged with it, and no less the manner in which he has conducted its affairs, have met with your undivided acclaim and esteemed approval.

"Furthermore, we know with what warm devotion and generous-hearted love the apostolic visitor, designated by us, follows the call to go to Germany. We know, too, with what zealous, objective, and benevolent impartiality he strives to enter into the purpose and duties of his important but also grave and at times thorny mission, and labors to rise to the hopes which Holy Mother Church and the Church of Germany place in his endeavors."

Bishop Muench became aware on this first visitation tour that a long-standing aristocratic tradition existed among German bishops. They were reserved and rather formal, businesslike in their contacts, and unaccustomed to friendly associations even among themselves. While the apostolic visitator was received everywhere with honors and quickly won the bishops' respect and confidence by his open and friendly overtures, he did not establish close friendships with the German bishops such as he enjoyed with American colleagues like Stritch, Mooney, Meyer, or Alter. There were two exceptions to this general pattern; one was Bishop Michael Buchberger of Regensburg and the other was Cardinal Michael Faulhaber of Munich. Both were Bavarian bishops from the land of Muench's ancestors. He immediately responded to their *Gemuetlichkeit*, and in the years ahead spent his most enjoyable hours in the scenic and Catholic surroundings of southeastern Germany, *Freistatt Bayern*.

It was Michael Faulhaber, firm and courageous opponent of the Nazis, scholar and senior defender of the Church and his people, who particularly became an immediate and close friend of Muench. When Muench arrived in Munich he took a room at the Excelsior Hotel near the railroad depot in order to spare the cardinal embarrassment because he could not receive him in his damaged house. When Faulhaber learned that Muench was in town he called him and said: "Bishop, you should not be staying where you are. There is too much riff-raff there." The cardinal then asked him to move to the Hotel Vierjahreszeiten where Faulhaber, with poetic justice, ordered for the apostolic visitator the suite Hitler always occupied when he stayed there. Faulhaber in referring to "riff-raff" was pointedly registering his protest against certain American occupation personnel with whom he repeatedly clashed over postwar policies in Germany, just as he had previously met head-on every Nazi infringement of the Catholic traditions of Bavaria. Faulhaber considered the American educational plans for Germany a direct assault on religious education by liberals and Freemasons. Nor was the aged cardinal enthusiastic about several aspects of the democracy which Americans were working to establish. Faulhaber's sympathies were with the monarchy and he would have preferred the re-establishment of the royal Wittelsbach family in Bavaria.

In their long conversations in the coming years during vacations at a summer villa at Adelholzen in the Bavarian Alps, Muench often had the opportunity to discuss these views with Faulhaber. Muench agreed entirely with Faulhaber's strong opposition to the imposition on Germany by Americans of doctrinaire, secular, educational procedures and joined him in battle against such moves. But the midwest German-American who loved and cherished the freedoms of democracy could not agree with a sacral or baroque monarchist restoration. The two men had a friendly and continuing dialogue on political preferences which left each unconvinced and unbowed.

When the first visitation tour of German dioceses had been completed and the report sent to Rome, Muench knew that he would be called by Pope Pius XII to discuss the completion of his first assignment. In early 1947 the call came, and Bishop Muench, Fathers Zeiger and Bertke left for Rome by train on 11 February 1947. Off and on for ten days Muench talked with Montini and Tardini at the Secretariat of State who, in turn, transmitted information to Pius XII.

During the first two years, Muench stayed in hotels on his Roman visits. After 1949, he always stayed at Salvator Mundi Hospital operated by the Salvatorian Sisters of Germany and his home State of Wisconsin. Here he felt at home and a deep friendship developed that would culminate in his final illness and death in their midst.

Muench reported to Father Howard Smith on the first interviews with Monsignor Montini:

"I think that I persuaded Monsignor Montini that it is necessary to send an experienced Italian to Germany with a view to taking up official relations with the new German government when and if it is formed. I was looking ahead — this is interesting work, but my heart is in the Diocese of Fargo. Furthermore, I am convinced, on objective grounds, that an American will be hampered in his work in consideration of the mistrust and jealousies of the Allied occupying powers. I have the confidence of the German hierarchy; that is one matter, but the French are quite mistrustful of me. I know that from a report that went in to Jacques Maritain, ambassador from France to the Holy See. He, himself, is a doddering old man. I had an hour's talk with him."[10]

Muench was not correct in his evaluation of the interviews with Montini, as he was soon to learn. During the intervals between talks at the Secretariat of State Muench also visited Father Leiber, personal adviser to Pius XII, accomplished his errands, left requests at various curial congregations, and awaited his audience with the Pope. This Roman pattern soon became familiar to Muench in his many visits during the years ahead. The long discussion of details was always processed through Montini and Tardini who filtered the information to the Pope. They discussed policy with Muench which Pius XII wished carried out in the future.

Pope Pius XII saw Muench for an hour and ten minutes on 18 February 1947. It was Muench's birthday and he termed the interview "quite a birthday gift." The conversation was, as always, in German. The Pope was pleased with the report and precisely outlined organizational, charitable and diplomatic steps which the apostolic visitor was to implement in Germany. The formation of a government for the new Germany was being discussed and was in a critical stage. The Pope was most concerned about relations between the Holy See and this German government-to-be. The possibility of a Christian Democratic Party forming in Germany along lines of Italian and French Christian Democratic parties was most encouraging to Pius XII. A new and promising opportunity for a fusion in Europe of religious and social aims was presenting itself for the first time in centuries. The Church would be able to continue the development of peace and social progress in a unique and hopefully permanent way. A society could take shape in which the person would be given primacy over the community. Political activity of a free people, imbued with authentic and vital Christian principles, could be essentially a lay activity. The institutional Church would not dictate and would not be committed by independent lay political action. The concordat of 1933 must be preserved, however, as a safeguard of the rights of the institutional Church.

Pope Pius was keenly interested in the charitable work being carried forward for the needy German people, the work of the German bishops, the situation of displaced persons, and the state of the Catholic theological faculties at the German state universities. German bishops had written to the Pope praising the work of the new apostolic visitor to Germany, and Pius XII congratulated and thanked Bishop Muench for his efficient progress in such a short period of time.

During the previous days Father Zeiger had also been having conversations with the Pope, as well as with Tardini, Montini, Kaas[11] and Leiber. Now Pope Pius summarized the consensus of the whole series of conversations. The juridically unclear situation in Germany would permit only one method of action, namely, to establish as many legal facts as possible. He repeated again and again that Muench should act courageously, and confidently said that all would be in good order.

The particular novelty of the German situation had demanded that Tardini and a special study group examine all facets of the Church's position in a Germany prostrate and without a central government. It was difficult for outsiders to penetrate and understand the chaotic conditions in Germany but Pius XII and Tardini and Montini were thoroughly convinced, according to their curial outlook, of the significance of the fact that, in all the previous years of upheaval, the papal nunciature had been continued at Eichstaett. This was a formal reality to them and it was essential, they insisted, to stress continuity in the months ahead. The recent death of Monsignor Colli, *chargé d'affaires* at Eichstaett was discussed, and it was recommended that Monsignor Hack continue the operation at Eichstaett while reporting to Rome through Bishop Muench at Kronberg.

It was not clear where the seat of the future papal representation in Germany would be set up after a German government was established. Because of the existing provisional juridical situation, all possible economies should be observed. Monsignor Montini recommended that real estate and a house should not be purchased. The present arrangement of living in a house requisitioned by the occupation forces should be appropriately changed to a rental agreement in order to return to normal conditions in a regular way. Muench should decide whether it was opportune to remain at Kronberg near Frankfurt for the time being.

Pius XII, Tardini and Montini were all concerned that refugees in Germany should be receiving spiritual and material care. Cardinal Frings was to continue to exercise protective care of refugees and the refugee council should continue to function. The Pope stressed that care of refugees should be entrusted eventually to the individual diocesan bishops. These tragic victims of war would, undoubtedly, continue to reside in Germany, and German bishops would have to begin to face this reality in their respective dioceses. If individual German bishops would, in agreement with Cardinal Frings, write to Rome for instructions, an answer would be given in conformity with the need to regularize quickly the state of refugees under their jurisdiction.

According to the practice of Pius XII of fortifying the continuance of concordats by establishing as many legal facts as possible, the Pope emphasized the necessity of undertaking positive written communications with officials on all levels. Pius was most anxious that the papal representative in Germany act on all possible occasions on the plain ground of facts in relation to occupation and *Laender* governments. Local conditions would determine upon what constitutions the bishops would take their oaths. Father Zeiger had pointed out that the bishops' oath had its origin solely in the Reich Concordat of 1933, and that it would now be possible to bring this oath in line with the forthcoming federal constitution. Pope Pius, however, remarked that the *Laender* constitutions should not be overlooked as they took form.

Pope Pius left the definite impression that, in order to avoid even the shadow of an indication of any breaking of the existing Reich Concordat, the Holy See would be willing to accept any legal or diplomatic sacrifice. Tardini had said that the contemporary Church was not going to construct problems based on questions of diplomatic procedure. Basic issues were at stake: the legal existence of the Church and the possibility of working for the salvation of souls. In order to assure both, the present Church was prepared to accept what would previously have been considered so-called diplomatic humiliations.[12]

As the conversation progressed Bishop Muench, with a sinking heart, realized that an early return to Fargo was not even under discussion. Finally, he diplomatically suggested to the Pope that his work as apostolic visitor was completed and a trained Vatican diplomat could now inaugurate the new approaches needed in Germany. The Pope looked up, smiled kindly, and told Muench that all reports he had received indicated that the apostolic visitor would be needed in Germany for an indefinite period. Pius XII understood and valued Muench's love for his diocese. But for the time being the Church needed his talents in their beloved and prostrate Germany.

Muench obediently accepted his assignment to return across the Alps. Pius XII sent his personal greetings and blessings to the Catholics of Germany, and before the audience ended asked Muench to accompany him to the Vatican warehouse where they examined medicines, food and clothing being loaded into another caravan of seventeen trucks which the apostolic visitor was to take back to Germany as a gift from the Pope.[13]

Muench then expressed his anxiety about his prolonged absence from his diocese. The Pope suggested that an auxiliary bishop be appointed for the Diocese of Fargo in the same way as Bishop Joseph P. Hurley, stationed in Yugoslavia in the Vatican diplomatic service, was in March 1947 to receive Monsignor Thomas J. McDonough, his vicar general, as an auxiliary for his Diocese of Saint Augustine. This suggestion took Bishop Muench by such surprise that he asked if he could give the matter a little thought.

Muench went back to the hotel in an agitated state to think and pray for hours. The vicar general at Fargo, Father Howard Smith, was too young in ordination at that time to be appointed an auxiliary bishop, and a priest from outside the diocese would only have complicated problems for Muench trying to keep an eye on Fargo diocesan affairs in the midst of his major worries in Germany.

In later years Bishop Muench often said that divine Providence, in his opinion, unquestionably directed his thoughts to Bishop Leo F. Dworschak, coadjutor with right of succession at Rapid City. If the latter could return to Fargo the diocese would be in the best of hands since he knew intimately its problems, was acquainted with and was liked by the priests, and had twenty years of experience in helping to direct its progress. Such a move would be quite unusual, however, since Bishop Dworschak had the right of succession in Rapid City. If he were returned to Fargo as auxiliary bishop he would, according to ecclesiastical procedures, be accepting a lesser status.

The next morning, February 19, Bishop Muench climbed the stairs of the Vatican to the Secretariat of State to discuss the whole matter with Monsignor Montini. As always, Montini listened sympathetically and expressed an interest in the proposal. He said he would see the Holy Father at once about the matter. Muench urged haste as Bishop Lawler of Rapid City, then eighty-four years of age, could die at any time and Bishop Dworschak would automatically succeed to that episcopal see. To make doubly sure, Muench himself called in quick succession upon two curial cardinals. Cardinal Raffaello C. Rossi, secretary of the Consistorial Congregation that had charge of episcopal appointments, was also sympathetic and said a cable would go off at once to Archbishop Cicognani, apostolic delegate in Washington. Before lunch Muench also paid a call to Cardinal Pietro Fumasoni Biondi, former apostolic delegate to the United States, and now also a curial member of the Consistorial Congregation.

To the astonishment of everyone concerned, the whole proposal was processed in the short period of twenty-four hours. Bishop Dworschak was in Saint Paul on 2 March 1947 for the reception tendered to Cardinal Konrad von Preysing by Archbishop John Gregory Murray, when he received a call from Cicognani to come to Washington. There he was told that the Holy Father had approved of the proposal of Bishop Muench, as had other Roman officials, and he asked Dworschak if he were willing to accept the transfer. The latter was completely taken aback by this turn of events which had never entered his mind. He had been in weekly correspondence with Muench ever since he left for Germany and this bolt of lightning had never even been hinted at in any of their lengthy and frank letters. Dworschak immediately agreed to accept the position of auxiliary bishop in Fargo both out of a deep and long-standing affection for Bishop Muench and in a spirit of filial obedience to the Holy See. Cicognani told Dworschak to return to Rapid City and await the public announcement of the transfer.

During the next six weeks all involved waited, not without much concern, for all pegs to fall into place. A new coadjutor bishop for Rapid City had to be found in the person of Bishop William T. McCarty, C.Ss.R., military vicar delegate of the United States armed forces and auxiliary of New York. This meant, of course, that Cardinal Spellman as ordinary of the American armed forces had a part in the new appointment to Rapid City as he had in so many appointments to American episcopal sees during these years.

Then on 11 April 1947 the new appointments for Fargo and Rapid City were publicly announced. On his name day Bishop Dworschak cabled Muench but he was absent in Berlin and did not return to Kronberg until April 14. The latter immediately rushed a long letter to Dworschak in which he could at last tell him what had transpired. Muench movingly wrote:

"Believe me, I am most happy and grateful to God too that you were selected as auxiliary. I know that you gave up a *jus ad rem*, but I need not assure you that I shall not leave you in the lurch. Unfortunately, I do not know when I shall return to Fargo, or whether I shall return there at all, or what else my future will be. Naturally, the Holy Father, not being able to look into the future, could not say anything nor make any commitments . . . Thank God, that all went off as planned. The Lord is really good to me . . . I want you to take hold of things as though you were the Ordinary, make decisions, parochial appointments, clergy assignments, approve building plans, administer finances, etc. . . . I was deeply touched by your expression of devotion and loyalty. A heartfelt *Vergelt's Gott*. I wish to assure you of my daily prayers that God's blessings may be on all your labors. Of my confidence in you I need not write. The fact that I asked for you is proof sufficient of that. May the Lord guide you in all your episcopal work. *Te cum prole pia benedicat Virgo Maria. Pax tibi.*" [14]

Back in Kronberg Muench began to realize that his work was only getting under way. So much had to be done and he felt unequal to the task. He was consoled by the interest and support of everyone in Rome, but especially by Pius XII's moving concern that the Church rise anew and that Germany be helped in every way possible to assume her rightful and worthy place among the free nations of the world. Muench meditated long upon the strange designs of Providence that had called Joseph's son to help his people in bondage.

Bishop Muench accompanies Cardinal-
designate Stritch to Rome for Consistory,
February, 1946.

Pope Pius XII visited the Vatican ware-
house on 18 February 1947 to examine
supplies packed for shipment to Germany:
l to r: Msgr. Andrew P. Landi, Rome
staff of War Relief Services of the National
Catholic Welfare Conference; Bishop
Muench, and Father Thomas F. Markham,
chaplain.

Villa Grosch, Kronberg, 1946.

Bishop Muench with Father Ivo Zeiger, S.J., 1946.

Bishop Muench addresses the First Catholic Youth Meeting in Fulda, Germany, following the war, September 1946.

Bishop Muench, as Apostolic Visitator to Germany, attends Fulda Bishops' Conference for the first time, 1946.

*Visiting the Lithuanian Refugees at D P Camp
in Hanau, 1947.*

*D P Camp at Valka, Catholic
church in foreground.*

*Muenster: bomb
damage to Cathedral.*

Consecration of Bishop Ferdinand Dirichs in Limburg an der Lahn,
21 November 1947.

l to r: Father Howard Smith, Bishop
Muench, and Father Robert Leiber, S.J.,
personal adviser to Pope Pius XII,
13 October 1948.

*Annual Cavalcade in honor of the Precious Blood, Weingarten, 27 May
1949: on court house balcony, l to r: Bishop Leiprecht, Bishop Muench,
Father Howard Smith, General M. Pierre Koenig, military governor of French
zone in Germany, Minister President Mueller.*

*A visit on 22 September 1949 to the Relay Camp at Friedland to see prisoners returning from
concentration camps in Russia. At right, Father Howard Smith and Bishop Leo F. Dworschak.*

*Visit on 28 November 1949
to Freiburg im Breisgau: l
to r: Bishop Muench, Archbishop Wendelin Rauch of
Freiburg and Prof. Leo
Wahlleb, head of state of
Land Baden.*

CHAPTER THREE

MISSION OF CHARITY

When Bishop Muench returned to Villa Grosch at Kronberg in March of 1947, with a clear mandate from Rome to continue and to expand the activities of the Vatican mission in Germany, the problems pressing for attention hung over the Taunus, as Father Zeiger said, like a thousand clouds. Which hat should Muench wear first: apostolic visitator to Germany, head of the Vatican mission, liaison consultant for religious affairs to the American Military Government, or military vicar delegate to American Catholics? Characteristically, Muench moved slowly and methodically. No detail was too small for his attention. A rigorous schedule of up to sixteen hours a day for seven days a week kept him at his desk to the despair of the staff. The Americans worried about his health, the Italians could never adjust to such a regimen, and the Germans marveled at such dedication.

The Villa Grosch, requisitioned by the American Military Government and attached to the civil affairs division of the general headquarters of the United States Army at Frankfurt, was a twenty-room house surrounded by gardens and an extensive wooded estate. The villa was assigned rent-free under Muench's title of military liaison consultant. Opportunities were afforded for an APO mailing address, travel permits throughout the four zones, and purchase of PX supplies and gasoline at army depots. Similar privileges were extended by the Americans to Protestant and Jewish missions, as well as to French and Canadian missions, at Frankfurt. The Vatican mission was to function, according to the original agreement of October, 1945, as a center providing spiritual and moral assistance to displaced persons and German nationals. It was to have no diplomatic recognition.

From this base Bishop Muench had an excellent opportunity to meet the needs of his several responsibilities. Operating expenses for the whole enterprise came from the American hierarchy. Bishop Muench received $109.00 a month from the Vatican as his personal salary which he always placed in the general fund. The understandably small annual Peter's Pence collection from Germany was directed toward the purchase of motorcycles for priests, especially in the East zone.

The staff at Kronberg included Monsignor Alberto Giovannetti, auditor (1946–48); Father Ivo Zeiger, S.J., chancellor (1945–51); Father Stanley Bertke from Cincinnati, secretary, and representative of the mission in Berlin. Bertke returned to the States in 1948 when Father Howard Smith was able to come from Fargo. Muench had originally intended to have both Bertke and Smith as secretaries, but the Secretariat of State in Rome recommended only one secretary. Father Smith was also unable to come as soon as Muench wanted him because he had to stay in Fargo to administer the affairs of the diocese until Bishop Dworschak returned from Rapid City as auxiliary bishop of Fargo.

Monsignor Giovannetti returned to Rome in 1948 to take up a position in the Secretariat of State and continued there to be most helpful to Muench in the following years. Giovannetti is presently serving as permanent observer for the Holy See at the United Nations in New York City. Other Italian monsignors serving at Kronberg and Bad Godesberg included Opilio Rossi (1948–53) and Ottavio De Liva (1950–1954). Both continued in the Vatican diplomatic service: Archbishop Rossi as nuncio to Austria and Archbishop De Liva as nuncio to Indonesia.

Two Germans, one a cleric and the other a layman, were invaluable assistants in the years ahead. Monsignor Bernhard Hack (1946–59) served the longest of all personnel. He was at first stationed in the former nunciature at Eichstaett and brought both experience and valuable contacts in German affairs to the Vatican's postwar work in Germany. The other, Robert Deubel (1947–52), served as secretary to Muench for American and German affairs. A close friendship developed between the young German and the bishop. When Deubel married Erika Titz who was Father Zeiger's secretary from 1945 to 1951, Muench witnessed their marriage, baptized their children, and spent many happy and consoling hours throughout his long stay in Germany with his *Kinder*, as he enjoyed calling them.[1]

Muench obtained the services of three Benedictine Sisters of St. Lioba from Freiburg im Breisgau for secretarial, household and cooking duties at the Vatican mission. In this way he continued the Fargo custom of having sisters working in the bishop's house. When Monsignor Bruno B.

Heim, secretary at Bad Godesberg, became apostolic delegate to Scandinavia in May, 1961, he asked for the Benedictine Sisters from Freiburg to manage the household at the Vatican post in Copenhagen in the same efficient and dedicated style he had experienced in Germany. Among the Benedictine sisters who served at Kronberg and Bad Godesberg from 16 May 1949 were Sisters Fridburga Gumbert, Genovefa Schwert, and Caecelia Rieger. When the nunciature was moved to Bad Godesberg on 10 May, 1951, a fourth sister, Sister Ilga Braun, O.S.B. joined them. She worked in the chancery and at the telephone exchange until Robert Deubel left in 1952 when she took over his work and a fifth sister joined the staff.[2]

The Sisters spent long hours in carefully processing the overwhelming volume of paper work that poured in upon the Vatican mission. Several German civilians were employed as cooks, maids and chauffeurs. Special favorites of Muench were two Polish refugees, Martin Wazny and Nikolaus Kramny, who had done forced labor under the Nazis, fled at the end of the war, and had come to the Vatican mission as workers in 1945. The latter, "Nicki" Kramny, was an adolescent who grew up at the mission and stayed on with Muench as chauffeur throughout the whole period at both Kronberg and Bad Godesberg.

The Villa Grosch consisted of twenty rooms on three floors. A large salon on the first floor with piano and fireplace was used as a reception center. Monsignor Giovannetti had an office off this salon. Bishop Muench worked and lived in one room on the second floor with a desk, bed and steel cabinet in the corner. Robert Deubel and Father Smith likewise had offices in bedrooms on the second floor, and another room was used as the center for distribution of goods. The sisters lived on the third floor. In a matter of weeks letters and incoming donations were spread throughout the whole house. Deubel said that only years later did he realize how poorly all was set up:

"Bishop Muench did not even have his own bedroom separate from his office. We never had an adequate guest room. All was most simple, most modest. Nothing was wasted, especially precious paper, paper clips and basic essentials of office operation and daily living. In the midst of Germany's total collapse and abject poverty, the Vatican mission was a model of simple and frugal living. Everything possible was distributed among the people. We wore donated clothing and often ate food sent to us.

"There were no big successes or disappointments. Day by day we experienced just ordinary events. But all of this quickly mounted to a remarkable contribution to Germany under the direction of a remarkable man. Bishop Muench was a hard worker, his heart was in everything he did. He was the good father of the house. If he was upset he never made a scene. He never sought official recognition of his merits nor was he ruthlessly ambitious. He made no attempt to demonstrate how a representation of the Vatican should be run. He was an example of simplicity, modesty and humility which I had never seen in a man of his position. He did not have any hobbies except his work. He enjoyed going out for a walk one hour a day. That was it."[3]

The bishop soon decided that his main concern was to come to the aid of the poor and helpless victims of the war. This was the Holy Father's deepest concern and the major energy of the mission was going to be directed to that end. Nothing could more please Muench's own personal inclinations. He considered that he could marshal forces and relieve suffering as a shepherd of souls should be doing. He had no inclination to interfere in the affairs of the German bishops, nor to attempt to influence occupation policy. He would respond to appeals for help from any source. He would make responsible and courageous protests against unjust, revengeful, or destructive tides in the political, economic and social rebuilding of Germany. It was his duty to articulate religious values in a society that had completely collapsed. Since there was no German government to deal with, Muench was determined to bring help to those who needed it most. They were the weak and powerless people of God, wherever they were and whoever they were, Catholics, Protestants, ex-Nazis or tragically displaced citizens of the nations of central Europe.

The apostolic visitator was painfully aware of how little any one person could do to alleviate the horrible suffering on all sides. How could one bring some hope to mitigate the congealed despair and resentment of the losers? How could one person lessen the self-glorification of the allied victors who were forming policies based solely on the legitimacy of international force? The best approach was charity, mercy and generous kindness toward all.

There was a moral passion and urgency of mission in this approach of Muench. These were the happiest years of his assignment in Germany. He said he never worked as hard in his life. He constantly referred to "my mission of charity." Some members of the staff at Kronberg criticized Muench for spending far too much time in this all-engrossing apostolate of charity. It was not traditional diplomatic procedure as learned in the schools. There were voluntary international agencies, United Nations bureaus, and German Catholic charitable societies, especially the *Caritas Verband*, which were able to perform these tasks if he would just direct the appeals to these quarters or advise his contacts to send aid through such organizations. But the bishop somehow never seemed to hear these suggestions and hints. He must have been conscious of such criticism which spread among those most conscious of protocol in the international Vatican diplomatic corps. As the years went by he was labeled as an amateur, a misplaced residential bishop over his head in the complex professional world of international diplomacy. Muench was always the first to admit this point. But somehow the hierarchy, clergy and people of Germany thought quite differently, as did obviously Pius XII and John XXIII. As for Muench himself, he never once doubted what the times demanded from a Christian presence and service. "This common effort to help the poor and distressed," he stated, "confided to me by the Holy Father through the Mission of Charity was my most cherished memory. The fact that I was awaited primarily as pastor, intercessor and helper gave me courage to take up my work in Germany."[4]

No nation in history as rich and prosperous as Germany was engulfed by such high tides of misery involving the sixty-six million people who suffered so much in the first years after the war. The problem was aggravated by the influx of fourteen million refugees. In relation to the United States, Muench liked to point out, this meant that in less than two years the equivalent of thirty million people were poured into an area no larger than the diocese of Fargo itself.

The large cities lay mostly in ruins. In Aachen eighty-five per cent of the buildings owned by the Church were destroyed; in Muenster every building used by the Church was destroyed. In the bishopric of Trier only 124 out of 834 parishes survived without damage; in the archdiocese of Cologne the 954 churches were reduced to 211. In the city of Cologne only one church remained of 104 previously used. The archdiocese of Paderborn lost 664 out of 1,284 churches.

Families were torn apart, wives searched in vain for their husbands, children wandered the streets and countryside. Millions of lost persons' names were registered in the files of the occupation forces and charitable organizations. Expellees were crowded into the homes of small cities or of towns and villages in the countryside. People lived for years after the war in air raid shelters, camps, attics, or cellars. Whole families frequently had to share one room with strangers. The strain of living under these conditions created new tensions and serious moral situations. Cardinal Frings of Cologne stated that he preferred consecrating a new home for the homeless to consecrating a new church.

If help had not come from outside Germany, millions would have died. People were dying in railroad stations and on the streets. Calorie intake was down in several areas to nine hundred a day. Bishop Hanns Lilje, Evangelical *Landesbischof* in Hannover, in an appeal to the Christians of the world, stated:

"It is the Church towards which all hopes are directed now. People lost confidence in public collections during the Nazi period. The only general body which enjoys confidence is the Church. She is trusted as being impartial.

"People set their hopes upon Christians within and without Germany. It is a tremendous alternative put before us: either Europe will see the starvation and death of millions of people; trouble and even strife and inner revolution will then be the dreadful by-product of this development; nihilism and chaos will be the end.

"Or the German people will realize once again that there is something, after all, in Christian love and forgiveness, and that they are not mistaken if they turn from the idols of nationalism and false racial doctrines to the Church of Jesus Christ who taught the world charity and mercy. They will realize that they do not hope in vain. . . .

"Come over and help us!"[5]

The Holy Father through the Vatican mission stimulated a response to such appeals. Other organizations such as the United Nations, the Red Cross, the Council of Relief Agencies Licensed for Operation in Germany (CRALOG) from the United States, the Swiss *Caritaszentrale* at Lucerne, France's *Sécours Catholique,* the Dutch Society for Spiritual Renewal and the Netherlands' *Caritas Missie*, the Belgian Caritas Mission, the Catholic Committee for Relief Abroad in London, Irish and Argentinean Catholic aid associations were early in the field.

Military occupation forces authorized existing German charitable organizations to receive and organize the distribution of relief supplies coming from abroad. This wise move prevented further geometric progression, according to Parkinson's law of bureaucrats, and encouraged the rebirth of Germany's traditional Evangelical and Catholic charitable organizations which had emerged from the catacombs following Nazi persecution and suppression.

The American Military Government set a noble example of magnanimity by bringing monthly from the United States government over 300,000 tons of foodstuffs, principally wheat. Voluntary food and clothing parcels poured in from the people of the United States; during the one month of August, 1947, 1,500,000 American parcels were distributed in stricken areas. CARE parcels and shipments made by CRALOG were not included in this total. The American contribution was all the more significant when the zonal divisions of Germany are considered. The Germans, with typical wry humor in their hour of collapse, passed among themselves the observation that the Russians were assigned their agriculture, the French their wine and lumber, the British their industry, while the Americans got their scenery.

The American clergy and laity, through their National Catholic Welfare Conference in Washington, D. C., were equally quick to respond. The executive board of the NCWC established War Relief Services under the direction of able and experienced priests and laymen. This efficient team had worked their way from North Africa through Portugal and Spain in the wake of Allied advances, and were now in a position to move into the prostrate nations of Germany and Italy.[6] Bishop Muench always worked directly with and through the organizational structure of War Relief Services of NCWC. He had good relations with members of its staff, and he directed the majority of his relief work through their well-organized distribution points in Germany. The apostolic visitator admired and leaned on War Relief Services directors Monsignor Edward E. Swanstrom, James J. Norris, Fathers Alfred Schneider, representative in West Germany, Wilson E. Kaiser, in West Berlin, and Fabian Flynn in Freiburg.

Pope Pius continued to send relief material into Germany which Muench helped direct through NCWC War Relief Services and the Catholic *Caritas Verband* of Germany. Beginning in the winter of 1947, papal relief supplies were brought into Germany by rail rather than in convoys. More than 300 freight cars filled with food, clothing, shoes, medicines, bicycles and tires came over the Alps from the Vatican. Through the instrumentality of Muench, the American army authorities generously brought these cars into Germany attached to their military trains running from Rome to Munich.

Muench had a long-standing respect for the *Deutsche Caritas Verband* headquartered at Freiburg im Breisgau. He had known its work from his student days in Switzerland, and considered this fifty-year old organization as the best of its kind in the Catholic world. Every parish in Germany had a *Caritas Verein* which served as the chief operating unit of the *Caritas Verband* in the community. Each parish society collected money and goods for the poor and distressed of the parish, and most of the parishes had trained, paid social workers. Then, in each *Kreis* or county there were central *Caritas* offices to coordinate parish work and to give emergency aid on a regional basis. Thirdly, there were diocesan *Caritas Verbaende* in charge of a diocesan director of charities who, with his staff, supervised and co-ordinated all diocesan charities, both parochial and institutional. All diocesan *Caritas Verbaende* were federated under the direction of the Freiburg central offices in the Werthmann Haus. Here special departments, with trained workers and experts in all social fields, directed the far-flung activities of the entire organization. The best library in the field of Catholic charities was also maintained at the Freiburg center. No supervision or control over diocesan activities was exercised from Freiburg, but suggestions, plans and conferences helped to co-ordinate and initiate effective activity. Although understaffed and overrun with the staggering volume of requests and petitions, this *Caritas Verband* was a strong arm in the rejuvenation of the Church in Germany. Its Lutheran counterpart, *Evangelisches Hilfswerk*, served the Evangelical community with equal thoroughness and dedication. Both societies were criticized for too much German organizational procedure, but no other charity groups ever met a challenge of such proportions as did these German societies in the dark night of their nation's postwar suffering.

Cardinal Stritch, Archbishops McNicholas and Alter, and other friends of Muench on the administrative board of the NCWC realized that the bishop of Fargo had no source of income in his German assignment. They generously recommended that the board send him $50,000 in 1947 for use as he saw fit. During the next three years the administrative board of NCWC continued to send Muench $25,000 from the annual Laetare Sunday donations of American Catholics. After 1950 the American hierarchy continued the annual stipend at a reduced figure of $5,000 yearly.

This most welcome assistance was for Muench a stirring testimony of American Catholics' generosity as well as a personal consolation that his brother bishops were supporting him and their religious confreres in Germany. Muench told the American bishops in his first annual report that wherever he went in Germany bishops, charity directors, welfare workers and pastors requested him to express their deepest gratitude to America's Catholics for such assistance. Without the aid supplied through War Relief Services and the donations directed through Bishop Muench the work of charity in Germany would have collapsed. The charity to Germany in these years was, in the minds of German Catholics, unprecedented in the annals of the Church.

Muench also busied himself in asking for donations from friends and acquaintances throughout the United States. A constant stream of letters went out from Kronberg and the response was phenomenal. Muench's best friend, Monsignor James W. Nellen of Milwaukee, led all in dedication and perseverance. Month by month "Boots" Nellen sent a total of 562 boxes of material goods and thousands of dollars. Clergy and laity in Fargo, both individually and through their societies, responded to the call with money and goods far beyond their means. Muench sent a letter to every priest with a German name in the United States and asked him to send personal help and to organize support from his parish. Now was the time to repay the stricken German Catholics for the donations which the nineteenth-century German Catholics had made in such quantity to the development of American Catholicism. William H. Regnery, sr., of Chicago, a friend of Muench for many years, sent $20,000 for relief work and told the bishop to call on him at any time he needed help. The names of individual donors were carefully and systematically recorded; their gifts checked through to final destination with scrupulous care. The staff soon understood that nothing was more important to the bishop. Endless hours were spent in receiving and distributing packages, acknowledging each gift with a personal letter, and distributing Mass stipends to needy priests according to a rigorous system of accounting.

The list of individual donors whose names filled the entry books and journals of the Vatican mission reads like a "who's who" of the great and small of American Catholicism. Muench stated that he always considered he was recording their names in heaven as year after year he acknowledged the flood tide of gifts. Repeatedly he would end his "thank you" letters with the traditional German phrase which his father had used: "*Vergelt's Gott.*"

It would be an important and significant overview of the depth and spirit of charity among American Catholics if a thorough sociological analysis could be made of these postwar gifts to Germany. Large numbers of American Catholics continue to reveal a superficial understanding of the significance of racial and social justice in their own country and particularly their own neighborhoods. They did, however, reveal in the same critical years of mid-century a remarkable awareness of international brotherhood and charity. Their gifts were a living testimony to the sacrifice and devotion that American Catholics of all national origins witnessed toward peoples who were so shortly before branded as their enemy and that of civilization itself.

There was, undoubtedly, a certain strain of anti-Communism in the motivation for restoring Germany, as was repeatedly evident in letters accompanying gifts from American Catholics. More apparent, however, was strong evidence of a living immigrant strain among the Catholics of the States. The twentieth-century descendant of European immigrants had not forgotten his origin, his debt to those who sacrificed for him, and his deep affinity with the descendants of those who made possible so much of the good life Americans now enjoy. Muench often wrote German Americans that their charity was an act of thanksgiving from grandsons on the American side of the ocean returned with love to their spiritual mother.

Only a few individuals can be singled out among the thousands of Americans who evidenced nobility of soul instead of smug revenge during these dark hours of western civilization.[7] For example, Fred P. Hansen of Chicago sent $5,000 worth of suit material for German clergy and laity, and Bishop Muench asked if he might have a Berlin tailor make him a suit from the material since he had only one suit. Muench, in turn, paid the Berlin tailor with seven cartons of cigarettes for his work, a most generous payment at that time when cigarettes were a prime exchange item on the black market.[8]

Donations came steadily from bishops, clergy and laity of the archdioceses of Detroit, Chicago, Cincinnati, Saint Paul, Milwaukee, Saint Louis; the dioceses of the Dakotas and Minnesota, Fort Wayne, Wichita, Covington and Baker. Seminarians such as those at Immaculate Conception Seminary, Darlington, New Jersey, organized collections for German seminarians. Catholic organizations including such old friends as the Catholic Central Verein of America in St. Louis, the Catholic Aid Association of St. Paul, the Catholic Church Extension Society of Chicago, the Saint Raphael's Society and the Leo House in New York, all sent regular support.

Especially gratifying to Muench were the donations from the Missionary Association of Catholic Women in Milwaukee who sent vestments, chalices and money to their former chaplain under the leadership of Mrs. Mary Gockel. Mrs. Leo J. Weiler and the Fargo Catholic Daughters of America sent 345 cartons of infant and children's clothing which they had collected in North Dakota. Hospital sisters organized drives and school sisters throughout the states organized collections and letter writing exchanges, under Muench's encouragement, between their students and German children, especially orphans. He wrote to the children in the Fargo correspondence school of the Sisters of Service: "Sometimes when you think making sacrifices is so difficult you should think of these unfortunate German children. They are forced to make even greater sacrifices. Like you, they do this with a spirit of love of God. And what we do out of love of God is no longer so difficult."

One of the most difficult and drawn-out negotiations Bishop Muench experienced during these first years was putting to the best possible use the first gift of $50,000 from the American hierarchy. After wide consultation with German bishops and officials it was determined that catechisms were more immediately needed than any other single item. Printing had been restricted during the Nazi period and the influx of refugees now added to the pressing need of instructing children in the rudiments of the faith. But the real problems only began after this decision was reached. Paper was non-existent on the German market and the occupation forces were slow to grant permissions for new printing. Lower officials proved particularly difficult when it came to religious printing. Muench had to appeal to top-level generals and directors of divisions who were more co-operative. After permission to print was obtained, further negotiations were opened with Swedish, Danish, Dutch and French milling firms. Finally a pulp mill in Belgium delivered 280 tons of pulp to a German paper mill in the American zone, and paper of a fairly good quality was produced. The German dioceses then supervised the printing and distribution of the million and a half catechisms. But the whole process took two years to complete and was a constant source of irritation to Muench during the years 1947 through 1949.

Muench received and distributed to needy priests, especially refugee and expellee clergy, over a million dollars in Mass stipends from 1946 through 1959. Usually an order was placed for a CARE package that would be covered by these stipends. It was a circumstantial and laborious way of helping, but the visitator knew of no better way. He had a special knack of finding the most needy and of rejecting pleas from those who should be taking care of themselves. He was ever vigilant that these stipends, given with such devotion, should reach the poor of God. Muench was fond of calling these refugee and expellee priests whom he assisted "God's eminences and most reverend, right reverend, and very reverend excellencies."

The donations of goods received at Kronberg were valued, during the same period by the apostolic visitator, at over $600,000. Muench collected a composite of quotations from clergy and people who had written letters after receiving these gifts and forwarded a copy to all American bishops. Among the hundreds of moving statements were:

". . . Your Excellency had the goodness to send me a food parcel. By this sign of neighborly love you have helped not only me, but my aged mother as well. We consider this not merely a gift of food, but more as a sign of Christian unity that transcends all borders and lands and political disharmony. Your gift gives me new hope and strength to carry on my priestly work in the diaspora. It will be my prayer that God will bless you and our other American benefactors . . .

". . . You know, certainly, how serious our plight is, especially among those who have lost their homes. How many knock on my door day after day begging for something to eat; 95% of them are refugees. The tower of our parish church seems to draw, as a magnet, people in need from all sides. They see in it a symbol of hope, a place where they will surely get a bit of warm soup, or a piece of bread, or perhaps even an article of clothing. Some things we can do, but much is left undone because there are no supplies. Consequently, deep is our gratitude for every gift that comes to us from your hands. God bless you and our benefactors . . .

". . . God bless you all for the food parcel and suit of clothes. How poor I am will be seen from the fact that I have worn the same suit for three years, ever since I had to leave my home in the Sudetenland. My joy in the Lord is great because he has filled the hearts of my American benefactors with neighborly love. I gladly work in the vineyard of the Lord, going long distances from post to post without sufficient nourishment and clothes. *Caritas Christi urget nos*, in spite of my sixty-two years of age. But I am not discouraged, for my Lord is with me and our Holy Catholic Church thinks of me . . .

". . . I am a refugee priest from Breslau. During the siege I was a witness to the destruction of our beautiful city which sank to rubble and ashes under the bombing and rain of fire. During these terrible months we had death next to us at table — death as a mess mate. I saw thousands die. But thanks to God I came out of this inferno of fire and bombing alive. This was to me a second birth. That I lost my home, my church, my beloved parishioners is like a sword thrust into my heart. But others have suffered even more than I. Today the need among refugees and expellees is great. They lack practically everything that is needed for a decent living — a home, clothes and foodstuffs. It is amazing to see with what docility they live through their misfortune. Many come this way, see our plight, and pass on. But the parcels received from Your Excellency remind us that there are still Christians in the world who have not forgotten Christ's command to love one another . . ."

Muench strongly advocated that people should first be fed and clothed before churches and institutions were rebuilt. The German bishops agreed with this policy, but repeatedly the Vatican mission had firmly to reject insistent requests from priests for aid in restoring parish churches. Several Americans had also to be dissuaded from directing their gifts to brick and mortar. For example, P. K. Mebus of Detroit gave $5,000 in February of 1947 for the rehabilitation of the Basilica of Saint Matthias in Trier, the city of his birth. Muench was able to convince Mebus that it was the policy of the German bishops that money go first to the poor. He recommended that the reliable CARE packages be sent to Trier rather than money which would have to be in marks — ten to the dollar — since no American account could be transferred to Germany. Moreover, a devaluation of the German mark would inevitably take place and a major loss of such a donation would follow. When the devaluation of the mark did come about on 20 June 1948, Muench then arranged through federal banks in the United States to exchange dollars for *Deutsche Mark*.

Gifts of money and goods never met the increasing demands and requests that flooded the Vatican mission. Each morning Muench would ask Deubel: "How many *Bettelbriefe* are there today?" The waiting room was time and again filled with petitioners who had come to plead for a relative in prison, a son who was lost, a house that was being requisitioned, a recommendation for amnesty, a student who needed housing, a mother whose fatherless family was undernourished. The word soon spread: "Go to Bishop Muench, he will help you." Some of these grass roots requests were a source of much amusement in the household.

Two widows in Bavaria wanted Muench to send American soldiers to kill a chicken hawk that was stalking their last two chickens. A household of old ladies in the Black Forest informed him that wild boars had eaten their potatoes. Muench sent them two cartons of cigarettes which enabled them to buy enough potatoes to see them through the winter of 1947. Muench often told with delight that more pastors asked for funds to restore church bells which had been bombed or melted by the Nazis than he thought existed in all of Christendom. There were stringent occupation laws against the use of any firearms by Germans. Father Balthasar Foerg of Haeder informed Muench that the cast of his parish play *"Volk am Kreuze"* were in trouble with the American military because they fired two old rusted side arms behind the scenes to signalize an incident in the drama. Muench called headquarters in Frankfurt to explain the incident. Nothing was unimportant to him; he would write to President Truman or to anyone in Washington, Frankfurt and Bonn if he could help the weak and innocent before the law. Here again he came in for criticism. So much time was obviously spent on endless minutiae that could be delegated. But the bishop would not be sidetracked. He was convinced that in this time of civil and social collapse the person and his welfare was all the more precious.

This was unquestionably the case during the bitter winter of 1947, the worst Germany had experienced since 1911. The whole of the country sank into the depth of depression. One of the worst droughts in the country's history had seared the usually rich crops. The lack of staple foods such as wheat, potatoes, sugar, meats and fat caused universal suffering. The allotment of potatoes was 100 pounds for each adult over an eight month period; bread was rationed to five ounces a day, meat from 100 to 300 grams a month, and fats such as lard, butter and cheese were almost non-existent except in agricultural areas where farmers were in no mood to share their only treasure.

Food riots broke out in the Ruhr. The German economy was disorganized, industries lacked raw materials, above all coal. Trade and commerce, when not shackled by restrictions in foreign markets by occupation policy, were severely limited by a lack of sound currency and credit in home markets. The outlook seemed to be hopeless. Chiefly because of a lack of materials, the reconstruction of the demolished cities did not get under way. Some 12,000,000 uprooted refugees and expellees were crowded into a Germany one-fourth smaller in area than before the war. Political life was divided and disunited; there was no central government; political parties that were allowed to function spent all their time in grappling with each other for power. Meanwhile the German people were totally uninterested in politics. They wanted something to eat; they wanted to keep warm; they wanted to work and earn their living.

If the Americans had not imported large quantities of foodstuffs, if food parcels had not come to Germany from individuals, millions of people would have starved. But, then, in 1948 a spirit of hope began to replace despair. The first evidences began to emerge of the *Wirtschafts-wunder* as the world called Germany's economic revival. The crops were abundant and a good harvest relieved the majority of the people from the stalking fear of hunger. Secondly, the currency reform of 20 June 1948 improved financial conditions. On that historic day every German, millionaire or pauper, received per capita forty *Deutsche Mark* for sixty *Reich Mark*, and on September 15 the balance of twenty DM. At the rate of .30 a mark the total was $24. Every individual possessing more than sixty RM had to turn in his excess holdings and received one DM for every ten revalued RM. If a family of six had savings of 5,000 RM, they now possessed seventy DM or the equivalent of $21. The currency reform exposed in a realistic manner the poverty of the German people, but at the same time it acted as a spur to greater production. Shops began to sell goods again now that money had value. Some social effects were negative, particularly among people with little or no earning power such as the refugees, aged, invalids, war veterans, widows, unemployed and students. These people had to depend even more on relatives or charity from abroad.

The third important factor in the economic revival was the development of the Marshall Plan which enabled Germany to co-operate with the countries of the western world and brought a flow of raw materials to German industry. Coal was shipped from England until German coal mining was fully restored and the Americans supplied badly needed raw materials. Both industry and labor began slowly to flourish although a balanced economy was still a hope of the future.

The economic revival pointed up the need of a re-evaluation of the Church's position in a new Germany. During the immediate postwar period all energy had been concentrated on the corporal works of mercy. This effort would continue for another decade, especially among the refugees and expellees, and normalcy would not be achieved in East Germany. In long conversations with Father Zeiger at the mission, and consultations with German Catholic authorities, Muench began to formulate certain basic ideas. He felt much at home in studying the social implications of religion's new position in Germany, and his academic training in the social sciences was an invaluable asset at this time. He carefully read and collected all literature on German conditions written at home and abroad, and held consultations with German academic, political and social leaders which he always found intellectually engrossing. In order to judge fairly and justly all sides of an issue Muench considered it indispensable to listen and to have an open mind. He thoroughly enjoyed contact with the academic and secular world and did not seal himself off from the forces that were re-making Europe. Few churchmen of his generation were so conscious of the complexity of political, social and economic problems of nations and of people outside the Church. This alert social sense, combined with a reflective spirit, enabled him to be more than a superficial insider participating in events.

The Kingdom of God is, indeed, within us, Muench knew, but it is born and grows socially. The visible Church is its source, instrument and expression. To renew the faith and the Gospel in the modern world, to establish peace in the world, churchmen would have to seek union with all men of good will. "We must dismantle discord," he said, "and drop an atom bomb filled with the energy of love on humanity."

Muench spent long hours studying the sources of the writings of Pope Pius XII. He wanted to express this thought exactly in his own speeches, contacts and writings. The German Jesuits Leiber, Zeiger and Oswald von Nell-Breuning were helpful in this regard since they all were contributing background work for papal pronouncements and writings. The Dominican Center for the Study of Social Problems at Walberberg, under the direction of Father Eberhard Welty, O.P., was another source of ideas. Monsignor Albert Buettner of the Auslandssekretariat, Beuel/Bonn; Heinrich Koeppler, general secretary of the Central Committee of German Catholics, Bad Godesberg; and Heinz Reuter, editor of *Deutschland Union Dienst*, Bonn, were valuable contacts for realistic understanding of the Church's new position.

The spiritual and intellectual recovery of German Catholicism, after a twelve-year interval of inactivity forced on the Church by the Third Reich, was actually a much more extensive building program than material restoration. How viable were former religious organizations and structures; would they function in a radically changed situation? The question was not only a problem of external organization and form. It reached deeper as an expression of an inner change, a new outlook on ideas and problems.

The first *Katholikentag* following the war was scheduled for Mainz on 1–5 September 1948. It was to be the seventy-second general assembly of German Catholics and the first since the Nazis suppressed these unique and valuable annual religious gatherings after the Essen *Katholikentag* in 1932. During these upcoming days of public worship, discussion and manifestations of the faith at Mainz, the first opportunity presented itself for the Church to place in public focus the problems of her postwar existence.

Bishop Muench was scheduled to pontificate and to bring papal greetings to a *Katholikentag* for the first time in sixteen long years. Father Zeiger was invited to deliver the keynote address at the first working session of the assembly of German dioceses, parishes and organizations. During the summer of 1948 Zeiger and Muench planned carefully for their appearances at the September *Katholikentag*, and they worked long hours in preparing what later came to be known as a basic platform for the Church in the years ahead. Zeiger consulted with his friend Leiber, adviser to Pius XII, and Leiber spoke with the Pope concerning the planned contents of Zeiger's address.

Zeiger's masterful address at Mainz on Thursday morning, 2 September 1948, deserves thorough summary.[9] This scholarly presentation of guidelines for a missionary Church in the diaspora was referred to by German Catholics in the years ahead as a platform policy statement. Under the title of "The Religious and Moral Situation of German Catholics," Zeiger began by stating unequivocally that it was a time for practical work, no longer a time for a theoretical laying of metaphysical ground plans for the Church's position. The religious situation would be determined by postwar conditions. The life of the Catholic Church in Germany was, in the same way as the life of the German people, in great material need. But the Church now stood stronger than ever before because of its freedom. The persecution and suffering of the Nazi era constituted an examination period, a purification, which like all crosses of Christ, was a holy blessing.

Is the Church needed in the postwar world? This question was being asked and it must be answered, Zeiger continued, with a strong "yes." The Church suffered with the State; in the fatherland's hour of suffering loyal Catholics stood to the end. The Church's freedom is a right not given as a gift from the State. Catholics defend God's holy right and his Church. They do not ask for special privileges or the rights of a special group, but they oppose every inroad on God's rights as a curtailment of man's rights.

After this general statement, Zeiger then asked: what did the war bequeath to German Catholicism? The answer is apparent. It is a new situation in the life and work of the Church. The work of the nineteenth and twentieth centuries is changed; the geographical and material situation is changed; above all the interior fundamentals of mankind are changed. "No pity, no tears, no longing will bring back the good old days for us," Zeiger stated. "Rather, let us be thankful for our freedom and the work to be done."

The Treaty of Westphalia in 1648 ended the Thirty Years' War between German brothers and stopped the previous hundred years of war between Christian confessions in Germany. Two hundred years later the Church lost her worldly position and lands through the secularization movement, but the geographical division of Germany between Evangelicals and Catholics remained throughout the nineteenth century.

Today industrialization, Hitler's Reich, and the displacement of thousands of people combined to break up traditional confessional lines. Both denominations sent their parish children forth from small villages to all parts of Germany. They turned the last village into a diaspora. There are no more territorial and geographical confessional distinctions; the confessions today are like the political map of the Federal Republic and the *Laender*. Nor would there be a return to "normalcy." The present political situation is here to stay as much as is the diaspora. Territorial Church unity was destroyed when God allowed the break-up of religious enclosures. The protective walls of Catholic particularity were torn down. The storm of the times spread Catholicism over the whole land, as seeds in the field, to enable the present generation to bear good fruit.

Is the Church in Germany ready for the new situation? Zeiger agreed with those critics who had been writing that Catholics are not mature, not ready for the dimensions of the diaspora. Catholics think first of strength, of truth, of faith, or of protecting Catholics who are separated from Catholic communities. The old Catholics in the original German diaspora of such regions as Mecklenburg, Saxony, Thuringia or Schleswig-Holstein learned that it was difficult to live there; so will contemporary Catholics who poured into these regions through forced migration. Over twelve million Germans from the East, of whom sixty per cent are Catholics, were now living throughout Germany and in the old diaspora lands. This new situation would not be met with the knowledge and strength of faith of believers living in an enclosed Catholic enclave. The Church must be conscious of herself as the seed of God that goes forth and fills the earth. Germany's forefathers built well interiorly since 1648, as soldiers standing firm. Today the challenge is an outward thrust, not critical of the past, but a recognition of a complicated problem due to new factors.

Father Zeiger again asked: Are Catholics inwardly prepared for this mission? There are still good Catholics and good pastors. A new government is forming under majority vote of a political party with the adjective "Christian". Organizations are strong, a conservative atmosphere exists. But there is a real difference between belief and practice. This has always been the case, but it is intensified today because a people become materialistic when they are building. Spengler said that a man who is a builder is a man lacking a sense of history. Modernity, technology and organizations based on reason have enveloped the land. The old methodology of land parishes will no longer work. Today's generation lived through the periods following 1918 and 1939. In this period of war, concentration camps and displacement, men became numbers without personality. If the Church continues to work in the categories of a family culture it will not reach modern man.

Modern man is acclimated to a film culture. Newspapers, sensations, cinema, sports, variety, dance, music, endless droning of radios, political propaganda and hundreds of other fantasies leave this generation struggling to find its soul. This is an epoch without *epos*, logic, peace or stability. Religion has been looked upon as a private affair since 1933. The German Catholic traditions of liturgical, community worship were seriously weakened among the young Catholic men who served in the army. This generation had Nazi propaganda poured into them; they had no opportunity to study Catholic theology or social teaching. What do democracy and freedom mean to the contemporary German; what are the lasting effects of totalitarianism on the new German? There is no deep understanding of the words of Scripture or the liturgy. Germany endured sixteen years without ethics or religion, and today's existentialism has been added to this atomizing of the person.

German Catholics must begin immediately to live in a Church which is a mission Church, Zeiger warned. The Catholic people of Germany are still good and survived well the war years. But they cannot rest there. They must build in a Germany that has become a mission land. There is a new diaspora, an interior mission. The displaced persons in their midst, the millions who need God's bread, the hundreds of thousands of children who need God's word — all will need churches, chapels, priests, sisters, active laity, books, food and money. A mission situation demands missionary methods. German Catholics must become as poor as a mission church, they must work in humility. Social help and charity mean motorcycles, catechisms, paper. The day of German particularism, egoism and attachment to a single region is gone.

Who will roll back the stone for us, Zeiger cried? Discussions atuned to old melodies will not answer the need to rebuild from within. Mission work with an apostolic tone is demanded in this hour of birth and building. A real apostolate built on a brotherhood of clergy and laity is the only road ahead or the Church will not primarily serve man himself. Practical work in a mission land concerns itself with souls and Christ. A current German writer declared that the tendency toward primitive Christianity lives today only in the apostolate of political movements. Zeiger concluded by denying this statement. The spirit of primitive Christianity must also live in the Church. This is the challenge for Germany's future if the people are to be claimed for Christ.

When the time came for Bishop Muench to give the closing address of the Mainz *Katholikentag* on September 5, he re-emphasized the thrust of Zeiger's opening paper. Muench praised the German Catholics for re-establishing the *Katholikentage*, emphasized the spirit of the noble Mainz social leader, Bishop Wilhelm Emmanuel von Ketteler, who was present at the first *Katholikentag*, and he then continued:

"With piercing insight Ketteler realized the demands of his century. He made himself their advocate with such great courage that it is impossible to think of a century of Catholic social work without remembering the name of Ketteler. Similar to our present situation, he, too, lived in a time of upheaval. Social tensions and transformations were clearly recognizable; false ideas were being spread abroad, wild passions were awakened. In this milieu he lifted high his voice against oppression and social injustice.

"We pledge now to follow him: not in passionate confusion, but with objective, clear ideas about social relations. Not in envy and hate between social classes, but in social justice and love. Not in class war that, like every dissension and war, brings in its wake only misery and destruction, but in mutual understanding and harmonious co-operation.

"Yes, harmonious co-operation, this is the serious demand in our age of tremendous upheaval. Will a people become strong and prosperous in division and discord? Look around the world and see the answer: prosperity and wealth are the fruits of peace.

"There will always be disagreements where there are human beings. But we are more than only human beings, we are Christians. Christ the Lord requires that we hold fast to each other and work together in the unity of faith and love.

"You carry the flame of faith in your hearts. Light the torches of deeds in your hands, carry them into your dark neighborhoods so that your fellow men may rejoice in the light of your holy Catholic faith and praise the Father in heaven because of your works of faith.

"You carry the fire of love of God and man in your hearts. What else does the Lord wish but that it also burn in the hearts of your fellowmen. Love kindles love; active, peace-giving love it must be.

"For these deeds of faith and love many small, individual efforts and much meticulous work is necessary, as well as dedicated, unified, mutual work. Let us not deceive ourselves and others: this *Katholikentag* at Mainz has again made evident how well organized your lay movements are. They are rightfully your fame and pride. However, organizations are but means to an end; they must never become the end itself. That would render barren the field of Catholic action. Catholic action is spirit and life; it does not allow itself to be made a slave by being handled and manipulated like a machine." [10]

The German clergy and laity reacted favorably to Zeiger's and Muench's first postwar tests at the Mainz proving ground. The issues were clear: what would be the relationship of Catholicism to postwar realities; the role of Catholicism as servant to a de-Christianized and overpopulated rural diaspora dominated by foreign refugees and emigrees; the danger of a disenchanted urban proletariat losing their faith; the challenges of religious art and liturgical developments in a new church under construction; the relationship of separated Christians in a newly forged *Una Sancta* that had developed under Nazi terror; the possibilities of entirely new relations with an emerging free civil society in the areas of church schools, Christian trade unionism and socialism.

All that had been discussed at Mainz existed in the form of problems rather than solutions. The Church in Germany during the late 1940's was not the Church of 1932. The Church had lost almost everything normally associated with the practice of the faith in a family and parish culture. Its structures and organizations were reduced to a sacristy operation. A prevailing sense of guilt and repentance existed among the Germans immediately after the war. Christians were conscious of the accusations that they had failed to provide the nation with more pervasive spiritual leadership in the Nazi period. When the Nazi Reich was defeated its *ersatz* religion also came to an abrupt end. Many Germans were ready to reject their former idolatry and to turn to a Church which had proved itself wiser and more enduring than the vain promises of the so-called thousand-year Reich. In 1945 there was a favorable opportunity for a mass return to Christianity. There were a considerable number of genuine and sincere conversions of former Nazis who willingly underwent a period of trial and instruction. But by 1948 there were few illusions about a national rebirth of faith and hope in either Catholicism or Protestantism. There had been too much evidence of opportunism, of people with a keen eye for the existential chance who were not really repentant, and who had experienced little interior change or acquired any fresh vision.

At the same time the Church had acquired new life through the blood of its martyrs. It had been purified by a flow of superhuman suffering, and had undergone an interior rejuvenation. A generous missionary spirit animated many people who were rediscovering the meaning and richness of a Christian community. There was a trained, if small elite, generously prepared for sacrifices, who could serve as a leaven for the masses. The problem faced at Mainz was that the Church needed to develop a corresponding response in bringing the message of grace and hope to a new situation. The Church was behind the times, did not fully understand how ordinary people were facing the problems of their everyday lives, and had not as yet any plans in hand to anticipate this need.[11]

The reasons for this time lag among German Christians were easily recognized. When National Socialism collapsed in 1945 and the Church regained her freedom, there had been a twelve-year period, from 1933 to 1945, of unlimited domination by a pagan system, time enough to suppress the regeneration and reinforcement of Christian life. Not only did Catholic organizations lose their leaders, but they were unable to train new people. For twelve years the education and instruction of a new staff of leading Catholics was stopped. Many of the younger generation had been lost during the Nazi regime so the gap could not be filled.

Antireligious governments of the right and the left in modern times worked according to carefully laid plans aimed at gradual and total extinction of all religious voices. At first God, the Church, sacraments, or bishops were not directly attacked. Groups of extremists attacked, rather, the "bad" and unnecessary, the anti-national, anti-governmental and capitalistic priests and laity. In this way confusion was spread among the faithful and deep conflicts aroused in their consciences. It was then easy to diminish through propaganda the prestige of the Church and Christian thinking. As domination of society becomes total, attacks upon the Church become direct and persecution constant.

The Nazis were particularly determined to wipe out the international character of German Catholicism. From a political and psychological point of view Catholicism was an international system based on higher principles than national ideas and state laws. Christians hold that the power and prestige of a nation always is dependent upon eternal principles, truths defended by a universal Church which, in the case of Catholics, has a universal center in Rome. The Catholic Church, an international organization directed by anti-national elements, the Nazis maintained, had to be isolated from the world outside as well as in the public life of the nation itself. All religious influences were to be eliminated from public life, from political and social life. As a result, Catholic organizations, parochial schools, trade unions, newspapers, journals and publications were abolished. Monasteries were curtailed or closed, religious orders limited, clergy ridiculed. Religion was erased from political, social, cultural and educational fields. Religious activity was limited to church buildings and their closest surroundings. Strong and powerful personalities among the German bishops — such as Faulhaber, von Galen and von Preysing — tried to break through the wall erected around them by the Nazis and to raise their voices in order to be heard by the whole population. But this effort had not prevented the Nazis from continuing their evil business.

The internal and external isolation of German Catholics, the destruction of their representation in public life, the essential break in organizational procedures — all constituted a heavy blow to the Church and religious life in Germany following the war. A Church does not exist only in its buildings, but primarily in the faithful themselves. The Church cannot exist without the spontaneous activity of Christians in different sections of public life. A real split developed between the spiritual life of a Christian and his activity in public life. The long years of National-Socialist propaganda and the demoralization of war, hunger, bad housing and overpopulation had destroyed the general moral level of society. The percentage of active Christians — fifteen to twenty-three per cent — was much lower than before the war, especially in the cities. The continuous education of the German people in a Christian spirit had been interrupted for too long.

The Zeiger thesis presented at the Mainz *Katholikentag* gained widespread attention outside Germany as well as throughout the nation itself. Among commentators was Dr. Karl Josef Hahn, professor of German language and literature at the Catholic University of Nijmegen in Holland, and author of a widely read study of the spiritual problems of postwar Germany (*Duitsland als geestelijk probleem*). Hahn stated:

"Father Zeiger, co-operator of Bishop Muench in Germany, stated in a major address that Germany has come to be a mission country. It was a surprising, in a way a shocking word because it sounds very unusual to use the word 'mission' in reference to the so-called civilized nations. We always lived with the idea that, in spite of all the difficulties in our West European civilization, the Church was more or less definitely established. Not only the Russians have spoiled such illusions. When we hear that in the center of Europe, in a nation which has contributed so much to Christian civilization and to the Church, a new mission is necessary, everyone will realize the seriousness of the situation. Certainly, in other countries of Europe the same problems are to be dealt with, but it seems that of the free countries of Europe, the Church in Germany is undergoing a very sad time.

"Yes, without any doubt, Germany is a mission country and new missionary techniques must be found to protect these millions of Catholics who are seriously threatened in their faith or have already lost it, to gain the souls of those who have never heard the name of Christ or never felt the real sense of his holy Name. But it is not easy to find these new methods or the people to put them into practice or the means to carry out the work. Therefore much patience and praying will be necessary to solve these questions." [12]

William H. Regnery, sr., Chicago:
"he helped me as none other
in my mission of charity."

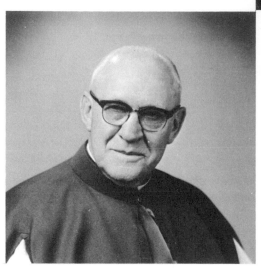

Monsignor James "Boots" Nellen
Holy Redeemer's parish, Milwaukee.

Charles M. Muench, sr., president of
Allen Silk Mills, New York, close friend of
Bishop Muench, donated vestment material
and clothing material for orphans.

Val and Mrs. Blatz visit their

daughter in the convent.

At home in Milwaukee on the occasion of mother's eightieth birthday, 13 December 1948.

On her eightieth birthday, "Liebe Mutti"
receives a papal blessing and rosary from
Pope Pius XII, 13 December 1948.

Addressing the first Katholikentag *since they were suppressed by Hitler,*
Mainz, 5 September 1948.

In conversation on 22 September
1949 with a priest in the
transit camp at Friedland. The
priest, a prisoner in Russia
since before the end of the
war, had been released that
morning.

Visiting prisoners
returning from Russian
concentration camps,
Friedland, 22 Septem-
ber 1949: l to r:
Father Howard Smith,
Bishop Muench, Bishop
Leo F. Dworschak.

Father and son sent to the DP camp at Friedland after their captivity by Russians.

A welcome for prisoners returning from concentration camps in Russia, Friedland, 22 September 1949.

Two apprentice workers receive new shoes from Father Alfred A. Schneider, NCWC-War Relief Services, Munich Youth Home, 22 May 1950.

Cardinal Faulhaber receives keys to nine trucks and a jeep for German Caritas from War Relief Services, 15 November 1949.

Refugees arrive at Seckach

*Refugees cared for
by Caritas at Buchen.*

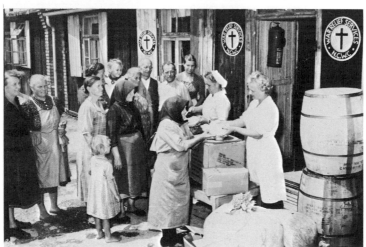

*Expellee families receive their daily share of government surplus
NCWC-War Relief Services' contribution of dried eggs and powdered milk,
Waldfriedhof, Munich, 2 July 1950.*

Hannover: Food and clothing distributed by War Relief Services of NCWC.

Delivered to the needy in Germany from one small county in Ohio: 256,000 lbs; $50,000 value.

Archbishop Muench speaking to Federal Minister for Refugees Lukaschek,
Schwaeb-Gmuend, convention of Ackermann Gemeinde (organization of Sudeten
Germans, Czechoslovakia), August, 1952.

Arriving in Frankfurt from Rome, 1953.

CHAPTER FOUR

FIRST PROBLEMS IN KRONBERG

Bishop Muench, in his methodical and thorough way, possessed the patience necessary to help German Catholics work out their own missionary methods and to take their own steps forward. The pressing nature of so many daily problems did not overwhelm him. He had, as Cardinal Frings stated, "a buoyancy of spirit that raised the hearts of those who lived in rubble." His skill as a lucid and balanced interpreter arose from an unfailing sense for continuity in the emerging shape and structure of a new Germany.

The first impression Muench made upon Germans was his precise and well planned approach to each issue in hand. From the very beginning he faced the complexity of postwar reconstruction with a slow pacing and sense of timing, a quiet and serene reflection that seldom at the time fully revealed the extent of his moral commitment and urgency of vision.

The unique contribution of the apostolic visitor was his understanding, tolerance and sense of mission that saw the possibilities of good in every person. As representative of the Holy Father, a responsibility he never forgot, Muench accepted all men as brothers while urging them to do the same. His clear mind never ceased to heed the message of the Christian heart: love is the saving grace of humanity, the ultimate justification of society, the saving weapon against hatred and exploitation. It was his task in a prostrate Germany to exemplify and advance love and understanding as the mechanism of a coherent international community. A profession of faith in human goodness and a practice of mutual trust could make negotiation respectable and possible.

Bishop Muench established a rigorous daily schedule which he never altered. He was an early riser and was the first in the household at the papal mission to offer Mass, always by 6:30 a.m., and often earlier.

After meditation and the praying of half of his divine office, he took breakfast which always had to be ready at 8:15 a.m. sharp. He liked an American style breakfast, beginning with cooked cereal the way his mother had made it in Milwaukee. While at table he started to read the papers. Often he would say to his co-workers: "What hat do I wear today? Am I apostolic visitor, chief of the Vatican mission, liaison consultant to the American Military Government, or military vicar delegate?" Shortly after breakfast he was at his desk and ready for the daily mail. Staff conferences, interviews with visitors and petitioners followed in regular order, but it was ever the mail that occupied him. Hours were spent in writing friendly and kind letters to everyone who sent alms, requested aid or asked assistance. A trained diplomat would set the majority of these so-called less important letters aside to be answered according to form by members of the staff. But Muench felt like a pastor of souls when he was responding to peoples' needs. His voluminous correspondence reveals that he seldom wrote formal or business letters. He always had a personal touch, and he would add some spiritual advice whether he could help or not. His constant model was Pope St. Pius X whom he deeply admired.

Muench's simple virtues stand forth in each encounter, virtues which endeared him to the German people: candor, straightforwardness, innate decency and good will, a determined moderate outlook, a patience in dealing with every occasion which was sent to him, he believed, as part of God's plan. He wanted all letters answered as quickly as possible, an assignment which took hours of typing by the staff. If a trip was to be made somewhere in Germany, he would expect Nicki, the driver, to have mapped out the route and timed the whole journey. He would leave his office at the last moment, often dictate letters in the car en route, and go immediately to the chapel or his office on his return to Villa Grosch. Often his systematic, precise planning was questioned by staff members who judged that he became too engrossed in details and did not allow himself enough time to consider the over-all implications of events.

The constant schedule of hard work from morning until evening astounded Monsignor Alberto Giovannetti who commented:

"I was very young at that time, and I had read a lot about the Americans. My opinion of Americans was that they are people who like nice, long weekends, like to enjoy themselves, like to enjoy life. I kept thinking, 'how can an American work as hard as Bishop Muench does?' I never worked so hard, and the American way of life hit me. I changed my opinion completely. I was completely wrong about the Americans."[1]

No spell was cast over the household by the presence of Bishop Muench. He did not stand on protocol; the staff was gay and relaxed. He was considerate, understanding and sympathetic with the feelings of everyone in the household. Monsignor Guido Del Mestri, counselor at Bad Godesberg, and at present apostolic delegate in Mexico, gave him the title of "Father of the Household," a designation which was repeated often by all involved.

Although Muench showed little emotion, he was always kind and considerate in his disciplined way. His normal attitude was first to judge all situations with the heart. This did not mean he was unintellectual; but it did mean that he was not cold, distant or intellectually superior. The secret of his success with both German hierarchy and laity was precisely that he was always a human being. He was not only an efficient diplomat, but was able to break through, to see people behind paper and formal occasions. His first reaction was not, "what is the law," and then to follow through wherever the blows might fall. He wanted to be a good representative of the Vatican and he wanted equally to help the German people. Here lay the source of his warm contacts with the Germans. In a conversational interview, Bishops John Pohlschneider of Aachen, Joseph Stangl of Wuerzburg, Adolph Bolte of Fulda and Edward Schick, auxiliary of Fulda, stated:

"Muench gave us assistance and help with extraordinary compassion and interest . . . He had an open heart for everything . . . Our bishops expressed their gratitude to Pope Pius XII for having sent Muench to Germany. They were convinced that Muench was the best possible nuncio for those times, and that he certainly showed more understanding of our problems than a nuncio coming from a Roman country could ever have done . . . He was unanimously accepted as a true friend of the Germans. Without exaggeration we can also say that the Protestants and other non-Catholics held him in high esteem . . . It was pretty much the general feeling that Muench did not run through diplomatic schooling, but that he was decidedly a pastoral bishop, taking care of priestly and pastoral duties in a special way. Most certainly this was very important for those early postwar years. His pastoral attitude impressed all of us tremendously."[2]

"What hat am I to wear today?" During the busy years from 1946

to 1951 the bishop found that the thrust of developing events and con-
testing personalities usually forced him to act in all four of his capacities
at the same time. The complex puzzle of German religious reconstruction fitted together along several horizontal lines. Muench had begun
his first assignment of contacting and working with all German bishops
as apostolic visitor. His on-going work as chief of the Vatican mission, as Catholic liaison consultant to the American Military Government, and as military vicar delegate for American chaplains in Germany
and Austria, was not as quickly or easily accomplished. The drawn out
occupation by the victorious allies, the protracted negotiations in establishing a new German government, the processes of de-nazification and
rehabilitation, and the increasingly pressing problems of expellees, refugees and displaced persons were all before him.

Bishop Muench's position in the American occupation setup was an
effective asset, as has been seen, in expediting his over-all work. He
personally enjoyed working as military vicar delegate with the chaplains, such as Major Thomas Corcoran, diocese of Alexandria, who as
deputy chief of chaplains was of invaluable assistance on many occasions, as was Captain Herbert Leger, archdiocese of Boston. Muench
granted and processed faculties, accepted as many invitations as possible
to confirm, preach, offer special Masses, dedicate chapels or give retreats
to American personnel in Germany. He cherished his visits to the camps
and meeting with the families of American servicemen in Germany.
Since he could not be at home in his diocese of Fargo, he looked upon
the American soldiers and their dependents in Germany as his pastoral apostolate. Thousands of Americans in Germany looked to him
as their spiritual father and during these years he established as close
relations as possible with his flock. For example, for three hours
on 7 July 1947 he confirmed 534 American children in St. Joseph's
Church, Bornheim-Frankfurt. Father Paul R. Kinder, in his farewell
letter to the military vicar on 11 March 1947, as he was completing his
chaplain's service, summarized the feelings of American military personnel toward Muench:

"I have counted the acquaintance of Your Excellency a real privilege
and grace. It was not my expectation that a writer, seminary rector
and bishop would be so gracious, humble, democratic and likable a
person . . . For Your Excellency's kindliness, for your Christian example, I heartily thank you. To many of us as you took your long
trips, ate in G. I. messes, slept in G. I. billets, forsook your cherished

life at home for a combination of strenuous and not-too-pleasant jobs over here, you were an inspiration."

But there were glaring incompatibilities as well in this spiritual activity of Muench among the American occupation forces. The Italian and German members of his staff at Kronberg constantly impressed upon Muench that his primary assignment was from the Holy See as apostolic visitator and chief of the Vatican mission. They warned him that he must not leave the impression, as he unquestionably did, that the special envoy of the Holy See to the Germans and displaced persons was there for the Americans. The Russians repeatedly made propaganda strikes at Muench's relation to the American occupation forces; the French never fully understood his four-fold role and generally persisted in not wanting to; the British were not pleased that they were not informed of Muench's assignments. Monsignor Richard L. Smith, a friendly and co-operative deputy controller of the religious affairs branch of the British zone of occupation, told Muench that he should have been accredited to the British section of the Allied Control Commission as well as to the American. British authorities were not informed of his coming and were not asked to grant him the usual faculties. As a result there were contradictory reports about him. Muench hastened to assure Smith on 31 August 1947 that he was anxious to work with British Military Government in Germany in complete harmony and co-operation. He was in Germany at the request of President Truman and the War Department to act as Catholic liaison consultant in religious affairs between the American Military Government in the American zone and the German episcopacy. He represented the Pope in Germany as an apostolic visitator learning about the state of religion and the problems of the Church. He was a military vicar delegated to assist chaplains and to serve the American Catholic troops. None of these assignments had a diplomatic character; rather, all were religious and spiritual in scope. While such explanations gained entrée for Muench to the British and French zones, and he was accorded all necessary courtesies, his position was clouded from 1946 to 1949 when the status of the nunciature in Germany was formalized by his appointment as regent.

His second hat, that of Catholic liaison consultant to American Military Government, proved to be a fruitful, demanding and exciting assignment. Secretary Patterson had instructed Muench to promote to the best of his abilities good will between the Army of Occupation and the German people in the interests of democracy. Monsignor Bernhard Hack, long-time assistant for German affairs at both Kronberg and Bad Godesberg, explained the nature of this operation:

"Muench tapped the rich resources of his home country, and with the co-operation and support of his fellow bishops and the Catholics in America he brought remedy to our manifold needs. He knew how to collect truly enormous donations, and how to direct them into the right channels. Muench was an exemplary administrator of all those donations. He did not choose the easy way; on the contrary, he checked and studied cases with meticulous care before he granted means to organizations and individual persons, and he insisted on getting reports on how the means had been used. His decisions were quick and therefore particularly valuable.

"What the walls in Kronberg would tell could they speak! How often did the rooms resound with the cry: 'Danger of dismantling; please help!' This pertained to a decision of Military Government that areas and plants of production still in working condition should be dismantled. However, these factories and plants were indispensable for reconstruction and to prevent unemployment. There were weeks in Kronberg when delegation upon delegation showed up in order to plead for Muench's intervention in this matter.

"Another issue was paper, a word that would re-echo in Kronberg. The Church press lacked the necessary paper for publications, and the materials had to be imported. Muench helped incessantly as much as he could.

"Or the issue would be amnesty for those condemned to death. A most difficult subject. Justice demanded its right. But was it really justice in each and every case? Muench never backed away from these difficult problems. He worked on them. He understood the mother who pleaded mercy for her twenty-one year old son who had committed war crimes at seventeen. Many times he succeeded in obtaining a reprieve, then an amnesty.

"One day he received a petition on behalf of a large group of people sentenced to death by an American court. It was discovered that this particular case had not been handled well. Muench saw to it that the responsible American authorities reconsidered the matter. And the judgment was quashed for all accused. These things received hardly any publicity: the misjudgments as well as Muench's successes. Who would have wanted to draw attention to those things at that time?

"Muench was a faithful and reliable American. In these matters especially the nobility of his character came to light. He was courageous and independent, and at the same time most tactful toward his fellow Americans. With prudence and frankness he intervened with the American Forces of Occupation when he noticed that they overstepped their competence or deviated from their instructions. He knew how to find ways and means, either by personally intervening or by delegating the proper people to turn such developments toward a better course. He felt completely at home in these and similar situations, and he knew his fellow countrymen well." [3]

When Muench came to Germany in the summer of 1946 General Joseph T. McNarney had succeeded General Dwight D. Eisenhower as military governor of the American zone. On 15 March 1947 General Lucius D. Clay became military governor and continued in that post until 15 May 1949. Muench visited Clay in Berlin on 3 August 1946 while Clay was still deputy governor and a close friendship developed at once between the two men. Muench highly respected Clay and consistently supported the policies which Clay tried to implement. Robert D. Murphy, Milwaukee native and political adviser to the military governor, was also a close friend of Muench, and the Catholic liaison consultant often turned to Murphy for help in difficult cases.

Muench was careful to point out that as liaison consultant for religious affairs he was representing the American hierarchy, in the same way as the American Protestant and Jewish liaison consultants were representing their official bodies. The Office of Military Government, United States (OMGUS), was located in Berlin. Father Stanley Bertke from Cincinnati, assistant liaison consultant and secretary, was assigned a house by OMGUS in Berlin — Dahlem across the street from the house occupied by General Clay, and Bertke made most of the direct contacts with American officials from there. Muench preferred to stay in Kronberg because of its central location, easy access for German Catholics, and more convenient travel contacts for himself. By remaining in Kronberg he hoped he would not be directly associated physically or in the minds of the Germans with the American Military or Allied High Commission. Muench slowly became more and more conscious that as a representative of the Pope it was not proper for him to be closely related to the occupation powers. However, during the first years, from 1946 to 1949, these contacts with the American occupation forces were invaluable aids to his mission. Father Bertke was of major assistance to the Catholic liaison consultant during the years 1946 until May, 1948, when he asked to return to Cincinnati because of recurring ulcers.

Muench made periodic visits to Berlin and remained usually for a week. He was, as he said, constantly looking for friends in high places who would be of help in expediting the urgent needs of the German people. General Clay from the very beginning informed Muench that he would be extended every facility as well as full freedom in working with the Catholic bishops of Germany. American policy was to turn all internal German affairs back to the Germans as rapidly as possible, and Muench was asked to collaborate toward this end with the German bishops. Clay believed, in the best American tradition, that Military Government should not take an active part in German religious life. The purpose of the religious affairs branch of OMGUS was to encourage German church leaders by helping them solve their immediate problems. The Americans had, furthermore, guaranteed with the arrival of their armies full freedom of worship to occupied Germany. As early as August, 1945, both Catholic and Evangelical church leaders had in turn expressed willingness to co-operate with Military Government. Church leaders were the first to receive permits to attend meetings outside of Germany. Theological seminaries were reopened in 1945. The churches were helped to resume publication of religious papers, although it was not until 1948 that an adequate supply of newsprint was made available through grants from the United States Congress. Scheduled time was allotted to the principal religious faiths to broadcast programs on religious subjects from each of the German broadcasting stations in the American zone. Freedom was granted to re-establish youth groups, a German Council of Christians and Jews was established in Munich, and Jewish synagogues and prayer rooms were opened in several cities. As General Clay summarized this program:

"Lasting reform in Germany must come from within. It must be spiritual and moral. While Military Government has not interfered in the internal affairs of the church in keeping with our own national policy, it has recognized that religious institutions are major elements in the German social structure which must participate in any program directed to the building of a peaceful and democratic Germany if it is to have hope of success.

"There is as yet little tangible evidence of a new spiritual growth in Germany. The freedom now accorded to its religious leaders, increased attendance in churches, and growing membership in religious youth groups do indicate that there is a revived interest in religious worship and teaching which may develop into a spiritual movement of deep significance in the future."[4]

While the actions of Clay and his collaborators on the highest levels in OMGUS never deviated from this statement of intent, the case was quite different with some lower echelon officials who carried out policy. It was on this level that Muench and Bertke continually ran into situations of obvious prejudice toward the German people and of misdirection of general policy. A spirit of revenge was all too often evident. A number of former German nationals had secured appointments to return to Germany after the war as officials in departments of the American occupation. Among them were some German Jewish refugees who had, understandably, all too vivid memories of the Nazi Reich's atrocities against the German and European Jews, the greatest massacre in human history. Then there were the American liberals intent on establishing a secular society according to their lights, and the educationists who planned in the name of democracy to impose an alien system of education on Germany's youth as the panacea for all social ills. As Muench told Dworschak on 15 November 1946:

"Right now we shall have a few battles with bigots in the matter of allocating newsprint to Catholic diocesan papers in Bavaria. The planners who got nowhere in the U. S. have come to Germany to foist their brand of democracy on the German people. Think of it, they succeeded in appointing a socialist as minister president in Bavaria [Dr. Wilhelm Hoegner], and another one as minister of education [Dr. Franz Fendt]. By overwhelming vote the people demanded their denominational state-supported school. The vote was so clear that the new Bavarian constitution (1946) provides for them against a group of secularist educators from the USA who want a school system such as we have in the U.S. Ambassador Murphy is a big help to us. I had a two hour conference with him in Berlin. I'm told that he asked pointed questions of the education branch in Berlin after my visit with him. It set up a heated row there in that division. Father Bertke is doing a good job. He does not take no from these fellows."

Muench handled each protest with care and delicacy because he did not want to seem ungrateful for the many acts of consideration which had been granted him in his work. But when the facts were in he was not slow to appeal wherever he could when apparent efforts were being made by secularists to eliminate all funds earmarked for assisting organizations with a religious association. As early as 17 September 1946 he appealed successfully for ecclesiastical students to be allowed to pursue studies in Italian and Swiss universities and seminaries. These students came from twenty dioceses and six religious communities. The Vatican had pledged financial responsibility. "Such a good-will gesture on the part of our Military Government will win new support for it in its arduous tasks," he stated. "We believe that the establishment of friendly relations among peoples in different lands will redound to the credit of our country, and will do much to secure the peace for which we all work." Muench also asked permission for German scholars to go abroad for research, and requested the Economic Co-operation Administration, OMGUS, to expand the German export program in respect to ecclesiastical goods, sacred vessels, vestments, liturgical books and craft works. Muench had brought this to the attention of the German bishops at their Fulda Conference in 1947, and the answer from American Military Government was that if Germans could show orders from abroad they would receive raw materials. Bishop Michael Keller of Muenster asked Muench to help dissuade the British from dismantling a synthetic oil plant at Gelsenberg, or to use it for another industry. Muench, in turn, wrote on 8 June 1949 to Leo Nemzek of Moorhead, Minnesota, then a member of the Economic Co-operation Administration in Frankfurt and pointed out that tens of thousands of workers and their families were involved in this dismantling. "There is much bitterness among them. Radical agitators are using the opportunity to foment trouble and to promote their leftist movements. Much of the good that a sensible occupation policy has accomplished thus far is being undone. This is not very promising for a well-ordered, prosperous economy and for future peace in the nation."

Muench requested in 1947 that German Boy Scouts be allowed to wear uniforms, but he was refused in this case on the grounds that such a permission would open the flood gates for unworthy organizations to do the same. The prohibition against uniforms of any kind applied to all groups as a means of deadening military activities. Military Government judged that the wearing of uniforms was so interwoven with militaristic desires of the German people that it would be unwise to open the doors in the slightest degree. In the summer of 1949 Muench obtained permission for 500 German children, under the direction of *Caritas*, to spend six months convalescing in Spain if they were under the age of thirteen. Muench also wrote a "thank you" note to Military

Government each time they supplied trucks for picnics for German children.

A steady volume of individual appeals was sent from Muench to the American Military. German bishops often sent him cases of mistaken identity, of people jailed by military authorities, and he forwarded them for review. These included requests that houses not be requisitioned; appeals for persons condemned to death especially when confessions were obtained under duress; release of seminarians from POW camps; diversion of food and fuel to student needs and the opening of military barracks as student dormitories; compassionate consideration for early release of POW's held in camps abroad; and building permits for needy institutions.

The most explosive conflict between American Military and German Catholics arose in Bavaria over imposed educational policies. The controversy had been brewing in Bavaria throughout 1947 as a result of American Military's direction on 10 January 1947 to introduce a plan for school reform throughout Germany. This plan was aimed at guiding and influencing German educational institutions toward more progressive methods and democratic educational ideals. American educationists in the educational division of Military Government in Berlin, whom Muench called "the John Dewey crowd in control," did not like the German system of education which required four years of compulsory education in the free public schools corresponding to American grammar schools. This German system was similar to the English, French, Dutch, Swiss, and Scandinavian systems all with strong democratic traditions. Yet the Americans formulated a plan for a twelve-year public school course to be made available to all German students. Reaction was immediate throughout Germany. Bishop John Baptist Dietz of Rottenburg wrote Cardinal Frings, chairman of the German bishops on 24 January 1947, that the school plan was an effort to introduce the American school system into Germany in order to achieve a democratic and socialized educational program. The main intention, Dietz stated, was to advance secular education, to separate Church and State as in the United States. The Nazis tried to do this, the bishop continued, and now the Americans were trying to destroy again the century-old diversified German educational program.

The Bavarians countermoved by submitting their own school reform plan to Military Government on 30 September 1947. But General Clay informed Dr. Hans Ehard, minister president of Bavaria, on 18 November 1947 that the school plan of the Bavarian Ministry of Cult and Education, under its director, Dr. Alois Hundhammer, was not acceptable because it was undemocratic, did not give an equal opportunity to all children, rich or poor, for higher education, and was especially inadequate in the proposed structure of the academic high school or *humanistisches gymnasium.*

Bavarians, strongly Catholic, traditionalist and free, feared that Military Government would impose the proposed school plan upon them against their will. On 7 January 1948 Cardinal Faulhaber urgently requested Bishop Muench to contact Murray D. Van Wagoner, former governor of Michigan and Land commissioner of Bavaria since November of 1947, and present to him a letter of protest from the cardinal archbishop of Munich in the name of the Bavarian bishops. Faulhaber stated:

"All responsible persons are convinced that the recovery of the spiritual and moral health of the people as well as the economic and cultural reconstruction of the nation demand a complete and thorough overhauling of the system of the schooling, training and education of youth. These are our most important and imperative tasks.

"We are in full accord with Military Government that our entire system of schooling and education of youth must be formed so that it can make the greatest possible contribution to coming generations in order to secure for them the blessings of peace, social justice, humanity and right. We hope that the school reform can be so implemented that the pupils will be trained in the spirit of democracy and of good will among nations, and that equal opportunity for education will be given to all children according to their abilities regardless of the economic and social standards of their parents."

But Faulhaber went on to stress the strong objections of Bavarian Catholics to the methods by which these objectives were to be achieved. The methodology of the proposed school reform plan would have completely unacceptable and unfavorable consequences for education. Faulhaber, ever suspicious of outside governmental interference, questioned the right of a victor power to impose cultural reforms on a vanquished nation unless it were indisputably shown that such reform was essential to democracy. The cardinal and the Bavarian bishops, as well as the Bavarian Evangelicals, under the leadership of Bishop Hans Meissner of Augsburg, were completely dissatisfied with the proposed school reform. Meissner even bluntly termed the American school reform plan in a public statement "dictatorship in the garb of democracy."

In his letter Faulhaber maintained that education is the supreme duty and right of parents whom the state must protect and support in fulfilling and exercising this natural right. "All disregard of this legal position, and over-emphasis of state authority in this respect, even if in the name of democracy, must lead once more to the catastrophe of totalitarianism." The American Military Government, in demanding that all education in Bavaria be free, that aids to learning must be free for all pupils, that kindergarten teachers receive university education, that the duration of education be extended, established procedures that would involve political aims in school reform.

The occupying power was, Faulhaber continued "obviously interfering in a matter that must be designated as an internal German affair, and from the federal point of view, as an internal affair of the individual German states." Military Government had repeatedly expressed the principle of granting the Bavarian people more independence and of allowing the representatives and the government constitutionally elected in 1946 by the people to govern their own affairs. Educational training was an internal affair of every country to be regulated independently by the people in complete awareness of their responsibility. To impose any definite school system on an occupied country would be a violation of natural law and would, therefore, lie outside the jurisdiction of the occupying power. Even if based on the intention of democratizing the school system, Faulhaber concluded, "such an intervention would be completely at variance with the spirit of real democracy and would be a severe blow to a belief in democracy."

Before he had seen this strong letter, Van Wagoner informed Minister President Dr. Ehard on 14 January 1948 that the directives of General Clay were orders and that Dr. Hundhammer should contact educational officers at Military Government in Munich. On 17 January 1948 Muench forwarded Faulhaber's letter to Van Wagoner and asked a special hearing of the contending parties before a decision would be reached. The bishop warned Van Wagoner: "Having a great deal of Celtic blood and spirit in them, Bavarians can be led but not driven."

Bishop Muench was alert to the seriousness of the situation. He had already rushed a long letter on 23 December 1947 to Archbishop McNicholas, chairman of the National Catholic Welfare Conference, in which he detailed the issues at stake in the approaching crisis.[5]

Murray Van Wagoner came to Kronberg with his special assistant, Edward Kennedy, to discuss the issues involved, and on February 2 he invited Muench to a staff meeting to present the anxieties and misgivings of Cardinal Faulhaber, widely known as the "uncrowned king of Bavaria." After a conference with Faulhaber, Muench accepted the invitation. The liaison consultant also met in May with General Clay and the New York lawyer, J. Anthony Panuch, special adviser for major problems, and told them about the vexing school problem in Bavaria.

Matters seemed to go along smoothly until July when it was learned that someone in Military Government at Munich had written to Cardinal Spellman attempting to draw him into the controversy by informing him of the opposition that Bavarians, under the leadership of Dr. Hundhammer, were fomenting against American occupation policies. It was reported to Spellman that Faulhaber was in agreement with American Military's school reform plan and would raise no further objections to it. Spellman, in turn, transmitted this information to Pius XII who shook his head negatively and found it difficult to believe since Faulhaber in a March interview had told the Pope the exact opposite. Pius XII asked his famed housekeeper, Sister Pasqualina Lehnert, who had served him during his years in Germany and who maintained a keen interest and many contacts in Germany, to write an informal inquiry to Faulhaber in the matter. Faulhaber was not pleased, to say the least, at this exchange of misinformation, and he fired off a letter in English to Land commissioner Van Wagoner on 19 July 1948 questioning the whole procedure.[6]

Van Wagoner stated in his reply that no letter had been sent by Military Government in Munich to Spellman. Since Pius XII had made inquiries based on information from Spellman, mistrust and suspicions grew in an already over-heated atmosphere during that summer of 1948. General Clay ordered an investigation which was carried out by Dr. Carl Friedrich of Harvard University. The mystery correspondent was never definitely identified due to regulations which prohibited files to be searched, and despite intense investigation by all concerned on the German front.[7]

Muench likewise soon found himself in the center of the controversy "with both feet", as he had said of Faulhaber. Van Wagoner sent a staff report to Clay on the controversy in Bavaria in which Muench was accused of the premature release of Faulhaber's letter. While Muench was in Berlin General Clay showed him the report of Van Wagoner, gave him a copy of it and asked him to respond in writing with his side of the story. Muench suggested that Clay inaugurate an investigation of the charge Van Wagoner made against him, but Clay said: "There is no need of such an inquiry because I believe what you say." It was later proved that Faulhaber had first written to Van Wagoner and then to Muench as evidenced by the certified postal dates of the two letters. Muench was particularly shocked because he had received a letter from Van Wagoner the day before the Land commissioner wrote to General Clay. Nothing was mentioned in this letter of the imminent rupture.

Muench then proceeded to prepare a statement with comments on the part he played in the discussions on the school reform plan for Bavaria, drawing on the notes he had taken after the several talks and discussions as well as on the correspondence bearing on the matter. He informed J. Anthony Panuch of his procedure on July 3.[8]

Personnel in American Military at Munich also wrote to the Department of State in Washington about the controversy, and Cardinal Spellman again received a report, this time about Muench's interference, from the department. Muench was in the United States in November of 1948 to attend the annual meeting of the American bishops. Spellman had left the meeting early and he called Muench from New York asking him to visit him before he returned to Germany. When Muench saw Spellman he explained the whole background of the controversy and together they prepared the answer that Spellman sent to the State Department. The incident was closed, but again Muench experienced personally the seriousness of the misunderstanding in Bavaria.

A new flareup occurred in August when Military Government issued an order to the Bavarian Government that beginning on September 1 they were to provide free schooling up to and through the universities, one of the pet projects of American educational experts, and to issue free text books to all pupils and students. The Bavarian Catholics and Evangelicals now became thoroughly aroused over this order and feelings ran high. Newspapers took sides and debate waxed strong in the Bavarian parliament. Religious leaders feared for the existence of private schools of higher learning because of the impoverishment of the Church through the new currency reform, as well as a lack of tradition in Bavaria, or for that matter throughout Germany, of supporting separate religious schools. Military Government allowed the Bavarian Government to grant subsidies to private schools, but religious authorities, pointing to recent experiences in France and Belgium, feared for the independence of their private schools.[9]

Dr. Alois Hundhammer, Bavarian minister of cult and education at the time, firm friend of Faulhaber and staunch supporter of the Bavarian tradition of education, explained the position which the Bavarians took on this important matter:

"In Bavaria we had confessional schools for several decades. Under the Hitler regime these basic rights were abolished and after 1945 while I held the office of Minister of Cult and Education, the reconstruction of our whole school system was at issue. It was my own as well as the Bavarian bishops' insistent desire to reintroduce and reorganize the confessional schools in Bavaria. This same aim was voiced by the Evangelicals and the Evangelical Land Bishop Hans Meissner.

"Influential persons in the Education Branch of American Military Occupation had different ideas, however, and demanded a completely changed school system. Their tendency was to sever our traditional connections in our high schools and colleges with Roman and Greek cultures, the very foundation of our educational system and of our intellectual outlook. They demanded that I abolish in our high schools the teaching of Greek and restrict the teaching of Latin to the extent necessary for future priests. I could not comply. Even the development of the ideology of national socialism cannot be blamed on Greek and Roman culture; other things were responsible for that. This was our first point of argument with the education officers of the Occupation Force.

"The second point at issue was the question of whether to have confessional or interdenominational primary schools. I stubbornly defended confessional schools, and the result was a number of discussions and arguments which ended with the consideration of my removal from my office as Minister of Cult and Education. According to the regulations of Military Government, which were then in force, the Occupation Powers had the right and authority to do so.

"All this resulted in a very hard discussion between Bishop Muench and the American officials. Bishop Muench naturally took the side of the Bavarian bishops and supported their efforts vigorously. In the fall of 1947 a conference was held in this very room with the American Director of Land Bavaria on the question of whether I should be removed from my office. During this conference one of the participants, I don't know if it was Van Wagoner himself, remarked: 'During this war we had to start classes for illiterates in practically all of our regiments. If Bavaria should ever again have its own army, Dr. Hundhammer would not have to organize classes of this kind for any member of the Bavarian army. Why, then, should we interfere so much with their educational system. Let him go ahead.'

"The whole question was relayed to Washington; I don't know the particulars about the proceedings. Finally Van Wagoner was replaced as Land commissioner by George Shuster . . . When Professor Shuster came over to us, peace was soon restored between us and the occupation forces. We retained our confessional schools. When we discussed our new Bavarian constitution in 1946 I had already taken a firm, definite stand in favor of our confessional schools. At that time I was chairman of my party [Christian Social Union] in the *Landtag* and had a strong influence on the committee in charge of the draft of the constitution. So with the arrival of Dr. Shuster, our school troubles were settled."[10]

Bavaria, along with North Rhine-Westphalia and Rhineland-Palatinate among the *Laender*, provided for denominational public schools in their new constitutions. Non-denominational public schools with religious instruction as a part of the curriculum were the exception. The Bavarian bishops held firmly to the traditional Catholic view of education for the children of predominantly Catholic Bavaria. All children from primary grades through high school were to have religious education as an integral part of their instruction. Under the German system of education the training of teachers also remained an issue of considerable importance for the Church because lay teachers were the authorized teachers of religion. Bishops insisted that teachers receive their training in denominational teacher colleges. If a thorough course in religion was not taken by teachers they would not receive their canonical mandate as teachers of religion.

Germany did not have a Catholic parochial school system such as existed in the United States. Primary and secondary schools, with some few exceptions in Bavaria, Westphalia, and the Rhineland, were public, tax-supported schools. Only in Bavaria were sisters engaged as teachers under conditions similar to those for lay teachers. There were private secondary schools in all dioceses of Germany operated by Jesuits, Benedictines and sisters, but generally both primary and secondary schools were public in structure. These public schools were either denominational, Catholic and Protestant, or interconfessional in character. In the interconfessional schools religious instruction was a definite part of the curriculum with Catholic teachers instructing Catholic students and Protestant teachers instructing Protestant children in religion courses.

It was difficult for Americans to understand and appreciate the association of religion and education which had such deep roots in Germany's religious past. The principles of separation of Church and State as known and applied in the United States had no frame of reference among Germans, and they found it difficult to understand what relationship American educational procedures had as such to democracy.[11]

The issue of free schooling and free textbooks in Bavaria became so critical that Minister President, Dr. Hans Ehard of Bavaria, intervened personally with General Clay and a compromise was worked out, at American initiative, by a commission of experts meeting in Wallenberg. The former three types of Bavarian secondary schools were to be maintained [*gymnasium, realgymnasium, oberrealschule*], each with an eight years' school term beginning after completion of the fourth year of elementary school. The American school plan, the *reformgymnasium*, was to be introduced on a trial basis as the fourth type of secondary school. Students would enter this *reformgymnasium* for a six-year term after completing six years of elementary school. With regard to free tuition and free textbooks, a second compromise was reached. Tuitions were to be reduced by fifty per cent, and because of the financial burden placed on *Laender* governments by the currency reform, only half of the expenses for textbooks would be borne by Bavaria in order to offer some aid to pupils from poor and large families. Teacher training norms were to be established by the majority of the teachers. The question of maintaining denominational, interconfessional and non-denominational schools was settled by following the Bavarian Constitution which had decisively preserved the traditional three educational divisions. Non-denominational schools, according to the new School Organization Law, could be established in places where the confessions were mixed, provided that both parents requested a non-denominational school through a signed statement for at least fifty children.

Bishop Muench summarized his concern and likewise his satisfaction at this turn of events to John Riedl of Religious Affairs Branch OMGUS on 6 December 1948:

"The Bavarian Catholic bishops are much concerned about the future of confessional schools. Fortunately, whenever a free vote was taken, Catholics and Protestants alike registered their wishes overwhelmingly in favor of confessional schools. If democracy will now be honored,

Military Government cannot but approve constitutional provisions in favor of such schools.

"Fortunately, top levels in Military Government want to respect the wishes of the people. Fortunately, too, Military Government honors the basic principles of the concordats, even though they are binding only technically. Fr. Bertke can tell you of our interviews with General Clay in these matters.

"The old ideological conflicts regarding religion and education are again making their appearance. We have to be vigilant. The Nazis destroyed the confessional schools, and the new enemies, the Social Democratic Party, Socialist Unity Party and Free Democratic Party are also seeking to destroy them. The Liberal Democratic Party joins hands with them. Liberalism in Europe is not of the American stamp."

A vacancy in the position of chief of the educational division of Military Occupation in Bavaria opened the possibility of filling this delicate assignment with an American Catholic. Bishop Muench was not slow in alerting Archbishop McNicholas in Cincinnati and Monsignor James H. Griffiths, chancellor of the Military Ordinariate in New York, of the situation. It was particularly urgent at a time when Cardinal Faulhaber and Dr. Hundhammer were so agitated over American Military Occupation procedures in the field of education. Muench also had vivid memories of one of his first difficult negotiations in the fall of 1946. Barely established in Germany, he was astounded at that time to learn from Cardinal Faulhaber that an American ex-priest had been appointed as the acting chief of religious affairs in Bavaria despite the directive that no ordained clerics could be officers in the religious affairs division. Faulhaber, noble anti-Nazi symbol throughout the world, was not only insulted by this blunder, but refused to receive such a representative of Military Occupation, and asked what the reaction would be on the part of an American cardinal if the United States were an occupied land and an occupying power would send a former priest to him as its religious representative.

Military Occupation favored the appointment of a Catholic educator to the Bavarian post as chief of the educational division, and stipulated only that the appointee have experience in public school administration. Dr. John L. Henley, superintendent of schools in Providence, Rhode Island, proved satisfactory to all concerned.[12]

When Clay retired as Military Governor of Germany on 15 May 1949, he was succeeded by John J. McCloy, former assistant secretary of the

Army. Muench enjoyed close relations with McCloy, as he had with Clay, and in an early conversation with the new military governor he was informed that Dr. George N. Shuster, professor and later president of Hunter College, New York, was being considered as successor to Van Wagoner whose contract as Land commissioner for Bavaria had expired. Muench was heartened at the prospect of having an American scholar of Shuster's quality, experience and understanding in the Bavarian post.[13]

When Shuster took up his position as Land commissioner for Bavaria in April of 1950 he was acclaimed in both the United States and Germany as a man unusually qualified for the tasks involved and not just a political appointment of the controlling American party. Nor did Shuster fail to live up to the high hopes placed in him. During the year and a half he served as Land commissioner in Bavaria he drew on his own wide educational and journalistic background as well as his personal experiences in Germany during the period of Hitler's first foreign adventures in the 1930's. To this day the Bavarians have a special attachment to this calm, gentle and wise American Catholic layman of German background, a pioneer in so many ways both in a maturing American Catholicism and in a Germany striving to build upon its own authentic and legitimate heritage. With Shuster's arrival an immediate cease fire ensued on the Bavarian front, much to Muench's satisfaction. Unnecessary misunderstandings and conflicts between Germans and Americans were a deep regret to Muench at a time when the two peoples were developing a natural and hopeful relationship based on common aims during the postwar period.

The Bavarian school question was the most difficult and delicate issue in which Muench was involved as Catholic liaison representative to American Military Government. Under its generous policy of religious freedom, Military Government did not directly interfere with the spiritual and religious functions of the German churches. The secular functions of German religious bodies was a direct concern, however, of Military Government in such areas as financing the work of the Church, administering its property, or making and enforcing ecclesiastical law in such matters as religious education. The three liaison representatives from the United States were authorized to provide assistance to their respective German churches in meeting needs arising from spiritual and moral functions. They were to serve as liaison representatives between their churches in Germany and the United States. They were contacts between Military Government and the German churches, providing information to Military Government about spiritual life and reconstruction, and making available to the German churches information and services pertaining to spiritual and moral functions of the churches which Military Government might possess. The liaison representatives were authorized to confer with German church leaders relative to spiritual and moral functions, assist them in finding means of developing these resources, and assist in the development of a peaceful and democratic Germany.

The liaison consultants were not to become special pleaders to Military Government for the churches in Germany, nor to assume responsibility in functional fields of operation directed by religious affairs officers of Military Government. In the emotionally charged issue of Bavarian school reform Muench found himself placed between Bavarian Catholics who considered themselves and their traditions misunderstood by Military Government, and some American officials who judged that Muench was becoming a special pleader for Bavarian Catholics. Muench considered that he had not overstepped his authorization. Despite the seriousness of Van Wagoner's charge, it is surprising that only one such incident occurred during the long years of Muench's service in Germany during which he was involved in a series of conflict-of-interest cases.[14]

Muench personally attributed this peaceful relationship to the wisdom and understanding of General Lucius Clay. Muench considered Clay, along with Chancellor Conrad Adenauer, to be the two outstanding statesmen he had the privilege to know and to work with in the reconstruction of Germany. Muench even encouraged Clay to be a candidate for president of the United States in 1956 if Eisenhower chose not to run again. When Clay was preparing to terminate his position as American Military Governor of Germany, Muench wrote him a moving letter on 10 May 1949:

"Before you leave Germany I deem it my duty to express to you in this way my sincere appreciation of your unfailing courtesy shown me on every occasion whenever I came to you with problems that arose in the course of my work.

"In particular I should like to express warmest gratitude for the assistance that you gave the Church of Germany through your administrative policies in the furtherance of her rights and freedoms having a bearing on her manifold religious works.

"The German people have every reason to be grateful to you. In the immediate postwar years you brought to them food and medicines with lavish generosity, without which thousands would have died of hunger and disease; you gave them new hope through your consistent policy, opposed in many quarters, of putting affairs into their own hands as fast as circumstances permitted; you helped revive their well-nigh lifeless economy and raise it to levels that have astounded everybody. We who have been witnesses of what was and what now is stand in admiration of the achievements that have been attained under your administration, despite the heavy odds that foes of your policies set up against you.

"From our own American history we know how difficult a period of reconstruction is under the best of circumstances. When, then, ill will and vindictiveness enter on the scene, peace and prosperity are given little chance to thrive. Your unyielding persistence to have a policy of conciliation win the day, inspired by fairness and justice even toward a vanquished foe, now brings to maturity rich fruits not only for Germany and the nations of western Europe, but also for our own nation.

"Our sincere regret is that you can not remain to enjoy the fruits of your indefatigable labors. For my part I shall always remember with gratitude the fair deal that you accorded me in an hour of need. Nor shall I forget your example of tact and prudence, patience and forbearance in dealing with others. What you said recently about humility with respect to decisions one in authority must make and then find that one was not right, made a deep impression on us in particular who hold positions of authority.

"My best wishes for all that is good under the sun and may the blessing of the Lord accompany you on your return to our beloved homeland."

The General deeply appreciated this tribute and in acknowledging Muench's letter, he remarked: "I have always felt that your influence did much to bring our own people to their senses and thus permit a change in policies which were more fitting to our national characteristics than was our initial policy of punishment and vindictiveness." [15]

Bishop Muench was convinced that the weak spot in American Military Government and later of HICOG was that they shied away from the churches. Secularists in high and low places, he maintained, were responsible for this attitude which "failed to touch the religious pulse of over 96% of the population of West Germany." The *Amerikahaeuser* information centers, cultural exchange services of HICOG, were in

Muench's opinion not portraying the United States accurately. To the end he continued in disagreement with the image of American life disseminated by these officially sponsored centers. The cultural affairs branch of Military Occupation fostered policies of active American aid to UNESCO, civic education, university projects, child guidance and community school projects, social service and public health projects. Religious life was consistently ignored as a major element in areas of proposed co-operation with the Germans. Muench continually requested that projects and programs be considered on their own merit by fair-minded officials, and that this judgment should include the whole hierarchy of values: political, economic, social, intellectual and religious.

Newspapers and their reports on Germany were also a constant concern to Muench who wrote hundreds of letters to editors, reporters and government officials concerning slanted or garbled news releases. He considered particularly the *Stars and Stripes*, American military daily published in Germany, guilty of consistently slanting the news by presenting only one side of the picture. "Half truths are just as bad, if not worse at times, than falsehoods," he said. Muench considered that Americans who flew across Germany and wrote value judgments at random as a result of their hegiras, were particularly hazardous to good German-American relations and to the cause of the West. A sympathetic understanding of the problems of the ordinary German people was too often missing in analyses of German conditions which appeared especially in papers published on the Atlantic Coast of the United States. The legend of Germany's "collective guilt" continued to be handed on despite a growing corpus of scholarly studies to the contrary.

Muench continued throughout his career to evidence a remarkable interest in professional journalism. He had printer's ink in his blood, as he said, and often repeated that he would have been a journalist if he had not become a priest. He had a passion for clipping articles and collecting massive files on social, economic, political and religious affairs. Every Sunday afternoon he took delight in working with his scissors through piles of publications. He was a dedicated writer of "letters to the editor," both public and private. He never missed an opportunity to meet newsmen or to issue press releases on every concern under his jurisdiction. "An informed people is a free people," he often stated, "and the Church has not adequately utilized the opportunity of free information to acquaint men of good will with her true purposes and programs."

No churchman of modern times relished an on-going dialogue with the press as much as Muench. His papers contain thousands of letters and clippings expressing his viewpoint on current affairs. This interest, which appears to have become a prime hobby, was not always received with understanding or sympathy. Muench's column, "The Bishop Writes from Europe," written for the people of Fargo in his own diocesan monthly on conditions in Germany, and an important journalistic survey of events during these years, became a case in point. These articles and his frequent interviews with reporters and quotations in the public press brought forth an expression of surprise from Archbishop Amleto G. Cicognani, apostolic delegate to the United States, who could not understand how a papal representative would make public utterances on current political affairs. This reaction was also passed on to Rome, but Muench was never directed to cease and desist. As a social scientist he simply could not understand why he should not observe the passing scene and comment as he saw fit. With the years he became more cautious, however, and began to direct his observations to journalistic friends who published them under their own names or as coming from "An Observer in Germany." He was assiduous in reporting all developments to Frank Hall of the Press Department of the National Catholic Welfare Conference in Washington, D. C., and he continued to encourage full coverage of religious news from Germany in the Catholic press of the United States. The Church, in this way, was enriched by the foresight of a dedicated pioneer in the apostolate of religious journalism and informational services.

Muench was in constant contact with personnel in the religious affairs branch, a division of the education and cultural relations department of Military Government. In each of the German states of the American zone there was a chief of this branch with assistants who headed sections conducting relations with German Catholic, Protestant, Free and Jewish religious authorities. These religious affairs offices were established to co-operate with the churches in the moral and spiritual reconstruction of Germany. Their officials worked to strengthen the efforts of the churches in making possible a Germany which would have the spiritual foundations on which democracy could be built.

All religious forces working toward democratic ends in German society were encouraged in their work. Muench was an invaluable aide and consultant to American officials of the religious affairs branch in opening doors of chanceries and identifying the social action programs of the Church which should receive attention. Special consideration was given to workers' movements. The Church in Germany had lost many of its workers during the Nazi period and after 1945 the German unions were largely under the control of socialist elements. *The Catholic Worker*, a German publication endeavoring to revive Catholic interest in labor union activities, received co-operation from religious affairs branch. Labor schools were established with American support for the training of young men and women in trade union participation. The former Catholic labor unions were not revived after the war and young Catholics began to participate in the life of the mainstream union activity. Muench often had nostalgic thoughts about separate Catholic trade unions, but he came to recognize the sound policy of realistic involvement in the existing power structure of German labor. The *Katholische Arbeiter Bewegung und Werkvolk* developed programs aimed at furthering labor objectives in industrial areas. In the seminaries courses were offered, with episcopal approval, on the practical application of the teachings of the papal encyclicals on labor.

In the field of education religious affairs branch tried to explain to major officials of the occupation the right of the German people to determine the kind of schools they should have. Their right to have confessional schools, guaranteed in the *Laender* and Reich concordats, was often challenged and misunderstood, as in the classic Bavarian controversy. The German people, in the first years after the war, strongly supported the concept of confessional schools and the churches insisted on their traditional rights in this matter. It was only in the late 1960's that popular support for confessional education began to wane.

Such questions as church taxes and state subsidies were left to the decision of the German people according to their new constitutions. Religious affairs branch strongly supported the teaching of religion in its traditional place as a regular part of the educational curriculum. To help bridge the gap between 1933 and 1945, the latest developments in the field of catechetics were made available to German catechetical associations.

Above all religious affairs branch attempted to guard jealously all aspects of religious freedom as an example to countries behind the iron curtain of America's intention to develop a free people morally and spiritually. Religious affairs branch did play a part in the "cold war" of the period by working to marshal those spiritual forces which would not only prevent the spread of Communism in western Europe, but also help lead Germany and Europe once more to a recognition of the spiritual foundation of its civilization.

The reaction of German Catholic, Lutheran, Free and Jewish religious leaders to the efforts of religious affairs branch were generally favorable and cordial. The American tradition of co-operation with and yet separation from religion was often incomprehensible to the Germans who could not see the value of the distinction. In the same way Bishop Muench and officials of religious affairs branch never fully understood the German state confessional outlook as a viable tradition.

The apostolic visitator formed several friendships with personnel in religious affairs branch during these years. Among them were Dr. Arild Olsen, prominent American Lutheran, who served as chief of the branch for the American zone. Dr. Urban Fleege, formerly a faculty member at Marquette University and the Catholic University of America, was chief of Catholic affairs for the American zone. In the different *Laender* Muench had many contacts with Dr. James M. Eagan, former professor of history at the College of New Rochelle, New York, chief of the Bavarian branch, largest German state in the American zone of occupation with a Catholic population of seventy-one per cent. In Hesse, Dr. George F. Donovan, on leave from his post as president of Webster College, Webster Groves, Missouri, acted as chief with headquarters at Wiesbaden. Edward J. Joyce, professional diplomat in the public affairs branch, Munich, Dr. John O. Riedl of the same branch in Bad Nauheim, and Edward J. Kirchner, cultural affairs officer in Munich, were also in constant contact with Muench.

Muench never tired of stressing to Military Government officials that when the occupying forces entered conquered Germany they found the churches the major center of social organization still remaining, battered but intact. Despite all claims to the contrary, the churches had been the primary effective resistance, such as it was, to the Nazi *Gleichschaltung*. They did not go down in the collapse of Germany's order and sovereignty as did those institutions which had lost their own identity. The churches — in contrast with business, law, medicine and labor — had a very low percentage of their professional leadership (3%) implicated by membership in the Nazi party or its major affiliates. Muench did not excuse the all too infrequent public and active opposition to the Nazis by churchmen and the churches, the confusion of German nationalism with Nazi policies, or the failure to support actively the far too few prophetic Christian opponents of war, injustice and terror. He only pointed up comparative records with other professions as a fact to be faced in reconstruction. Justified reflections on the failures of Christians should not be ignored in any country of the west or east. But recrimination and sweeping generalizations from incomplete data should not impede the opportunity for a new beginning in the postwar world.

The churches were among the major instruments in the reconstruction of West Germany in the three zones where they were allowed to operate with a degree of freedom. As the major intact institutions, and because of their pastoral activities, the churches also continued to be a major center of independent opinion as they had been during the Nazi period. On occasion, Muench warned, this meant criticism of certain policies of the occupation which ignored principles of due process and justice to individuals. Such was especially the case during the denazification processes of the Americans. But a wise democratic leadership should not be led to suppose that church leaders were not on the whole co-operative with the re-orientation and reconstruction program in its positive aspects.

No other German institution recovered its international contacts more rapidly nor was more eager to participate in international conferences, exchange of persons and social reconstruction along democratic lines. Even such a controversial figure as Lutheran Church President Martin Niemoeller, who disagreed spectacularly with much of the postwar military policy of the west, co-operated in the main with the western churches. He emerged, furthermore, as one of the most effective leaders in inter-denominational co-operation and in leading German Protestantism from its former enslavement to political power into a vigorous social action program. In the movement toward European union the churches were foremost in activity. Even during the Nazi period, church centers in Rome, Geneva and Stockholm were a major effective channel between the west and the German underground. Since the war American voluntary agencies in Germany, the vast majority church-supported, and German church societies worked in close co-operation toward the common objective: an independent church in a free society. In Europe the Catholic Church alone operated over twenty international Catholic organizations. Several international Catholic organizations were formed for the primary purpose of promoting European unity. The Catholic Church was recognized for its international character.

The most remarkable growth of interfaith work in the world in the decade following the war occurred under the auspices of the National Conference of Christians and Jews and the religious affairs branch in West Germany. Nine councils were started in Germany in the first five years after the war, and three other councils quickly followed. Significant progress in interfaith co-operation was effected by Protestant and Catholic organizations in areas of social action, including religious youth activity, in forming interconfessional workers' societies. An Evangelical Academy at Tutzing and a Catholic Academy in Munich developed creative and significant postwar programs in lay leadership and social action. The former was termed, at the founding meeting of the World Council of Churches at Amsterdam in 1950, one of the foremost postwar developments in lay leadership on social action. The Evangelical *Kirchliche Hochschule* in Berlin and the Catholic seminary in Koenigstein began training over 500 pastors yearly for religious work in the Soviet zone of Germany.

One of the American postwar programs in Germany that cost Muench much time and personal involvement was the de-nazification procedure established in March, 1946, and carried on long after its original hoped-for effectiveness had seriously diminished. The public safety branch of Military Occupation in the American zone undertook the extensive program with the active support of the military governor, General Clay; and Muench continued to disagree with Clay throughout the whole period as to its merits and value.

The United States, as well as the British and French turned the procedures over to the *Laenderrat* in their zones to determine who the main Nazis were, and to purge major Nazis from positions of leadership while new German leadership was developing. Four classes were defined by law: major offenders to be punished by as much as ten years' imprisonment, confiscation of property, and permanent exclusion from public office; offenders subject to imprisonment, fine, and exclusion from public office but entitled to probation; followers, or nominal Nazis, who were subject to fine but could exercise their rights of citizenship; and those exonerated as a result of the investigations.

It was an immense legal undertaking involving 545 tribunals with a personnel in excess of 22,000. The procedure required all Germans over eighteen years of age to register and complete a questionnaire. There were thirteen million registrants in the American zone, of which three million were chargeable cases under the law. Three-fourths of the German population were to render judgment on the remaining one-fourth;

and the one-fourth had innumerable relatives and friends among the three-fourths. As General Clay stated: "Perhaps never before in world history had such a mass undertaking to purge society been undertaken." Clay maintained that the program drove the major Nazis from hiding and excluded them from leadership for years to come. If the nominal Nazis had not been restored to citizenship, political unrest, he felt, would have developed. Judgments were administered by Germans responsible to the electorate. "They may not have cleaned their own house thoroughly, but they at least removed the major dirt," Clay stated.

Reaction of German churchmen to the de-nazification program was strongly negative, however, and they constantly requested Muench to intercede on their behalf. As far as the clergy was concerned it was no issue. Less than four priests in a thousand had joined the Nazi party, and the German bishops insisted that in most cases these priests were irresponsible, emotionally unbalanced, or disgruntled, disappointed troublemakers in their dioceses or religious communities. The hounding of priests and religious in the immorality and foreign exchange trials of 1935, the stand of the bishops against the antireligious measures taken by the Hitler government, the elimination of religious instruction in the public schools, the planned strangulation of private Catholic schools, the dissolution of Catholic societies, confiscation of their properties and eventual suppression of the Catholic press — all these measures conspired to place the large majority of priests and people behind their bishops in standing against the Nazis as and when they could.

The vote in Catholic areas of Germany in the last free election of March, 1933, records that the Nazis received less than half of the total vote — 47% — while in Bavaria, Baden, Wuerttemberg, the Palatinate, Rhineland, and Westphalia the vote was considerably less than that. Hitler came into power not with the support of Catholic Bavaria, as was constantly charged, but with the misguided hopes of a General Erich von Ludendorff and the Prussian landowners, as well as misled and naive aristocrats such as Franz von Papen. Conscientious Catholics concerned about moral responsibility were shocked in 1959 when the papal honors of the Catholic von Papen were restored. Such a blunder, despite the inability of the judges at Nuremberg to convict as guilty such financial and diplomatic creatures as Hjalmar Schacht and von Papen, only increased bitterness and recrimination in the years ahead.

Muench was concerned with the problem at hand. In the wake of de-nazification trials, deep resentment and even hatred was developing.

Every pastor, even in the smallest village, was harassed by disunity. Recriminations and feuds were tearing neighbors apart and destroying peace and unity in families. The "Persil-vouchers," ironically so-called by the German people after a well-known German cleanser, and obtained from the courts as evidence of de-nazification, were a major cause of dissension. Bishops and pastors, as well as governmental and civil servants who had been victims of Nazi brutality, clamored for an early end of de-nazification. The internal strife that was generated was good for neither Church nor State. Muench never tired of stating that what was happening in Germany through de-nazification procedures was a bitter reminder of the reconstruction procedures carried out by carpet-baggers in the southern states of the United States following the Civil War.

Total registrants of thirteen million under the de-nazification Law of Liberation produced over nine million non-chargeable cases. The chargeable cases, 3,436,690, were 26.1% of all registrants. Of this number, 2,489,730 were amnestied because, despite affiliation in some degree with the Nazi Party or associated organizations, nothing incriminating could be brought against them. In the trials, 18,386 were exonerated, and in 315,176 cases the proceedings were quashed. Consequently, 613,398 Germans in the American zone were found to be offenders, a total of 4.6% of all registrants. Of this number, 0.26% were major offenders; 3.57% offenders; 17.33% lesser offenders; and 78.84% fellow travelers. Clay admitted, "In looking back, it might have been more effective to have selected a rather small number of leading Nazis for trial without attempting mass trials."

The Catholic and Lutheran bishops of Germany worried about mitigating the bitterness that had been aroused, of preventing the resurgence of emotional nationalism as a consequence of de-nazification, and of fostering unity in a spirit of the mercy of God and the charity of Christ. As early as 24 December 1946, the Catholics, Cardinal Michael Faulhaber and Archbishop Conrad Groeber of Freiburg, along with President Dr. D. Wurm of the Evangelical Church in Germany, issued a public letter to the Christians of the United States:

"We feel obliged to speak to the American people about a problem which at Christmas time is an especially heavy burden on us.

"For eighteen months a large number of people are detained in the internment camps of Germany, who — aside from a small group of real criminals — are under automatic arrest on the grounds of supicion and calumny because of their membership in the National Socialist Party or of the official rank they held. Some of them are detained only because they are needed as witnesses in trials which have not even been assigned a date.

"Among these people are officials, officers, doctors, scientists of outstanding quality and absolutely unobjectionable background. There are even thousands of women and mothers who, as members of the National Socialist Party, did social and welfare work in the party, but who did not participate in active propaganda. Some of them have borne children behind barbed wire. Many of them are separated from their children and worry about them, who, since they are not under parental guidance, are exposed to physical and moral dangers. Among the male inmates there are not a few amputees whose detention can only be considered a special hardship.

"There are no Germans who do not want those who are really guilty to be tried. But we cannot understand why so many men and women who will not be proved guilty of any crime are detained for such a long time while no preparation is being made for their regular trials. In many ways we have already experienced much help from the American people, above all with food supplies for our starving population. We therefore hope that the American people will understand our longing for justice and will redress a situation which otherwise will lead to a prolongation of hardship, in many cases undeserved, as well as to a general deterioration of morals in Germany."

Cardinal Faulhaber and the bishops of Bamberg, Wuerzburg, Regensburg, Augsburg, Eichstaett, Passau, Freiburg, Rottenburg, Fulda and Limburg also asked Muench to forward a formal appeal to General Clay in behalf of their people. Muench transmitted this formal and detailed protest through Ambassador Robert Murphy on 4 August 1947 and penned his own comments as a preface:

"In intimate contact with priests and people, the bishops are much worried over the growing disaffection in wide circles of the population toward the American authorities of Military Government.

"They all realize that the army of occupation will have to remain in Germany for some years. Indeed, they are anxious to have it remain because, if it were no longer here, chaos and civil war would ensue. They are anxious, therefore, that points of friction be removed, and that respect for the authority of Military Government be not undermined.

"Within recent months they have expressed to me their appreciation of the stand which the United States is taking in behalf of a better and more prosperous Germany. They are grateful to General Clay for his efforts to bring relief supplies into Germany and to rebuild, in co-operation with the Germans, the German economy. Among the big powers Germany today has no better friend than the United States.

"They are much concerned, then, over the increasing resentment and bitterness in the people over the policy and practice of de-nazification. The exploitation of the bitterness by agents of Communism, in particular, causes them much anxiety. The reports which they are receiving from their priests on this point are not at all reassuring.

"In asking me to transmit the memorandum Cardinal Faulhaber assured me several times that the bishops wished in no way to offer anything but helpful criticism. His reverence for legitimate constituted authority is really edifying." [16]

Dr. Martin Niemoeller, president of the Evangelical Church of Hesse and Nassau in the American zone, also spoke out forcefully against de-nazification procedures: "Servants of the Word must be told that any voluntary activity by Christian pastors in carrying out the de-nazification law constitutes a scandal to the community of Jesus Christ, as confidence in the usefulness, justice and humanity of the procedure is not merely shaken but completely shattered. For the sake of their offices and our parishes, we must therefore forbid pastors any longer to bear the responsibility for this nuisance."

As an American, Muench had no official relations with German civil authorities, and as apostolic visitator he could not allow himself to be drawn into affairs that were tied to internal political feuds. He advised Germans who turned to him to appeal directly to Military Government, helped in translating their affidavits to be forwarded to the latter, and sometimes, in the cases of bishops, forwarded the appeals himself to Clay or Murphy. Again as an American, Muench personally appealed to American senators to investigate the entire de-nazification procedure. He wrote his own Senator William Langer of North Dakota on 25 January 1947:

"Many of our American officials are disgusted with the grave miscarriage of justice in handling de-nazification cases. I am enclosing a copy of part of a letter which one of them wrote me. He has since quit his job at Camp Dachau.

"If a Congressional Committee would come to Germany and hear such men, and Germans too, we could clean up a stinking mess of injustice, and possibly save whatever is left of our efforts to restore democracy in Germany.

"The very threat of an investigation would do much to save our good name for fairness and justice.

"The War Crimes Commission also needs to clean house, as the enclosed summary of cases in Gage I and Dachau shows. I am informed by reliable authority in Berlin that the report is an understatement of the real facts."

Langer informed Muench that he could "depend on my whole-hearted, unqualified, active support; and I shall assist you in every way I possibly can because you are doing a magnificent job." The Case Sub-committee of the House Select Committee on Foreign Aid made a unanimous report to Congress in February, 1948, that the de-nazification proceedings be closed on May 8 with full amnesty for lesser offenders and followers. But the official ending of the de-nazification proceedings did not take place until the Germans had established their own government after 1950. As late as 26 November 1951 Muench was still concerned with the problem, as he informed Dr. Paul Seabury, instructor in government in Columbia University:

"De-nazification has been ended officially in Germany but unfortunately is still carried on endlessly by certain people who are alarmed over the fact that former Nazis, for the most part merely party members, are back in the government.

"They do not see that by their agitation they furnish fuel for men like General Otto Remer and the Socialist Reich Party.

"They ought to read the history of the occupation of the South after the Civil War.

"The capable white people of the South, who for various reasons gave their adherence to the Confederacy, were 'derebelized' with what results we Americans well know. The 'damn Yankee' attitude still prevails in many sectors of the South as a consequence of stupid policies in the Reconstruction."

Another major area of Bishop Muench's concern in the postwar years was the agonizing war trials that dragged on and attracted world-wide attention. The trials of war criminals in Germany consumed, perhaps, more of Muench's time even than the de-nazification procedures. The files from the Kronberg and Bad Godesberg days contain literally thousands of letters and petitions from bishops, pastors, wives, children and relatives of the accused. Muench had arrived in Germany just as the

Nuremberg trials of the major Nazi criminals were being held. Because of strong world reaction to the international basis of the Nuremberg trials, particularly the Soviet participation in judgments of justice, the Americans came to the conclusion that they would, under Military Government, conduct their own legal procedures.

Muench was requested by Pius XII repeatedly to remain vigilant, in the passionate climate of postwar Germany, that justice be tempered by the spirit of Christian mercy. The Nazi philosophy of life had corrupted and perverted humane values; the war had resulted in the release on both sides of the basest human passions during combat action. The period after the war had at first brought forth a spirit of enmity, revenge and a determination to occupy Germany as a conquered not a liberated people.

A consistently correct procedure was followed by the apostolic visitator in cases that came to him on an appeal basis. How often he wrote or testified during fourteen years: "While trial matters are beyond my competence, nevertheless churchmen have always been accorded the privilege of interceding when a human life is at stake." Muench wrote, telegraphed and called officials of Military Government, the State and War Departments, congressmen and senators, lawyers and judges, and members of the United States Supreme Court. He neither recommended nor condemned, but only asked for reconsideration of cases warranting amnesty, probation or reduction of sentence. In each case he took in hand, however, he made it unquestionably clear that he supported the petition already submitted to proper authorities. For example, he wrote Senator Francis Case of New Jersey on 22 April 1949: "It seems to me that death sentences ought to be commuted in cases where a reasonable doubt still exists. A life once extinguished cannot be revived, nor also our honor, if, through cowardice in the face of an outcry from pressure groups, falsely labeled as public opinion, we violate our principles of jurisprudence, rightly esteemed throughout the world."

Names of living persons who were accused as war criminals and amnestied through the exclusive or co-operative intercession of Bishop Muench can only be passed over at this early date. Their number, the story of their releases, and subsequent contributions to democratic life in West Germany would more than fill a separate volume. Several types of cases can, however, be recorded at this time as an indication of the extent of Muench's mission of mercy.

One case that he never tired of talking about was that of a seventeen-year old boy, just drafted at the end of the war, who, in his first and only combat action, in panic had shot and killed a grounded American airman. When the boy was sentenced to death, his mother appealed in despair to Bishop Muench who, as time was running out, called for hours trying to locate General Clay. When Muench finally reached Clay by phone in London, Clay, as always, was not only willing but anxious to review the extenuating circumstances, stayed the execution, reviewed the case and eventually the boy was released.

Other typical cases in which court decisions were reversed were: a policeman at Offenbach am Main who was falsely accused of having given orders to shoot an American pilot; a physician and medical adviser at Dachau concentration camp who, through letters and con· versations of Muench with Clay, had his sentence reversed from death to life imprisonment; a member of the SS (*Schutzstaffel*) elite guard who was not a member of the Nazi Party and who had been forced to join the SS, had his sentence of ten years reversed; a high official of the postal service, in charge of field mail service during the war, and who was not a Nazi, had his sentence reversed; a civilian physician who cared for prisoners at Anrath near Krefeld in the Rhineland was cleared of party affiliation.

Not all cases were favorably considered. The family of Erich Wentzel, who was accused of participating in the killing of American airmen, appealed to the apostolic visitor who, considering the circumstances warranted a review, intervened on 30 November 1948, but Wentzel was executed on December 3. The Baroness Constantin von Neurath petitioned that her husband be transferred from Spandau Prison to a prison in West Berlin, and was refused. Muench likewise intervened for an easing of conditions at Spandau Prison, under quadripartite control, in behalf of Admiral Erich Raeder. Baron Ernst von Weizsaecker, German ambassador to the Vatican during the Nazi period, was accused of anti-Semitism in June of 1949. The Vatican Secretariat of State, as well as Muench, intervened on Weizsaecker's behalf with President Truman, and Muench warmly took part in working for Weizsaecker's release.

The famed Malmédy Massacre case became a major object of Muench's concern. From 16 May 1946 to 16 July 1946 hearings were conducted at Camp Dachau involving seventy-four members of the SS First Armored Division who were accused of killing seventy-one unarmed American prisoners of war at Malmédy crossroads in Belgium on 17 December

1944. One case was separated because of French nationality and, interestingly enough, as a forewarning of what was to come, the French judiciary discontinued the charge because prosecution evidence in the Malmédy trial was not recognized as valid. Of the seventy-three accused former German soldiers, forty-three received death sentences, twenty-two life sentences, and eight imprisonment of from ten to twenty years.

A cry arose in Germany and abroad centered on accusations of improper methods used by the American prosecutors in extracting evidence. Proofs adduced by the prosecution consisted of stage settings, stool pigeons, and testimony of the prisoners themselves obtained under coercion in pre-trial investigations in the Schwaebisch Hall Penitentiary.

A long process of review began immediately after the decision and continued into the 1950's. General Clay asked for independent review by the Simpson Commission of the United States Army, and on the basis of their conclusions that improper methods of obtaining evidence had been employed, Clay reversed and reduced fifty-four sentences on 20 March 1948. Twelve death sentences were confirmed and Clay ordered execution on 18 May 1948. But Secretary of the Army Kenneth C. Royall ordered a stay of execution the next day after the United States Supreme Court by a tie vote of 4-4 had refused to consider an application for release of the accused by writ of *habeas corpus*. Justice Simpson recommended commutation of the twelve death sentences in September of 1948; Clay reaffirmed six of them and commuted six to life imprisonment in April of 1949; General Handy commuted the remaining six death sentences on 31 January 1951; and in August of 1951 thirty-one sentences were reduced by the Modification Board.

The bishop of Fargo became deeply involved during these days in a considerable number of the appeals of accused German soldiers in the Malmédy trial and its long drawn out aftermath. Muench held the opinion that grave injury had been done to the reputation of American justice among the German people; that the honorable tradition of American jurisprudence had been offended against by the first American prosecutors and judges. As he told Justice William Clark of New York, guilt had not been established beyond dispute. Muench considered Clay in this case, as in so many others, to have carried out the spirit of American fairness by the care with which the cases were reviewed to prevent injustice. "No one who knows the situation here blames General Clay," Muench informed Judge L. W. Powers of

Denison, Iowa, on 21 May 1949, who had written the dissenting opinion at Nuremberg:

"General Clay's administration was excellent, but he was unfortunately harassed and embarrassed by personnel who should never have come to Germany. His close friends are bitter about the kind of men in lower administrative levels who had in their hands the implementation of the policies of occupation . . .

"What is now happening justifies the position you took. As an American I love the good name of our country and suffer not a little because of the sharp and caustic things that are being said and written about us anent the trials not only in Germany but in other countries of Europe as well. I have in mind in particular the best press of Switzerland."

European Communists, of course, made as much political capital as possible out of the furor over the Malmédy case, while, ironically, patriotic and veterans' groups in the United States protested equally as vigorously against any mitigation of sentences. Muench, in this regard, tried to prevent the removal of Edwin A. Plitt, American member of the Mixed Review Board dealing with clemency and parole in German war crime cases, after the Malmédy sentences were mitigated.[17]

Muench was in close contact throughout the entire procedure of the Malmédy case with Colonel Willis M. Everett, jr., Atlanta, Georgia, lawyer, who had defended the accused German soldiers. After the first trial Everett continued as a civilian in working for review and reversal of the original judgments. He spent more than 2,000 hours and over $1,000 of his own funds to see that justice was done. With remarkable perseverence he carried the case to the United States Supreme Court and as a result of its split decision forced a re-examination of the whole case. "Often I am told that I should be hung with the Germans. For two years I have done nothing constructive except fight for justice and fairness trying to carry out the Army's announced policies on democracy and giving the Germans a fair trial," Everett explained to Muench. He added: "The Malmédy story is fantastic and I could relate some unbelievable incidents. Your work, I hope, will prove of much benefit, but so much corruption and ungodliness existed while I was there that my memories are surely varied."

In reply, Muench told Everett on 26 May 1948:

"May I say that no one in the whole case has done so much as you in clearing our fair name for right and justice, besmirched by men who, hardly Americans, played such a foul role in obtaining evidence. I hung my head with shame when I read what happened in the original trial, but raised it again with pride when I saw what you did to rehabilitate our good name."

Both Everett and Muench were referring to the malfeasance of the prosecution staff, research analysts, interpreters and interrogators who had among their numbers many former German nationals who had fled Hitler's Germany and had recently taken out American citizenship. After the war they returned to Germany in the occupation personnel lacking an understanding of the Anglo-Saxon democratic jurisprudence and filled with a spirit of vindictiveness, personal grievance and racial desires for vengeance which precluded objectivity. Repeatedly Muench received protests regarding the activities of these former Germans. Warren E. Magee, Washington, D. C., lawyer, who was the first American attorney to represent a German defendant at Nuremberg, had even filed a formal protest with Pius XII regarding the Nuremberg trials and the activities in those proceedings of these "new Americans, many of whom have imbedded in their very beings European racial hatreds and prejudices." Magee continued, "While individual judges may seek to be personally fair, judicial fairness is precluded by the procedure. I fear these 'trials' will go down in history, not as history's greatest trials, as extolled by Justice Robert Jackson, but as history's greatest mistrials."

A case to which Bishop Muench gave continual attention for years was that of Major Josef Diefenthal in the First SS Army Division at Malmédy. Diefenthal, then twenty-nine years old, was leading Combat Group Peiper from Cheneux, Belgium, toward Werbomont in the afternoon hours of 17 December 1944. An American knocked-out jeep blocked the route of advance and Diefenthal ordered his sergeant, Paul Zwigart, to remove the destroyed jeep while he remained in his armored troop carrier studying maps and transmitting orders via radio. Diefenthal insisted that he did not give orders to his battalion that prisoners of war should not be taken, was not present at the Cheneux crossroads at the time that Zwigart and others were accused of massacring the Americans, and that his guilt was due to his failure to prevent the crime rather than to any affirmative action on his part. Zwigart was condemned to death as was Diefenthal in the first Malmédy decision. Zwigart insisted he was acting on orders, but his own affidavit as well as others did not implicate Diefenthal in these orders. The latter insisted that General Clay had not seen these affidavits in his review of the case.

Diefenthal's sentence was reduced to life imprisonment by General Handy on 30 January 1951 because of discrepancies in testimony and "the confused, fluid and desperate combat action, a last attempt to turn the tide of Allied successes and to re-establish a more favorable tactical position for the German Army." Mrs. Magda Diefenthal pleaded with Bishop Muench to enter a plea of clemency in behalf of her husband who was imprisoned for life at Landsberg. After studying the testimony and documents of the trial, and after long discussions with Everett, defense counsel for the accused, as well as with Clay, Huebner and Handy, Muench appealed on 20 November 1953 to General William H. Hoge, commander-in-chief at Heidelberg for a retrial. Hoge received the request and recommended that a petition for clemency be submitted to the Interim Mixed Parole and Clemency Board. Diefenthal had been a prisoner for nine years, expecting the death sentence for five years of that period. His wife was sick and he had an eleven-year old daughter who did not know him. He had lost a leg in the war and suffered a seventy per cent disability.

Muench obtained legal help for Diefenthal in preparing his petition which was submitted on 20 July 1954 and he was granted release on 1 July 1955. It was one of the happiest occasions of the bishop's many works of mercy in Germany. He invited Diefenthal and his family to make the one-hour trip from Euskirchen to Bad Godesberg for an afternoon visit that ended with "Kaffee und Kuchen" which the sisters at the nunciature prepared. All were filled with joy and thanksgiving. Thousands of Germans have never forgotten the persevering charity of Muench who worked for almost a decade to help obtain freedom for a friendless major languishing in prison. Muench told his good friend, William H. Regnery, sr. in Chicago, on 12 April 1954:

"Our prestige has not been helped by some of the things that were perpetrated in Germany, largely by men in lesser positions who hardly deserve the name of Americans. The whole occupation story should be written in order to give our good name a place of honor again.

"It would tell a sad and tragic story of the cruelties which have been committed by some false representatives of our government who parade before the world as having fought against brutal men, guilty of atrocities. Despite the Nuremberg and Dachau trials, the rights of men are not secure and justice does not prevail."

Bishop Muench, Cardinal Josef Frings of Cologne and Archbishop Michael Buchberger of Regensburg at Flensburg, 3 October 1949.

In garden of Father Wilson E. Kaiser, NCWC representative in Berlin: l to r: Father Kaiser, Bishop Muench, and Father Howard Smith.

Christmas eve Pontifical Mass, St. Boniface Church, Heidelberg, assisted by members of the U. S. Army stationed at Heidelberg, 24 December 1949.

*Bishop Muench and Father Howard Smith enjoy Christmas dinner
1950, with the family of Colonel O'Neill at Army Base in Heidelberg.*

*German Bishops' Conference: Crypt of St. Boniface Cathedral, Fulda, 22 August 1950: first
pew, l to r: Cardinal Konrad von Preysing (Berlin) and Bishop Muench; second
pew, l to r: Archbishops Lorenz Jaeger (Paderborn) and Josef Kolb (Bamberg); third pew,
l to r: Bishops Albert Stohr (Mainz), John B. Dietz (Fulda), and Simon Konrad
Landersdorfer, O.S.B., (Passau); fourth pew, l to r: Bishops Julius Doepfner (Wuerzburg)
and Michael Keller (Muenster).*

Last visit to his mother, September, 1953, with sisters, Mrs. Mary Herrick and Teresa.

Private audience with Pope Pius XII, Castel Gandolfo, 20 October 1953: standing, second from left: Archbishop Muench; third from right, Bishop John F. Dearden, Pittsburgh; far right: Rev. Gerald M. Weber; kneeling, fourth from left: Raymond W. Lessard; fifth from left: James D. Schumacher, Fargo seminarians at the North American College, Rome.

Nuncio Muench enters Olympic Stadium in Berlin for Pontifical Mass at Katholikentag, *13 August 1958.*

Archbishop Muench addressing crowd in Olympic Stadium, Berlin, on occasion of centenary of diocese of Berlin, 19 June 1955.

Conversing with Lt. Gen. Clarence R. Huebner, chief of staff, Army of Occupation, in St. Ignatius Church, Heidelberg, 31 October 1948: at left, Mrs. Huebner; right: Julia Huebner.

First visit to the Benedictine Archabbey of Beuron, Ascension Thursday, 1949.

CHAPTER FIVE

THE HEROIC YEARS

On 1 July 1948, as a result of the London Six Power Conference, the three military governors of West Germany directed the premiers of the *Laender*, or state governments, to convoke a constituent assembly for all of West Germany. The purpose of this early move, only three years after the occupation began, was to achieve, on the basis of a free and democratic form of government, the eventual re-establishment of German unity. The rapid recovery of the German economy, based on the principles of a social free market economy, and acclaimed by the world as an "economic miracle," was also instrumental in this move toward Germany's independence.

The premiers accepted the task and took steps to form the parliamentary council of delegates representing major political parties in the twelve *Laender*. From 1 September 1948 to 8 May 1949 this national constituent assembly worked in Bonn on a "Basic Law," the first federal constitution of the postwar period. During the protracted discussions regarding the new constitution the German Catholic bishops took a firm stand on 11 February 1949 concerning basic human rights and principles which they considered of vital importance to the establishment of a sound political system. Bishop Muench was active in support of the German bishops in this important matter.

The issue was whether the new constitution would recognize natural law; would the dignity of the free, morally conscious individual be protected by safeguards enabling him to shape his life and that of his family according to his conscience and in obedience to divine law. The German bishops were all too aware of the disregard of God-given rights of individuals and parents by the previous Nazi regime. Secondly, the Vatican and the German hierarchy wanted the Concordat of 1933 recognized in which parents were defined as responsible for the education of their children in their families as well as in state schools which guarantee parental rights. Cardinal Josef Frings, president of and acting in the name of the Fulda Bishops' Conference, wrote on 11 February 1949 to the Parliamentary Council:

"How can any constitution safeguard and assure the peaceful future of our people as long as such basic rights are deliberately ignored? The struggles and sufferings of these last years would have been in vain if the federal constitution were not to contain provisions making it impossible for the state to violate the Christian conscience, in vain if the state were again allowed to prevail over parental rights in matters of school education. We want here and now plainly to decline all responsibility for developments which might ensue.

"We bishops resolutely repudiate attacks which, during the discussions on the *Reichskonkordat* (1933), were launched against the Holy See by the press and in parliament. These attacks have deeply offended both us and the whole Catholic population. They were the more offensive to the Holy Father, considering that during the time of our humiliation the Holy See never ceased to consider Germany as a party capable of concluding treaties, considering also that the Holy See has constantly proved itself the friend and helper of our suffering people, regardless of the opinions of the world. We expect, therefore, that the federal constitution will contain guarantees for the maintenance of the concordat concluded between the Holy See and the Reich."

Long and sometimes passionate discussions concerning human rights took place between Christian Democrats and Socialists in the parliamentary council. The Socialists, generally centralistic with regard to the new German federal state, now became federalistic in their position on human rights. They did not want to include in the constitution the right of parents to decide the religious character of a school for their children. The Socialists wanted the various *Laender* to decide this matter since there were several German states in which the Socialists held a majority.

The German bishops, Catholic organizations and Christian politicians worked hard and did all they could to have this right registered, a right which was acknowledged in article twenty-six of the United Nations Declaration of Human Rights. But their efforts were not successful. When the final document was approved the new constitution did not include a declaration of parental right to decide the religious character of a school for their children.

A special problem was also created in the "*Clausula Bremensis.*" In the state of Bremen, in the British zone, an enclave under United States jurisdiction because of the harbor, state-controlled schools were recognized with simultaneous religious instruction by state-appointed instructors for Catholics and Protestants. The German Catholic bishops were not satisfied with this arrangement. On 23 May 1949, after passage of the constitution, the bishops published a declaration in which they expressed their definite wish to fight on until all their demands should be fulfilled. They considered this question of grave importance because in the future the whole problem of education and confessional schools would depend upon the rights of parents and acknowledgment of the Reich Concordat of 1933.

In the case of the concordat, the second issue at stake in the new constitution, better results were realized. These months were busy ones for Bishop Muench since Monsignor Domenico Tardini of the Vatican Secretariat of State made it repeatedly clear that Pius XII wanted the Reich Concordat of 1933 preserved at all costs. The Vatican always maintained that by signing this concordat, it had in no way approved of National Socialism, but wished to safeguard religion and the rights of the Church. Hitler accepted this agreement only to break it, but it was never annulled and neither party ever declared its validity ended. The concordat was of special value to the Vatican because it regulated the relations between the Church and the German Reich as a whole whereas formerly the Vatican had to try to reach an agreement with the separate German *Laender.*

The fact that Cardinal Eugenio Pacelli, both as nuncio to Germany and Vatican secretary of state, had the prime influence in forming this concordat played no small part now in papal determination to preserve it intact and as valid until such time as a new agreement were negotiated. As early as 27 July 1933 an article in *L'Osservatore Romano,* in an attempt to counter interpretations by National Socialists and opposing sides, stated that "such an agreement did not mean the approval or recognition of any particular current of thought or political tendency. The purpose of the Holy See in negotiating with States was to guarantee the rights and freedom of the Church, without any ulterior motive."

Most countries rejected the argument that to come to an agreement with a foreign state necessarily implied approval of its form of government. The famed Reich Concordat was a treaty freely negotiated between two sovereign powers. The Vatican consistently relied on international law and precedent in claiming that this argument was still valid. German Catholics generally believed, moreover, that the main reason why the concordat was being met with such bitter opposition by Social Democrats and Communists was because it safeguarded confessional schools and recognized the rights of parents to ask for their establishment.

A minority of Catholic intellectuals and critics of German Catholicism's record before and during the Nazi period, however, began to raise their voices against continuing the concordat. They questioned whether Catholic leaders had not capitulated to and collaborated with Hitler because they gained through the concordat a clear agreement between Church and State, an agreement that had not been possible under the Weimar democratic republic. In this way they hoped to maintain Catholic "solidarity." Such writers as Heinrich Boell, Ernst-Wolfgang Boeckenfoerde and Carl Amery would intensify a decade later their rejection of concordat-Catholicism and its results in Germany. As Carl Amery stated: "The concordat's fate is well-known — exactly the same incidentally as that of all or almost all concordats before it — and historical evidence raises doubts about the famous or notorious serpentine wisdom of the thousand-year-old Vatican politics." [1]

During the eight months of late 1948 and early 1949 Muench had to master an entirely new corpus of background materials concerned with the establishment of the Basic Law. Father Howard Smith, his former secretary and vicar general of the Diocese of Fargo, arrived in July to assist him as secretary at Kronberg. This was a major help to Muench who had been waiting for two years to have Father Smith at his side. Muench told Dworschak that they had done two months' work during the first month Smith was there. Father Ivo Zeiger, S.J., and Monsignor Opilio Rossi, of the Vatican Secretariat of State, were also staff members. Monsignor Bernhard Hack moved from Eichstaett to Kronberg in 1950 and served as special assistant for German governmental and educational matters.

Muench had just completed making contact with all of the *Laender* governments and now was faced with the formation of the Federal Republic.[2] Fortunately, the major parties in Germany — Christian Democrats, Social Democrats, Free Democrats, as well as a minority of the Christian Socialists — supported the new Basic Law and were anxious to reach agreement. In this way they could go to the country with a constitution that was likely to receive the backing of an overwhelming majority of the people, and the Federal Government would be a reality. A majority of the delegates were willing to recognize tacitly, until review by the federal court was possible, the validity of the Reich Concordat of 1933. A general article of the new federal constitution declared that the international treaties of the Third Reich were valid until new ones were agreed upon. The battle, however, would have to be fought over and over in the future as to recognition of the concordat by the various German states.

Four years after the capitulation of the Nazis, on 8 May 1949, the Basic Law was passed by a 52-12 vote of the delegates. Two-thirds of the *Laender* also approved the constitution, with only Bavaria, according to its strong regional traditions, rejecting the Basic Law.[3] At the same time the Bavarians made it clear that with the acceptance of the Basic Law on 23 May 1949 they would become members of the new Federal Republic of West Germany. Meanwhile, the military governments of Britain, France and the United States still remained responsible for German internal and external policies.

No fewer than nineteen articles of the Basic Law were devoted to fundamental rights. This development was due to the strong inclination of the occupation powers, the majority of the German legislators themselves, and citizen groups such as the German bishops had represented. The individual received constitutional guarantees including freedom of the person and development of personality, freedom of belief, conscience and religion, freedom of the press, and freedom of science, research and teaching. Protection of the family, freedom of assembly, inviolability of correspondence, the right of association, and the protection of home and property were also safeguarded.

Simultaneously, the passing of the constitution also marked a new stage in occupation policy for West Germany. On 10 April 1949 the three allied military governors proclaimed the occupation statute which was linked to the Basic Law and extended self-government and administration to Germany. Veto rights, security, disarmament, demilitarization, foreign affairs, foreign trade and exchange control were retained for a one-year period by the occupying powers. Military governors became high commissioners and military law was replaced by civil administration. The three high commissioners formed a high commission which made joint decisions from its new seat on the Petersburg in the seven mountains near Bonn.

The West Germans selected Bonn as their provisional federal capital until Berlin could hopefully again become headquarters of a united Germany. But the Berlin blockade from June, 1948, to May, 1949, indicated that the political realities of the period made any possible agreement with the Russians a remote eventuality. The division of Germany was temporarily accepted by the West as a political necessity and the West Germans by strong majorities aligned themselves with the West.

On 14 August 1949 the West Germans held their first elections for a Federal Diet, elections which founded the Federal Republic and initiated the work of the principal federal organs. With thirty-two million citizens entitled to vote, 78.6% of the electorate cast their ballots. There was a choice of candidates representing thirteen parties in a mixed system of voting along lines of proportional representation. The Christian Democratic Union and its Bavarian counterpart, the Christian Social Union, won 139 seats, the German Social Democratic Party secured 131 seats and the Free Democratic Party obtained fifty-two seats. Together with the German Party, which obtained fifteen seats, a coalition of the CDU/CSU and the FDP was formed as a majority government. The SDP went into opposition. Dr. Conrad Adenauer, former mayor of Cologne and president of the Parliamentary Council, was elected federal chancellor of the first government by 202 votes, the required majority of all delegates. He was proposed by the new federal president, Professor Dr. Theodor Heuss, of the FDP.

Bishop Muench knew that the fast changing developments of these months would affect the status of the Vatican mission at Kronberg. Although the high commission of the Allies still retained administrative controls, an independent German government was now in the offing. During the uncertainty over whether the seat of government was to be at Bonn or Frankfurt, Muench asked Hack to investigate suitable housing for the Vatican mission in both cities. Frankfurt, for economic and financial reasons, was the more logical choice as provisional capitol. Bonn, a small city and badly damaged, had inadequate air, rail, highway and telephone connections. But Bonn secured a narrow victory over Frankfurt in the Parliamentary Council by 33 votes to 29, and the center of future events was now definite.

While the new government was taking shape Muench was preparing to give another report to Pope Pius XII and Roman curial officials on German affairs as well as to make his *ad limina* visit as bishop of Fargo. He received authorization to come to Rome on 6 October 1949, and he traveled as usual via Munich, taking Bishop Dworschak with him, to visit his close friend Cardinal Faulhaber. Auxiliary Bishop Dworschak of Fargo had come to Germany to accompany Muench to Rome for the *ad limina* visit.[4]

In Rome, Muench reported on developments to Montini and Tardini and awaited his interview with Pius XII. The meeting with the Pope was well over an hour in length. Father Leiber noted that Muench's sessions with Pius XII were lengthy and were conducted with a rare informality, an indication of Pius' interest in German affairs and his personal liking for Muench. The latter was moved by the warm cordiality with which he was received and noted that Pius XII was, as usual, intensely interested in the Church in Germany and "manifested an amazing grasp of the whole situation."

Pius XII informed Muench during the meeting that he was going to appoint him regent of the nunciature in Germany. Up to that point Muench was an apostolic visitator and chief officer of the Vatican mission in Germany. Since the death of Archbishop Orsenigo at Eichstaett, no nuncio had been named to succeed him and Muench had acted unofficially as representative of the Vatican during the first years after the war. Now, with independent German governmental status in process, Pius XII stressed that when German autonomy came with its right to exchange diplomatic representatives, he would appoint a papal nuncio to represent the Holy See at Bonn. Pius also wanted to make it clear that the Vatican did not consider papal representation in Germany to have been terminated, in the same way as he did not consider the concordat to have ceased. Although the nunciature had lost its diplomatic character in 1945, it still existed ecclesiastically. Pius also stated that the nunciature was to be the ecclesiastical co-ordinator for the whole of Germany, both West and East, without the Holy See taking a position concerning the division of Germany into eastern and western governments. As Muench wrote Bertke on 5 December 1949 after his return from Rome:

"My appointment will again give the nunciature some sort of official standing. Accreditation with the German Federal Republic via HICOG, and not with the Eastern "German Democratic Republic," involves serious complications for the Holy See, no matter from what point of view one looks at it. We are watching developments closely."

Reaction throughout West Germany was favorable to this move and Muench received a large volume of congratulatory letters and messages upon his return to Kronberg. Archbishop Wilhelm Berning of Osna-brueck stated in a typical letter on 26 November 1949: "Your activities in Germany to this very day have been visibly accompanied and supported by the grace of God. Your nomination as regent of the apostolic nunciature has caused great joy all over Germany."

The new title did not alter Muench's operation at Kronberg in any appreciable degree. The work load was increasing daily and in areas quite remote from the world of diplomacy. From the first days in Germany one of the insoluble concerns of Bishop Muench, which now assumed major proportions, was the problem of displaced persons, expellees and refugees in Germany.

Muench never tired of explaining the plight of these poor and helpless people who had been thrown upon the collapsed German economy. Displaced persons were non-Germans who had been citizens of countries that were allies of the Western Powers and who had been brought into Germany by the Hitler government as slave laborers, or who had fled before the invading armies. At the end of the war they remained in Germany. Hungarians and Romanians were not classed as displaced persons because they had come from former enemy nations. Most of the Italians returned home soon after the war, but a large number of Hungarians and Romanians remained in Germany because their homelands had been taken over by the Communists. Thrown on their own resources in an impoverished and overburdened German economy, their plight was desperate.

The Allied armies advancing in Germany had discovered almost 6,500,000 displaced persons performing forced labor. Some 4,000,000 were returned to their homelands by mid-1945, but over 2,000,000 remained in assembly centers and camps throughout Germany. They were people without a country who could not or did not want to return to their homelands because of their religious and political beliefs. They included the Baltic people — Lithuanians, Latvians, Estonians — the western Ukrainians, Poles, Yugoslavs and Russians along with the Hungarians and Romanians. Over 342,000 of these displaced persons were Catholics.

Some 150,000 displaced persons in Germany were Jews who had come from Poland, Czechoslovakia and Hungary after the war. The creation of the state of Israel helped in the resettlement of Jewish displaced persons in 1948 due to the courageous policy of the new Israeli government. American-Jewish agencies were particularly successful in placing Jewish displaced persons abroad and in raising morale in the camps through establishing self-support, handicraft and vocational training.

Displaced persons' camps in Germany were protected by authority of the military occupation and administered first by UNRRA of the United Nations and then by the International Refugee Organization. General Clay was deeply concerned with the plight of displaced persons and vigorously pursued a policy of granting priority in employment to them in labor and guard units. The camps were located in the countryside because of bomb damage in industrial areas. Displaced persons were remote from the labor market and did not, understandably, want to work in the German economy. Clay strongly advocated more liberal immigration laws for these victims of war who were not wanted in Germany, did not want to return home and were not allowed to move freely to new homes.

Many displaced persons remaining in Germany wanted to emigrate but the immigration laws of western nations had set up such high barriers that only relatively few could be resettled. Bishop Muench told the American bishops in his first annual report of 1947: "In taking displaced persons, receiving nations use a method of selection reminiscent of slave trading. Only able-bodied young men and women qualify for immigration; the sick, the aged, women and children are not wanted. There is very little charity in the whole process of taking these unfortunate people." He then went on to press a point which he constantly stressed:

"If immigration barriers were lowered in the United States, our country would receive, for the greatest part, persons that would really be an asset to our nation. At this point the observation may be made that for economic reasons we need a larger population. We need to become a larger importing nation if foreign countries are to obtain dollars to purchase the things that our enlarged industrial and agricultural capacity is able to produce. Of course, we can give foreign countries dollars by way of gifts and loans, but clearly that cannot be a permanent policy. In the long run we would lose both our goods and our dollars. If we are to prosper, we have to have a larger market at home, not only for the things that we ourselves produce, but also for the things that are produced by other nations. Today foreign countries are dollar-poor. We could make them dollar-rich by buying from them the things that they produce and are anxious to sell us.

"Aside from such purely material reasons, however, the duties of

Christian charity compel us to take in the homeless and give them a chance to live."

Pope Pius XII was much concerned about the problem of displaced persons. In each conversation with him and Monsignor Montini, Muench was directed to exert every effort toward mitigating the tragic conditions of displaced persons in the camps. The Vatican Migration Bureau was established and Father Edward J. Killion, C.Ss.R., former American army chaplain, was in charge of German and Austrian affairs while working closely with the International Refugee Organization centered in Geneva, Switzerland. Monsignor Paolo Bertoli, formerly at the nunciature in Berne, was sent to South America by Pius XII to open doors on that continent.

The third Vatican mission which was sent to Germany during October of 1945 had as its main objective the aiding of displaced persons and refugees, and the occupation powers accepted it on that basis of operation. This mission, headed by Archbishop Carlo Chiarlo, preceded the arrival of Bishop Muench on the scene, as has been said. Muench realized from the very beginning the importance Pope Pius XII attached to this aspect of the work of restoration in Germany. Eight priests were assigned to represent the different nationalities: Italians, Poles, Ukrainians, Lithuanians, Hungarians, Slovaks, Croatians and Romanians. These priests moved out from Kronberg to the different camps visiting the displaced persons, refugees and expellees, collecting information, and organizing pastoral work among these peoples who could not possibly be cared for by the dismembered and disorganized German Church.[5]

Muench maintained that if every nation of North and South America, as well as those of western Europe, would assume a quota of immigrants, the problem would be quickly solved. He kept asking for a sort of Marshall Plan for displaced persons to be devised and put into practice. He felt strongly that the Church in the United States would stand only to gain if more displaced persons were allowed to enter. The fact that most Catholic displaced persons did not want to be repatriated for religious reasons was evident proof to him of their qualities as Catholics.

Although Western governments repudiated the false and inhumane assertion that these displaced and uprooted people should be forcibly handed over to their political and religious enemies, as the Russians repeatedly asserted, they were slow to establish policy for resettling the uprooted in countries where they could begin life anew.[6]

Representatives of Catholic War Relief Services, the charity arm of the NCWC, had been in the field caring for these displaced persons immediately following the cessation of hostilities. Their representatives visited camps in Germany, Austria and Italy and over the years brought 68,000,000 pounds of supplementary food, clothing, educational, religious and recreational supplies to displaced persons. In addition, over $2,000,000 in supplies and funds was given to Catholic War Relief Services for distribution by the International Refugee Organization. The European staff of this Catholic organization undertook the task of selection, processing and transportation of displaced persons to some twenty-five countries, and approximately 6,500 persons were assisted in the first stages of the operation.

Bishop Muench often spoke in praise of the noble and courageous efforts of the priests engaged in this work such as Edward E. Swanstrom, Emil Komora, Aloysius J. Wycislo, William E. McManus, Stephen A. Bernas, Alfred A. Schneider, Wilson E. Kaiser, Fabian Flynn, C.P., George McSweeney, O.P., and laity like James J. Norris, Patrick Boarman, George Donovan, C. Joseph Neusse, Sylvester Theisen and Joan Christie. In commending the team work of the NCWC National Catholic Resettlement Council Muench told the American bishops:

"They have given new hope to the homeless, helpless, hapless displaced persons, unable to return to their homeland, but filled with eagerness to start life anew in some other country, regardless of the hardships that such new beginnings may involve. For, life in barracks and camps has become unbearable; how unbearable can be realized only by those who have seen such camps with their crowded living quarters, inadequate sanitation facilities, common kitchens and tables. The heavy atmosphere of hopelessness is oppressive.

"The National Catholic Resettlement Council has reason to be proud of its setup. Today it is the best in the field. Its representatives here are men and women not only experienced for their tasks but also alive to their grave responsibilities, and aware of their obligations of charity toward these unfortunate, uprooted people.

"Under the general direction of Mr. James Norris they have held conferences among themselves, with IRO officials, with representatives of the Displaced Persons Commission, with American consuls and their staffs, as well as with the German and American voluntary emigration agencies, among them the revived St. Raphael Society of Hamburg, tried and tested in aid of emigrants. Their aim is to coordinate their work with a view to cutting red tape to a minimum, breaking bottlenecks, and in general rendering the processing of prospective emigrants as easy as possible. Their work is one of large proportions."

Also helpful in arranging immigration of displaced persons into the United States was Monsignor John O'Grady, secretary of the National Conference of Catholic Charities, Washington, D. C. He reported to Muench on 25 May 1949 that 30,000 displaced persons had already arrived in the States, but O'Grady regretted that more displaced persons had not been sponsored in agricultural dioceses of the mid and far west. The Relief and Emigration Service for Catholic Displaced and Refugee Students sponsored by the Relief Department of *Pax Romana*, under its secretary Edward J. Kirchner in Munich, served students in exile who totaled throughout Germany at this time around 5,000.

The surface of the displaced persons problem had scarcely been touched by the presidential directive of 1945 under which only some 42,000 refugees were welcomed to the United States. The United States Congress, moved by its international commitments and pressured for three years by public opinion, passed on 25 June 1948 the Displaced Persons Act under which 205,000 displaced persons were authorized entry over a two-year period to the United States on quotas unused during the war years.

After his return from Rome in the fall of 1949 the new regent of the nunciature accelerated his campaign to place displaced persons in countries of the west. Daily letters went out from Kronberg to French, Canadian, Australian and American bishops and religious superiors begging them to accept displaced priests, sisters and laity in their jurisdictions. Muench wrote to American senators and congressmen encouraging them to investigate conditions in the camps and to liberalize immigration quotas. By March of 1949 only 7,129 displaced persons had gained entry into the United States under provisions of the Displaced Persons Act while Israel had received 8,427 displaced persons, Australia 2,160 and Canada 2,010 by the same date.

Muench was deeply disturbed at this slow pace of resettlement and carried on an extensive correspondence with North Dakota's senators, William Langer and Milton R. Young. The latter conducted a survey in North Dakota and found that of the 4,424 people who responded, 2,026 were in favor of admitting more displaced persons while 2,398 were opposed. Young informed Muench on 26 March 1948 that there was a need for greater publicity and information on the plight of the displaced person. "In North Dakota," he said, "many of our World War II soldiers are the ones most opposed. I assume that this is because while in Germany they came into contact with some of the less desirable displaced persons. However, there, too, I think their attitude is due somewhat to the lack of information and understanding of the whole problem." In his reply of 20 April 1948, Muench stated:

"Your letter of March 26 brought me much encouragement. I thank you for your interest in the displaced persons.

"If our soldiers of World War II would see the plight in which these poor, hapless people are, and if they would meet them as I have, they would at once open the doors wide to admit them.

"They are victims of a system which to crush they sweated and feared, bled and died.

"Soldiers will benefit from an enlarged home market. We can best give jobs to them if we can use to the full our expanded capacities in industry and agriculture. For that we need larger home markets. Foreign markets are dollar-poor. At present they can buy goods because we lend or give them the dollars with which they buy.

"We should have a population in the States so large that we shall have to import more than we do. Only if we buy from other countries, giving them in this way our dollars, will they in turn be able to buy from us.

"It is a very shortsighted policy not to look beyond the affluence of the present day. We know what surpluses have done to farmers and to workers in the factories. In the face of the experience which we made we can not pursue a short range, narrow population policy.

"We cannot talk in one breath of an economy of abundance in production and in the next of scarcity of population.

"Our country grew rich and prosperous in the decades when we opened our doors wide to immigrants. Thanks for listening to me."

The bishop was so aroused over the deteriorating situation among displaced persons that he determined to fly to the United States to talk with Archbishop McNicholas, chairman of the Administrative Board of the NCWC, contact friendly clergy and laity across the country on behalf of displaced persons, and solicit support personally wherever he could find "a friend for the friendless." Muench also determined to seek an interview with President Harry S. Truman to present the case for accelerating the resettlement of these homeless victims of war in a "haven of refuge." On 8 February 1949 Muench was granted an interview at eleven a.m. with President Truman in the White House. Muench's notes on this session are included in Appendix VI.[7]

Voluntary religious organizations and labor groups continued to give strong support throughout the United States for a revision of the Displaced Persons Act of 1948. The provisions of this act proved to be so discriminatory that Congress, following public pressure, added 104,000 to the quota for displaced persons in amendments to the law on 10 June 1950. Provisions were also made for an additional 119,744 from special groups such as German ethnics expelled from Eastern Europe, members of the Polish army in England, orphans, Greeks and refugees from Trieste.

At their annual meeting in November, 1947, the American bishops anticipated the passage of the Displaced Persons Act of 1948 by establishing the Bishops' Resettlement Committee to better focus the attention of American Catholics on the problem of displaced persons and to direct planning for their resettlement in the United States. Resettlement directors were established in 118 dioceses and lay organizations and nationality groups were represented on the diocesan resettlement committees. A National Catholic Resettlement Council was established with representation from the National Catholic Welfare Conference, the Catholic Committee for Refugees, the National Catholic Rural Life Conference, the National Conference of Catholic Charities, the Saint Vincent de Paul Society, representatives of other national Catholic lay organizations, and some fifteen nationality groups. This council undertook the huge task of organizing and educating Catholic America to the full implications of the displaced persons resettlement program. The council also co-operated with Protestant and Jewish representatives and other voluntary organizations concerned with American resettlement programs.

Father Stanley J. Bertke, secretary to Bishop Muench, was particularly helpful in investigating conditions among the displaced persons. "Without sparing himself," Muench informed the American bishops, "living out of a suitcase and traveling thousands of miles to interview displaced persons," Bertke had collected authentic first-hand information for a plan of action which the regent now wished to place before them and the National Catholic Resettlement Council. Monsignor Montini at the Secretariat of State was also much impressed with Bertke's report of September, 1947. He assured Muench that Pius XII intended to write to the bishops of North and South America and Australia encouraging them to accept displaced persons — priests and laity — into their dioceses.

The International Relief Organization discontinued its operation on 30 June 1950. There were 700,000 displaced persons still to be resettled before that time. It was estimated that about 150,000 to 170,000 displaced persons would have to stay in Germany because of mental or physical disabilities, age, political undesirability or criminal records. These were the hard core who would be thrown upon an already overburdened German economy. Muench recommended that American Catholic relief agencies co-operate, along with voluntary relief agencies of America and other countries, in assisting the Committee for the Rehabilitation of Political Refugees, a new organization of the German Federal Government established to assist stranded displaced persons. German charity organizations — *Caritas, Evangelisches Hilfswerk* and others — were anxious to co-operate but they were burdened with the responsibility of caring for their own German unfortunate along with millions of refugees and expellees from the East.

Muench asked that Americans open their hearts to the hard core remnant, except for the political undesirables and criminals, work toward further easing of immigration restrictions in line with the American tradition of humanity and charity for people in need, and open contacts for displaced people to emigrate to relatives, friends or religious institutions in the United States. "Neither age nor physical disability should bar people, otherwise acceptable," he said, "from enjoying the good life of our country as long as the charity of others is willing to care for them." Secondly, he recommended that the charity work of War Relief Services be extended in a special way to the hard core displaced persons. James J. Norris and his staff of workers of Catholic Relief Services again rose to the occasion. They helped obtain visas for 60,570 of the 160,000 displaced persons who came to the United States from Germany and Austria during the period following the war until 1 September 1950, and 14,532 were still in process. This was a major accomplishment of the small NCWC staff in Germany considering the complexities of the law, red tape involvements of bureaucracy, the general attitude of mistrust toward emigrants and the false reports spread abroad about them.

The problem of displaced persons was never fully resolved. In the American zone of Germany alone there remained a total of 175,197 displaced persons: 97,440 in IRO camps; 9,549 in civilian labor service;

and 68,208 on the German economy. Those in the camps were cared for by the respective German state governments, subsidized by the Federal Republic government, and partly by voluntary agencies of relief and charity for cases of need. The residual group which could not shift for themselves had to be cared for by charity. In the years ahead Catholic Relief Services directed help to *Caritas* which had to share the heavy burden. Consignments of clothing, shoes, food and medicine were especially valuable. Monsignor Franz Mueller, president of *Caritas*, conveyed to American Catholics through Bishop Muench the heartfelt gratitude of *Caritas* directors and workers in West and East Germany. Year after year wherever he went in Germany Muench received touching expressions of gratitude from the displaced persons themselves and the German people for help given to those whom Monsignor Swanstrom aptly characterized as contemporary "pilgrims in the night."

Bishop Muench endeavored especially to place in American dioceses the 448 displaced priests who had not found positions in the German Church. There were, besides the displaced priests in Germany, 100 in Austria and 191 in Italy, the latter mostly studying in Roman seminaries. This was one of his pet projects that he never tired of advancing. Displaced priests who had followed their compatriots in flight to Germany often were unable to continue with them in resettlement in western countries. Muench asked the German ordinaries to accept them into their respective dioceses. "In every case," he stated, "the German bishops promptly expressed their willingness to take these priests, provided only that their knowledge of German was adequate for the care of souls." The bishops were anxious, however, about financing the displaced priests, especially since the diaspora dioceses were flooded with poor expellees who could not financially care for their priests. Muench worked out an arrangement whereby the German bishops and Catholic Relief Services together supplied subsidies to displaced priests.

At the same time Muench labored year after year at a project close to his heart, namely, arranging for displaced priests to be invited to the United States by American bishops and religious superiors. He tirelessly contacted bishops who had a shortage of clergy and encouraged them to take displaced priests. He collected complete dossiers on individual displaced priests, with the careful assistance of Father Bertke, and kept informing American bishops that these exiled priests were, with rare exceptions men of sound character, devoted to their priestly tasks, and self-sacrificing in service to the people entrusted to their care. As a result of these efforts American dioceses accepted over 400 of these Latin Rite displaced priests and seventy-two Oriental Rite priests. Bishops of Canada, Australia and South America also took displaced clergy from Poland, Lithuania, the Ukraine, Hungary, Latvia, Czechoslovakia, Romania and Yugoslavia. Father Bertke's "Report on Displaced Priests," requested by Bishop Muench for the information of the Vatican and the American bishops, is included in Appendix VII as a summary of the violation of the dignity of the human person that emerged from the man-made wreckage of World War II.

When the International Refugee Organization closed its books on 31 January 1952, after fifty-two months of existence, more than 1,000,000 displaced persons had been resettled in at least fifty-two countries. Of that number, some forty-five per cent were assisted by Catholic resettlement agencies in the United States, Canada, Australia, New Zealand and South America. War Relief Services provided new homes and opportunities in the United States for 145,074 Catholic displaced persons and refugees representing thirty-five nationalities. An estimated 25,000 Catholics entered the United States with the help of other participating agencies to bring the total Catholic figure to 170,074 out of 390,744 persons benefited under the Displaced Persons Act.

This record of charity, in which Muench participated for so long and with such intensity, was one of the major gratifying experiences of his tenure in Germany. There had never before been such a planned and supervised mass resettlement of family groups regardless of label. The original injustice suffered by the large majority of these displaced persons had been rectified. It was an example of the application by free nations of the solidarity of human society. As Wycislo wrote:

"These are our new neighbors, our new Americans, our fellow Catholics; men and women whom we have transplanted, whom we must nurture and introduce into the life stream of our land, our institutions, our traditions, and in the process enrich the patrimony of that faith bestowed on us by the generations that preceded them." [8]

During his remaining years in Germany Bishop Muench tried to do whatever he could for the remnant of 160,000 displaced persons, the hard core, who remained in the displaced person camps. He encouraged all involved in the difficult work of trying to help these abandoned refugees. For example, he told his fellow American, Archbishop Gerald P. O'Hara, nuncio to Dublin, on 12 May 1954:

"The charity workers are confronted with a serious difficulty in this:

the more aid that comes to the displaced persons in the camps, the less inclination there is among them to find work. It is the PWA attitude which we became acquainted with in the United States in the bad thirties. On the other hand, one cannot let the people suffer, certainly not the women and children because the men refuse to work or give themselves over to drink or immoral practices."

New housing projects cared for 50,000 of the hard core, but the housing projects were often at a distance from job opportunities. Approximately 42,000 who remained in the barracks did not want to be integrated into the German economy because of racial, nationalistic and political prejudices. Assimilation was out of the question and they were undesirables for emigration due to old age, illness or moral turpitude. *Caritas* opened several homes for displaced persons. The first was dedicated in Munich on 17 May 1953 accommodating 350 persons under the direction of the Sisters of the Most Holy Saviour.

While the problem of displaced persons in Germany attracted worldwide attention in the years following the war, there was another even more serious problem of the refugees or expellees in Germany which received far less attention. The group of expellees, or *Ostfluechtlinge*, comprised some 12,000,000 Germans from the East who, according to the Potsdam Agreement of 2 August 1945, were forcibly resettled in Germany. The expellees or refugees were, undoubtedly, the gravest problem faced by the new Federal Republic and by the Church in Germany after the war. Never before in history had such a large migration taken place and on such short notice. Little did the National Socialists of the Hitler regime imagine that their orders to exterminate millions of people and to hunt others from country to country would bring home a few years later such a cruel punishment to their own nation and to displaced persons of German ancestry from occupied nations.

After the war the formerly German-occupied nations to the East sent back to Germany all German-speaking persons, even if they had lived in the country for generations and had never been German citizens. The expellees and refugees comprised first, those who were resettled as a result of pacts made in 1939 to 1941 with the Soviets and with the Baltic and Balkan states; secondly, those who fled to the West before the invading Soviet armies; thirdly, those who were deported from the territory east of the Oder and Neisse rivers, from Czechoslovakia (Sudetenland), and from Hungary in accordance with the Potsdam Agreement.

In all, as a result of this influx of some 12,000,000 people, there was an increase of eighteen per cent to a total German population of 66,000,000 people. They were suddenly dumped into an area smaller than Montana, Texas or California, or, as Muench always stressed, not much larger than the two Dakotas. The expellees and refugees came from the Balkan countries, Russia, Poland, Silesia, Czechoslovakia, Hungary, Austria, Croatia and Romania. During their migration, according to first-hand reports, between one and two million more expellees disappeared. They were never found again. It was reported that they either died or were deported to eastern Russia. Likewise 2,000,000 refugees stayed in the East zone and 10,000,000 refugees were dispersed throughout the zones of West Germany.

As the expellees poured into a truncated and demolished Germany they had nothing but the clothes on their back, no currency and were suffering from undernourishment. The deportation was anything but "orderly and humane" as the Potsdam Agreement provided. Bombed-out cities could provide no shelter for them, except in the ruins or in ill ventilated bunkers. No plans had been made for the resettlement of these expellees. They were crowded into homes everywhere, including rectories and bishops' houses. They moved into abandoned camps, barracks, air raid bunkers, on abandoned river barges, in unused factories, warehouses and store rooms, in huts and hovels which they constructed out of materials cast about in the ruins. The living conditions among the refugees and expellees was not only bad, but as Bishop Muench repeatedly pleaded, unworthy of creatures made after the image of God. The situation was aggravated by the fact that Germany's territory was one-fourth smaller than it was prior to 1939. The richest agricultural, mineral and timber resources of the eastern hinterland had been cut off and now belonged to nations behind the Iron Curtain.

Through air raids during the war about 5,000,000 of 18,000,000 dwellings in Germany had been destroyed or damaged so badly that they were not habitable. The occupation powers forced the expellees and refugees to be quartered for the most part in country areas. Up to four families lived in the same house, whole families in one room, young and old, married and unmarried. The dangers to morality and the stresses on harmony and peace in these confiscated rural homes were apparent and immediate. There were one-third more women than men among the expellees and older age groups outnumbered younger persons. As a result of this forced, rushed deportation and no planning, industrial workers and miners were allocated to farming areas while farmers were sent to industrial areas. The first place available was allocated, especially in the winter months, to the incoming millions. The arrival of these new war victims added another complex dimension to Germany's problems. The highly industrialized areas of the western section of West Germany could not produce enough food for this added population. The agrarian lands of West and East Germany were overrun with new German nationals who now had political rights with all the resulting implications of their votes for the struggling new nation. Bavaria, for example, traditionally agricultural, had increased its population by twenty-seven per cent, and Schleswig-Holstein by sixty-six per cent.

A new class in the population of West and East Germany was created by this mass migration. From an economic point of view the expellees were proletarians; but by origin and psychologically they were aristocrats, intellectuals, businessmen and farmers. Now spread across the German countryside, these uprooted people with their experiences, fears, hatreds, resentments and passionate hopes for a sudden solution of their hopeless situation, soon came into conflict with the relatively stable population of the towns and villages of the West. The original inhabitants, shocked survivors of the war and bombardment, were not enthusiastic about receiving these *Neubuergere* into their homes in a time of hunger and cold. Muench informed Pius XII that, although there were faults on both sides, there was more to say in favor of the impoverished refugees and expellees.

Conditions in the countryside and villages became especially difficult. The traditional customs and ways of country life were now threatened anew by a growing black market. Poor and idle townfolk, with different, often liberal and non-Christian ideals, lived in the same houses with the old German peasantry. They had no work and were unwilling to labor in the fields as tenants. Their resentment and irritation threatened the structures of the country folk in such areas as Schleswig-Holstein where the country villages grew by 120 to 150%.

Archbishop Conrad Groeber of Freiburg im Breisgau expressed his strong resentment to Bishop Muench on 5 February 1947 at these developments, as well as his own consistently reactionary nationalism. He wrote:

"I have just now received a report concerning the refugees in Nordbaden from Professor Kuenzig who was sent by us to investigate. The description of distress has filled me with deep sorrow. I am of the opinion that there is only one policy which would correspond to justice, and that is a policy of return. Should the refugees remain with us it will result in a constant source of danger. For these people will never forget their home country and the injustice done them.

"I have learned through statistics that there are only twenty-three million inhabitants in Poland while the rest of Germany still in existence has to make room for seventy million human beings. Furthermore, according to the so-called peace policy, the German people are being deprived of all possibilities of normal development. All public statements made to the contrary, the fact remains that the intention is to destroy us. We constitute a danger for other nations solely by the fact that we managed to recover even before Hitler assumed control. His war actually was only a long awaited occasion to break down the German people. And now they expect us to become the slaves of others for an indefinitely long time.

"No wonder that nationalism is again increasing, and as a result, the thought of revenge is increasing. It is really strange that the German people who were overwhelmingly against Hitler should now do penance for Hitler and his gang. Hitler lied to us and the Allies have proved, as far as lies are concerned, that they have the same virtuosity. Radios screamed into our ears that the Allies came as saviors of the German people. And now we have the results. America took from us our patents and France took from us what was not solidly nailed to the ground. The mood of the German people, unfortunately, becomes more bitter by the month, so much the more since the so-called democracy, in regard to religion and culture, is developing into an excellent imitation of the Hitler regime.

"You will say, why does the Freiburg archbishop write this to me? I answer, because the Holy See should remind the whole world that a peace has to be arrived at that is just and according to the will of Christ. As in the field of charity we should not allow ourselves to be outdone by the Protestants, as has already happened, so much the less should we be outdone in approaches to true peace. Instead of taking care to control the inclination for war in the German people, our former enemies try their best to foster it in as short a time as possible."

Bishop Muench did not respond to this letter. It all too well summarized the attitude of those German Catholics who had opposed Hitler only after he attacked the Church, but who had pursued and continued to pursue a nationalistic defense of their homeland in war and peace. Muench was conscious of the growing questioning of the position of the Church in Germany as represented by such older leaders as Groeber of Freiburg. He knew that more and more such a stance would be challenged on moral grounds, on the basis of the compliance of the established Church with Hitler's nationalistic adventures, on the basis of a lack of defense and support for the individual's conscience and the needs of all suffering men in the world. He preferred to support those in the German Church who were looking toward a new future and who were, with penitence and courage, building an open awareness of the needs of all God's suffering servants.

Nor was Groeber's position typical of the majority of Germany's Catholic leaders and laity whom the regent encountered. Before the end of 1945 the German bishops had met in conference and established a special refugee bureau in Frankfurt, *Die Kirchliche Hilfsstelle*, to meet the immediate needs of the 12,000,000 expellees and refugees of whom roughly half were Catholic. Expellee priests were inducted into pastoral service for their people, emergency space was found for religious services, and liturgical articles for divine worship were provided. The situation was chaotic and the German bishops ordered a special annual collection in their dioceses under the slogan: "Carry One Another's Burdens." *Caritas* was charged with supplying elementary aid such as food, clothing and household goods to the unfortunate expellees. Self-help projects were started in the camps which included small industries in glassware, toys, leather goods, ceramics and wood work. Plans for housing projects were formed.

The *Saint Bonifatius Verein*, similar in purpose and activity to the American Catholic Church Extension Society, immediately swung into action and exerted more leadership and initiative than any other Catholic group throughout the whole period. The Saint Boniface Society expanded its program to include aid to refugees and expellees. Through its affiliated groups — the Catholic Diaspora Aid for Children, the Guardian Angel Society, the Society for University Students, the League of Academic Groups of Students and Professors — a mass attack on the problems of refugees was launched with typical German thoroughness. It was often stated during these years that no other Church in a European country could have faced and solved a problem of the magnitude of the refugees in the German diaspora. In addition to rebuilding churches destroyed and damaged by the war, there was a new need for over 2,000 churches for expellees. Mass was offered in schools, inns, meeting halls and homes in some 3,700 communities where Mass had not been celebrated since the Reformation. The German Protestants in the diaspora generously opened their churches to Catholic expellees and refugees. Equipment for liturgical services, bicycles for refugee priests, furniture for their rooms, religious and devotional materials were all collected within Germany from parishes that were spared in the bombings. Cardinal Frings of Cologne, chairman of the German Bishops' Conference, was the first to ask for such a collection from his archdiocese despite the heavy losses to church properties in that industrial area.

The Saint Boniface Society also inaugurated an extensive program of training parish workers and catechists in short and long courses at various society centers during different periods throughout the year. Some became paid full-time helpers, but the majority were voluntary lay workers. Catechetical centers and child welfare institutions, which the Saint Boniface Society had been supporting for sixty years, now became active centers of daily service.

Cardinal Frings as chairman of the Fulda Conference of German Bishops was at first the protector of the refugees. Pope Pius XII, after being informed by Bishop Muench and the Fulda Conference of Bishops of the gravity of the situation, appointed Bishop Maximilian Kaller, exiled from the Diocese of Ermland, as protector of the expellees. But Bishop Kaller died within a year on 7 July 1947 due to his arduous labors. The newly consecrated Bishop of Limburg, Ferdinand Dirichs, was appointed as Kaller's successor, but he died in an automobile accident on 27 December 1948. Muench was particularly grieved at this loss since he was a friend of Dirichs and often visited him at Limburg an der Lahn, which, close to Kronberg, was his favorite cathedral and diocesan center. At the Fulda Conference of 1949 Dr. Franz Hartz of the Prelature of Schneidemuehl was designated as Dirichs' successor. Bishops Julius Doepfner of Berlin and Heinrich M. Janssen of Hildesheim later served as directors of this important apostolate.

The German bishops, Muench observed, devoted special care to the expellees in their respective dioceses. Expellee priests, although not incardinated, received the same treatment as diocesan priests. In practically all dioceses a priest director was appointed for expellees. This director was charged with keeping the bishop informed of the needs of the expellees, protecting their interests against heartless people, finding job opportunities for them, and providing comfort and help for those who were unemployable, sick or aged. Everyone realized that quick solutions were impossible since the refugee problem baffled not only the Germans but the occupying powers. The German bishops discussed the refugee problem not only at each annual Fulda Conference but also in special regional conferences each spring and fall. Muench kept the Vatican informed about the extremely dark picture, and Pius XII wrote Archbishop McNicholas, board chairman of the NCWC on 24 December 1948:

"A true affection for our fellowmen as well as the law of nature itself urges us to find a way of unimpeded emigration for these unhappy people. The Creator of the universe has provided all his good gifts primarily for the good of all. Consequently the sovereignty of individual states, however much this is to be respected, ought not to be carried so far that free access to the earth's bounty, which is adequate everywhere to support multitudes of human beings, should be denied to needy but worthy persons who have been born elsewhere. Reasons for this are altogether insufficient and unjust, especially when such free access will not be detrimental to the public welfare properly weighed and considered."

Pope Pius sent tons of foodstuffs, clothing and medicine as well as several carloads of paper to the German bishops for religious literature and prayer books. Papal charities were now directed mainly to the poor, impoverished refugees as the German people began their remarkable economic recovery. Cardinal Frings sent a letter to John J. McCloy, United States high commissioner in Germany, recommending emigration of skilled refugees to underdeveloped countries, and Muench endorsed Frings' recommendation with a covering letter.[9]

The refugee problem continued to grow to such dimensions that the United States Congress sent several delegations to Germany to survey the facts and to offer recommendations for remedial measures. McCloy, as high commissioner, directed special attention to the problem because to a large extent the refugees and expellees were retarding the economic recovery of Germany, and provided radical and nationalistic agitators with explosive materials. The homeless expellees, in their desperate situation, became an easy prey to unscrupulous politicians in the first years, and they played an important role in national elections as they were courted by political adventurers.

With all this in view, Cardinal Frings appointed a special commission composed of laity and clergy, Germans and Americans, to study the problem. James J. Norris, head of the NCWC mission in Germany, was a member of the commission. The American bishops, in response to the Pope's request for aid, sent $300,000 from the American Catholic people to Pius XII for the building of small churches and chapels to serve expellees and refugees in the diaspora. No other national hierarchy assisted the refugees in such an organized way. It was a unique overture of charity in response to distress. Archbishop Lorenz Jaeger of Paderborn, president of the *Saint Bonifatius Verein*, planned for 150 churches and chapels to be built with these funds. The expellees donated labor for the new buildings. They were simple, functional, creative in contemporary design and constructed in areas where no Catholic churches had been built since the Reformation. In September of 1949 Bishop Muench laid the cornerstone for one of these small churches at Bordesholm in Schleswig-Holstein, and Archbishop Berning of Osnabrueck in his sermon on the occasion said that Muench's presence was symbolic of the unparalleled generosity of the American people.

Following the desire of the Holy See, Bishop Muench directed the charities of the Vatican mission at Kronberg to the refugees and expellees. In particular he and the staff tried to help priests, sisters, lay catechists and parish welfare workers in the missionary diaspora areas of Germany. Through good contacts it was possible to get food parcels, clothing, suit materials and Sunday missals into Berlin and the Russian zone, even throughout the Berlin blockade of 1948–49. This was achieved by sending sealed trucks from *Caritas* — Copenhagen over Luebeck to Berlin. The Russians, to everyone's surprise and gratitude, allowed these trucks to pass without hindrance. In the period of a year, from October, 1948, to October, 1949, relief supplies such as food, clothing and shoes valued at $71,416.25 was distributed from Kronberg to refugees. During the same period over $100,000 in Mass stipends was directed to expellee priests, especially in the Russian zone, in the form of *Deutsche Mark*, food parcels, suit and cassock material, motorcycles and food in bulk. Monsignor John Zinke, director of Catholic charities for the Soviet zone, was Muench's invaluable contact in Berlin for this extensive undertaking. Muench aimed each year during his tenure in Germany at collecting $100,000 in Mass stipends from friends and helpers in the United States for these refugee priests. Each year he was overwhelmed at the response that he received and which enabled him to meet these quotas. An exact and conscientious accounting of the Mass stipends was kept in both Kronberg and Fargo, money was banked in New York, and distribution of goods and marks was always made through existing charity organizations at work on the scene.[10]

A quite different evaluation of the response of Muench and the German bishops to the needs of expellees and refugees was given by Monsignor Dr. Gerhard Fittkau, professor of theology, Essen. Fittkau had been active in the work of the *Saint Bonifatius Verein* during the years following the war and had traveled, with an introduction and recommendation from Bishop Muench, throughout the United States soliciting funds for work among the German expellees and refugees. He stated:

"Bishop Muench didn't understand the problem. Nor did the German bishops. They just wanted at that time to keep the expellees at a distance. Theoderick Kampmann, theologian from Munich, even wrote that the refugees had no rights; it was a political problem. But it was really a question of international justice.

"Linus Kather, co-founder of the CDU and its second vice-president, did most to help the refugees and to save them. But he left the party in disgust. He always insisted the refugee problem was one of national and international justice. No matter what was left of Germany — one-fourth of the entire nation — the expellees needed more than charity according to the norms of justice. The expellee farmers were mostly forced to pay more rent to the German farmers for living quarters than the farmers paid before in taxes to the state for their entire farms. The question was one of principle, an equalization of burdens. It was not a question only of having cheap labor, but one of compensation from the government so the expellee could hope to have his own land. The expellees fought in the CDU for a just compensation. Cardinal Frings even said at first that this was Communism. We said: 'No, you are Communists by not giving a just compensation.' In spite of themselves and of their shortsightedness, the CDU did grant compensation to the expellees and won them for the party. Otherwise they would have gone elsewhere. As soon as the new currency was established, freedom of movement granted, and help in building houses begun, the ten million workers that expellees supplied were the backbone of the German revival. And the expellee priests saved these people for democracy and convinced them of the expiation that was necessary.

"Muench had a poor start. He co-operated with the regular German Catholic organizations. The director in charge of *Caritas* in Frankfurt gave gift packages only to *Caritas* people who were not the ones in the greatest need.

"The German bishops saw the appointment of Bishop Maximilian Kaller [of Ermland] by the Pope as an infringement on their jurisdiction. Bishop Kaller had been driven out by the Gestapo and dumped in Halle in the Soviet zone. With a piece of cardboard he tried while there to start a tracing service for expellee priests. He found forty-five of 400 priests in the first year. The priest was the focal point and he then helped to find people. Kaller asked for a central service but it was not allowed. He could only work locally. He tried to get scattered families back together. In camps in Denmark, for example, there were 250,000 expellees from the eastern provinces, mostly women and children. They were there sometimes as long as three years since the military was processed first and civilians were left behind. This is why Bishop Kaller worked at the first job of getting human rights restored. Archbishop Berning's [Osnabrueck] man was Monsignor Albert Buettner [*Katholisches Auslandssekretariat*, Beuel/Bonn] who was absolutely unacceptable to us. He was nationalistic and placed questionable characters in the seminary for expellees at Koenigstein. Buettner was a classmate of Zeiger who advised Muench. Buettner didn't like Kaller's job. Kaller went to Frankfurt and set up an office for the position given him by papal decree. It was in a Frankfurt apartment rather than at Koenigstein. Muench was told that Kaller was a papal delegate in competition with himself and Muench was not friendly. Muench asked Kaller in the parlor at Kronberg what he wanted. Bishop Kaller had a bad reaction to this treatment when he wanted to cooperate with Muench. Kaller died in 1947 from the over-all conditions. He was never recognized. I told Cardinal Frings that if Kaller did not get some money I would report him to the Pope. The first to give money, 10,000 marks, was Groeber [Freiburg], Frings gave 10,000 marks, and the *Ludwig Missionsverein* gave one-fourth of the money for the Koenigstein seminary."[11]

Monsignor Fittkau then explained what he considered to be the condition among the expellee and refugee priests:

"There were 2,500 expellee priests in Germany; 1,000 died or were deported to prison. These priests had no guidance and had to look for a place to put their heads. Most German bishops saw them as part of a transitory situation. They were granted no rights, no incardination. Accordingly, many of the old canons, monsignors and archpriests had to be satisfied with a room in a rectory, take their knapsack and go out and teach catechism to the expellees.

"The enormous expulsion of six million Catholic people made a great transformation in the pastoral scene of Germany. Four of the six million expellees were dumped by the occupying governments into rural areas already crowded with evacuees from bombed-out cities. So the refugees were really a second flow. The four million dumped in the diaspora, the rural areas where no Catholics had lived since the Reformation, found themselves in rural parishes with no church but where there were farm houses in which they could find a room. There was no freedom of movement for anyone who was not a citizen in 1939, and a work permit was also required.

"It was very difficult to care for these people pastorally. The expellees went especially into Archbishop Berning's diocese of Osnabrueck; there were 250,000 in Schleswig-Holstein alone. The absence of elementary decency and charity, the atomization of the Mystical Body was so complete, that no one realized how much National Socialism had affected everyone. When I saw Berning he said: 'Are you usable?' I had just come back from three years in Siberia; there were seventeen patches on my pants and I had no shoes. I had to go to public welfare for shoes. Berning said: 'When you are functionable, come to me. I have sixty priests coming in on me.' I said: 'Yes, but there are a million people to care for.' 'Yes,' he replied, 'and the priests bring their mothers with them in a wagon.'

"The German bishops were unwilling to give any special pastoral attention to the expellees. Archbishop Groeber in Freiburg said to me: 'Here come the Poles and Prussians to spoil our good manners.' I said: 'I'm very inclined to dress as you please if you dress me up. My grey suit came from a non-Catholic dentist. I have nothing so far from Catholics.' He feared us as Prussians.

"Expellee priests had to go wherever they could. The German dioceses, scarred and bombed as they were, didn't want them. When four of us came to Berlin from Siberia, the vicar general of Berlin said to us: 'We have at least fifty of such junk as you to get rid of.' So our first efforts were directed toward self-help and organization to keep the expellees and refugees from radicalism of either the right or left; to convince the Church of the great potential among the expellees for a positive contribution. Germany could only be restored by work. The expellees and refugees needed home industries in which they could use their skills. The Sudeten Germans from Czechoslovakia were eighty per cent industrial and urban. The 2,500 priests who had gone through ordeals with great heroism and remained with their parishioners now were excardinated by Czech and Polish bishops. They were not wanted at home and not wanted in Germany. In time the German bishops and Muench came around to realize the whole picture and a major achievement of incorporating the expellees was achieved. But Muench did not once help me nor the *Saint Bonifatius Verein*. Muench had the trauma of proving himself a German as a second generation German-American. Zeiger and Buettner influenced him." [12]

Fittkau's reactions evidence the deep-seated feelings that were aroused between refugees who poured into Germany and the beleaguered German people themselves. Whatever was done was never enough. The problems created by an influx of 12,000,000 expellees would have more than taxed the most stable and wealthy of nations. Fittkau was correct in insisting that the refugee problem had to be resolved on a basis of justice and not only of charity. The Federal Republic and the *Laender* governments utilized budget funds and passed the General Law of Equalization of Burdens to expend 25.8 billion marks by 1952 for relief of expellees. Governmental efforts were pointed toward restoring the faith of the refugees in political freedom, and to accord them a social status under which they would no longer consider themselves as recipients of charity but could earn their own livelihood.

This herculean task of the incorporation of the refugees was undertaken with vigor by the Federal Republic. The federal chancellor, Dr. Adenauer, and President Eisenhower agreed in the spring of 1953 that an international obligation existed toward Germany on account of the obligation borne in caring for refugees. However, emigration did not solve the problem. For example, in 1952 about 80,000 Germans emigrated of whom half were refugees. But in the same year more than 200,000 new refugees escaped from the Soviet zone of occupation. Social expenditures for expellees in the form of pensions and social benefits could be met only by a constant and vigorous increase in economic activity. The Federal Republic strove, and with considerable success, for a productive form of support rather than pure welfare. The refugees found employment in agriculture and industry through filling the gaps left in the West German economy by millions who had died and other millions who were still prisoners.

The new census of 13 September 1950 revealed that of the 3.1 million employable persons among the 7.9 million expellees in West Germany, 2.6 million were already employed. Eighty-five per cent were employed and fifteen per cent, or half a million persons, were unemployed. This remarkable achievement was dampened by the fact that the percentage of unemployed among the expellees was twice as high as among the indigenous population. Moreover, many of the refugees could not find employment in keeping with their abilities. Average wages for expellees, tax paid, amounted to 39 marks per head compared to 180 marks for the indigenous population. Only 40,000 of the 300,000 expellee farmers had acquired their own land and the skills of farmers from Eastern Germany in cattle breeding and plant cultivation were not fully utilized. An expellees' bank was established which granted credits at low rates of interest and supervised the use and repayment of loans. Due to this measure some 7,000 small and medium industrial enterprises, 59,000 crafts shops, and 50,000 trade and transport businesses were established for and by refugees. Firms formerly located in the areas beyond the Iron Curtain were re-established in the Federal Republic, and such industries as glass articles, toys, artificial jewelry and musical instruments made a promising new start in West Germany.

Long-range productive use of the expellees necessitated their moving from the countryside of Schleswig-Holstein, Lower Saxony and Bavaria to the industrial cities. The effort to build new houses for the expellees became the major thrust of the entire period. According to the statistics of the census of September, 1950, some 2.6 million refugee families needed houses of whom not even one-fourth had found homes by that time. During the period 1949 to 1952 approximately 350,000 dwellings for expellees were built while some 500,000 old dwelling places were allocated to them. Another 900,000 dwellings were needed and gradually throughout the 1950's this need was met. Because there were not heavy defense expenditures, housing construction advanced at a rapid rate. Germans were convinced that the construction of housing was just as important an asset in the struggle for preserving a free and democratic Germany and Europe as a military defense contribution would be.

The social and religious assimilation of the expellees was also gradually faced by German Christians as not only a matter of almsgiving but of seeing that justice was realized. The reality of the diaspora was upon them. Three-quarters of the Catholic refugees, for example, were directed into districts that had formerly been ninety per cent Protestant. Since six million Catholic expellees had arrived in the country, every fifth Catholic in Germany was a refugee. As an illustration of the situation, the diocese of Meissen in Saxony had 209,000 Catholics before the war; the refugees brought that total to 725,000, an increase of two hundred fifty per cent. But the number of priests increased by only 303 because this half a million Catholics brought only 105 priests with them of whom sixty-three were fully active in pastoral work, the others being ill or too old to work. The Commissariat of Magdeburg, a part of the Archdiocese of Paderborn in the Russian zone, had 150,000 Catholics and after the migration included 700,000. Fulda and Hildesheim were in the same situation. Osnabrueck increased in Catholic population from 467,908 to 1,041,000. In Schleswig-Holstein where there were formerly only 3.5% Catholics, between two and three hundred thousand Catholic refugees from Silesia arrived. One parish with 300 parishioners before the war now had to care for 11,000 souls. In Mecklenburg, in the Russian zone, there were 400,000 Catholics among 900,000 refugees. Pomerania, Brandenburg, Thuringia and central Germany revealed the same picture of expellees from Silesia, Bohemia and Moravia forced out of their safe surroundings and set down with no pastoral assistance as beggars in strange surroundings.

The *Saint Bonifatius Verein* reported that there were eight million Catholics living in the diaspora, 3,631,855 more than formerly. Only 1,232 priests came with these more than three and a half million people. Priests reported that they were not able to offer Mass, administer the sacraments and conduct church funerals as needed; home visits and confessions were impossible. The secretary general of the *Bonifatius Verein* reported he visited villages where formerly thirty Catholics lived and where there were now 2,000. He met children of fourteen years who had not received their first communion and children of three years who had not been baptized. The most faithful parishioners of several Protestant pastors in the region were Catholic Silesian refugees who came regularly to the Lord's Supper. The dean of Magdeburg said: "I need priests now; in five years I shall have no Catholics left."

Lay people tried to help the situation by visiting the most deserted districts on Sunday to assemble the Catholics and to read the Gospel. Parochial schools were abolished in the Soviet zone and religious instruction was next to impossible. Instruction in Marxism, the Russian language and state youth organizations were required in primary schools. The bishops of the Western zones were not allowed to visit the Soviet zone. Catholic publications were forbidden because of an alleged lack of paper. A situation exactly similar to the Nazi period was rapidly developing for the Church in the Soviet zone.

As one means to meet the growing antireligious thrust of Soviet zone educational and cultural policies, Bishop Muench strongly supported a unique idea advanced by Archbishop Josef Otto Kolb of Bamberg. With the joint endorsement of Lutheran Bishop Hans Meissner of Augsburg, Kolb planned a Christian and ecumenical radio station in Bamberg to be called *Christlicher Sender*. Kolb worked from 1946 to 1948 to obtain permission to establish a Catholic and Protestant voice which would restore the Christian point of view and be a stronghold against Communist infiltration from the East. Kolb wrote General Clay on 24 March 1948:

"By broadcasting Christian ideals, drawing from the cultural resources of the occident, we will be able to present our listeners with programs of the highest entertainment and educational value. By so doing we hope to be a stronghold of democratic ideals, of human rights and world peace. American statesmen often have emphasized the need of religious leadership to bring about the good will and pacification of nations.

"I beg you to bestow this gift to both Christian confessions. I assure you by making possible this broadcasting station you will set up to yourself the greatest and most permanent monument of eternal thanks in the hearts of millions of the best German citizens."

Muench heartily endorsed the project to Clay on 31 March 1948 and told him democratic interests would be well served by such a Catholic and Protestant broadcasting station. At first American Military was interested in matching the joint donations of German Catholics and Protestants to establish the station. But the project never developed because technical difficulties, due to overcrowding of the radio frequencies, prevented any further allocation of licenses. Kolb was informed that the project, which was in complete agreement with American policy to encourage free competition in the field of public information, had to await technical developments such as frequency modulation which would increase the number of available wave lengths. Because of the delay this imaginative and important project never materialized.

In the west the diaspora situation was not as critical as in the east, but the purely Catholic districts had disappeared. As Zeiger had said at the Mainz *Katholikentag*, all Germany was a diaspora. Everywhere Catholics and Protestants were living together. The social revolution in the Catholic villages had dissolved their former religious solidarity. In a Bavarian district of 120 communities where formerly 600 Protestants resided, 20,000 Protestant refugees now were living. During 1947 in Munich, the capital of Catholic Bavaria, for every marriage in which both parties were Catholic there were no fewer than 51.14 mixed marriages. A questionnaire in one of Munich's secondary schools for boys revealed that only ten per cent of the pupils received the Eucharist and twenty per cent attended Mass. Of the patients at a Munich women's clinic, fifty per cent had not gone to confession in over six years.

Catholic laymen began to raise their voices in protest against the slow pace of assimilation of the refugees and recognition of existing spiritual problems on the part of the German hierarchy and clergy. Dr. Karl Josef Hahn, in a series of lectures during the summer of 1949 at the University of Fribourg, Switzerland, stated:

"In the western districts of Germany, life seems more normal. But when one has an opportunity to look behind the somber screen of the damaged towns, to come into more permanent contact with the clergy, the population, the individuals, one has the impression that these long years of National Socialist propaganda and the demoralization of war, hunger and bad housing, have brought down the general moral level. The percentage of active Christians is much lower than before the war, especially in the cities. The continuous education of the people in a Christian spirit has been interrupted for too long a time." [13]

Otto B. Roegele, editor of the independent Catholic *Rheinischer Merkur*, spoke up sharply against what he considered the institutional inertia of conventional Christianity before the challenge presented by the refugees and expellees. The Church in Germany needed a "now" expression of a Christianity committed to values of universal import such as justice, human dignity, community and charity toward the refugees. Roegele called for an ability to witness.[14] He recommended strategies for breaking the cycles of institutional servitude which held back what he considered a dedication to human renewal:

"Germany has become a mission country, and that in a double sense, territorially and spiritually. The apostacies from 1933 to 1945 have shown Christians to be in a minority. Instead of the propertied class of previous times there remains an army of millions of diaspora Catholics who were unprepared for diaspora conditions and whose unhappy material, personal and spiritual state makes normal forms of orderly apostolic work quite impossible.

"Catholicism in Germany has lost its traditional social fiber, its heritage of interior and exterior habits. Either directly or indirectly its interconnection with the distress of the nation as a whole is clearly marked. German Catholicism lives under a threat because the lack of priests is steadily increasing and the priests are rapidly becoming old; because the Orders are receiving fewer novices (although this is by no means true of the contemplative orders), and because too few of the laity are both willing and able to help. The Church is suffering from the general crisis of the times, from the perpetual shifting of German affairs, and from the arbitrary changes in zonal and provincial boundaries. In the Russian zone it faces even severer hardships because there the authorities hate religion. It suffers from uncertainty and anxiety for the future, but it suffers most of all because its members are so weak, so many of its members are devoid of imagination and because it throws off a continuous smokescreen of illusion so as not to have to face up to realities. The bourgeoisie, from whose ranks most of the faithful come, has changed into a proletariat; it is exhausted, disoriented, and unable to cope with its responsibilities; it is devoid of both political vitality, fertile ideas and trustworthy leaders. The working classes to a depressingly large extent hold aloof from the Church. Throughout Germany a type of conventional Marxism influences quite a large proportion of the people. A few intellectuals have undergone genuine conversions and found their way back into the Church which they have frequently infused with some of their own energies; but most intellectuals still adhere to liberalist doctrines (such as the leading scholars have abandoned) and are in practice banal materialists. The country folk display a terrifying lack of solid religion and practical Christianity. Taken in conjunction with their refugee neighbors, these country folk present the most crying spiritual problem of the day. According to Spengler, when the peasant's cottage stands outside world history, then it gets flattened out by world history. Nor has anyone given an answer to the question of the returning soldier who has been unsettled and disillusioned by the war. The epidemic of divorces, the marriages of returning soldiers, mixed marriages, birth control among the newly married, all represent tasks which have yet to be mastered.

"It must be confessed with shame that official German Catholicism's reaction to these trials has been to a large extent pathological. Instead of trying to answer the extraordinary demands of the territorial diaspora by an exchange of priests and by other means which would have equalized the strain in different parts of the Church, the dioceses have hermetically sealed themselves up. Nothing more promising than a sort of restricted guerilla tactic has been evolved in order to meet the unbelievers, when what was needed was generous and ambitious strategy."[15]

Roegele made several concrete suggestions for model new communities which would be genuinely involved doers of the word. Instead of seeing the widespread destruction of seminaries and theological colleges as an opportunity for educating priests in a new way that would open them to the world's needs, too often efforts had been directed towards rebuilding a ghetto. The refugee priests should have been welcomed into the circle of diocesan religious life, but they had been generally treated as strangers and interlopers who were not wanted. Instead of taking to heart their experiences under a totalitarian state and erecting institutions and organizations as remote as possible from direct state interference, in general the German Catholics had clamored even louder for those tax privileges which depend upon the benevolence of the secular state. The majorities of the Christian parties were accustomed to advancing claims dating from as distant a time as 150 years to squeeze from a bankrupt state the interest which had collected in the meantime. Instead of encouraging lay movements, both outside and within Catholic Action, in order to compensate for a lack of priests, most of the attempts at independent lay action were being treated, Roegele claimed, with the utmost caution by the hierarchy and clergy. The bishops and priests had never missed an opportunity to demonstrate their authority, even upon issues where their authority did not apply. Instead of learning from experience under a totalitarian state and recognizing the family as the ultimate and most secure stronghold of belief, morality and Christian education; instead of invoking its massive collective energy to fulfill the task God had laid upon the Church; instead of taking advantage of the unique opportunity now that German Catholics were members of a missionary Church, every effort had been made, according to this critic, to restore the *status quo* without considering that what had formerly produced some good results could be more harmful in a society which in the meantime had been turned inside out.

The profoundest hopes of German Catholicism, according to Roegele, centered upon Christ who had brought them to their time of trial. Their hopes were also founded upon their fellow-Catholics in foreign countries who had already answered their appeals in a most encouraging and practical manner either directly or through the Pope's requests. Now German Catholics hoped they could share with their fellow-Catholics internationally the lessons they had learned under totalitarianism, could share their sacrifices, as well as their seeking for mutual understanding with Christians who had grasped what had been happening on both sides of the fence.[16]

Monsignor Fittkau and Dr. Roegele held similar views that diaspora conditions and the assimilation of the refugees supplied the testing ground of German Catholicism. Fittkau stated that the new people of the diaspora contributed a strength and dimension to German Catholicism which it had not previously evidenced. Several of the progressive developments in German Catholicism following the war arose from this milieu. The inspiration came from the people themselves and not from chancery offices. Liturgical celebrations, by necessity, were open and developing; 2,000 new churches were built in former Protestant ghettos of Germany. There was not a small diaspora community that did not become acquainted with Catholics for the first time. Over 7,000 Protestant churches were used for Catholic services, and separated Christians who had lived back to back for centuries were now at least face to face for the first time. The Adam Moehler Institute in Paderborn, and the ecumenical encounter that developed in that important center was advanced by the forced mixture of separated Christians in that archdiocese. The new German catechism of 1955 developed from work in the Soviet zone. The joint Protestant and Catholic participation in the political action of the CDU was a first since the Reformation.[17]

Bishop Muench, in his position as regent of the apostolic nunciature, was conscious of these variegated patterns of deeply felt commitment that were developing in Germany. He was ever alert to prophetic voices asking for social change and rejoiced in any evidence of a sense of compassion for other human beings. But he was the representative of the official Catholic Church in Germany and ever held to his deep conviction of the viability of the Church, human and sinful as it was in every place and time. Moreover, he had to live with and respect the contributions of dedicated churchmen who did not agree with and did not understand the dissent from "churchianity" that was developing in the postwar world.[18]

Groeber mentioned the expellee and refugee seminary at Koenigstein in his letter. This project was of paramount importance for the German diaspora and Bishop Muench had supported it enthusiastically from its inception. Cardinal Frings of Cologne, Archbishop Jaeger of Paderborn, Bishop Berning of Osnabrueck, Bishop Wendel of Speyer and Bishop

Kaller for refugees met at Koenigstein on 4 February 1947 to discuss starting a special missionary seminary for expellees. Muench entertained them afterwards at Kronberg which was only three miles away. Monsignor Albert Buettner, director of the *Auslandssekretariat*, Beuel/Bonn, was an early moving force behind this unique project to train priests for the diaspora from among refugee students and by refugee professors. Soon after his arrival in Germany, Muench visited Buettner in his one-room office and residence in Frankfurt. Muench made a deep impression on Buettner because he came inconspicuously dressed in a simple black suit without a sign of rank. Germans were not accustomed to such simplicity from persons in authority. Buettner had directed the work of the secretariate for Catholics in foreign countries from Berlin before and during the war. Muench offered any support possible for refugees. Muench and Buettner talked about the need to help refugee priests and students of theology because it was so difficult for them to find a place in the seminaries of Germany which were either in part destroyed, in part occupied by occupation forces, or in part still housing army hospitals. The danger was that expellee students of theology who had an intention to continue their study of theology or whose studies had been interrupted would drift away to some other field of work. They decided that a new seminary should be established as soon as possible which would exclusively serve expellees and refugees.[19]

This Saint Albertus Magnus Seminary at Koenigstein im Taunus near Frankfurt remained a special interest and concern of Muench throughout his German years. He supported it in every way possible and watched its growth with much satisfaction. By 1952 there were 260 students in the minor and 150 in the major seminary with forty expellees to be ordained that year for work in the refugee diaspora. In 1953 Koenigstein was named a pontifical seminary.

No one in Germany or the United States was greatly surprised to learn that Pius XII on 28 October 1950 conferred the personal title of archbishop upon Muench in recognition of his labors in Germany. Muench had gone to Rome for the proclamation of the doctrine of the Assumption during the Holy Year. A Holy Year pilgrimage of old friends from Fargo had landed in Frankfurt on October 10 composed of Monsignor Lucian J. Arrell, pastor of the Fargo cathedral, Father Frank J. Nestor, pastor of Saint Anthony parish, Fargo, and twenty lay people from the diocese. After a visit at Kronberg the group went on to Rome, and Muench and Smith followed by train from Frankfurt on October 13. The Fargo pilgrims attended the papal Mass in Saint Peter's Basilica and when Muench had his interview with Pius XII some days later the Pope told him he had seen him on that occasion. When Muench expressed surprise that Pius had noticed him in the great throng, Pius replied: "But, why not? I know you very well." Pius went on to say that Muench had been named an archbishop because of his labors under most difficult circumstances. Montini likewise expressed satisfaction with his work. Muench was grateful for this further recognition and looked upon the title as symbolic of the major contribution of all who had been involved in the reconstruction effort in Germany. The eighteen days spent in Rome were most enjoyable for Muench and Smith, particularly since the latter had experienced a set-back in health on September 22, a warning of an injured heart condition. Muench was most considerate of Smith and tried to help him relax in Rome. He was worried about his secretary's health and repeatedly stated to Bishop Dworschak that he did not know what he would do if he did not have his beloved secretary at his side.

Letters and congratulations poured in upon the new archbishop from friends, admirers and co-workers. Throughout these letters the refrain was repeated that the title of archbishop was just an indication of what was to come when Germany gained sovereignty as a nation. Pius XII, by naming Muench an archbishop, clearly indicated that he intended to have him remain in Germany. During their conversation on 30 November 1950, the day before the public announcement of Muench's personal rank as archbishop, the Pope had told him that as soon as the German Federal Republic would regain its diplomatic status in international relations he should proceed at once to present credentials of the Holy See to the German government. In this way continuity would be preserved for the papal nuncio as dean of the diplomatic corps.

Pope Pius moved in this appointment clearly and definitely on his own. There had been much speculation among papal diplomats during the previous months about the German appointment. There were several Italian ex-diplomats from Iron Curtain countries in Rome who looked toward Germany as a possible position for themselves. The posts of papal nuncios in France, Spain, Italy and Germany were top level appointments, usually leading to a red hat. The Italians of the Vatican diplomatic corps did not look favorably upon any alteration of their traditional succession to these posts. An American territorial bishop who had no diplomatic training, and who had served as head of a papal mission under extraordinary postwar circumstances in Germany, was not a member of the established order. If the appointment had been made *pro forma* through the Vatican Secretariat of State, it would undoubtedly have been directed to one of the senior Italian career members of the system. Tardini had clearly indicated this preference several times during the past years both in conversations and in his questioning of Muench's abilities as a permanent representative, without in-training and friendships, of the oldest diplomatic corps in international relations. But Pius XII acted in this case, as in so many others during his tenure, as his own secretary of state. The personal relationship of Pius and Muench was an important determinant in the decision. The universal esteem and respect for Muench which Pius had learned about in no uncertain terms from German bishops and leaders was also a major factor in the decision. The Germans wanted Muench and they did not hesitate to make their opinion clear both before and after the appointment. "It could have been nobody else," Monsignor Hack stated, "although this was not entirely self-evident. At this point Muench's mission to Germany could have been considered fulfilled. There were some considerations in that regard. But the fact that Muench enjoyed the complete confidence of all in Germany, which fact was brought to the attention of the decisive authority insistently and warmly at the right time, resulted in the nomination of Muench to this new high office."

Chancellor Dr. Adenauer guided the new Federal Republic with determined steps toward independent sovereignty during the last months of 1949. On 20 September 1949 he announced to the Federal Diet certain guiding principles for a foreign policy of the first Federal Government. Referring to the "Occupation Statute" by which Germany functioned under High Commission control, the chancellor expressed the desire for an extension of German competence in legislative, executive and judicial matters as provided for in the revisionary clauses of the statute. The primary aim of the Federal Republic was to attain sovereign status with an independent German policy. "The only way to freedom is to attempt, with the approval of the High Commission," said Adenauer, "to extend our liberties step by step and gradually to increase our spheres of competence."

The way to sovereignty for Germany was opened at the New York Conference of Foreign Ministers from 12 to 18 September 1950. The London Six Power Conference two years previously, in February of 1948, had led to the formation of the Federal Republic and the parting of the ways between Russia and the West over Germany. Now, in September of 1950, the western foreign ministers laid the foundation for a partnership between the Federal Republic and the free world, the democracies of the West. A "little revision" of the Occupation Statute was advanced on 19 September 1950 which included three decisions on foreign policy. The Federal Republic was authorized to establish a foreign ministry, the state of war between victors and vanquished was terminated, and the Western Powers guaranteed the territory of the Federal Republic against armed aggression. The "little revision" of the Occupation Statute was delayed for nearly six months because Adenauer was not immediately able to agree to the *quid pro quo* demanded of the Federal Republic. This was the acknowledgment of the prewar debts of the former German Reich. The initially incalculable extent of this commitment caused the foreign affairs committee of the Federal Diet to express doubts which prevented Dr. Adenauer from signing the agreement until 6 March 1951. On that date the Federal Republic re-established its own missions abroad, staffed by its own diplomats. Accredited diplomatic representatives to the Federal Republic were now possible. Germany had regained its status in international law.

During these months Archbishop Muench was in constant contact with Montini and Tardini at the Vatican Secretariat of State receiving instructions on rapid and proper procedures for the presentation of the credentials of the apostolic nuncio to the Federal Republic. The Vatican wanted it definitely understood that the nuncio was to have the title of apostolic nuncio in Germany. In this way it was clearly stated that the Holy See refused to acknowledge the division of Germany. Rome also wished Muench to be the first diplomat to present credentials to the Federal Republic both to preserve continuity, as had been the consistent policy of Pius XII since the end of the war, and in this way to indicate the concern of the Holy See that the dean of the future diplomatic corps in Germany would be the first to seek accreditation from the government. The papal nuncio in the international diplomatic corps was traditionally accorded the deanship or position of honor. Pius XII was concerned that this position which he had personally held in Germany after World War I should be continued there after World War II.

Four days after Adenauer signed the "little revision" of the Occupation Statute on 6 March 1951, Tardini informed Frings, as chairman of the Fulda Conference, that Pius XII had sought agreement from the Federal government for the appointment of a nuncio to Germany and that the Pope had appointed Muench as nuncio on the same day as the signing of the little revision "because of his gifts of mind and singular achievements." Through an indiscretion at Bonn the news of Muench's appointment as papal nuncio was released to the press on 12 March 1951 before the Vatican had received the usual letter of agreement from the newly established foreign office of the Federal Government. The German chief of protocol of the foreign office informed Nuncio-designate Muench on March 12 that the Federal Government would be happy to receive him as dean of the diplomatic corps.

Several democratic governments of the West had sent chiefs of mission to the Federal Republic in 1949 when the new government had been established. The Vatican had not done so because these missions had to be accredited to the high commission of the occupying powers and not directly with the Federal Republic. Since the nunciature was the only diplomatic mission which had continued its activity without interruption through the collapse in 1945; and since Muench, while serving as apostolic visitor, had acted as regent upon the death of the previous nuncio, Archbishop Orsenigo, the Vatican wished to be accredited directly to the Federal Republic. This procedure conformed with the repeated statements of the Vatican throughout the whole period that the Reich Concordat (1933) and concordational conventions with Bavaria (1924), Prussia (1929) and Baden (1932) were still in force. By tolerating the appointment of Muench as regent of the nunciature, the occupying powers tacitly accepted the Vatican theory with regard to the continued unbroken existence of the nunciature.

The German chief of protocol announced that Muench would be received first and separately by the federal president, and that the other chiefs of mission, previously accredited to the high commission, would be received subsequently as a group when they all had credentials. This arrangement was planned because the original chiefs of mission to the high commission had already been received previously by the president. The chief of protocol also stated that the decision of the Vatican to appoint a nuncio was welcome in Bonn as it was an ideal solution for the problem as to who should be dean of the diplomatic corps.

On the day of the press announcement that Muench was to be the nuncio, the archbishop was offering Mass in the Cologne cathedral, commemorating the twelfth anniversary of the coronation of Pius XII, in the presence of the president and chancellor of the Federal Republic and the Bonn diplomatic corps. Muench received congratulations from all sides. He, naturally, was not surprised at the news which he had known about for over six months, but was grateful for the good will so universally expressed. That evening Muench telephoned Dworschak in Fargo to announce the news. During the following days the nuncio-designate received a steady deluge of calls, letters and telegrams from across the world. All the old friends hastened to express their joy and pride. The files of congratulations trace his associations from Milwaukee to Fargo, along with the American, German and Italian episcopacies and clergy, government officials in the United States and Germany, co-workers among the laity in American and German societies, relief organizations, military services and the diplomatic corps. James Farley, former postmaster general of the United States, wrote on March 21 that he rejoiced that Muench was the first American to receive such an appointment to Germany and he added: "Knowing you as I do, I understand full well that you will achieve success where it would seem insurmountable to others." William C. Bruce of the Bruce Publishing Company on March 12 "could not help regret that all this is taking you further and further away from all your friends here in Milwaukee." Father William McNamee, pastor of Saint Michael's Church, Grand Forks, North Dakota, wrote on March 19:

"They say great responsibilities are thrust upon great people. The mantle of the great which has fallen upon your shoulders will be worn with honor and distinction. The Church in wisdom has chosen you as her representative at one of its most important outposts. She knows that a prelate of your sound judgment and deep faith will fulfill her mission with the greatest satisfaction. We shall miss you in the Diocese of Fargo. You inspired all of us to work with greater zeal for the glory of God and the growth and progress of the Church. Though you may have left us, the lessons you silently taught us remain."

And Monsignor Paul Tanner, general secretary of the NCWC, a former student of Muench's in Saint Francis Seminary, Milwaukee, said on March 12:

"You know without our saying it that all your friends are rejoicing without qualification in the good news that came today, the twelfth anniversary of your predecessor as nuncio in Germany. The ways of Providence indeed are strange and little did any of us twenty years ago foresee the circumstances that are enabling you to serve the Church in Germany in her difficult hours in a way that amply repays all that the German missionaries ever did to establish Catholicism in Wisconsin.

I don't want to wax historical or hysterical but I do feel quite deeply about the whole matter."

Muench prepared carefully during the remainder of March for the formal presentation of his credentials as apostolic nuncio and new dean of the diplomatic corps to President Dr. Theodor Heuss at Villa Hammerschmidt, the Bonn "White House" of the Federal Republic on 4 April 1951.[20]

It was a memorable and moving occasion for all concerned. Muench called it "an historic day." Of all the congratulations received, none moved him more deeply than the one from Father Ivo Zeiger, S.J., his original co-worker at Kronberg in the first uncertain days of 1946. There was no one to whom he owed more for where he was at that hour. Zeiger, now in his last illness at Munich and on the thirtieth anniversary of his own vows as a Jesuit, wrote a moving letter to Muench on the evening of April 4 after hearing on *Deutscher Rundfunk* the entire preceedings at Villa Hammerschmidt:

"Today is truly a significant event, a very clear and warm heartfelt recognition of the Holy Father and his work for Germany. It all came in a straightforward way from the mouth of our head of state himself. In my memory of the German nation this has not happened in such a way since the Middle Ages.

"Today is equally a grateful recognition of your love and help for the German people in the last five years. It is also unique in history that the accrediting head of state would give such thanks and praise to a new diplomat.

"Lastly, today is a worthy recognition of the firm association of the Catholic Church with Germany, a recognition that will bring joy and happiness to the Holy Father.

"So permit me, on the evening of such a day, to congratulate Your Excellency from the bottom of my heart. When I left Rome in the fall of 1945 I meditated that it was during the same days that Saint Peter Canisius in 1549 went north, after his well-known vision in Saint Peter's Basilica of the Sacred Heart in which Germany was laid on his heart. His blessing has gone with us on all our journeys. If Your Excellency will do me a favor, I request that in your new nunciature, after Saint Boniface, the second apostle of Germany, Peter Canisius, will not be forgotten. On May 8 it will be 430 years since Saint Peter Canisius was born. And my entire heartfelt joy goes out to you that it '*so weit nun ist.*'"

While all of the official protocol was being carried out, the staff at

Kronberg was preparing for the move to Bad Godesberg. Monsignor Hack had spent considerable time searching for a proper headquarters in or near Bonn. Since Bonn was a relatively small city on the Rhine, housing for the governmental and diplomatic personnel of the Federal Republic was at a premium. Hack located a beautiful villa on the banks of the Rhine river in Bad Godesberg, adjacent to Bonn. While not large, it was more suitable than Villa Grosch and adequate for nunciature needs. The building was called "Turmhof," and was currently used as a rest home for older citizens operated by nuns from Cologne after their own convent across the street had been requisitioned by the British Military Command. Negotiations were begun between the Archdiocese of Cologne, British Military Government and the city of Bad Godesberg for purchase of the building by the Holy See. Monsignor Wilhelm Boehler, representing Cardinal Frings in the negotiations, and Monsignor Hack were able to obtain a favorable price of 100,000 marks ($25,000) for the building, which as Muench said, was "a real bargain" since there were several interested parties.

Extensive decoration and refurnishing was begun after the purchase. Hack supervised this operation and he and three of the sisters moved to Bad Godesberg in May of 1951. Muench moved back and forth from Kronberg to Bad Godesberg checking on the progress of the work during that spring. He was disturbed, particularly, at the shower in his bathroom which had been placed in the middle of the tub. "Can you understand such stupidity," he said to Hack on a visit, "to put a shower there?" Muench went on to explain where and how a shower should be placed. Hack continued:

"Muench called the workers in and showed them where things belonged. He certainly had his own ideas about this or that installation. It took them four weeks to get everything fixed the way he wanted it. He had very precise ideas, and he was right. But at that time there were only second or third class materials available in Germany which he might not have quite realized. Production was just slowly starting again. To get a new faucet, a new door handle, was a major operation. There just were not first class materials available. Later most of what was put in was replaced. Economic development was only slowly coming to life at that time. Many of our best men had died in the war. A mechanic or craftsman was king in his own right. They had to be treated like his majesty personified in order to get them to do anything. They were more important than a nuncio. And there were less and less experts in the field. They irritated him because he was used to excellent work in this regard in America.

"But I must emphasize that he lived more frugally than any of the German bishops. He did not want comfort for himself. In Kronberg he had only a very small room for all those years. Long after many of the bishops had returned to their residences and lived in spacious, well-furnished rooms, he was still satisfied with accommodations like those of the youngest assistant priest. He had one room, barely furnished. In all things he was very modest and never spent money for unnecessary things." [21]

Auxiliary Bishop Dworschak from Fargo was there during preparations for the move from Kronberg to Bad Godesberg. He had visited Switzerland and returned to Kronberg on May 15 so that he and Muench could go to Rome on May 25 for the beatification of Pope Pius X. In an audience requested by Bishop Dworschak on May 29, the twenty-fifth anniversary of his ordination, Pius XII asked the two bishops, with a smile, how they could both be away from their diocese at the same time and they replied because of the good priests of Fargo. Pius enjoyed this rejoinder and went on to congratulate them on developments in the diocese of Fargo. Pius was conscious of how deeply Muench felt about his diocese and never suggested that he relinquish it in spite of the fact that he was now nuncio to Germany. Muench always hoped for the day when he could return to Fargo and looked upon his tenure as bishop there as his one stability in an ever-changing scene. He was often criticized for holding tenaciously to his episcopal see even when he had acquired nuncio status. But Bishop Dworschak understood completely Muench's love for Fargo and supported him at every step of the way. In the years ahead Muench's attachment to Fargo became even more intense, especially when he began to decline physically. Muench was mentioned repeatedly for such American sees as Milwaukee, Chicago, Newark, Saint Louis, Detroit, Saint Paul or San Francisco. [22] But Muench knew that as long as Pius XII lived he would never leave Germany. He worried about what would happen to him afterwards and always dreamed of returning to Fargo as his final terminus. Particularly, he feared that he would have to retire to Rome; little did he know in that spring of 1951 that what he feared the most would eventually take place.

Muench returned to Germany on June 9 and the nunciature staff moved to the new *Turmhof* home on the Rhine on the same day. It was an exciting hegira as they gathered the cherished files of the postwar years and traveled from Kronberg in the Taunus to Bad Godesberg. Americans, Germans and Italians made the short trip together and joyfully explored their new home. With Muench were Father Howard Smith, Monsignors Opilio Rossi and Bernhard Hack; Robert Deubel, secretary, the sisters of the clerical and domestic staff; and the household staff of Germans and refugees.

The *Turmhof* was surrounded by a large enclosed yard and set back from the road. The villa contained two chapels, twenty-nine rooms, and seven bathrooms on three floors. A large circular reception hall on the first floor was surrounded by a parlor, a reception room, a library which was stocked with current German, Italian and American publications, a salon, a chapel, the dining room and kitchen. On the second floor Archbishop Muench had a study and bedroom suite for the first time since he had come to Germany. On the same floor there was also the chancery and separate offices and bedrooms for members of the staff. The third floor housed guest and staff bedrooms, and part of this level housed the sisters and their chapel. Altogether, it made for functional and gracious living.[23]

Muench loved the "new home on the Rhine." From their windows looking east, they could see the "seven mountains" on the opposite side of the Rhine. He found the *Turmhof* and its 5.3 acres most congenial. He said Bad Godesberg was called the "Riviera of Germany," because there was little snow, unlike other parts of Germany, and he could watch from his window the steamers and barges going up and down the Rhine. He felt at home, as in Fargo, where he formerly checked from his window in the bishop's house the moving of the Great Northern trains across the Dakota prairie. Muench never tired of saying: "It is beautiful here. There is a lot of sunshine, gorgeous flowers, trees in blossom, song birds everywhere praising their creator. It is tragic that the madman Hitler brought all the misery that he did on the good German people."

Accompanying Cardinal Faulhaber to Munich's Frauenkirche on his eightieth birthday, 6 March 1949.

In Rome for the ad limina *report, October, 1949, a visit to Villa Nazareth, a home for war orphans founded by Msgr. Domenico Tardini. Standing, behind children: l to r: Msgr. Domenico Tardini, Bishop Edward J. Hunkeler, Bishop Dworschak, Bishop Muench, Msgr. Alberto Giovannetti, and Msgr. Alfredo Ottaviani.*

Bishops Dworschak and Muench, Father Howard Smith, on day of consecration of Bishop Johannes Bydolek, Hildesheim 21 September 1949.

Centenary of St. Boniface-Verein, Regensburg, 2 October 1949: 2nd from left, Bishop Muench; Cardinal Josef Frings, Cologne, Bishop Michael Buchberger, Regensburg, and Archbishop Lorenz Jaeger, Paderborn; behind Bishop Muench, at left, Bishop Dworschak; at right, Bishop Albert G. Meyer of Superior, Wis.; between Bishop Buchberger and Archbishop Jaeger: Bishop Julius Doepfner of Wuerzburg.

"For the first time in my life," with Archbishop Jaeger of Paderborn aboard
a six-span open coach, escorted by horseback riders on their way to the
Cathedral in Paderborn to celebrate the patronal feast of St. Liborius,
23 July 1949.

Meeting of representatives of War Relief Services of NCWC, Frankfurt, 25 February 1949.
James J. Norris is at right of Bishop Muench.

Holy Year pilgrimage group from the Diocese of Fargo, received in special audience by Pope

Pius XII at Castel Gandolfo, 17 October 1950. The pilgrimage was headed by Msgr. L. J. Arrell.

*The nunciature,
"Turmhof", a block
from the Rhine, Bad
Godesberg, May, 1951.*

*View of the Rhine from
the Turmhof.*

*In the nunciature chapel, Bad Godesberg. The
chapel carvings were by Brother Notker, O.S.B., of
Maria Laach Abbey.*

At the nunciature, Bad Godesberg,
July 1952. Seated, l to r: Archbishop
Muench and Msgr. Opilio Rossi;
standing, l to r: Msgrs. Ottavio
DeLiva, Bernhard Hack, Father
Howard Smith.

Visit of the Vatican Substitute Secretary of State, Monsignor Giovanni Battista Montini, now Pope Paul VI,
at the Benedictine Abbey of Maria Laach, 28 August 1952: l to r: Fr. Theodor Bogler, O.S.B., head
of 'ars liturgica' workshops at Maria Laach, Msgr. Montini, Msgr. Bernhard Hack, Archbishop Muench,
Msgr. Joseph McGeough of the Secretariat of State (presently nuncio in Dublin), Abbot Basilius Ebel,
O.S.B. and Fr. Emmanuel von Severus, O.S.B., prior.

"Germany is a land of processions and conventions,"

Freiburg, 21 September 1954.

Corpus Christi procession,

Huefingen, 9 June 1955

Archbishop Muench and Bishop Julius Doepfner arriving in Berlin, 25 March 1957.

Officiating in nunciature chapel, 1958, at baptism of Daniella, daughter of Robert and Erika Deubel, former secretaries at the nunciature. Gerald, age 2, stands in front of Erika while Erika's mother holds the baby.

On the grounds of the nunciature, with Gerald and Daniella, children of Robert and Erika Deubel, October, 1959.

CHAPTER SIX

AMERICAN NUNCIO ON THE RHINE

A new chapter of Archbishop Muench's work in Germany opened in Bad Godesberg in 1951 and continued for the next eight years. The Kronberg years from 1946 to 1951 were filled with organized charitable works which because of his training and inclination were his forte. Then he could meet and help people as a bishop and pastor. This work was an inner necessity for him, the flesh and blood experiences of Christianity. Now as nuncio the bonds of cordial and brotherly love which he cherished so much were slowly but surely circumscribed. Monsignor Hack, who worked closely with him throughout the entire period as adviser on German affairs, explained:

"It should not be kept a secret that many sacrifices were part of Muench's life as nuncio in Bad Godesberg. As an American it was easy for him to understand the administration of American dioceses, the American political system and society. However, even an experienced European has difficulties in comprehending the political and social situation of European countries other than his own. So much the more for Muench, even though he was not a stranger to Germany. His German forefathers, his travels and studies in Europe, and other factors facilitated his orientation and information. But the bishop of Fargo had never encountered such kind of chains — if I may use this comparison — as he did here again and again which impeded the accomplishment of certain ecclesiastical aims."[1]

There was no doubt that the legal details in which he now was involved were alien to Muench's training as a religious sociologist, professor of social science and pastor of souls. Notwithstanding all the explanations given him in Rome by Pius XII, Montini and Leiber, as well as his awareness that the German bishops, clergy and laity were solidly behind him, Muench continued to wonder why he had to serve as a nuncio. Germany, in his opinion, badly needed a development of religious sociology and experimentation with new structures in social action such as were emerging in Belgium, Holland and France. Qualified persons were not writing and acting in the field of social justice to the extent that they should. There was a significant lack of interest and realization of its importance among the Germans. If he could return to his diocese, Muench thought, he could make a contribution across national frontiers, with his background, experience and contacts, through writing, conferences and general encouragement of ideas in Christian social justice. "The ideas of social justice were part of his very being. He realized the needs of the people, he felt with them, and he envisioned the constructive tasks that lay in the social movement for the improvement of the present situation."[2] Far from the encounters with Coughlinites and the social problems of the 1930's, this papal diplomat on the Rhine repeatedly came back to the challenges and application of Christian socio-ethical principles.

Muench had no illusions that he was trained for the papal diplomatic corps.[3] Father Robert Leiber, S.J., personal adviser to Pius XII, directly and pointedly revealed the source of Muench's uneasiness during his years as nuncio in Germany. Leiber stated:

"For the Holy See the most important question was the continued validity of the *Reichskonkordat* of 1933 signed by Cardinal Eugenio Pacelli, secretary of state to Pius XI and former nuncio to Germany, and Franz von Papen, vice chancellor of the German Reich under Adolph Hitler, chancellor, and General Paul von Hindenburg, president. The question was of such importance because the concordat guaranteed the fundamental right of existence of the Catholic Church in the German State. I do not have to quote the different opinions on this particular question. Pope Pius XII insisted that the concordat retain its validity. He had also been informed that the Allied Powers favored the interpretation that the concordat remain in force; that, if any international treaty at all would survive the capitulation, then the concordat would undoubtedly be among those whose validity would not be questioned. Since the concordat obviously survived the capitulation, it consequently retained its validity and effectiveness. German President Theodor Heuss [1949–59] was of the same opinion and he expressed this in a letter to Pius XII.

"The one who had first drawn attention to this issue was Father Zeiger [Kronberg/Taunus, 1945–51]. He was a singularly capable man and he was the best informed on the legal relations between the Holy See and the German government because before his assignment to Kronberg he was the first to draw attention to the necessity of clarifying and regulating this matter so that nothing would be lost.

"The ecclesiastical-legal situation in Germany, and that includes negotiations concerning the concordat, was unknown territory to Bishop Muench. An important German ecclesiastic, who held Muench in high esteem, once remarked that the nuncio would never succeed in really understanding this specific situation. Muench grew up in the atmosphere of American Catholic life and mentality, which is ideal in its own way and country, but which completely differs from our own situation. This is just what I heard from others.

"At one time only, when Nuncio Muench was in Rome for a visit, did I talk to him about this. He asked me different things, what the opinion of the Vatican was on this and that, and then he mentioned this matter of the concordat. I gave him the very cautious reply: 'Your Excellency, it is expected that the nuncio to Germany keep a sharp eye on these things.'

"Muench answered: not a week has passed that I did not concern myself with and study this question, the validity of the concordat, its adaptation to the new situation, etc. In other words, he protested against the doubt that he would not give this question the necessary attention, that he would not take it seriously enough. I had the impression that he knew about and suffered under this doubt. The fact is, and I cannot forego saying it, that Pro-Secretary of State Tardini did have the conviction that Muench was not well qualified for dealing with these difficult questions. It is possible that Pius XII shared this opinion. This fact may have cast a shadow over the otherwise excellent relations between the Pope and the Nuncio.

"Zeiger died on Christmas of 1952. It was in the years after 1952 when more activity was expected from the nuncio in this regard. Later on these things were well taken care of.

"A new, more or less grave, difficulty arose between the nuncio and the monsignors at the Vatican, Monsignor Tardini and also Pius XII, with the establishment of a new office, a sort of liaison office between the Church in Germany and the German government; between the bishops and other ecclesiastical offices on the one hand, and the government and members of parliament, politicians, leading officials, on the other. Pius XII was not in favor of such an office because he was afraid it might aim at replacing the nunciature. And when the French Catholics started to establish a similar office, Pius became nervous. The French wanted to copy the Bonn office of Monsignor Wilhelm Boehler [1891–1958; representative of Cardinal Frings, chairman of the Fulda Conference, at the West German Federal Government]. The fact was that Monsignor Boehler, a very capable man, took over quite a number of duties of the nuncio and succeeded in solving many problems. I had a look at the list of subjects worked on by Boehler, and I had to admit that there were many things that he treated in a better way than a nuncio could have done. And that not because it was Muench who was nuncio at the time, but because these subjects could not have been taken care of by any nuncio as successfully as by Boehler. These things did not really belong to the competence of the nuncio and had to be approached and solved in a different way. There were many topics that had been presented to the government by a nuncio that were rejected with the remark: 'Excellency, this is a strictly internal German matter and does not belong to our respective interests.' I had the impression, and I also said so to Pius XII, that most of the matters Monsignor Boehler took up were of strictly internal German interest and could be handled much better by him than by a nuncio. I said that in defense of the nuncio, but also because I was convinced of this. I do not know whether the Pope shared my opinion.

"When Monsignor Boehler came to Rome, together with Cardinal Frings, the Pope bestowed on him an exceptional honor, the personal title of 'excellency,' although he was not a bishop, in recognition of his merits and accomplishments. Boehler, however, told me that he was only too well aware of the Pope's dissatisfaction with his office and activities. Since I could not deny the truth of his remark, I did not answer at all; I just kept quiet. Soon afterwards Boehler died. I did have the impression that the relationship between the Holy See and the nunciature in Bonn was overshadowed by all of this a little bit. I am sure that Muench suffered under this fact. It was impossible for him not to notice and realize this.

"It is true that by his training Muench was more at home in the realms of practical pastoral work, social justice and welfare. In Fribourg he studied social sciences and there is no doubt that this was his favorite subject. These legal matters were not close to his heart, he took them up rather by duty than by personal interest. Muench always struck me as a personality of genuine kindness who was predominantly moved by motives of benevolence and compassion with a great awareness of matters pertaining to social and charitable works rather than by considerations of a diplomatic and legal nature. His kindness made a lasting impression on me, his readiness to help, and his deep piety. He was a man of simple, convincing piety.

"He longed to get in contact again with young people, with students. I do not say this as a generality but rather explicitly, remembering his remarks, his nostalgic talks about his former work. For me, it seems a great tragedy that this man, instead of being able to return to his country, had to stay in the nunciature for eight more years and leave it as a sick man and a cardinal to spend a few miserable years in Rome without being given a task worthy of him."[4]

Although the references are lengthy, the only possible way to obtain a first-hand background for Muench's difficulties during this period is to quote directly from interviews with those contemporaries who were most closely and personally involved with him. Cardinal Frings of Cologne completed the portrait from his perspective as chairman at that time of the Fulda Conference of German Bishops. He said:

"The most important question was the recognition of the *Reichskonkordat* of 1933. Pius XII insisted on its recognition in a most persistent manner. The first representative of the Vatican after the war was Father Ivo Zeiger, S.J. He came as early as 1945. He visited me in a rather undignified position, namely, as assistant driver of an American officer. We talked until the small hours, and he kept returning to one point in our discussion: the concordat and the necessity of keeping this concordat meticulously or we would lose the basis of negotiation with the German government to be established later.

"Muench also worked hard on this matter although concordats were not really close to his heart. As an American this topic was not quite familiar to him. But the efforts had good results; right from the start the German government recognized the validity of the concordat. Later on we had the major legal proceeding at the Federal Court of Justice in Karlsruhe. But it was beyond Muench's power to influence this development. The effectiveness of the concordat was considerably limited by the decision of the Karlsruhe Court.

"The first purpose was to get the concordat's validity recognized and, without doubt, Muench worked hard to reach this goal. But concerning the enforcement of detailed regulations of the concordat, as far as the bishops were concerned, he did not strongly emphasize this point; he certainly never annoyed or bothered us with this.

"I myself once joined the Christian Democratic Union party and got quite a reprimand pointing out that this step was against the regulations of the concordat. The rebuke came from papal quarters, from the Vatican. I was informed that this step was contrary to the agreements of the concordat because in the concordat it was stated that a priest should abstain from political activity because the Third Reich took care of this. I took this step after the war but this shows the opinion of Pius XII. He insisted that the concordat be kept to the last dot in order to prevent others from telling us that we did not keep it ourselves. It was his concordat; he had drafted it personally. And it was good that he was so insistent. If this concordat had not been kept at that time, the ground would have been cut from under our feet. But by maintaining this firm stand the concordat was accepted as belonging to international contracts. Thus Heuss, first president of the German Federal Republic, recognized it as such and it was provided for in the constitution. I am certain that it was considered of utmost importance in Rome by Pius XII, that the nuncio succeeded in attaining this end.

"Muench was highly esteemed by all; I know for sure that Chancellor Adenauer had a very high opinion of him. Muench acted as intermediary in the negotiations between Germany and America. There were several tight spots and I had the impression he helped to ease the tension.

"In regard to the school question, this subject was rather foreign to him. He could not quite make himself familiar with the German educational situation. The system of government-owned and supervised Catholic schools was too different from the school situation in his own country. It was Monsignor Opilio Rossi at the nunciature who was the expert on the German school question. I remember well how impressed Boehler was. Rossi was the best informed on German educational conditions which differ so completely from those in Italy and in the States.

"All our present relations with the government started with the concordat of 1933. After its ratification the bishops' hands were tied. At the time it was enacted I did not yet belong to the hierarchy. How much agreement among the bishops was there with the concordat? I do not think one can say that the Bishops' Conference had been asked, or listened to, or that the Conference had given its consent. Not all of the bishops at that time favored the idea. Several maintained that we should try to live with the new regime; others, however, were bitterly opposed.

Particularly Galen and Preysing belonged to the opposition, and the Bishop of Wuerzburg, Matthias Ehrenfried. The Nazis called him 'Stoerenfried' [trouble maker], this Bishop Ehrenfried. Archbishop Groeber favored the Nazis in the beginning but then he turned against them forcefully and became a fierce opponent.

"In regard to the recognition of the Nazis given by the concordat, I do not think the German bishops can be blamed in any way. The reaction among German Catholics also differed widely. I remember well the day the concordat was announced. I was a pastor then, and I was surprised, very, very surprised . . ."[5]

As nuncio Archbishop Muench found himself immediately in the center of bitter disputes over the validity in postwar Germany of the concordat of 1933. The question was aggravated by the constituent states of the German Federal Republic as they began to revise or enact new legislation in educational matters, an area which was placed under the jurisdiction of the different *Laender* by the new constitution. Articles twenty-one through twenty-five of the concordat, dealing with schools and teacher training, became the subject of fierce controversy. The validity of the concordat was attacked mainly by socialists and liberals on the ground that it was a fascist pact concluded by the Hitler government with the Holy See.

The nuncio and members of the staff at Bad Godesberg worked long hours preparing briefs proving that this charge did not do justice to the facts. They pointed out that the Reich Concordat was drafted more than ten years before Hitler came to power on 30 January 1933. On the one hand, Nuncio Eugenio Pacelli, under instructions received from Pope Benedict XV, undertook to draft articles for a concordat shortly after presenting his credentials to President Friedrich Ebert of the German Reich on 30 June 1920. On the other hand, the government of the Reich likewise took steps to work out a draft, known as the 'Delbrueck Draft' under the authorship of Dr. Heinrich Delbrueck of the Foreign Ministry. Thus two drafts were on hand in the early 1920's, twelve years before Hitler assumed power.

Both drafts were made the basis of preparatory negotiations between the Vatican and the Reich. Some progress was made, but a succession of short-lived federal governments and protests entered by the Bavarian government brought the negotiations to a stop. In Munich preparations had also been initiated for a concordat between Bavaria and the Holy See since the Bavarians feared that if a concordat were concluded with the Reich before one with Bavaria its interests would be jeopardized, an attitude reflecting the traditional tension between Munich and Berlin.

The concordat with Bavaria had been concluded on 29 March 1924 and ratified on 24 January 1925. The success of the Bavarians brought Prussia into action. After several years of negotiation, a second *Laender* concordat was concluded by Pacelli with Prussia on 14 June 1929 and ratified on 5 August 1929. Approximately four months later Nuncio Pacelli was recalled to Rome. He left Germany on December 10 and was made a cardinal six days later. When Cardinal Pietro Gasparri resigned as papal secretary of state Cardinal Eugenio Pacelli succeeded him on 7 February 1930.

On 30 January 1933 President Paul von Hindenburg invited Adolph Hitler, whose Nazi Party had received the most votes but not a majority in the national election, to form a new government. The government of the Catholic Chancellor Heinrich Bruening was overthrown and the plans of Hitler had succeeded. Bruening, in Canadian and American exile during the years ahead, never could believe that his government was not sacrificed by short-sighted opportunists. The Center Party voted for the Authorization Law of 21 March 1933 granting police power to the government and power to rule without parliament.

Chancellor Hitler obtained from the Reichstag special emergency powers. Germany, like other countries such as the United States, was in the throes of a serious depression. Millions of men were out of work and the Communists profited from this situation by adding large numbers to their party membership. In order to strengthen his hold on the Catholics of Germany, Hitler took the initiative in reviving negotiations with the Vatican to conclude a concordat. On 23 March 1933, Hitler, the new chancellor, in an address before the Reichstag, declared that the government would respect pacts made with the churches, Catholic and Evangelical, and that every effort would be made to foster and strengthen amicable relations with the Vatican.

In April of 1933 he sent his Catholic supporter, the aristocrat, Franz von Papen, then assistant chancellor, to Rome with the Delbrueck Draft in his briefcase. Cardinal Pacelli, papal secretary of state, brought to the conference the draft he had made as nuncio to Germany. Since these two drafts were used in the negotiations, the concordat was concluded by July 20 and ratified on 10 September 1933. Everything was carried off in such a brief period because very few alterations had to be made. Hitler's cabinet, composed of eleven members of whom three were Nazis and the other eight members of coalition parties, approved the concordat. Hindenburg, not Hitler, signed the document.

In the controversies of the 1950's, the nunciature staff at Bad Godesberg, tried to point out these facts in refuting the assault on the concordat as a fascist or Nazi covenant. A further charge was made by socialist opponents of the concordat: its signing gave prestige to Hitler. Muench replied that undoubtedly it did, but so did the thirty-eight bilateral and five multilateral international pacts the Hitler government made with other governments before the conclusion of the concordat. These facts the adversaries of the concordat, he stated to the press, conveniently ignored in their intemperate polemics against its validity. However, an observer of Muench's own personal viewpoints and inclinations during the whole Nazi period and after it cannot but question if the new nuncio was not now put in a position of following orders from the Vatican. Now he was defending the tragic compromises and historical institutional involvements of continental Italians and Germans which did not advance the cause of Christianity during the totalitarian period. The catholic and moral stance of the Church was without doubt compromised by the pacts with Hitler and Mussolini. A post-factum defense of the worn-out concordat system found less and less support as the lines between morality and politics were more carefully scrutinized. The democracies of the West went through a similar soul-searching as they re-evaluated their own wartime pacts with Communist Russia.

Muench pointed out that Pius XI had misgivings about concluding a concordat with the German Reich under Chancellor Hitler. In his celebrated encyclical of March, 1937, "*Mit Brennender Sorge*," on the condition of the Church in Germany, Pius XI stated: "We were guided by the solicitude incumbent on us to safeguard the freedom of the Church in the exercise of her apostolic ministry in Germany and the salvation of souls entrusted to her, and at the same time by the sincere wish of rendering an essential service to the progress and prosperity of the German people." Pius XI, Muench stated, would have been blamed if he had rejected the offer of 1933 because in later years difficulties arose for the Church in regard to matters that were now safeguarded by pertinent articles of the concordat. Pacelli as Pius XII set forth in some detail to the cardinals on 2 June 1945 the reasons why the Vatican entered into a concordat with the German Reich and noted the benefits that accrued to the Church from the fact that a juridical basis had been given for the protection of her rights and interests. However, few knowing observers missed the point that it was Pacelli who was defending his own concordats. And in the postwar, ecumenical and post-Christian world, as it was often evaluated, the concordat system became less and less functional and acceptable.

However, Nuncio Muench had a job to do in Germany during the 1950's and he carried through with his usual dedication. In 1954 an opportunity for a test case of the validity of the 1933 concordat presented itself and its opponents in Germany were not slow to seize on the opportunity. The state government of Lower Saxony, with socialists in control, enacted a school law in April, 1955, which the Federal Republic contended violated article twenty-three of the concordat providing for the maintenance of existing confessional or denominational schools and the establishment of new ones only if parents demanded it and circumstances warranted erecting such schools. Lower Saxony embraced the Diocese of Osnabrueck and part of Muenster where Catholics composed less than twenty per cent of the population. When negotiations for settling the dispute between Lower Saxony and the Federal Republic failed, the latter took the case on 25 March 1955 to the Federal Constitutional Court, the supreme court, located at Karlsruhe. Because the docket was crowded with constitutional cases, the first senate of the Constitutional Court set the hearing for June of 1956, more than a year after the case had been submitted.

Both the Federal Republic and the state government of Lower Saxony were represented by some of the best jurists in Germany. The governments of Land Hesse and the City-State of Bremen joined forces with Lower Saxony and also sent a group of eminent jurists to Karlsruhe. The case attracted international interest, especially since the three states were controlled by socialists and liberals who denied the validity of the concordat chiefly for the reason that its school articles provided for confessional or religious schools.

The case was argued for five days from 5 to 9 June 1956 before a bench of eleven justices. An early decision was expected. However, the justices could not reach the required unanimous agreement. Justices who dissent from the majority opinion are not given an opportunity in Germany to present a minority opinion. After innumerable sessions a decision was finally rendered on 26 March 1957.

The eighty-eight page opinion was composed of two parts. In the first section the court declared that the concordat was validly concluded, continues in force, and obliges both the federal and state governments since together they form the German Federal Republic, the successor of the Third Reich, possessed of all its rights and bound by engagements made with foreign governments. This decision was a major reversal for the socialists and liberals who had marshaled their best constitutional lawyers to win a decision against the concordat's validity.

The second part of the court's opinion proved to be a disappointment to the concordat's defenders. It showed marked traces of compromise and indicated why the justices could not reach a unanimous agreement as demanded by law. Muench stated that the second part of the decision lacked clarity of thought and precision of argument. Its language and reasoning were involved and resulted in a complicated exposition of the issues before the court.

The court held in the second part that the federal government lacked constitutional powers to compel the state governments to carry into effect the concordat's educational provisions. All cultural affairs, including schooling and education, were subject to the sovereignty of the several state governments. The states were to decide whether they would permit their sovereignty to be limited by an international pact such as the concordat.

As soon as the opinion of the Karlsruhe court was released, the contradiction it contained was pointed out by defenders of the concordat. On the one hand state governments were obliged by the articles of the concordat even in areas of their sovereignty, and on the other hand, they could not be obliged to discharge their obligations. Eminent jurists disagreed with the court decision, and Muench realized at once that the decision would give rise in the future to many problems. Satisfactory solutions would not be found unless the existing uncertainties were removed. The Church would have a difficult time, Muench stated, to obtain recognition of her interests in cultural matters as protected by the articles of the concordat. Traditional ideologies still played a major role in the educational life of Germany as the nuncio learned repeatedly in the controversies ahead.

Muench told Giovannetti in Rome: "*So geht es hier: immer Konkordat.*" He wrote to his fellow American, Archbishop Gerald P. O'Hara, apostolic delegate in England, on 28 January 1956: "In my work here one may paraphrase the saying: 'The nuncio proposes, but the concordat disposes'." While thanking his friend Archbishop Albert G. Meyer of Milwaukee on 8 April 1954 for his generous contribution to the German mission of charity, Muench sadly commented that no one could realize how heartened he was to be able to give assistance to the poor and needy, especially in the East zone. "It is the one thing," he remarked, "that brings sunshine into my daily work that bristles with concordat problems. Often I have reason to think of the dictum: '*Historia concordatorum, historia rixarum*' ".

Until the Nazi regime came to power in 1933 public elementary schools were as a rule denominational, either Catholic or Lutheran. Only Baden, Hesse and certain provinces of Nassau in Prussia had interdenominational public elementary schools where the teachers were both Catholic and Protestant. Religion was a recognized branch of the curriculum and was taught by pastors and teachers in the schools. These schools of Baden and Hesse were *de facto* Catholic or Protestant because of the composition of the population especially in the rural towns and villages. In the larger cities interdenominational schools were the rule because of the religious mixture of the population.

The school system of Germany was an historical mortgage. Until the beginning of the nineteenth century, schools in almost all of the *Laender* were the concern of the churches. Ecclesiastical supervision of the school existed even in Prussia where the public school had been introduced during the reign of Frederick the Great. But as a result of the on-going arguments between Church and State in the nineteenth century the Church lost this previously recognized right and the State alone controlled the schools. Accordingly, the Church took steps to guarantee religious education in these public schools through concordats and agreements. This was in contrast to France where an automatic development toward private schools began after the separation of Church and State in 1905. This was never the case in Germany where neither Church nor State was interested in such a separation. An attempt was made, rather, to come to an agreement regarding the *res mixtae*, and education remained as one of the most contested political issues.

The Hitler regime abolished Catholic and Protestant denominational schools and when the war ended secularists in the Social Democratic and Free Democratic Parties supported this position. German Catholic bishops and parents, however, demanded denominational public schools, both Catholic and Protestant, according to the provisions of the concordat, and they were successful in establishing their rights in Bavaria and North Rhine Westphalia. The latter state constitution provided for denominational, interdenominational and non-religious schools according to the desires of parents. The North Rhine Westphalian school system was, in Muench's opinion, the most democratic and fair among the nine states comprising the Federal Republic. The Rhineland-Palatinate had a confessional school system and Baden an interdenominational one.

However, since the Federal Republic was a federation of states, each of the nine states directed its own school system and exercised sovereignty in cultural matters. The Karlsruhe decision of 1954 supported this constitutional provision and created continual complications, especially in Hesse and Lower Saxony, where only interdenominational schools were established by the legislatures. So many restrictions were enacted that the establishment of denominational public schools was made practically impossible. Such measures were in violation of the concordat which guaranteed Catholic public schools and the establishment of new ones when numbers in a community warranted them. Minister Presidents Heinrich Kopf of Lower Saxony and George-August Zinn of Hesse were both Social Democrats and supported this development. Evangelical Land Bishop Hanns Lilje of Hannover also strongly supported traditional Lutheran rights in Hesse against Catholic intrusions. Although Catholics of the diaspora were still a minority in such traditional Protestant areas as Hesse, Bremen and Lower Saxony, they were present in increasing numbers. As the conflicts of the 1950's are viewed in the dimension of Vatican Council II, it is apparent that the pioneer period of the ecumenical movement, even in Germany which was more advanced than any other country in the West, did not permit a new development of interfaith activity to germinate in the field of education. The interdenominational school, in an open ecumenical climate, could have been a strong base for breaking down the ancient Christian separation in Germany which became less viable in the years ahead. Such a development, however, was not possible at the time, and the Vatican's insistence on enforcing the concordat ever remained as the determining policy.

Muench was a completely dedicated representative of the Holy See and Pius XII in the matter. He considered Pius not only as his official pastor but was also personally attached to the Pope. The nuncio was anxious to find out what Pius desired and to follow through with orders from the Secretariat of State. There was never a question of reservation in this regard and the staff completely understood this orientation. Muench also received understanding during the entire education controversy in the different states from Chancellor Adenauer. The Federal

Republic supported the concordat in principle. In exchange of notes with officials of the *Laender*, Muench first presented his position to Adenauer before forwarding it to representatives of the states. The federal secretary, Dr. Hans Globke, was a sympathetic intermediary for Muench in these negotiations. Globke, confidant of Adenauer, was a loyal Catholic who had served in the civil service during the Hitler regime at the request of the Catholic bishops who had asked him to stay on as a possible deterrent of even worse persecution during that period. Adenauer's government was the object of continual opposition to Globke from leftist fronts; yet the chancellor never buckled under this pressure but rather supported this faithful public servant of unquestionable integrity.

Years of political wrangling continued during the 1950's in Bavaria over the maintenance of Catholic teacher training schools. The Free State of Bavaria had a long tradition of such schools which the Nazis abolished and which the Christian Social Union, Bavarian arm of the Christian Democratic majority party, had revived after the war. When a four-party government was established in Bavaria during the early 1950's, composed of Socialist, Liberal, Bavarian and Expellee parties, this coalition introduced a new bill on teacher training in the Bavarian *Landtag*. Under the provisions of this educational bill the traditional Catholic teacher training schools were abolished. The nuncio sent a note to Dr. Wilhelm Hoegner, Socialist minister president of Bavaria, charging that the measure would be in violation of article five of the Bavarian Concordat of 1925. The government disagreed and proceeded with the first and second reading of the bill. Meanwhile a bitter fight ensued between the four-party coalition government and the Christian Social Union. The latter charged that the education bill would be in violation of both the concordat and the Bavarian constitution. Muench brought another note to Hoegner in order to prevent the bill's adoption, but after a long and sharp debate the bill was adopted by the Bavarian parliament following its second reading. Some alterations were made, but the controversial Catholic teacher training schools were excluded.

Article fifteen of the Bavarian concordat provided that in cases of difference of interpretation the two parties, the Vatican and the Bavarian government, should seek an adjustment of the difficulties that had arisen. Minister President Hoegner requested that such negotiations be opened, but the Bavarian bishops held to their traditional position. The Vatican directed Muench to reply that the bill was so out of accord, both in wording and meaning, with the concordat that it offered no basis for negotiations. The Holy See was prepared to open negotiations, however, as soon as the Bavarian government would present a bill that offered an acceptable basis for discussion. Catholic organizations in Bavaria stood strongly behind their bishops in the encounter. The Association of Catholic Educators, the League of Catholic Families and the League of Catholic Parents marshaled their forces to preserve traditional institutions of education as well as in defending the rights of parents to engage teachers who had received an integral Catholic training and formation.

The whole controversy was a repeat performance for Archbishop Muench of the earlier conflict of the Bavarians with American Military Government. This time, however, he found himself in the center of the century-old encounter on German soil between Socialists and Catholics. Now the on-going battle was rendered more difficult by the fact that the Lutheran Church in Bavaria was not as interested in denominational teacher training schools. Nor did the Bavarian Lutheran Church have a concordat with Bavaria but only a pact whose provisions on the issue of teacher training were less stringent than those of the concordat. The Society of Bavarian Teachers, firmly liberal and anticlerical, further aggravated the problem by taking a strong supporting stand behind the coalition government's bill.

A stalemate of the contending forces continued until the Bavarian legislative elections of 1958. The Catholic support of the Christian Social Union candidates over the Social Democrats and Free Democrats brought them a strong majority to the new *Landtag*. An education law was then passed in quick order providing for Catholic teacher training institutes which the Bavarian bishops and Catholics strongly supported at that time. Since, with few exceptions, elementary schools were public and mostly Catholic, the Holy See, the Bavarian bishops and Catholic parents wanted teachers in these schools to be trained in Catholic teacher training institutes. According to the new educational law, public school teachers in Bavaria were to be trained in a three-year course at one of the seven teacher training institutes affiliated with the three Bavarian universities of Munich, Wuerzburg and Erlangen. An interdenominational teacher training institute was to be established for teachers in interdenominational schools. The Bavarian bishops also decided to establish a private teacher training institute at Eichstaett which the Bavarian government subsidized. In the university cities where teacher training institutes were established the Bavarian bishops began building dormitories for student teachers which included a chapel, library, dining and conference rooms. A priest would direct these residence halls.

In the other states of Germany the problem of teacher training institutes was not solved as satisfactorily from the Catholic viewpoint. In Lower Saxony the Social Democrat and Free Democrat government would not recognize the repeated pleas of Bishop Helmut Hermann Wittler of Osnabrueck that Catholic students attending the teacher training institute there be given a Catholic training. In Baden-Wuerttemberg the four-party coalition government reached a compromise. The state established five interdenominational, one Evangelical and two Catholic teacher training institutes. It was apparent that the potential of an ecumenical educational dimension was not possible in the 1950's just as it did not develop in the more favorable climate of the 1960's. Centuries of ideological conflict die slowly, as separated Christian communities in western nations have learned by hard experience. Despite bitter awareness of the results of their divisions, a positive and trusting ecumenical engagement developed only reluctantly among many German Christians.

The nuncio had another eye-opening experience of the complicated Church-State traditions of European nations when negotiations were begun in the 1950's to establish a new diocese in Germany. For an American bishop who had taken for granted the *laissez-faire* policy of the United States government toward ecclesiastical developments, Muench found the negotiations to create a diocese at Essen enlightening, and frustrating. The separation of Church and State, he said, has its definite drawbacks, but in the long view it is a major advance over Constantinian continental procedures.

The last German diocese to be established in twenty-eight years was at Aachen (Aix-la-Chapelle) in 1930. The rise of the Hitler regime, the war and postwar problems excluded the possibility of planning new ecclesiastical jurisdictions. Yet the rapidly increasing population in the highly industrialized Ruhr area pointed up the long-overdue need of a new diocese there, and Cardinal Frings, Archbishop Jaeger and Bishop Michael Keller realized this fully. Their jurisdictions had grown into what had been repeatedly termed a "mammoth diocese." These bishops decided that Essen, in the heart of the Ruhr, would be the appropriate city for a new diocese.

In order to begin procedures to this end the concordats with the Reich of 1933 and with Prussia in 1929 had to be respected, studied and followed in every detail. An agreement was finally worked out with the government of North Rhine Westphalia and signed by Nuncio Muench and Minister President Fritz Steinhoff, as well as Professor Dr. Luchtenberg, minister of cult and education, on 19 December 1956, an historic event that took place at the nunciature at Bad Godesberg to Muench's special delight.

After this preliminary step the agreement had to be approved through three readings by the legislature of North Rhine Westphalia. Upon ratification, documents signed by Pius XII and Minister President Steinhoff were exchanged at Duesseldorf, capital of the state, with Muench as intermediary. Here again the entire procedure was governed by the Concordat of 1933 which stipulated that a new diocese or ecclesiastical province or changes in diocesan circumscription must be submitted to the agreement of the competent government of the state concerned. The entire process was not completed until 1 January 1958 when Nuncio Muench presided at the installation of Bishop Franz Hengsbach as first ordinary of Essen.

These negotiations had resulted in a territorial division of Cologne, Paderborn and Muenster. Essen was the smallest of the twenty-three dioceses of West and East Germany, covering only 695 square miles. In population it was the most densely occupied area of Germany and of Europe. An effort was made to limit the territorial area of Essen since at its establishment it comprised 1,300,000 Catholics among a total population of 2,900,000 inhabitants. If the diocese had embraced the whole Ruhr area it would have included 3,000,000 Catholics and would have been but another "mammoth" diocese of which Germany already had too many. The eight largest cities of the Ruhr, with the exception of Dortmund, were in the Diocese of Essen. The new jurisdiction was deeply rooted in Catholic tradition. In the city of Essen alone there were six churches from 800 to 1100 years old. In the Middle Ages Essen was a center of Catholic culture and missionary enterprise. After the industrial revolution this moderately large city rapidly increased in size. Between 1816 and 1955 its population increased from 21,500 to 689,852 people. The clergy and people of Essen were known for their strong Catholic roots; vocations to the priesthood and to the religious life were especially numerous there. Bishop Hengsbach had a sympathetic understanding of the problems of miners and steel workers in the Ruhr, and Muench judged that "a future of great promise lay ahead" for this first and only diocese he saw to gestation in his thirteen years of service in Germany.[6]

The nuncio frequently spoke informally with German bishops about his own experiences in a living community as bishop in the small diocese of Fargo and the pastoral advantages of closer contact with clergy and people. On social occasions at the nunciature and on visits across Germany he recounted anecdotes and humorous incidents pointing up the close relationship of Catholic people in a small diocese. He hoped in this way to encourage more flexible thinking on the part of the German hierarchy in regard to breaking up some of their immense dioceses. But ancient traditions and firm attachment to precedence and protocol were too solidly established. At a time when the German dioceses were beginning a recovery from years of persecution the bishops were not convinced of the advantages of dissection while they were trying to reorganize. Muench was far too considerate of a national hierarchy's autonomy to interfere or attempt to impose his own preferences through behind-the-scenes maneuvering with Vatican officials as was done all too often elsewhere by nuncios and apostolic delegates. The German bishops deeply appreciated this straightforward and sensitive approach of the nuncio. He was personally convinced that there should be more and smaller German dioceses; he observed that there was too much rigid impersonalism and that the lines of communication were formalized. But he did not try as a foreigner to remake the ecclesiastical map of Germany.

In the same way Archbishop Muench refrained from unwarranted personal direction or interference in the selection of German bishops. He understood perfectly that one of his main tasks as a papal representative was to assist Pius XII and the Consistorial Congregation in the appointment of good bishops to govern dioceses. If he accomplished this task well he would render the best service to the Church in the country where he was carrying out his mission. During his thirteen years in Germany twenty-five new bishops and twenty-three new auxiliary bishops were appointed. In each case of a new appointment Muench scrupulously followed correct procedure and did not try to influence appointments that would be in his own image and likeness. He collected the recommendations of the cathedral chapters and the German bishops and forwarded them to Rome. His own recommendations were appended, but invariably they coincided with the majority opinion he was transmitting. He was particularly careful not to work against local preferences for advancements by recommending names of clergy or bishops who had the same ideological outlook as himself. The nuncio did not see each appointment as an opportunity to place a so-called conservative rather than a progressive in a bishopric. He was rather inclined to look for promising clergy who showed initiative, courage, balance, devotion and proved administrative ability. If there was one quality Muench continually looked for in episcopal candidates it was that of service to the needs of contemporary men and an openness to the real problems of the world.

The nuncio was particularly noncommittal about episcopal appointments before, during and after they had been processed. When he was asked by the press who would be the first bishop of Essen, the nuncio replied, with a laugh, that the Holy Spirit had not revealed that information to him. He was determined with skill and humor to preserve his position above party politics. He seldom indicated pleasure or displeasure with individual episcopal appointments. However, he was clearly pleased with the appointment of Ferdinand Dirichs as bishop of Limburg, the episcopal see he felt closest to and where he often pontificated, assisted and visited during his time in Germany. When Dirichs died in an automobile accident on 27 December 1948 after only one year in office Muench was deeply grieved. The advancement of Bishop Julius Doepfner from Wuerzburg to Berlin and then to Munich pleased the nuncio as he considered Doepfner the type of strong character needed to revitalize German Catholicism. In fact, Muench encouraged Doepfner to accept the appointment to Berlin in 1957 as a call to be of service in a place where religious fortitude was especially needed by the Church, the nation and the world.

After long discussion and careful study of the different organizations for religious care of members of armed forces in Europe and America, the German bishops in 1956 established a military ordinariate of a new type in Germany. Many features of the American Military Ordinariate were included in the new German setup as a result of investigations of Monsignor Georg Werthmann, vicar general of the *Wehrmacht* in World War II, and pastor of Germans employed in American labor units after the war. Werthmann worked in close collaboration with the office of Catholic chief of chaplains in Heidelberg and traveled to the United States to study the chaplains' service in the Pentagon, in army camps and at American schools for the training of chaplains.

In the former German *Wehrmacht* a bishop with titular rank, not a

member of the German hierarchy, was specially appointed by Pius XII
as ordinary of the armed forces. Subject to military authorities, he had
his office in the defense ministry at Berlin. The appointment of an
army bishop had been provided by the concordat in 1933, but it was
not until 20 February 1938 that Franz Joseph Rarkowski, acting head
of the military chaplaincy since 1929, was consecrated as bishop of the
army. The German bishops had not wanted an army bishop while the
Hitler government demanded an exempt military chaplaincy. The
bishops finally accepted an army bishop with the stipulation that he
not attend the deliberations of the Fulda Conference except when
matters affecting the military chaplaincy were discussed. The army
bishop was also obliged to carry out all decisions of the German bishops.
The latter were not favorable to Rarkowski while the Nazi regime was
as enthusiastic toward him as he was about them. His speeches and writings to the German Catholic troops during the war were extremely
nationalistic and militaristic and have been used by authors since the
war as evidence of German Catholic support of the Nazis.

Painfully conscious of this bitter experience, the German bishops determined after the war to establish a military vicariate independent of
army authorities. The defense ministry at Bonn agreed to the arrangement for the new defensive German army, and the Vatican gave its consent in accordance with the provisions of the concordat. Cardinal Josef
Wendel of Munich was appointed military vicar by Pius XII. He was
assisted by a vicar general who supervised religious work in the military
from an office in the defense ministry, while serving as liaison representative between the military vicar and the ministry. Deans were appointed
for the six military areas of the new *Bundeswehr* who organized and
supervised the religious and spiritual work of military pastors. Two
pastors, one Catholic and one Evangelical, were appointed for every
1,500 officers and soldiers where there had been previously but one
chaplain for an entire division of 15,150 men. The military vicar made
all appointments of pastors or chaplains, not the defense ministry as
before. Pastors were not to wear uniforms except on maneuvers and they
held no military rank. They served for five years and then returned to
their respective dioceses or religious communities.

The German bishops considered these arrangements a real advance
over the former practice of chaplains being members of the army. Now
the organization of religious service in the army was patterned on
general diocesan procedures. Thirty army pastors were to function

after the war over against some 500 during the war. The new system was a distinct improvement over the former compromising arrangement. However, to place the military ordinariate under the archbishop of Munich was as confusing as the American practice of continuing their military ordinariate under the jurisdiction of the archbishop of New York. An independent military bishopric was desired by competent and experienced military chaplains in both Germany and the United States as a more efficient and personal pastoral arrangement for modern armies.

During the years in Germany Muench followed closely the progress achieved by German Catholics in liturgical reforms. The liturgical movement was older and better established among German Catholics than it was at home. In Fargo he had followed closely the liturgical activity of the Benedictine monks of Saint John's Abbey and the Liturgical Press of Collegeville, Minnesota. His auxiliary was an alumnus of the Saint John's Seminary, as were a large number of his priests, and Muench was in close contact with Abbot Alcuin Deutsch, O.S.B., Fathers Virgil Michel, O.S.B. and Godfrey Diekmann, O.S.B. Much of the inspiration for the American liturgical apostolate from the 1930's through the 1950's had come from northern European countries. Now in Germany as papal representative Muench had close relations with the Benedictines of Maria Laach and Beuron abbeys as well as the Liturgical Institute at Trier, a center for study and publications on liturgical matters.

On 21 March 1950 the Roman Congregation of Rites approved a new *Ritual* for use in German dioceses. Apart from the essential rites in the administration of the sacraments, the German vernacular was to be used. A commission of theologians had worked for five years in preparing this new ritual which was approved by the bishops at their Fulda Conference in 1949 and forwarded to Rome for final authorization. The first volume containing the rites for the sacraments was issued at once but the second volume of various sacramentals and blessings did not appear until 1952. This vernacular ritual met the long-expressed wishes of clergy and laity and grew out of the German liturgical movement which had developed in strength before the Hitler regime and became a major consolation to Catholics under Hitler who were compelled to live their Christian lives more and more at community worship. When Muench first came to Germany there was not much demand for the use of German in the Mass since there was a widespread tradition of the use of the missal and of dialogue Masses. Nor was there much agitation for a vernacular divine office for the clergy since priests used a German and Latin version which had been issued by Pustet Publishing Company as early as 1939 and revised with a translation of the psalter by Monsignor Romano Guardini of Munich.

Then two liturgical congresses were held at Frankfurt in 1950 and at Munich in 1955. Over 700 priests and 300 laymen attended the first sessions at Frankfurt which were sponsored by the Liturgical Institute of Trier. Four petitions were sent to Rome for the restoration of the Easter Vigil service, evening Mass, mitigation of the eucharistic fast and the reading of the epistle and gospel in the vernacular at Mass. Following this conference the first three of the four requests were approved, not only for Germany, but throughout the entire Catholic world. It was obvious that Pius XII was interested in liturgical reform. Muench experienced in conversations with the pontiff how deeply concerned he was to promote sound liturgical advances.

At the Munich conference five years later some fourteen bishops, seven abbots, 1,200 priests, 1,400 laity and guests from over a dozen nations discussed liturgy and piety. An intense discussion of the use of the vernacular at Mass developed as delegates participated in the German high mass, *deutsches Hochamt*, at which certain parts such as the Gloria and Credo were sung in German according to an approved century-old custom. During the days of the conference the ordinary of the Mass was sung by the entire congregation. Since there was no opportunity for all of the 1,200 priests to celebrate Masses, they attended the community Mass and received communion in alb and stole. Bishops at the sessions recommended that Benediction or Exposition of the Blessed Sacrament during Mass and side altar Masses during the community Mass be discontinued; that communion bread be consecrated at the Mass in which people receive communion; that as a minimum the people respond to the prayers of the Mass; that communion be distributed only at communion time; that only adults or those confirmed serve Masses. At the conclusion of the conference a second petition was forwarded to Rome for permission to read the epistle and gospel in the vernacular at all public Masses as well as a revision of the whole liturgy of Holy Week.

The second petition was granted but the other reforms did not take place until after the International Assisi Liturgical Conference of 1956 was held. Rome was slow in granting complete use of the vernacular in the liturgy until Vatican Council II because of a strong curial position that Latin and universality were synonymous. During all the years of preliminary jockeying for liturgical advances Muench, as nuncio, strongly supported the requests of German bishops and people for the use of the vernacular in the liturgy. He realized the importance of this need among northern European Catholics for a full and understanding participation in worship. He particularly saw at first-hand its necessity in such areas as the East zone of Germany where Christian community life and meaningful participation in worship were indispensable to survival. Unlike some other nuncios and apostolic delegates who actively and intemperately tried to suppress liturgical studies and renewal in western nations during the same years, Muench did not associate catholicity or Italian hegemony with a preservation of the Latin language.

More than that, Archbishop Muench worked year after year to interest American bishops in liturgical developments that were taking place in Germany, France, Belgium and Holland. Archbishop Edwin V. O'Hara of Kansas City told Muench that it was he who had set the American chain of events in motion when the nuncio enthusiastically gave O'Hara a copy of the German ritual in 1951 at Bad Godesberg. Three years later on 3 June 1954 Roman approval was given for an American vernacular ritual with the form of the sacraments, unctions and exorcisms restricted to Latin. Muench saw a copy of this new ritual at the Bruce Publishing Company in Milwaukee when he was visiting at home. While he thought the translation was good, he also judged that several prayers needed revision and simplification. He also sent a request to the annual meeting of the American bishops that three statements be added to the marriage ceremony to be said by the bridal couple regarding the sacredness of the marriage bond, the value of the child in the sight of God and the blessing of family prayer in the home.

Archbishop Muench was particularly interested in liturgical reforms that were pastoral in character. He was aware that the majority of the American bishops were progressive in social action and charitable activities while they were equally conservative in liturgical and theological matters. He tried through correspondence and conversation to convince as many as he could of the pastoral values of liturgical renewal and to praise theological studies that flourished in Germany. The so-called leaders of the American hierarchy, especially those in the east, were opposed to a vernacular ritual and liturgy. Their arguments were that in many dioceses there were still large numbers of various language groups and they asked what would be the vernacular for such people. Muench held that such difficulties could easily be overcome, as was being done in Europe, by either using Latin or special temporary language editions in such cases. There was more understanding and leadership in liturgical developments among the bishops in the Midwest, and Muench often wrote his friends there about European advances in the use of the vernacular, dispensations from antiquated fasting rules, the preparation of a new German catechism and the restoration of the evening Mass. He strongly favored the practice of offering Mass in the evening, such as was begun in Germany on 12 January 1951, as a major pastoral advance in meeting the contemporary needs of an industrialized society and in helping pastors and people in missionary and rural areas.

Progress was slow in the United States. Muench wrote Dworschak on 25 March 1953:

"History is repeating itself. As with frequent and early communion the diehards will offer passive, even though respectful, resistance. I am thinking of experiences in the early years of my priesthood. Then even good and zealous bishops and pastors shook their heads in doubt about the reforms of Pius X."

Archbishop Muench continued to send information to his fellow bishops in the United States about German Catholic experiments in liturgical and pastoral renewal. The Fulda Bishops' Conference had eight permanent commissions among which was a commission on religious life. Bishops Simon Conrad Landersdorfer, O.S.B., of Passau and Albert Stohr of Mainz headed a subcommittee of this commission which reported on liturgical matters. The Liturgical Institute at Trier, while not functioning under the authority of the German bishops, supplied background studies and proposals. A Liturgical Commission advised the two bishops and was composed of research scholars, practical liturgists and representatives from institutions which were prominent in the beginnings of the German liturgical movement such as Maria Laach, Beuron, Klosterneuburg and the Oratory at Leipzig. Muench was pleased when the American bishops established an *ad hoc* episcopal committee on the liturgy in 1957 composed of Archbishops Karl J. Alter of Cincinnati, William O. Brady of Saint Paul and Auxiliary Bishop Dworschak of Fargo. Cardinal Stritch had encouraged the development of this committee which recommended the establishment of a permanent Bishops' Commission on the Liturgical Apostolate. The American bishops established such a commission at their annual meeting of 1958 and Archbishop Joseph E. Ritter of Saint Louis was elected chairman of the five member bishops' group. For years the American Liturgical Conference had requested some official episcopal contact with their organization as an indispensable aid in implementing Rome's liturgical reform program throughout the dioceses, in overcoming indifference, in eliminating abuses and excesses and in up-dating further reforms.

Muench was happy at this development which provided official support for liturgical reform in the United States. The archbishop was convinced that a Christian social apostolate could never be formed without liturgical renewal. He was not, however, as sympathetic to all forms of contemporary liturgical art and architecture. His tastes in art were definitely centered in the Maria Laach school and he was less than enthusiastic about modern art and architectural developments in Germany and the United States. He worried about the piety of the people and the pastoral implications of contemporary artistic idioms which he never understood. The new functional churches which were being built so rapidly in Germany impressed and fascinated him, but their contemporary forms and art were not to his liking. He often called these churches "airplane hangars." However, here as in all other developments the nuncio did not interfere and restricted himself to disputing about architectural and artistic taste in private.

Another religious movement in Germany which was *a terra incognita* to the nuncio was the pioneer ecumenical movement. But in this case he adapted more easily than in the field of contemporary art and architecture. Called the *Una Sancta* Movement, the ecumenical apostolate had been started some thirty years earlier by the Nazi victim, Father Max Joseph Metzger, and now had chapters throughout the country. *Una Sancta* aimed at promoting better understanding and eventual reunion between separated Christians in the land of the Reformation. Priests and laymen met in small, semi-private gatherings to discuss in friendly and frank terms the causes of the split in Christendom, to study in the light of more recent and unbiased historical data the Protestant Reformation and the subsequent Catholic reform, and to create mutual good will which could be a foundation for eventual religious unity.

Germany was a pioneer again in this long-overdue apostolate which was eventually recognized by Vatican Council II. The German Bishops'

Conference officially recognized the *Una Sancta* movement and a commission of twelve Catholic theologians under the leadership of Archbishop Lorenz Jaeger of Paderborn was established. The Lutherans established a similar commission of theologians under the direction of Bishop Wilhelm Staehlin. In September of 1954 these two commissions sponsored a three-day conference at Berlin in which 150 Catholic and Protestant theologians, scholars, pastors and laymen discussed the obstacles to reunion. Compromise in belief and practice was declared unacceptable in ecumenical dialogue, and a serious study of the elements which divided and united Christians was begun.

Muench was fascinated by this exciting ecumenical breakthrough and closely followed its writings and activities. His reports to Rome on the movement were positive and encouraging. There were, naturally, accusations of heresy sent to Rome against *Una Sancta* activities by intransigent and reactionary elements in German Catholicism. The nuncio repeatedly calmed the Roman curia's suspicions of doctrinal indifference and assured them that the German bishops were not going too far in ecumenical activity. When Archbishop Jaeger was named a cardinal in 1965 it was an encouraging recognition of his efforts in this apostolate. Muench also attempted to inform his American colleagues about the possibilities of a similar movement developing in the United States, but there were no official developments in the States until after the council. In Germany the climate was more favorable since the nation had twice in a single generation been torn by war and subjected to pagan persecution under the Nazis. Catholics and Lutherans had been drawn together in suffering. Those German Christians who had together lived through the concentration camp experience were never again the same. Polemics and parochial competition were downgraded while common prayer, study of the Scriptures and holiness of life were emphasized. Co-operation in the social, political and moral issues affecting Germany and the world was developed as a basic step toward eventual Christian reunion. The form and structure of such a future unity was placed in the providence of God. The nuncio found most promising the Johann Adam Moehler Institute which was established in Paderborn under the patronage of Archbishop Jaeger. The German hierarchy and academic world respected Jaeger for his clarity of thought, well-balanced views and common sense judgments. The ecumenical movement in Germany made solid progress with Jaeger's strong support. Catholic theologians, historians and writers studied at the Johann Adam Moehler Institute to equip themselves better for conferences with Protestant scholars. The irenic spirit of the nineteenth century theologian Johann Adam Moehler (1796–1838) was the guide for lectures and discussions held at the institute. The contemporary scholarly demands of ecumenical work were met by the establishment of the Moehler Institute. Archbishop Jaeger clearly stated that Protestants would be welcomed in a brotherly spirit of tolerance without compromise in the fields of faith and morals by either side in a continuing dialogue.

Muench considered the co-operation of Lutherans and Catholics in charity and welfare work an auspicious step forward. Catholic and Lutheran support of the Christian Democratic Party in Germany also opened further avenues of joint action. Less promising was the continuing emphasis in the postwar period by both confessional groups of their contrasting outlooks on society. Institutional forms and structures continued to erect psychological blocks to ecumenical advance. An emphasis on prewar institutional separations limited ecumenical activity to small circles and the important second step toward reunion did not develop as rapidly as its proponents had hoped. But a deep-seated longing for unity existed among German Christians which resulted in an openness that had not been possible for 400 years. A growing awareness, despite differences, of what the two churches had in common awakened in both communions a new consciousness of their obligation to serve together the needs of all men.

One of the major concerns of the nuncio which remained an unsolved problem throughout this entire period was his relation to the Catholics in the East zone of Germany. The Vatican and the Federal Republic carefully recognized the nuncio as papal representative in all of Germany but in fact he was free and operative only in the western section of the former German nation. The partitioning of Germany following the war into four military occupation zones — British, French, Soviet and American — was not meant to be permanent. The Big Four had agreed that Germany would be unified at the earliest possible date, but in the intervening years Russia held firmly to its zone and created the German Democratic Republic there. Germany was cut in two economically and politically so it would no longer be a danger to Russia. East Germany became a part of the series of satellite states in central Europe serving as a buffer zone for Communist interests.

In West Germany there were eleven states with a population of 51,000,000; in East Germany 22,000,000 people lived in five states. The

Federal Republic of the West made a strong economic recovery after the war while the Democratic Republic of the East suffered from dismantling of industries, reparation payments, socialization of industry and agriculture. Business stagnated, goods never met demand, food and clothing were rationed, and a black market developed. The East mark currency was depreciated and sold at a discount of five to one West marks. East Germans continued to flee to the West in an increasing number.

There were two Catholic dioceses in East Germany, Berlin and Meissen in Saxony. There were also five other ecclesiastical jurisdictions: the Vicariate of Goerlitz, a small remnant west of the Oder-Neisse line of the former large and flourishing archdiocese of Breslau; and the areas of Saxon-Anhalt, Mecklenburg, Thuringia and Meiningen which belonged respectively to the archdiocese of Paderborn, and the dioceses of Osnabrueck, Fulda and Wuerzburg in West Germany.

Catholics composed a small minority of less than three million among the twenty-two million inhabitants of East Germany. The Lutheran Church was more seriously affected by the division. More than half of the three million Catholics in the East were expellees from East Prussia, Silesia and the Sudetenland who were scattered over an area of some 46,000 square miles. This area had always been diaspora territory for German Catholics but missionary problems were intensified after the war. The eastern state governments continued to pay the customary surtax to the churches as was done in West Germany. But religious census figures were never taken, and since the church tax was based on the income of church members, the total amount of tax money received by the churches in the East was inadequate in every way. The dioceses of West Germany helped as best they could. Papal relief and American assistance were directed primarily to East Germany after 1950. Muench asked the American bishops for a policy change in the distribution of their relief funds in Germany. He informed them that the recovery in West Germany was now advanced to the point where future goods and money should be directed to the needy in the East. Muench often told the story that he realized West Germany had recovered on the day a pastor asked American help to purchase a Carrara marble altar for his church that already had a main altar and two side altars.

The nuncio directed relief assistance to the 1,600 priests laboring in difficult eastern outposts and for the religious, educational and charitable work of fifty-two religious communities in 423 localities. Over 4,500 sisters were conducting kindergartens, day nurseries, catechetical centers, hospitals and homes for orphans and the aged. Shut off from contact with their fellow Catholics in West Germany and other parts of the world, these priests and sisters were conducting an heroic apostolate. Churches were open although local Communist officials created as many difficulties as possible. Observers reported that attendance at Mass and religious exercises was two to three times higher than in West Germany. The attachment of the suffering Catholics of the East to their Church was much deeper and warmer than in the West. Unusual daily sacrifices to keep the faith alive in their families intensified religious fervor.

There was considerable discussion in Lutheran and Catholic circles about the pros and cons of state support and encouragement of religion as a result of the eastern experience. Heinrich Koeppler said that western governmental authorities did everything in their power to aid the Church. While this good will was appreciated it did not always advance or fertilize the religious atmosphere in Germany. Even socialist state governments in the West aided religion whenever objective requests were presented. A general Church tax was levied throughout Germany and distributed to the Churches according to the religious preference recorded in census figures. A growing number of religious voices were raised against this milieu Catholicism or Lutheranism which possessed several characteristics of a state-church relationship. What can the Church do if she is loved by the State, Koeppler asked:

"It is not easy for the Church to be met with benevolence by the State and to enjoy a favorable public opinion. There is always danger of some corruption. I have often been in the Soviet zone and I certainly do not find only negative results in a situation where the Church has to take a stand against the State. New sources of vitality and awareness in the Church and in individual religious life spring up that are hard to find in the West. But I would not go to the extreme and say that the ideal condition for the Church's spiritual welfare is martyrdom. Each situation has its advantages and also its disadvantages. We can clearly see that when we look at the extremely different conditions on this side and on the other side of the East zone border."[7]

Muench respected highly the able director of Catholic charities in West Berlin, Monsignor John Zinke. Charitable assistance to the East was channeled through this courageous man who was called "a wanderer between two worlds." Priests and religious, welfare workers, widows, orphans, war veterans and prisoners of war, children, the sick and the aged were all assisted by papal relief from Bad Godesberg. Year after year Communist officials in eastern Germany continued to place obstacles in the way of free religious activity which the constitution of the German Democratic Republic and its five states guaranteed. Religious instruction was impeded or rendered impossible by ingenious pretexts. Censorship of the Catholic press prevented the distribution of publications of the Morus Publishing House, West Berlin, and the diocesan weekly, *Petrus Blatt*, was forbidden throughout the East zone. The Benno Verlag, Catholic publishing house in Leipzig, was never allowed enough paper for publishing Catholic books, pamphlets, leaflets and papers. Catholic publications from West Germany were not allowed in the East.

Catholic youth were under particular pressure as were their Lutheran companions. Pressure was put upon boys and girls under fourteen to join the Young Pioneers, a youth organization patterned after similar societies in Soviet Russia. After the age of fourteen young people were forced to join *Freie Deutsche Jugend*, the Free German Youth organization. Youth dedication ceremonies were held each year during the Easter season to replace first communion and Protestant confirmation ceremonies. Ten weeks of indoctrination were given before the rite by state functionaries who called themselves "shock troops against God." If young people did not participate they were not allowed to continue higher studies and their parents suffered economic recrimination and loss of jobs. Students in eastern universities were subjected to similar pressures and Marxist dialectical materialism was required subject matter in courses and teacher training materials.

Collections for religious purposes were impeded wherever possible inside churches or at meetings in homes. Priests could not be sent by bishops from their western jurisdictions to the East. Priests in the East were constantly subjected to surveillance and blackmail threats in a way that was reminiscent to all Germans of Hitler's Gestapo methods. Efforts were made, as in all countries behind the Iron Curtain, to separate clergy from ecclesiastical superiors, and the Lutheran Church was placed under special pressure in this regard. Clergy were pressured to participate in the National Front, in the Stockholm Peace Movement, in the Society for the Promotion of German-Soviet Friendship, and in pastors' conferences for peace. Pastors were accused in the press of being "warmongers in cassocks, saboteurs of peace, and stooges of the western powers." Lutheran Bishops Hanns Lilje of Hannover and Otto

Dibelius of Berlin, as well as the successive Catholic bishops of Berlin, Cardinal von Preysing, Bishops Wilhelm Weskamm and Julius Doepfner, stood up firmly with apostolic fortitude under such terroristic pressures. Muench told Rome that the clergy and people were exhibiting in the East a fortitude equal if not surpassing that of the early Christians. A Catholic spokesman went on Berlin radio (RIAS) in 1950 to declare: "Either the Church subjects herself to a materialistic state and makes herself a slave of might, or she remains faithful to her high aims and goes into the catacombs. Every true disciple of Christ knows that he will choose the latter way. The might of the rulers in the Soviet zone will perish as tyrannical might has always perished in the eras of persecution during two thousand years in the Church of Christ."

Efforts in the East were intensified year by year to make the Church an instrument of the State or to crush religion. Muench watched events closely but was not able to visit the East zone until 1954, eight years after his arrival in Germany. After the revolt of June, 1953, restrictions were somewhat relaxed and the nuncio was allowed to attend the 1200th anniversary on 23 May 1954 of the martyrdom of Saint Boniface and his companions at Erfurt in Thuringia. Two months of negotiation with different East zone ministries preceded the granting of a three-day pass to Nuncio Muench and Bishop Wilhelm Weskamm of Berlin. The group visited Bishop Frederick Rintelen, auxiliary of Paderborn, who resided at Magdeburg while caring for the eastern province of Saxon-Anhalt. At Erfurt Muench was deeply moved at the manifestations of faith and devotion to the Holy Father. On Saturday evening, May 22, Catholic youth from throughout the whole East zone formed a candle-light parade from the cathedral to the bishop's house to serenade the papal nuncio on his first visit with songs and by spelling out in light: "Long live Pius XII." On Sunday over 70,000 people participated in a Mass honoring the apostle of Germany which the nuncio offered on the steps of the cathedral in the public square. Newspapers in the West gave wide coverage to this historic visit, the first since Nuncio Orsenigo had left Berlin before the approaching Russians in 1945.

Muench had an opportunity to observe conditions and developments during this short trip into the East zone. He was particularly impressed with the small and struggling seminaries which had been established. Neither Berlin nor Meissen had seminaries of their own before the war; priests were trained for the area that was now East Germany either in the Breslau seminary, now behind the Oder-Neisse line, or in western seminaries. A seminary, the Bernardinum, was established shortly after the war at Neuzelle in the jurisdiction of Goerlitz, a small area of the former archdiocese of Breslau in an old, secularized Cistercian Abbey. The Bernardinum had grown in enrollment from twelve to fifty philosophers and theologians who lived in primitive conditions; seventy-four priests had already been ordained. Dr. Ferdinand Piontek, a septuagenarian and vicar of the cathedral chapter of Breslau, had courageously worked to establish this pastoral training center for future clergy.

There were no minor seminaries in the East and this situation presented a serious problem of preparing students in the classics and humanities for the major seminaries. The nuncio was impressed with a novel preparatory seminary he was shown, the Norbertus-Werk, which accepted only young men who had passed their examination in some trade or craft such as carpenter, mason, electrician, mechanic, or painter. Carefully chosen for their qualifications, the young men numbering 220, were all over eighteen years of age and were an inspiring group. Later minor seminaries were established in Schoeneiche, East Berlin, for 120 boys and at Halle in the Magdeburg jurisdiction with room for forty students.

The critical shortage of priests was also being met at another seminary established by Bishop Weskamm in a former Ursuline convent at Erfurt. Here seventy seminarians were at first studying, but when the restrictions on travel were temporarily lifted after the uprising of 1953 a large number of young seminarians courageously left their safe seminaries in the West to study in this pioneer Saint Pius X Seminary at Erfurt. Enrollment jumped to 220 students and offered encouraging hope for missionary work in the future.

The nuncio was touched by the apostolic spirit of the priests he met in the East zone who were working in an atmosphere of fear and anxiety. Refugees were continuing to pour into Berlin from the East zone at the rate of 8,000 a month. Some 153,693 people had sought freedom there during 1954 while 306,000 had passed through Berlin in the previous year. Fifty-four camps were in operation in Berlin to process the refugees. Muench had to organize assistance for the legal and welfare workers who were striving to serve these pilgrims fleeing from the intolerable political and economic restrictions of life in the East's Democratic Republic. Father Wilson Kaiser maintained the high traditions of NCWC War Relief Services in Berlin. An exodus of over two million people from the East continued until the Communists in August of 1961 erected the wall which sealed off the East for an indefinite time. Muench stated that the theoretical principles of atheistic Communism had become a cruel reality for Germany.

Conditions in the East zone improved slightly following the attacks of Premier Khrushchev on Stalinism and the uprising in Poznan, Poland. But after the Hungarian revolt of 1956 General Secretary Walter Ulbricht and Prime Minister Otto Grotewohl were hurriedly called to Moscow and given orders again to tighten restrictive measures throughout the Democratic Republic. Students had become restive in the East and Russian troops were brought in. So many teachers and professors had fled to the West that the quality of education had declined. The Church had to warn continually against the intensified Communist propaganda and indoctrination courses among youth. Parents did an ingenious job of catechizing their children at home. Priests were forbidden to visit state welfare institutions and prisons. Building permits were practically stopped; the Church was fortunate to hold what it possessed. A new Office for Church Affairs was established in 1956 headed by a Moscow trained fallen-away Catholic as an effort to control all activity of the Church in the East. Protestants and Catholics took a firm stand in defense of rights guaranteed by the constitution but local officials were encouraged to harass religious persons whenever possible. The solidarity of the clergy, with hardly an exception, when confronted by these oppressive governmental measures, was the chief factor in the continuing strength of the Church. The regime wanted to root out all religion but feared to take drastic steps among a restive people. There were few defections from the faith among the people despite constant pressure to abandon membership in the churches. Muench reported that the sensual, materialistic and easy-going life in West Germany resulted in more defections than were achieved by the oppression in East Germany.

The archdiocese of Cologne assumed sponsorship for the diocese of Berlin and the archdiocese of Munich for the diocese of Meissen. In 1957 the nuncio obtained a second permit to visit in the East zone for five days on the occasion of the 750th anniversary of the birth of Saint Elizabeth of Thuringia. Archbishop Muench returned to Erfurt accompanied by Father Joseph Senger, his secretary, Bishop Doepfner and Monsignor Zinke of Berlin. Economic conditions had not improved, the political situation was still one of harassment and infringement of individual liberties. The loss of population, as a result of the mass flight of thousands to the West, had created such a serious problem for the

Democratic Republic that the East German Parliament had imposed heavy legal fines and imprisonment on those who attempted to leave. Particularly serious was the loss of professors, scientists, engineers, physicians and writers. Since the end of the war an estimated 3,200,000 people had left East Germany, of whom a large percentage were Catholic. The Federal Republic had established 3,000 refugee camps in the West and built 2,500,000 homes for the refugees. Bishops, clergy and religious were no longer granted entry permits to the Soviet zone. The nuncio saw at first hand the continuing restrictive measures imposed by the Communist regime on any social manifestation of religion.

The work of the nuncio embraced the whole horizon of developments in Germany as they affected the Church. A nuncio should promote the relations of the Vatican with the civil government, watch the state of the Church and inform Rome of the same. This meant that Muench had to inform Rome about everything which might be of interest or importance in forming a judgment about German conditions, about its persons, problems, assets; its economic, cultural, artistic, military and spiritual life; about its desires and policies. The more abundant and precise, the more objective the information that a diplomat reports, the more it helps in forming right judgments and policy toward a specific country.

In this area Muench felt very much at home and thoroughly competent. As his reports to the Vatican are analyzed in terms of objective developments there can be little doubt of his competence. As an academic social scientist and a pastoral bishop he was uniquely qualified in the papal diplomatic corps to supply Rome with thorough analytic progress reports. His annual fifty page reports to the American bishops on German conditions were equally professional. American bishops of the period repeatedly stated that Muench's annual report to them, which he prepared over a twelve month period and presented sometimes in person and always in precise written form, were among the best they received at their November annual meetings. Both in Rome and the United States these reports on the condition of the Church in Germany were studied and used by officials. The Muench reports from Germany to the American hierarchy during the postwar years would make a unique volume of primary source materials for students of the development of religion. There is no similar corpus of commentary by an official visitor available in the field of socio-religious studies of German affairs.

Topics which the nuncio analyzed in these annual reports included family welfare, home building, industrial relations, labor developments, population studies, films and publications, Catholic organizations, diaspora needs, rural life, charity work, education, youth activity, religious celebrations, marriage problems and liturgical reform. To the Holy See the nuncio reported on relations with the federal government, concordat problems, rapport between Catholics and Protestants, general religious developments, clerical and lay status, education, religious statistics, political parties and the situation in the East zone.

Each report was carefully organized as an academic position paper. The reader has the impression that Dr. Muench had prepared his annual lecture on the state of religion in Germany. All is in syllabus form; statements were objective and supported with references and bibliography. Each topic was treated in its historic, sociological, cultural, intellectual, political, economic and religious dimension. There was a striking absence of slanted reporting and analysis. All sides of a question under discussion were presented and statistical data supported conclusions. Pius XII was stimulated by the quality and carefully balanced insights of these reports, and Monsignor Montini told Muench on 28 November 1956 that his pastoral activity and diplomatic reporting were an intelligent and assiduous service to the Church and the Holy See.

The social scientist was not, however, equally at home in the realm of diplomatic protocol. As Dr. George Shuster stated to the writer on 19 September 1963: "Until the time when full sovereignty was conferred on Germany Muench was happy and very effective. As a papal nuncio in Bonn he felt the walls closing in." Muench was harassed by protocol and the endless correspondence associated with his position as dean of the diplomatic corps at Bonn. He kept a current file on all diplomats who called formally on him as dean when they came to Germany and as they left. Frequently his assistance was sought by these diplomats and their staffs in their relations with the Federal Government or in matters such as housing. Each year he had to prepare a formal address on behalf of the diplomatic corps at their traditional New Year's reception by President Theodor Heuss. Muench always insisted he was not a born diplomat and judged he was wasting time on the diplomatic circuit that he could be devoting to people and their needs. He found particularly wearing the continual round of receptions, luncheons and dinners. As dean he could not evade these social affairs so highly prized by the diplomatic corps as indispensable opportunities for exchanging news and information. He much preferred to be administering the sacraments, helping people or joining in an academic discussion on social problems of the day. He found diplomatic personnel too often to be faceless people, as he quaintly said, professionals in a world apart from hearth, altar and work bench. Here was a striking confrontation of the milieu of a German immigrant's son from the United States with the ancient structure of international diplomacy.

And yet, paradoxically, Muench was effective in the area in which he considered himself most inadequate. Frants Hvass, senior ambassador to Germany from Denmark during the entire postwar period, said of him:

"The nuncio's humanity made a deep impression upon people. He was not restricted to church work only. Archbishop Muench was very mild, more than kind to all, Catholics or not. He was reserved, kept back, never entered into politics. Not once did difficulties arise during his tenure as nuncio. Things went most smoothly under him as dean. He was always supported by his colleagues. The fact that he spoke English and not only Latin or French or Italian helped to break down stereotypes. I never heard one word that was unkind about him in the entire diplomatic corps. He was open and ever asking for practical solutions to problems. He was so simple; at one reception he was placed in a room by himself and he asked me to come and sit with him because he didn't want to sit alone. We were all impressed with his lack of any officiousness."[8]

Walter C. Dowling, minister under Ambassador James Conant in Germany, and then American ambassador to Korea, spoke warmly of Muench's influence on the diplomatic corps. There was not one person in the Bonn diplomatic group, Dowling said, who did not consider Muench as a personal friend. Some even affectionately called him "Red" because of his reddish hair and the cardinal's robes they all wished for him. Mrs. Erika Pappritz, chief of protocol in the Federal Republic's foreign office, commented:

"Nuncio Muench was very kind, gentle and personal on every occasion. Monsignor Hack often came to me to ask questions about protocol. He said that Archbishop Muench did not like diplomatic procedures. Once he asked what the archbishop was to do about dinners; should he go to dinners where women were wearing low cut gowns? I replied that both Pacelli and Orsenigo attended such dinners and that Muench should consider himself invited as a diplomat and not a bishop. If a picture were taken the Holy Father would understand because he attended such receptions himself. Or, if necessary, the women can be informed that they should wear scarfs.

"There was a great difference between Orsenigo and Muench. Orsenigo was a trained diplomat; Muench was in the first place a priest. He was modest in a touching way. He did not commit any mistakes; he would do everything he was told but did not like it. You would expect that when the dean of the diplomatic corps appeared that he would stand and receive greetings. But not him; he would move around and talk with everyone. He was uncommonly well-liked in the diplomatic corps. Sometimes there are mishaps in the diplomatic corps, but never with Muench. He and Adenauer both had a good sense of humor and got along well. Adenauer appreciated Muench for being so natural and sincere. In 1957 the German Government evidenced its appreciation for Muench's contribution by conferring on him the Grand Cross of the Order of Merit.

"I remember well a call from the Spanish ambassador who was having a visiting cardinal and Muench to dinner. He wanted to know how to place them at table. In the first place, I answered, you should never invite both. But the cardinal precedes even if Muench represents the Pope. So he placed the cardinal above Muench who didn't care at all. This was so typical of him.

"At another reception, during the time Germany was deciding on a new national anthem, it was directed that only the third verse of 'Deutschland, Deutschland ueber alles' could be sung, Muench said to me: 'I don't see why everyone is worried about this. It is a question of patriotism and not of nationalism. But many foreigners and Germans objected to the first two verses and they were not sung. Muench's view endeared him to the German people." [9]

The nuncio enjoyed his own annual official reception at *Turmhof* on the occasion of the anniversary of the Pope's coronation. Muench was repeatedly told that these receptions were the highlight of the diplomatic receptions in Bonn because of their dignified and careful preparation. The selection of those to be invited was done with care by the nuncio and his staff. Diplomats liked to come to the house of the Pope's representative and the archbishop did not shy away from preparations for these celebrations. A special honor, never forgotten by his guests, was the fact that he invited their wives as well. Muench said he did this as a special recognition of the sacrament of marriage. The nuncio met all guests in his typically warm and uncomplicated way, put all at their ease and moved about talking to all who came. He was always in good humor on these occasions and was a genial host.[10]

In the same way Archbishop Muench enjoyed visitors both at Kronberg and Bad Godesberg. In Fargo he had established a tradition of hospitality and good conversation. In Germany he was soon known for a welcome that the Germans found *gemuetlich* and fondly referred to as reminiscent of nineteenth-century immigrant patterns of reception. In the early years at Kronberg Muench looked forward to American and other visitors. They stayed at Villa Grosch, were given guided tours of the new Germany and enjoyed long and informed discussions of hopes for the future. American bishops and their parties touring Europe were given a special welcome as a sign of appreciation for their generous support of the papal mission to Germany. But as the years passed and the number of bishops, priests and laity visiting Germany grew to major proportions, the constant stream of guests began to take its toll. There were over 200 American bishops and a good proportion found their way to Muench's doorstep as Americans began to visit Germany in a steady stream during the 1950's. For example, in a week's period during July of 1950 he entertained for several days two priests from Fargo, Bishop Joseph H. Schlarman of Peoria, Bishop Albert R. Zuroweste of Belleville, Monsignor Frank A. Kaiser of Belleville, Father George A. Carton of Peoria, while having Bishop William T. Mulloy and Fathers Charles J. Hoffer and Elmer J. Grosser of Covington as house guests for the whole week. This entertaining continued while he was pressed on all sides by German visitors, petitioners for charity, official mail and his ordinary schedule. Archbishop Muench became simply worn out by this pressure and never found a way to say no. "Visitors, visitors," he exclaimed, "they all take this caravan route." In desperation he wrote on 2 June 1957 to his classmate and friend Bishop Mariano Garriga of Corpus Christi, Texas: "If only you were one of the many tourists who call here, some of whom I do not even know. They are recommended by some friends back home. Believe me, it would be a real pleasure to have you here for a number of days as our guest. Take a jet and come over."

The archbishop never tired throughout the whole period of attending German Catholic religious celebrations, pilgrimages, conventions and especially the annual *Katholikentage*. Germany, he said, was a country of congresses and meetings and while he could not accept all invitations, the number of events in which he participated, gave addresses, offered

Mass or delivered sermons broke attendance records. He judged that the nuncio could meet the people in this way and come to know their interests and needs.

Muench's papers contain folder after folder of speeches given at meetings and on special occasions before groups that ranged from youth organizations to scientific societies.[11] Newspapers, radio and television covered his major addresses since nuncio and Muench had become synonymous to the German people. In spite of his official work he continued to accept invitations to officiate as a bishop. He liked to ordain men to the priesthood and went to Limburg, to the Jesuits at Saint-Georgen in Frankfurt and Maria Laach Abbey where he ordained Fargo seminarians who had studied at the North American College in Rome. The archbishop was fascinated by the colorful traditions of German Catholic assemblies, their pageantry, piety and enthusiasm. Cardinal Jaeger of Paderborn thought the nuncio enjoyed participating in large Catholic celebrations because he had come from a diaspora diocese at Fargo. American Catholicism had fewer public pilgrimages and national manifestations of the faith. The continent of the United States was too large for such organized expressions of religion while Germany was more regional. The nuncio enjoyed participating with the common people in pilgrimages to shrines of the Virgin Mary in the Rhineland, Westphalia and Bavaria.

Each year's *Katholikentag* found Muench in attendance to celebrate the final pontifical Mass. He faithfully attended the conferences and meetings of the days' sessions and learned from the spirited discussions the German Catholic positions on problems of the day. The Cologne *Katholikentag* of 1956, with 800,000 participating in the closing function, and the Berlin *Katholikentag* of 1958 particularly impressed the nuncio. When he offered the final Mass in Hitler's Olympic Stadium with 130,000 participating there and 40,000 more in nearby bleachers the archbishop was filled with gratitude that Germany's Catholics had survived their frightful ordeal and were again free and strong.

The stories about the nuncio at these Catholic gatherings spread across Germany and became part of contemporary folklore. The people had just never experienced such humane and disarming kindness from high churchmen. When the papal visitor first came to Limburg there was much preparation on the part of welcoming committees who greeted him solemnly by genuflecting and kissing his ring. To their astonishment he arrived in a plain black suit, shook hands with them instead and deposited in their hands a package of American cigarettes. Shop-keepers in Limburg still recount the times Muench walked down the street from the cathedral talking with the children and distributing candy to them from large bags. At the diocesan seminary of Cologne he passed out cigarettes to the seminarians and in the presence of Cardinal Frings jokingly promised the seminarians that if they joined the Fargo diocese as missionaries they would be pastors within three years. While he was celebrating Mass for the Cologne seminarians the servers came before him at the wrong time to wash his hands. He said: "Well, as long as you are here let's go through with it anyway."

The cigarette technique which Archbishop Muench used so often did not always work in the complicated world of European protocol. When he went down to Wuerttemberg for a public occasion and slipped a package of cigarettes into the pocket of the Prince zu Hohenzollern that startled and offended high personage handed the cigarettes to his servant instead of accepting them with pleasure and good humor. Such acts, unimportant in themselves, played an important role in structured European relationships. The aristocrats and servants of the protocol considered the nuncio's natural and simple behavior all too typical of his Bavarian craft and immigrant background. Muench secretly enjoyed it when an especially class-conscious or pedantic soul did not understand his American sense of humor. However, the unique good will from all sides and the experience of Muench's noble character and warm heart quickly emerged. The archbishop frequently pontificated at the Muenster Basilica in Bonn and the people gathered inside and outside the church to cheer him with warm enthusiasm. It was a unique expression of gratitude for all he had done for Germany. Monsignor Hack summarized this development:

"It is absolutely astonishing how Muench captured the simple people. They loved him, adored him; it was really amazing. They felt that here was an unassuming man who talked right to their hearts, not a traditional prince of the Church. It is rather interesting, this instinctive turning to Muench, because there were many persons who found it difficult to get in contact with him, who on first sight did not feel drawn to him. The simple people, however, held him in warm esteem. They loved him." [12]

An interesting case in point occurred at a workers' session in the *Singakademie* during the first Berlin *Katholikentag* of 1952. Josef Gockeln was president and, as was customary, the bishops and the nuncio passed from meeting to meeting to listen for a time. When the party of cardinals, bishops and the nuncio arrived Gockeln was speaking. The workers broke into thunderous applause as the nuncio took his seat. Observers said this was the most prolonged applause they had ever experienced. Gockeln finished his speech and then told the audience he was in a major dilemma. Custom required that he now ask one of the cardinals or bishops to speak, but would they excuse him if he asked the nuncio instead. Gockeln then delivered an extemporized tribute to Muench in which he praised Muench's work for Germany in a moving way. He ended by addressing him: "Your Excellency, we shall never forget the talk you gave to the miners at the Bochum *Katholikentag* in 1949. At that time you said the hands of those who work so hard in the bowels of the earth should be kissed. We know you meant this in a symbolic sense, but in fact you not only kissed our hands, you showed us a respect and gave us such honor as will never be forgotten by the workers in the mining districts of the Ruhr." [13]

In his approach to the responsibilities of the German assignment Muench was not only being himself but was also acting shrewdly and according to a carefully considered necessity. He had often been told in Rome and diplomatic circles that he held the most difficult of diplomatic posts. He wanted to settle affairs in a smooth and efficient manner. He was also conscious of the growing underground reaction among Catholics throughout the world in the 1950's, a reaction that would break forth on the floor of Vatican Council II, that there should be an end to the paraphernalia of nuncios and delegates as outmoded due to new communications media. Michael de la Bedoyere had called for an end of the "tradition of triumphalism," and a realistic facing of the contemporary realities of the Church's nineteen millennia of existence. Voices were raised in missionary and established Christian communities asking for a radical revision of Vatican diplomatic procedures. The presence of nuncios, internuncios, and delegates in countries left the impression that the Church was imitating secular powers, as was historically the case. The need of foreign representatives of the Vatican was continually questioned since modern communications made instant contact with Rome possible from all parts of the globe. Regular meetings of the Synod of Bishops was another new vehicle for meaningful exchange between Rome and local churches. Bishops and observers were more and more asking why patriarchs and bishops designated by their regional or national conferences could not represent them to the Vatican. The latter would know their own country better than outsiders, would be thoroughly familiar with local traditions and languages, and could be in a better position to evaluate problems and decide on appropriate solutions. If papal representatives must be continued, then a growing number of competent observers also preferred laymen instead of foreign clerics in a Vatican diplomatic corps of the future.

Muench, accordingly, wanted his tenure in office to reflect these growing demands for a new style in papal diplomacy. He worked hard at constituting a minor breakthrough in papal diplomacy, a pastoral technique rather than an innovation which would have to come from a future pope and a reformed Roman curia. He was conscious that there had been a favorable public response to his strong, personal involvement in the problems of the German people, but he was equally conscious that he had not been prepared for the spirit he was striving to establish. The nuncio was criticized by papal diplomats for not operating the nunciature at Bad Godesberg according to the book, for disturbing traditional procedures and also for working so hard. But Muench said the times were extraordinary and demanded extraordinary procedures. The future Pope John XXIII, as Archbishop Angelo Giuseppe Roncalli, nuncio at Paris, had expressed similar sentiments in May of 1950: "To tell the truth, I have always believed that, for an ecclesiastic, diplomacy (so-called) must be imbued with the pastoral spirit; otherwise it is of no use and makes a sacred mission look ridiculous."

Archbishop Muench held a deep conviction that the nunciature household must be a first example of charity and mutual trust. He strove to maintain peaceful relations between his Italian, German and American staff. The Italian monsignors who assisted at Bad Godesberg were aides in preparing memoranda to Rome and in interpreting the wishes of Pius XII and the Secretariat of State which, Muench said, "is always our guiding principle of action." The German staff members helped the nuncio in governmental, ecclesiastical and diplomatic contacts. The Americans were there primarily to assist the archbishop in his continuing duties as bishop of Fargo. There were difficulties along the way as individuals tried to advance their own ideas on proper procedure. The nuncio was not always regarded by members of his own staff as being competent in certain areas where they considered themselves particularly qualified. Conflicts arose and Muench ever insisted on charity as normative. Once when a protest came to him about a staff member who was accused of upstaging the nuncio and advancing himself, Muench suggested that he and the accuser go to the chapel and pray for the accused since they all needed prayers. The nuncio was aware of second level tensions among the three national groups at Bad Godesberg but he never failed to support the staff. They, in turn, and despite occasional differences, were unanimous in their loyalty to and appreciation of their benefactor.[14]

Archbishop Muench worried about the health of his close friend and secretary, Father Howard Smith, who suffered from a congenital heart condition. From 1948 to 1953 Smith was at his side caring for all exchange of charity money and working long hours on the English correspondence. The nuncio did not escape criticism for imposing his own rigorous work schedule on his secretary. In July of 1953 Monsignor Smith returned to Fargo and after being hospitalized in November of 1954 he died prematurely at the age of 53 on 8 February 1955. Muench far away in Bad Godesberg was deeply grieved at this personal loss. Monsignor Smith was succeeded in turn by two young priests from Fargo, Fathers Gerald M. Weber and Joseph Senger, who served the nuncio during the remainder of his tenure.

Muench tried to establish an atmosphere in the nunciature at Bad Godesberg similar to the family life he loved in Milwaukee. He was particularly attached to the Benedictine sisters who did some of the secretarial work and managed the household. Monsignor Alois Eckert, director of charities of the Archdiocese of Freiburg, on a visit to Maria Laach Abbey, had suggested to Muench that he engage these sisters from Freiburg and they were a constant consolation to him throughout his German years. Monsignor Guido Del Mestri, counselor of the nunciature and later apostolic delegate in Nairobi, Kenya, and Mexico gave Muench the title of "father of the household," and he enjoyed carrying out this role. His paternal kindness was remembered by all who were at Bad Godesberg in the 1950's. They lived not only with a professor of sociology but with a priest who was social in his attitudes and actions. Although he was absorbed in his official work he did not forget the nunciature family. Each evening there was conversation in the library when the nuncio was home, and he came daily to visit anyone who was sick to be sure they were being cared for and to give them a blessing. There was a relaxed family atmosphere at all times.

But it was the big feasts that everyone remembered. Muench wanted to join especially in the preparations for Christmas. He gave money to the sisters and employees which they were to spend for gifts for their own families. Christmas was always a family feast at the nunciature, exactly as it was celebrated in Milwaukee and Fargo. After Benediction of the Blessed Sacrament in the chapel on Christmas eve, the whole staff assembled in the large reception room. The nuncio would first read the Christmas Gospel while he stood near a carefully chosen large Bavarian tree. Underneath the tree there were many packages, all gaily wrapped which was not the German custom. Then all assembled would sing the beloved German Christmas carols before the nuncio passed gifts among them. Champagne was served as well as cognac and benedictine; home made cookies made the rounds, including those from his mother and sisters in Milwaukee. This *Bescherung*, or distribution of gifts, was Muench's special delight; he sang with the staff, made the rounds with chocolates and cookies and stayed until 10:30 p.m. when it was time to prepare for the midnight Mass which he was to celebrate at the Muenster Basilica in Bonn. Christmas day dinner had to be exactly as his mother's was: consomme, goose, dumplings, sauerkraut, apple sauce, chestnuts and apple dressing and German Christmas sweet roll. A particular problem over the years was the cooking of a turkey and plum pudding for Thanksgiving which all worked at but never really achieved according to form. American guests were welcomed magnanimously and the sisters tried to cook their dishes for these occasions, not always with success but to the enjoyment of all. On special occasions such as First Fridays and other feast days all assembled in his chapel for Mass. The nuncio's chapel had been executed by Brother Notker Becker, O.S.B., of Maria Laach Abbey with woodcarvings, reminiscent of the craft of Muench's father, according to themes of sacrifice from the Hebrew and Christian Scriptures. On these occasions Muench wanted all to join in singing German hymns, especially to the Virgin Mary, such as "Maria zu lieben, ist allzeit mein Sinn." Gifts were distributed to each member of the staff on their name days. On fast and ember days he was strict in enforcing the Church rules. But on feast days such as Easter he insisted on numerous colored eggs throughout the octave along with the cherished old-fashioned wood smoked ham (*Bauernschinken*) that Josef Reiss obtained each year from his relatives in Baden. Each Easter Sunday the eggs and cakes had to be blessed before breakfast. The Christmas tree was sent every year from the *Bayerischer Wald*. It was a gift from Father Josef Krottenthaler, pastor at Neukirchen hl. Blut on the Bohemian border. Piety and family traditions were ever the emphasis.

The Muench family preserved close ties with one another throughout the years. Interest and activity centered on their mother who lived a long life in their midst. The nuncio considered her to be a model of Christian family virtue and strength. She lived in Milwaukee with the archbishop's sister Teresa and took great interest in her family, parish, friends and garden. The archbishop never failed to write her a weekly longhand letter in German full of news and small events and was consoled by the prayers of his "Liebe Mutti" for him. He anxiously awaited letters from her and his sisters and brothers and talked much about their families. His mother missed him very much and he would plan for months ahead the infrequent trips to the States so he could spend the majority of his time in Milwaukee and Fargo. Nothing refreshed him more and the German bishops commented often on the nuncio's exemplary devotion to his mother and family. He was always preparing some gift, photo or German keepsake to send to his mother, and during meals and recreation the staff heard more about his brother Joe's bowling lanes in Neenah or his sisters' activities in Milwaukee than international or ecclesiastical politics. German dignitaries on tour in the States visited Muench's mother and a parade of cardinals, bishops, governmental and military officials, to the delight of the family, passed through the Muench home in Milwaukee. Newspapers carried accounts of these visits in both the United States and Germany. Pope Pius sent telegrams for celebrations or when his mother was sick. On 6 December 1954 the mother fractured her hip and never fully recovered. The nuncio planned on visiting her during July of 1955 but she died suddenly on 24 May 1955. Because of the pressing concordat problems in the *Laender* and the pending Karlsruhe court decision Muench could not leave his post to attend her funeral. After so many years of close ties it was the greatest sacrifice he had to make. Archbishop Meyer offered the requiem Mass and Bishop Dworschak paid his mother "a loving tribute" in Muench's name. Bishops John B. Grellinger, auxiliary of Green Bay, and Roman Atkielski, auxiliary of Milwaukee, along with a large number of clergy and laity assisted at the last rites which brought Muench, far from home, "more comfort than can be expressed in words." In the years ahead he always returned to Milwaukee for vacations but it was never quite the same for him.[15]

Archbishop Muench's relations with his diocese of Fargo during the German years were also an intimate and personal attachment. No one who knew the bishop of Fargo had any doubts about where his heart was throughout the entire period. He tenaciously held to his title there despite continual questioning both at home and abroad of his dual offices. Even after becoming an archbishop and a nuncio he still hoped he could return to his diocese despite the obvious impossibility of such an eventuality. As his health began to decline he was even more adamant in this position. After 1951 he realized that he could never return to the Red River Valley but he held to his diocese with the hope that he could come back for one year and then retire. During the German years he was continually mentioned as a possible successor to several American archdioceses as they became vacant. Personally, he would have liked such a development, but ever loyal to Pius XII and the German bishops and people who wanted him at Bonn, he always had Fargo to look forward to when sooner or later he would come to the end of his long service abroad. He plainly did not want to retire in Rome and could not see what he could do in the Church after the German assignment was ended.

Fargo and its life were a daily joy to him. He kept in contact through voluminous correspondence and visits. His auxiliary, Bishop Leo Dworschak, was a consolation to him at every turn. He repeatedly told Dworschak that he was actually the bishop of the diocese and tried in every way to support him. Neither Muench nor Dworschak suspected that the latter would continue as auxiliary for eleven years. Muench was solicitous to have Dworschak looked upon by the priests and people as ordinary of the diocese. He obtained the faculties of a residential bishop for his auxiliary so that he could function as the ordinary. Since he had to be away for so long he wanted the auxiliary to have a free hand at every step. He wrote his faithful Fargo secretary, Larry Boyle, on 12 November 1957:

"Two decades have sped by fast, and who would have dreamed that half of my time as bishop of Fargo would be spent away from the diocese. Our Holy Father has given me an honorable position in Germany, but believe me I am more than grateful to him that he continues to allow me to be bishop of a diocese I learned to love for its priests, religious and laity."

Bishop Dworschak wrote long and detailed letters to Muench on every development in the diocese. Telephone calls and frequent visits between the two friends also helped in maintaining contact. Muench and Smith at Bad Godesberg were always thinking of the staff in Fargo and living through the problems at home. One of their continuing pastimes was to compare the time on the North Dakota prairie with theirs on the Rhine and to talk about what was then going on at 608 Broadway in Fargo. A constant stream of banter was exchanged between the separated friends as a cover for their loneliness and homesickness.[16]

Dworschak consulted Muench on every major appointment, explained existing problems, asked advice on building programs and, in his exact manner, detailed each step that was taken. Muench responded promptly with memoranda on all points; he encouraged his auxiliary and when he disagreed with him he never insisted on his viewpoint being followed. He would say: "You know, of course, that I want you to proceed with whatever arrangements you think best. I merely want to recall all things as a sort of guide for action. I want you to feel completely free to make whatever decisions you think should be made in the diocese." Muench revealed here as in so many instances how objective he could be. He never was jealous of his authority in Fargo and the unique experience of a bishop absent for so long did not impede the progress of the diocese. Moreover, he firmly and promptly rejected any appeals to him over the head of Bishop Dworschak. Muench was fatherly when problems arose among the clergy and gave detailed advice on procedures that would be kind, generous, patient and reasonable. His auxiliary carried through in a spirit that created confidence among clergy and laity in Fargo.

The first two years after Dworschak came to Fargo were the most difficult. During that period he had to face a shortage of priests, bad floods in the Red River Valley, the anti-garb law in North Dakota and building programs in several communities. The building responsibilities were the heaviest for Bishop Dworschak since there was so much to be done and there were so few resources to complete the undertakings safely. Fargo was a missionary diocese and money was scarce during the first years after World War II. Muench helped as much as he could in soliciting priests through correspondence with Archbishop Richard Cushing of Boston. The latter on one occasion replied that "anything we can do for the bishop of Fargo will be readily and willingly done for him." Priests were also obtained from Bishop Mulloy in Covington on a lend-lease basis. The problem in Fargo was that there was no seminary, monastery or college in the diocese that could be turned to in an emergency situation. Muench always dreamed of a monastery in his diocese, but that never materialized since there was already the Benedictine Assumption Abbey at Richardton, North Dakota, in the Bismarck diocese, and the state of North Dakota could never have supported two abbeys. The minor seminary of Fargo, named in his memory, was established after his death in 1962 by Bishop Dworschak. Illness and deaths among the clergy created a severe shortage and Bishop Dworschak took to the road to obtain temporary assistance where he could. Muench supported him by writing to American bishops asking for the loan of priests to serve the people of Fargo. The archbishop also worked incessantly to direct priests from among the displaced persons in Germany to the Fargo diocese. Eleven priests came to Fargo as a result of his efforts. If every diocese in the United States had done as well there would have been no priest shortage and no problem of helping needy priests who wanted to be of service. Only one of the eleven displaced priests who came to Fargo left the diocese for a larger place. The others are faithful pastors in the diocese of their adoption.

The "anti-garb" bill placed before the people of North Dakota during 1948, presented a major problem to the State's two dioceses of Fargo and Bismarck. A North Dakota citizens' group obtained sufficient signatures to petition that an initiated measure be entered on the special ballot of the 29 June 1948 general election. This initiated measure prohibited teachers in public schools from wearing any garb denoting a religious order or denomination. The proposed act was aimed at preventing seventy-six sisters from teaching 2,051 children from rural areas throughout the State. These sisters were teaching in public schools at the request of local school boards due to teacher shortages and because parents wanted them.

A spirited controversy developed and the Catholics of the two dioceses organized opposition to the bill on the grounds that it was discrimination based on the clothes teachers wore; that Catholics and Protestants wanted sisters so licensed and that this bill would divide Christians at a time when they were working closely together; that local school boards should solve local problems; that no religion was being taught by the sisters in public schools; that the sisters did not challenge the right of any other licensed teachers because of race, religion or creed. Proponents of the measure held that the teaching sisters constituted a threat of the Church taking over the public school system and that the procedure effected a union of Church and State.

A Committee for Defense of Civil Rights was organized to oppose the measure with two lawyers, Herbert G. Nilles of Fargo, a Catholic, and Clifford Jansonius of Bismarck, a Lutheran, as co-chairmen. This committee issued 63,000 copies of a thirty-two page pamphlet written by Bishop Ryan under the title: *Facts About Sisters Teaching in Public Schools in North Dakota* as an attempt to counteract distorted and emotional stories about the teaching sisters. A campaign supporting the measure was organized by forces outside North Dakota who opposed religion in any phase of public education and who supported strict separation of Church and State. A similar bill was being prepared in Missouri and challenges were being raised in New Mexico to sisters teaching in public schools.

An unfortunate and heated exchange of accusations was soon waxing strong. Bishops Dworschak and Ryan, along with their clergy and laity, tried to keep the whole issue on the level of the bill's discriminatory aspects but the American tradition of religious bigotry soon was dividing communities and religious groups that had made much headway in interfaith activity during the war years. When the votes were counted on June 29 the anti-garb initiated measure passed by a 52–48% majority of 9,000 votes. Catholics represented only nineteen per cent of the North Dakota population. The strong negative vote indicated that a large number of Protestants had joined their Catholic neighbors in support of the *status quo*. The anti-garb measure was defeated in every county where sisters were teaching in the public schools except two, Cass and McHenry.

Bishop Muench, who had been following the controversy closely and giving advice on procedures, stated in his *Catholic Action News* column "The Bishop Writes from Europe" of September, 1948:

"The Catholics of the State of North Dakota, supported by their non-Catholic friends, anxious to have basic civil rights prevail, put forth a truly superb effort. We have reason to be proud of them. Looking in retrospect at the campaign from a land where Catholics and Protestants are marching arm in arm to protect parental rights in the interest of religious education in the public schools of Germany, it is disturbing to an onlooker, to say the least, that Protestant clergymen put themselves in the forefront of the anti-garb campaign, in association with avowed enemies of religion, in order to bar American women, fully qualified to teach, from accepting positions in schools to which they had been invited by parents, merely because they chose to wear a religious rather than a secular garb. We can well understand why good Protestants are dismayed, mortified and chagrined over such a spectacle. The Protestant Church lost more on June 29 than its leaders seem to realize, or are willing to admit. The bigotry that was unleashed in connection with the campaign strengthened the Catholic Church, as it always has in the past, and weakened that of the Protestants in proportion."

The North Dakota incident was one phase of the strong anti-Catholic movements in the United States following World War II. The growing influence and position of Catholics internationally and at home gave rise to a contemporary revival of the nineteenth-century Know-Nothing spirit. The personal position of Pius XII, the growth of Christian democratic parties in Europe, the strength and development of Catholic schools as well as the emergence of several national Catholic political leaders all brought forth a negative reaction. Such organizations as Protestants and Other Americans United for Separation of Church and State, the writings of a Paul Blanshard and stepped-up Masonic activity particularly in the hinterlands all created religious tensions.

Muench, Dworschak and Ryan were now faced with a hard decision: what should be done about teaching sisters in public schools where they were wanted by local communities? Their imaginative and, for the times, startling solution became the American religious news story of the year. The bishops stated in their cathedrals at Fargo and Bismarck on Sunday, 11 July 1948, that the American constitution guaranteed that no law could discriminate on the basis of religious membership or belief. Since the so-called anti-garb measure prohibited the wearing of any religious habit by a public school teacher, and because this act would force the withdrawal of sisters and close some public schools in North Dakota, an emergency situation existed due to teacher shortages. Consequently the sisters would arrange to wear in school "a respectable secular dress" which in no way indicated the fact that such teachers were members of a religious order or denomination. Where school districts found it necessary and desirable to retain the services of the sisters, these teachers would continue to teach attired in a manner in strict compliance with the law. "In contests of this kind," Muench stated, "one should in my opinion try everything. There were many who thought Mrs. McCollum would not win her case in the supreme court after she lost it in the lower courts."

The effect of this thunderbolt had national repercussions. Secularists were confused and dismayed that their tactic had backfired, and no anti-garb bill was initiated in any state after 1948. The forces who believed that local control was the best expression of democracy were heartened. Progressive groups in the American Catholic community were encouraged by this realistic and open solution. Muench was proud of this breakthrough, but he feared that conservative American bishops might consider this step as a dangerous precedent for the sisterhoods. He, accordingly, wrote several letters to American churchmen explaining and defending the North Dakota decision as a precaution lest their Fargo-Bismarck experiment would come under attack on the floor of the annual conference of bishops during their Washington meeting in November. With his strong backing and the careful explanations of Dworschak and Ryan the breakthrough went unquestioned. When Muench was in Rome during the autumn of 1948 he also vigorously defended the North Dakota experiment at the Congregation of Religious and gained approval through a rescript for sisters to wear secular garbs in public schools.

As a result this interesting pre-ecumenical and pre-Vatican Council II experiment was far from a set-back. It became a pacemaking precedent and a striking foreshadowing of post-conciliar developments among the sisterhoods. Stritch with a smile told Muench: "Fargo has led again." Muench replied on 2 November 1948 that he knew several officials at the NCWC as well as leading American conservative ecclesiastics were strongly against "Catholic public schools," and sisters teaching in secular garbs in public schools. But these eastern cardinals and archbishops had larger financial incomes to support Catholic schools in such dioceses as New York, Brooklyn or Philadelphia and they should not impose their favored position on missionary dioceses. "More important," Muench continued, "there is a fundamental principle at stake here. It seems to me that when civil liberties of our religion, to say nothing about the rights of parents regarding the education of their children, are involved, we should use every means at hand to create new structures for our apostolate."

The bishop of Fargo through the years also watched with interest the attendance at the annual Fargo Catholic Action Days, his little *Katholikentage* as he called them. Each year he continued to write a Lenten pastoral and during the years in Germany Muench prepared thirteen such pastorals.

Rural retreats continued to be held, and the pastoral and missionary care for Mexican Catholics from Texas who worked in the sugar beet fields in the Red River Valley was augmented by trailer chapels which the Catholic Church Extension Society supplied. Muench had advocated the same technique for work among refugees and expellees in Germany and Dutch Catholics had supplied these mobile units for the German diaspora. The Bishop's Diocesan Charity Fund was organized in 1946 as successor to the Orphans' Collection for Saint John's Orphanage and as an effort to establish the various charitable undertakings of the diocese on a secure and permanent basis.[17] The number of priests in the diocese increased from 127 in 1935 to 161 in 1959, and the priesthood scholarship fund steadily grew until it reached a total of $560,306 in 1959. In 1948 Muench asked for a survey of Catholic families who would be willing to take German displaced persons into the diocese. Sixty-five families offered to accept displaced persons in their homes, 210 promised aid in some form, and 285 jobs were offered on farms, in construction, for mechanics, domestics, nurses and doctors. The results were not as positive as he had hoped, but at least a beginning had been made.

When Muench went to Germany the Fargo Diocese included 69,622 Catholics and he happily watched it grow during his stay abroad to a total of 85,449 by 1959. The growth and development of his beloved diocese was the major consolation of the first American nuncio to serve the universal Church. If one key to the effectiveness of Archbishop Muench as nuncio to Germany can be traced, it will be found in the patterns of missionary and diaspora action that he knew and cherished in his prairie diocese in the American heartland.

During the Bochum Katholikentag, *on 1 September 1949,*
Bishop Muench and Father Howard Smith went 2,500 feet
into a coal mine to see working conditions of the miners.
Above ground Gemuetlichkeit *with the miners.*

Officiating at the wedding in the nunciature chapel of Patrick Boarman,
cultural representative of NCWC in Bonn, 12 December 1953.

*Archbishop Muench, Cardinal Josef Frings of Cologne and Cardinal
Theodor Innitzer of Vienna on the occasion of the twelfth centenary of
the martyrdom of St. Boniface, Apostle of Germany, Fulda, 13 June 1954.*

*Behind the Iron Curtain for the first time
in Erfurt, 23 May 1954. At left is
Bishop Dietz of Fulda.*

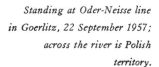

*Standing at Oder-Neisse line
in Goerlitz, 22 September 1957;
across the river is Polish
territory.*

While attending the 750th anniversary of the birth of St. Elizabeth of Thuringia, behind the Iron Curtain, a visit on 21 September 1957 to a children's home in Erfurt.

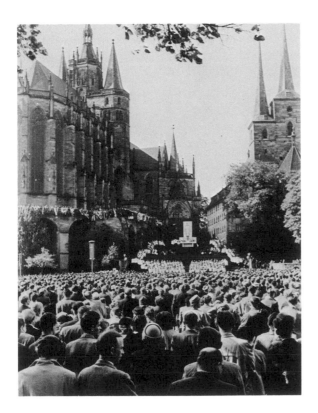

Celebrating Pontifical Mass at altar on stairway leading to the Cathedral and the St. Severn Church, at right, on occasion of 750th anniversary of birth of St. Elizabeth of Thuringia, Erfurt, 22 September 1957.

Twentieth anniversary of Archbishop Muench as bishop and twenty-fifth anniversary of profession of Mother Augustine Weihermueller, O.S.B., St. Walburga's Abbey, Eichstaett, 15 October 1955.

Officiating at the ordination of Dr. Max Jordan, international correspondent, author and radio commentator, who became a priest at the age of fifty-seven on 8 December 1951 at the Archabbey of Beuron.

Officiates at ordination of Father James D. Schumacher, a priest of the Diocese of Fargo, 8 December 1954, Maria Laach Abbey.

President Theodor Heuss presents the Great Cross, highest category of the West German Order of Merit, in recognition of the nuncio's "meritorious services to the German people," Bonn, January 1958.

Conversing with Dr. Ludwig Erhard, Minister of Economics, at a Bonn reception, 1951.

At Indian reception, talking with his friend, Frants Hvass, senior ambassador to Germany from Denmark, Bonn, 1 January 1955.

Attending reception given by Ambassador and Mrs. Hoe on National Holiday of Philippines, Bonn, 4 July 1958.

Chancellor Adenauer, new Indian chief, smokes pipe of peace, Milwaukee, July, 1956.

With Chancellor Adenauer at diplomatic reception, New Year's Day, 1957.

*A moment with Theodor Heuss, president of the German Federal
Republic, at annual dinner for Diplomatic Corps, Bonn, 29 January 1958.*

CHAPTER SEVEN

CARDINAL IN CURIA

In 1951, on the occasion of the 250th anniversary of the Pontifical Ecclesiastical Academy, training school for Roman diplomats, Monsignor Montini, substitute secretary of state for Pius XII, stated that modern diplomats no longer defended the interests of their countries in a spirit of rivalry and opposition. The best diplomat now proposes the broadest of programs, suggests interests that have universal value and finds solutions suitable for all concerned. Civil diplomacy tries to reduce antagonism in the world, to let reason prevail over force and to increase the prosperity of each country. Diplomacy is at the service of peace and the Church endeavors to look for earthly good as much as for true peace. Papal diplomacy can add to this effort by advancing the ideal which is the basis of its diplomacy, the universal fraternity of men.[1]

According to this definition, Nuncio Muench's relations with the Federal Republic of Germany were productive and effective. Cardinal Frings, in the name of the German bishops, told him on 31 August 1954:

"During the years of your stay with us you have become one of us in the best, most beautiful sense, and a bond of strong mutual trust embraces us. You have helped all those who were or are in need with most generous charity, mostly in complete secrecy.

"You have fostered in a most excellent and outstanding manner the prestige of and respect for the Holy See both within the Church as well as with the governments of the Federal Republic and the *Laender*.

"May we enjoy for a long time to come your wise, strong and kind administration in our hard struggling fatherland."

Archbishop Muench had to learn the methods of secular diplomacy the hard way. He became a good papal representative because he worked at it. His instincts of simplicity and natural goodness won people to him. Germans who before were indifferent to or suspicious of the

Catholic Church and its head now evidenced good will toward the nuncio. He looked out to the world at large and stressed that the Church was at the service of all men. In his frequent speeches he kept repeating that Christianity cannot be lived in isolation from the world. From his studies in the field of social science and his wide experience, he understood the Tridentine siege mentality that had intensified in the Catholic Church after the loss of temporal power in 1870. A sectarian withdrawal of Catholicism from the modern world became official Vatican policy. In the period before and after World War I the Church had stressed its role of saving souls and protecting its inheritance wherever possible.

A new opportunity for service and involvement opened for the Church following World War II. A reaction against totalitarianism and a revival of religious spirit developed in the free world. Muench as visitator and later nuncio considered as one of his prime tasks the help he could give Germans in re-establishing international contacts. During the Nazi years German Catholics and their fellow citizens had been cut off from contact with the free world. Lay and clerical leaders repeated as a constant refrain that Muench was one of the few who helped Germany regain friendly exchange with former enemies and mistrustful neighbors. He spoke out strongly against the early shortsighted occupation policy of non-fraternization and worked with American officials to end it. He totally rejected the theory of the collective guilt of the German people. He petitioned for intellectual and cultural exchange permits. To the nuncio international co-operation was basic to a policy of peace.

The emergence of the Christian Democratic parties in European countries, particularly in Germany and Italy, offered another encouraging opportunity. For the first time in the modern age viable political structures developed which brought together national and religious leaders. Nineteenth-century liberalism and its accompanying secularism was a thing of the past. Church and State were offered an opportunity to work together in achieving the legitimate aims of religion and society. Too many churchmen could not see what was taking place and continued in baroque isolation from the movement of the times. Classical and triumphant religion in the Constantinian spirit of Europe's past was dead despite the exaggerated importance some prelates continued to attach to themselves. Muench associated no outward signs of theocracy with his position as dean of the diplomatic corps at Bonn. If the spirit of Kronberg and Bad Godesberg was one thing it was not ornamental baroque. Cardinal Faulhaber, on his first visit to Kronberg, said that "it would be impossible for our friend Muench to live any simpler than he does." The Germans could not believe that a bishop coming from one of the victorious powers could live as frugally as he did.

The nuncio understood that universal misery demanded as a minimum that he participate in it. His own modest home background prepared him well for his responsibility to give an example of Christian simplicity. Muench took an intense interest in the social welfare programs of the Christian Democratic Union and watched each program as it developed in the planning stages of legislative action. A rare opportunity was at hand to forge new social programs based on Christian moral principles for the common good.

The nuncio considered Conrad Adenauer to be Europe's leading statesman of the period after the war. Adenauer had made a beginning for a new Germany, re-established the nation in a position of friendship and mutual confidence with the free world, as one of the century's major "architects of Europe." In a letter of 4 April 1953 Muench detailed to Archbishop Cushing of Boston his high opinion of Adenauer:

"In the first place, I should say that he is a very good Catholic, fearless and uncompromising in the profession of his faith. One of his sons is a priest of the Archdiocese of Cologne.

"Born in Cologne seventy-seven years ago, he started his career as a lawyer. Among the distinguished achievements during his administration as Lord Mayor of Cologne from 1917–1933 are the Cologne University, the Rhine River Port, the City Planning which gave the city of Cologne its large 'Ringstrassen,' the Fair Grounds and Exhibition Buildings, and the Stadium.

"Member of the Center Party, known for his sterling qualities of leadership, he was chosen President of the Prussian Council of State, which office he held from 1920–1933. In this position he proved himself to be a consistent and courageous opponent of Nazism. In consequence, Goering, Minister President of Prussia, deposed him as President of the Prussian Council of State and as Lord Mayor of Cologne. Twice imprisoned, he spent one year in hiding at the Benedictine Abbey of Maria Laach.

"At the cessation of hostilities in 1945, the American Military Government of Occupation, impressed by his anti-Nazi record, appointed him Mayor of Cologne, but within six months after taking over the city and county of Cologne, the British Military Government deposed him in

October of that year because he did not see eye-to-eye with its policies, refusing to do what was not in accord with his convictions.

"In February, 1946, he was elected President of the CDU (Christian Democratic Union) for the State of North Rhine-Westphalia, and became the President of the CDU for all of Germany in 1950.

"As President of the Parliamentary Council in Bonn, to which office he was appointed in September 1948, he was called by President Heuss in 1949 to be Chancellor of the German Federal Republic, which office he holds to this day; since March, 1951, he also assumed the duties of Foreign Minister.

"Of his great achievements in the interest of a United Europe, won by his patience and tact in negotiations, his unswerving co-operation with American policies, there is no need of further comment. The American press has been reporting that fully. Among Americans who followed his postwar career closely he is acclaimed as Europe's outstanding statesman."

Muench respected Adenauer as a man of peace and the architect of a united western Europe. He was the catalytic agent of the process that created and consolidated the German Federal Republic. He personified a cultural and historical continuity, especially among Rhinelanders, that had been destroyed by Bismarck, Wilhelm II and Hitler. He was the representative of an age-old spiritual underground. Golo Mann, German historian, said of Adenauer: "The appearance of this patriarch, free of every form of hysteria, incapable of assuming a false pose, pursuing his foreign political policy steadily and unerringly, produced a beneficial effect after all the frightful vagaries, all the tortures and insanities."

Adenauer's premise was in the Goethe tradition: the true course of the German people was not to unite as a centralized nation but to remain integrated in the center of Europe in order to act as bearer of civilization for the continent and the world. A lack of natural borders on the East and on the West rendered Germany unstable as a nation-state. Adenauer considered nationalism to be "the cancer of Europe," and as early as 1919 led a movement for a Rhine-Ruhr republic that was to remain united to the Reich but which would act as a balance to the power of Prussia and stabilize the East-West pull of traditional German foreign policy. When the opportunity came after the war to build a new Germany, Adenauer directed all his talent and conviction to establishing a federalized republic. He commanded primarily moral authority and respect; his integrity was unquestionable. He did not consider the unconditional surrender of Germany in 1945 as implying a complete transfer of governmental authority into the hands of the Allies. To Adenauer such an interpretation was wrong both from the viewpoint of international law and the practical impossibility of the Allies' running Germany from the outside. The occupying powers, with the exception of Russia in the East zone, gradually realized this fact and supported the formation of the republic. This position of Adenauer had been the firm stand of the Vatican which Muench was instructed to advance. From his first days in Germany, accordingly, Muench had ideologically been attracted to Adenauer. Their hopes for a united Europe also quickly forged a friendship and respect which grew with the years.

Adenauer helped the German people regain their freedom and human dignity after years of suppression. The individual citizen experienced the benefits of personal and political freedom as well as the opportunity to develop his talents. The Germans gradually again acquired the self-esteem essential to national life. Thousands of people in the Soviet zone and East Berlin also watched hopefully as West Germany developed during Adenauer's fourteen years in office. The Berlin air lift and wall, the mine-infested death strips along the demarcation line and the twenty military divisions at war strength in the Soviet zone were evidence of the terrorism and suppression which the Communists had to use to prevent the desire for unity and freedom in the East to prevail.

Germany's revival was not, as Adenauer emphasized, his work alone. All citizens contributed to it, including the minority political parties, and especially the German people through their hard work. With political insight to the needs of the postwar years they continued to give the Christian Democratic Union the majorities which made it possible for Adenauer to pursue his policies. He applied coolheadedness and shrewdness in making these forces politically and economically effective. Ludwig Erhard, vice chancellor and minister of economics, also played a key role in the rebirth of Germany. Erhard directed the establishment of an economic system that was a blend of freedom and astute planning. A prosperous society rapidly developed that supported the best system of social services on the continent. There were no extremes of poverty and wealth, no slums or ghettos, and over a million foreign workers had to be brought in by the end of the 1950's to supply the expanding demands of German industry. Economic prosperity was the general norm for the whole of society.

Adenauer saw that the plight of Europe after the war would force a new and intensified economic integration across national boundaries. When the Federal Republic was being established Adenauer held that the Basic Law did not mean an endorsement of the Ten Commandments but merely the enactment of a law which would be transitional. The Federal Republic was provisional since East and West Germany were not united. The federal structure of the new Germany was also an open door for progressive integration with western Europe. The Basic Law was not for Adenauer a constitution since the people had not voted for a constitution. Adenauer continued to insist that Germany was not united and until it was through free elections in both the East and the West a transitional situation existed.

The federal chancellor never tired of asking the Allies if they judged Germany to be a greater threat than Russia. The outbreak of the Korean War helped supply an answer to that question and from 1950 on there was intensified interest on the part of the Allies in a European Defense Community which would include Germany. Adenauer saw in the EDC an opportunity for nations to unite in common defense of western civilization and to abandon an obsolete nationalism and dismemberment. Although the EDC never materialized because of French opposition, Adenauer continued to advance the idea, along with the Coal and Steel Community, the Common Market, Western European Union and NATO. He aimed at making war impossible in Europe in the future by binding Germany to the West and thus enabling European nations to remain free from Russian imperialism. He was ever grateful to the United States for assistance in rebuilding Germany, but he held to the position that the Americans must lead in helping Germany resolve the interim problems of a divided country.

Adenauer's ideals and hopes for Germany and Europe coincided so closely with Muench's that their relationship became a consolation to both men in their difficult posts. Walter J. Donnelly, American official in HICOG and later ambassador to Venezuela, told Muench on 5 January 1953:

"I have great faith in Adenauer and his colleagues, as well as in the German people, to face the problems not only of their own making but also of the European nations, and of their determination to identify themselves with a united Europe. I'm still confident that Adenauer will succeed with his program despite the articulate opposition and the instability of the political situation in France. I am sure it is most comforting to him to know that he can look to you for advice and certainly spiritual guidance during these critical days."

Whenever he had the opportunity the nuncio explained what Adenauer was doing for Germany:

"In my opinion, Adenauer is Europe's greatest statesman. Not only has he regained for his country an honorable place among the nations of the West, but he has also promoted with a persistence that is exceptional the idea of a united Europe. For the first time in modern history such unity has been achieved. While it is still far from perfect, having laid the foundation for it will be to Adenauer's lasting credit. Among the statesmen of Europe he is doing everything in his power to keep the idea of concerted action against Communism alive and vigorous."[2]

The Vatican's policy of strong anticommunism under Pius XII was carried out by Archbishop Muench with conviction. Pius XII was uncompromising in his rejection of Communism, a policy that would be re-evaluated under his successors. Pius continually warned against the perils of coexistence and even issued a decree in July, 1949, excommunicating Catholics who voluntarily accepted Communism. This Vatican policy of anticommunism was influenced by the suffering and persecution of Catholics behind the Iron Curtain as well as by the internal Italian political situation. In Italy, as in Germany, for the first time in the modern period there were Christian Democratic political majorities. In Italy the Vatican was obsessed, excessively, its critics insisted, with the fear of a popular front government controlled by a Communist in the postwar years. Despite this strong anticommunist stand, never once did Pius XII lead a "crusade" against Russia or Communism. He practiced the same diplomatic restraint in this area as he had done earlier toward the Nazis and for which he was so strongly criticized. The Vatican's position against Communists was stronger than it was against the Nazis and Fascists because Pius considered the latter totalitarian movements as passing phenomena. Although conservative curial cardinals pushed hard for a clear union of the Catholic Church with the West against the East, Pius never made such a formal association. However, his anticommunist policy was clear and predominant in all Vatican diplomatic procedures. Muench followed this policy with determination. His observations in Europe as a student following World War I, his academic orientation, his social and political preferences as a professor and bishop in the United States, and his experience in Germany after World War II — all combined to convince him that Communism was the prevailing danger to free men and religious life.

Neither Adenauer nor Muench considered that peace could be fortified in the postwar world, accepting Russia's power and position, unless Germany identified itself with a united Europe. A policy of *détente* was considered unrealistic by Adenauer. His underlying assumptions were the danger of Soviet military incursions to the West; the unification of an armed Germany allied to the Atlantic Pact; the organization of a "little Europe" dependent for its protection on the United States; and the ultimate re-unification of Germany. Socialists in Germany called Adenauer "the chancellor of the Allies," and American diplomats such as George Kennan held that Adenauer's assumptions were not only questions of fact and fulfillment, but productive of persuasive fear and suspicion. There never was a lack of opposition to Adenauer's firm policies which to the end were based on a rejection of the thesis that Germans should meekly accept the reality of a divided Germany. A united continent, the chancellor maintained, could not evolve without a federated central Europe as an integral part of the whole.

Adenauer told Muench he only hoped that people in the future would say of him that he had done his duty. In the period of the cold war and the Soviet threat of the 1950's the chancellor's first steps toward establishing peaceful international order in Europe were clear evidence of his vision and foresight. However, the defensive posture of both West and East in the time after the war prevented free and friendly reciprocal exchanges from developing in political, economic, social, scientific and cultural fields. Adenauer held to an intransigent policy in East-West relations because he considered it indispensable to the construction of a free Germany that would survive. His successors could begin to build bridges between socialist and democratic nations in Europe upon the solid piers he had firmly erected. "The western world should seek peace through a treaty with the Soviet bloc," Adenauer said in 1954, "but only after making itself strong militarily and economically. We in Germany are particularly well informed about the difficulties which must be surmounted on the way to easing tension with the Communist-dominated world. We also know that extreme caution and vigilance are called for."

Adenauer visited the United States in 1953, 1955 and 1956. Muench worked hard in making arrangements for him to visit with American Catholics as well as civic and governmental officials. Adenauer was aware of the strong interest in Germany's revival among the descendants of German American immigrants in the Midwest, and he told Muench at a reception for Winston Churchill in Bonn on 11 May 1956 that he would like to visit some Catholic institutions there. Muench acted as liaison in arrangements for a stop in Chicago and an honorary degree which was given the chancellor by Marquette University, Milwaukee, on 15 June 1956.[3] Stritch later remarked to Muench that seldom had the American press been so unanimous in praising a distinguished visitor from abroad, "Our people understand his importance and worth." Adenauer characteristically assured the American people at Yale University on 12 June 1956 of his "firm conviction that in the struggle between totalitarian oppression and the free self-determination of peoples, a vigilant and united West, upholding its spiritual and moral values, can never be defeated."

Muench often entertained Adenauer at the nunciature. In January of 1956, for example, the nuncio as dean of the diplomatic corps, had a dinner for the chancellor on the occasion of his eightieth birthday. Muench presented him with the papal insignia, the Order of the Golden Spur, and invited his seven children, several Bonn officials, and Cardinal Frings for the happy occasion. At table Adenauer, who under his rock-like appearance was warm and witty with those whom he knew well, told Muench that he was envious of his watered silk archbishop's robes. If he had lived in the Middle Ages, the chancellor said, he would have had something equally colorful to wear rather than the business suit or formal black tails to which he was restricted. That evening after the celebration Muench asked the sisters at the nunciature to make a bow tie from some extra pieces of his *ferraiuolo*. The nuncio then sent the tie across the Rhine to the chancellor's home at Rhoendorf as a gift which Adenauer delightedly wore at later receptions. Both he and Muench enjoyed the questions and comments that this tie evoked among the perplexed guests. For relaxation Adenauer read history, geography, poetry and listened to classical music. Muench enjoyed finding atlases and good new books in the field of American history to present to his friend; while Adenauer, proud of his gardening art which he had learned during the years of enforced isolation under the Nazis, would send Muench some of his best specimens of roses for the nunciature chapel.

The nuncio was able to suggest several solutions to problems that the Bonn government faced. In the same way as he had served as liaison representative to the American Military governor during his first years in Germany, Muench now explained German positions to embassy officials in Bonn and to government and Church officials in the United States. But his wide personal contacts became more circumscribed. As nuncio he cautiously had to preserve his position above involvement in American concerns in Germany, in German Church matters and in governmental affairs. He would consistently say: "It would be highly improper for me as nuncio to Germany to interfere or pass judgment. My jurisdiction does not extend to these matters. In my work as nuncio I have to observe the propriety due to my office."

A problem of special delicacy arose with the re-establishment of the German Embassy at the Vatican. The near numerical equality of Catholic and Protestant citizens in Germany, with the Protestants slightly in the majority, made the assignment of offices a particularly crucial matter. The appointment of the German ambassador to the Holy See was further aggravated by the fact that formerly a Protestant always occupied the office. After the war Catholics began to insist that one of their members be appointed to that post. This dispute attracted considerable attention and was discussed in the press as well as privately in government circles. Muench worked toward a solution in a typically American pragmatic way. He recommended that an alternate mode of procedure be used, namely, that for one term a Catholic, the next a Protestant, would hold this ambassadorial position. This system was inaugurated by the Federal Republic and continues to the present.

Heinrich Koeppler described another of Muench's observations which relaxed tensions when he said:

"Nuncio Muench was down to earth. He also had a spontaneity which we hardly ever, if ever, witnessed with our bishops in Germany. I admired the independence of his opinions. We were in Erfurt for the jubilee celebrations in honor of Saint Elizabeth in 1954. It was shortly before the bishops' conference at Fulda. At dinner a very lively discussion developed among the bishops on the main topic of the coming Fulda conference: mixed marriages. Muench listened quietly, smiled and then laughed. When the excitement reached a peak he remarked dryly that he could not understand all this agitation of the German bishops over the question of mixed marriages. At home, in the United States, the problem was looked at from a different angle. There the saying was: 'a Catholic marries a Protestant; that makes two Catholics in the future.' Why, then, all this excitement? His words had the effect of a bomb. For me, who had listened to this discussion with a certain uneasiness, it was a relief. His natural, straightforward manner was not only charming, personally convincing, but also a great help in creating a friendly atmosphere in the Church in Germany."[4]

A difficult situation with which the nuncio had to live during his term in Germany was that Poland kept pressing the Vatican for recognition of the Oder-Neisse frontier that had been imposed on Germany after the war. If the Vatican had recognized Poland's demands it would be a transgression of its own policy of not recognizing new frontiers until they had been sanctioned by international treaty. The Holy See had insisted that Muench was nuncio for all of Germany. If the Polish administrators of the former German dioceses, now in Polish territory, were appointed diocesan bishops, the concordat would have been broken with Germany which guaranteed governmental approval of episcopal appointments. Nothing was done, accordingly, during Muench's stay in Germany and he had to walk a tightrope in regard to the lost territories of eastern Germany. He could not agree with German demands, or support the Polish requests, or go against the Vatican's policy of non-involvement in a strained political situation.

As nuncio, Muench also had difficulties with curial officials, especially in trying to explain to them the actual situation in Germany. The predominantly Italian curia of the Vatican for centuries had been suspicious of German religious developments as far back as the Middle Ages, during the Reformation period and in the following 400 years. Italians in modern times tended to look upon Germany as the home of the Reformation. There was a constant undercurrent of feeling, unexpressed for the most part, but apparent to all involved, that the Germans were difficult to handle and that their innovations had to be braked.

Muench respected deeply the spirit and structure of the Church in Germany. He admired the theological studies pursued by German . scholars and defended them before the Holy Office. He did not judge that the vitality and life of German Catholics should be obstructed. He never failed to praise and explain the strong and vital Catholic life he witnessed among the German people. He considered the religious development of the German people equal to that of any other national group. He favored the freedoms of American Catholicism but recognized the depth of thought and culture which the older society of Germany supplied. Muench unconsciously but strikingly anticipated the developments that took place in Vatican Council II. He often talked about the collegial position of bishops in the Church and questioned why they could not exercise what was theirs by tradition and right. He personally accepted and believed in the principle of subsidiarity which was enunciated in papal documents for economic, social and political matters, and could never understand why regional and local ecclesiastical procedures did not equally come under the same umbrella. To Muench, Catholicity did not mean conformity. If life had taught him one thing it was that unity and diversity could co-exist and even flourish in a relationship of mutual interaction.

The continuing ecclesiastical and diplomatic problems began to press in on him. As early as 1954 Muench began to say: "The years are taking their toll." Actually he enjoyed excellent health throughout the entire German tour of duty. He was treated by his doctor, Theodor Moellers, chief surgeon of the Marienhospital in Bonn, only for occasional colds until 1958 when he began to experience some heart trouble and had a blood pressure problem which, however, was easily kept under control. He was not incapacitated in his work, but because of his age and habits of work, with little or no relaxation, he periodically became exhausted. His doctor advised him to take a few days off, to withdraw somewhat from too many visits and conversations, to retire earlier at night and to take a siesta. He was as mentally alert as ever but long interviews, extended visits, lengthy public addresses and formal gatherings irritated him and he shunned them as much as possible. He more and more preferred to stay in his office working among his papers, reading and praying. When he was exhausted he became distracted and irritable which was entirely out of character for him. Later, when he was moved to Rome, he began to evidence marked signs of progressive cerebral arteriosclerosis.

On the occasion of the coronation of Pope John, 4 November 1958, a large reception was held at the Beethovenhalle in Bonn. Archbishop Muench's memory slipped temporarily and he had trouble recognizing people. He was having another temporary "black out," a certain passivity and confusion which occurred at intervals of several weeks especially when he was exhausted from work. On such occasions it was impossible to suggest anything to the nuncio because he would not react normally and would stubbornly refuse to co-operate. In order to save the situation Monsignor Hack called a waiter and instructed him to go up to the nuncio who was surrounded by people and tell him that he had a long distance telephone call. Muench said: "But is that really necessary now?"

Hack then came forward and answered: "Yes, Excellency, it is urgent. Please come at once." He went along and Hack led him into a dark lecture room where Hack sat down on a chair and Muench took the next one. The nuncio without asking any questions took Hack's hand and said: "I am so grateful to you. You did a splendid job. Where is the car?" Hack told him it was a few yards away in a dark side street and that nobody would notice their departure. When they arrived home at the nunciature Muench went directly to bed.

The deaths, one by one, of his close friends in the Midwest also depressed and saddened him as he, far from home, learned of their loss. First there was Monsignor Howard Smith on 8 February 1955, then the unexpected death of his patron, Cardinal Stritch, in Rome on 27 May 1958 before he could begin his new work as pro-prefect of the Congregation of the Propagation of the Faith. A few weeks later, on 19 June 1958, Muench was shocked to learn of the death of his classmate, Monsignor Joseph Adams, pastor of Saint Mathias Church, Chicago. "What makes such happenings hard to take is the fact that I cannot pay my last tribute of friendship by attending the funeral services," he said. Then Cardinal Mooney died suddenly a few hours before the opening of the conclave in Rome on October 25 of the same year and Muench realized that his two closest friends among the American cardinals were now gone. On every trip home he had unfailingly visited Mooney and Stritch and found he could count on their advice and support for his work in Germany. Unlike Cardinal Spellman, who never could quite forget that Germany had been at war against his United States, Stritch and Mooney had through the years strongly supported Muench's mission of charity among the German people. Bishop William T. Mulloy of Covington died on 1 June 1959 and Muench's brother-in-law, Ray Ott, was the victim of a sudden heart attack on 19 June 1959. Finally his closest companion throughout the years, Monsignor J. W. "Boots" Nellen of Milwaukee, died on 24 August 1959 and Muench realized that he was more and more alone.

The archbishop was also worried about his own future. Pius XII was still in office but his health was declining. There would be no change at Bad Godesberg as long as Pius lived, but Muench realized that his own age precluded him from future consideration for an appointment to an American archdiocese. When Pius XII died on 9 October 1958 and Cardinal Angelo Giuseppe Roncalli of Venice was elected his successor as Pope John XXIII there was considerable speculation about future developments. Muench had known and worked with Roncalli when the latter had been nuncio at Paris from 1944 to 1953. He looked forward to his first meeting with Pope John in February of 1959 at which time he expressed his filial obedience and gave the new Pope an extensive report on the progress of the Church in Germany.

Bishop Dworschak came to Bad Godesberg for a visit in the fall of 1959 and the two friends met in Rome for the centennial celebration of the North American College on 2 October 1959 and the *ad limina* visit and report of the Diocese of Fargo to the Holy See. Four days later Muench had an audience with Pope John. At this time the archbishop learned from the Pope that he was being considered for an early appointment as a cardinal. When Bishop Dworschak and the delegation from Fargo came into the Pope's study they all observed how much Pope John and Archbishop Muench seemed to be enjoying each other's company. Muench, of course, could say nothing of their conversation, and he returned to his German assignment.

Five weeks later on Sunday, 16 November 1959, Archbishop Muench was in his office at the nunciature when he telephoned Monsignor Hack and asked him to come to his room. Hack explained what then happened:

"It is never very convenient for members of the staff to live in the same building that serves as office because they are continually on duty, day and night. Private life is almost non-existent, as with a monk.

"So I went to see him. On a Sunday morning one is usually more relaxed, having no pressure of weekday work. He said: 'Here, I have a few letters, I wonder what they are about.' Among them I saw a large envelope with the address written by hand. I remarked: 'Your Excellency, this is a handwritten letter; it seems to be for you personally.' 'Oh,' he replied, 'please open it and take care of it as you see fit.' And without reading it, my first guess was this is a thank-you letter from the Holy See for some princely personage in Germany because those letters usually had elaborate handwriting and special formats. I was about to put it with the other letters when I started glancing through it, wondering whether this letter was addressed to the Prince zu Hohenzollern or some such personage, when I suddenly stopped short, having seen his own name on the inside address. I exclaimed: 'Your Excellency, this letter is addressed to you personally. I have read something special — Your Eminence!' He did not catch on, took back the letter and said: 'Oh, it's addressed to me, then I'll have to read it myself.' That was the way he officially learned of his having been created a cardinal.

"That day he was in fine shape, but somehow the state of his health showed, fear of a change welled up in him. But he was most controlled, and he gave no outward sign of it. But, undoubtedly, fear filled his heart, fear of a change.

"He did not say anything. He only repeated, 'I can't understand this, how is this possible?' Of course, I think he was happy. That was only natural for he had such an admirable attitude toward the Holy Father and an absolute devotion to the Holy See. He was touched but he did not like to show his emotions. He was very disciplined, sometimes to the point of giving the impression of being cold, hard and unbending, which he wasn't at all. But to those who did not know him it could appear thus. He often walled himself in; so this not giving expression to joy, this being so controlled, does not imply that he did not feel joy. We all rejoiced with him over this honor. Above all, we were happy that this nomination offered such a dignified and deserved end to his career, for his illness had been steadily progressing. He had worked and accomplished so much in the past years that we could not imagine a worthier conclusion to his term of office as nuncio." [5]

Pope John named eight new members to the college of cardinals in these appointments of 16 November 1959. Besides Archbishop Muench, a second American, his former colleague at Saint Francis Seminary, Archbishop Albert G. Meyer of Chicago, was also named a cardinal.[6] It was a unique honor for the archdiocese of Milwaukee to have two of its former priests elevated to the college of cardinals at the same time. The Pope's action increased the college to seventy-nine members, its highest number to that time. All of the new appointees were to serve in the Roman curia except Cardinal-designate Meyer. The curial cardinals would be increased from twenty-four to thirty-one and would include an American for the first time in history. Cardinal-designate Muench would take the place of his old friend Cardinal Stritch who had died in Rome in 1958 before he could begin work there.

When the news of Muench's appointment was released in Germany there was an outpouring of articles, congratulations and expressions of gratitude. As Heinz Reuter described it:

"With the publication of the news that Pope John had made him a cardinal and that he would have to leave the Federal Republic in a short time, the whole German press was full of long articles on Muench, his life and his work that went on for days on end. On that occasion everyone realized that Muench had become an accepted great authority in the mind of the public in Germany. Perhaps this could be best expressed by this formula: 'Nuncio equals Muench.' The word had become a synonym, and that, I think, shows best how well Muench had succeeded in blending his personality with his position so that it received a certain personal color and was unanimously accepted in Germany with great sympathy.

"Those who read the many commentaries published on his leaving Germany could not help being convinced that these farewell eulogies were not of the usual formal kind, but that they were honest expressions of esteem and gratitude for all Cardinal Muench had done for Germany. They came right from the heart.

"Not one nuncio to Germany had ever been in the same situation as Muench, ever since there had been nuncios in Germany, and that covers quite a period of time if one starts with the nuncios of the late Middle Ages. I think that none of them ever had to deal with and manage a situation as difficult as the one Muench was confronted with. Nuncio Pacelli had to overcome some very difficult political situations after the revolutions of 1918–19 and during the crises of the Weimar Republic. But all this happened in an externally functioning state, even though it may not have been too well organized at times and was suffering from economic depression. But Muench in 1946 met with the aftermath of a terrible catastrophe that had led into the next disaster. A similar situation had never existed in Germany before, not even after the Thirty Years War in 1648. Muench helped a country that was completely destroyed, split up and with millions of peoples expelled and displaced from their homes."[7]

Archbishop Jaeger and Heinrich Koeppler confirmed Reuter's analysis of the Germans' appreciation for Muench. Cardinal Frings came to the *Turmhof* to offer congratulations in the name of the German bishops and to express his own personal joy at the appointment. A generous purse from the German bishops enabled the nuncio to take care of his expenses for cardinal's robes and the move to Rome.[8] The cardinal-designate was flooded with telegrams and letters from around the world which he and the staff tried to answer in the midst of a round of governmental, diplomatic and ecclesiastical farewell receptions. The German press detailed his contributions in the previous years and called him "friend and defender of the German people." President Theodor Heuss wrote him in the name of the German people on 17 November 1959:

"I am anxious to write you these few personal lines of congratulation to assure you once more how happy I have been to know you in your post, in such difficult times, a person of manly objectivity and yet endowed with an irenic heart. I was afforded the opportunity not only to respect you as the dean of the diplomatic corps, but also to honor the warm friend of the German people and a kind-hearted soul. I am moved to express this to you in friendly affection at this decisive moment in your priestly life."

Muench was deeply moved by the warm expression of thanks which President Heuss made publicly, and he was overcome with emotion when Chancellor Adenauer, in the name of the Federal Republic, presented him with a Mercedes-Benz automobile as a farewell gift. This Mercedes became a symbol to Muench of the attachment of his dear German people, and in Rome during the remaining years he cherished with real delight this one material object he owned.

In less than twenty days all the farewells had to be made, cardinal's robes acquired, and the personal papers, books and accumulated keepsakes of his years in Germany packed and forwarded to Rome. The staff was invaluable in assisting Muench in meeting the demands of what was for him a most trying and sad time. Each letter and call, every personal farewell with friends opened before him the cherished experiences of the past thirteen years. Finally, when all the official acts were completed he went to the community room of the sisters at the nunciature on the evening before his departure. He sat at the table with the sisters who had done so much for him and was visibly moved while they tried to keep back the tears. Finally he said: "To depart does hurt, it does hurt to part, but the will of God fills the heart with peace and joy."

The next morning Father Senger accompanied Muench to Rome and took care of all arrangements. The cardinal-designate was very tired and somewhat apprehensive. They went to Salvator Mundi Hospital on the Janiculum hill and he was shown to the two rooms across from the chapel on the third floor which he was to occupy for the remainder of his life. The Salvatorian sisters who had welcomed him so often in the past on his frequent trips to Rome were honored and overjoyed that Muench had chosen to make their hospital his home. Monsignor Giovannetti from the Secretariat of State came by to cheer him up as he always did; Archbishop Guido Del Mestri, apostolic delegate in Kenya, who had been a counselor at Bad Godesberg until the previous September, arrived for the occasion and Muench was pleased to have two of his former Italian aides beside him to make him feel more at home.

On December 10 Muench went to Ciampino airport to welcome Cardinal-designate Meyer and delegations from Chicago and Fargo; a half hour later the Muench family arrived from Milwaukee including his three sisters Mary, Teresa and Dorothy; two brothers Joseph and Frank, a brother-in-law Frank Herrick, a sister-in-law, Mrs. Frank Muench, and five nieces and nephews. Muench revived in spirit as soon as his family came on the scene and for the next four days he visited and toured the city with them and his Fargo friends as they had done in former years. However, the family observed that he seemed to be weeping every time he looked at them.

When Muench met Dworschak at Ciampino airport he said: "We must go to see Cardinal Cicognani immediately. I want to consult him about making a request to retain the title of bishop of Fargo for another year, after which I will retire." Cicognani explained to Muench when they arrived at the Vatican that this request was not possible since it was contrary to established protocol. Muench, accordingly, received notification that he would have to relinquish his diocese of Fargo and be assigned the titular archbishopric of Selymbria. This was another blow that depressed him; all the meaningful ties seemed to be breaking.

The first of the traditional and official ceremonies in connection with the creation of new cardinals took place on December 14. At the North American College, the two Milwaukee friends, Meyer and Muench, were to receive their bigliettos informing them that the cardinals in secret consistory with the Pope had approved of their nominations as new members of the college of cardinals. Some 500 guests including thirteen American bishops and the United States ambassador to Italy, James D. Zellerbach, were present for the formal presentation of documents. The next evening Cardinal Muench hosted a reception and dinner for his guests at the Michelangelo Hotel, and on December 15 a semi-public ceremony was held in the Consistorial Hall of the Vatican at which the new cardinals were given their red birettas, the insignia of the cardinalate. The final event of the elaborate and drawn out ceremonies, on December 17, was a public consistory at the altar of the chair in Saint Peter's Basilica. Pope John presented the symbolic red hat to seven of the eight nominees since Cardinal Paolo Marella received his red biretta from Charles de Gaulle, president of France. A final brief private consistory at which the cardinals were given topaz rings and formal assignment to their titular churches in Rome ended the long day. An exhausted Cardinal Muench had difficulty finding a ring small enough for his finger among those proferred to him and he became momentarily confused.

But the next morning he was in good spirits as the relatives and friends accompanied him to his titular Church of San Bernardo alle Terme across the street from Cardinal Cushing's titular Church of Santa Susanna, the American church served by the Paulist Fathers. San Bernardo, a circular church converted from a former indoor game room on the site of one of the four corners of Diocletian's baths, was served by Cistercian monks.[9] At this time of taking possession of the church, Muench had to relinquish his titular see of Selymbria which he had held for only six days according to the complex procedure required of a cardinal who is not an ordinary of a diocese. Cardinal Muench spoke in English, German, French and Italian during his acceptance speech.

On December 19 the Muench party was received in a twenty-minute private audience by Pope John after Cardinal Muench had spent a half hour with the pontiff. Muench translated the Pope's jovial and friendly remarks into English. At one point, in response to Bishop Dworschak's short speech of thanks to the pontiff in the name of the diocese of Fargo, Pope John said: "Cardinal Muench, you may tell your successor that we do not always intend to appoint a cardinal to Fargo." Everyone laughed and clapped. Pope John was most affable and cordial and won all with his unusually paternal gift of putting everyone at ease. It was a memorable climax to the entire occasion and Cardinal Muench bid farewell the next day to the Chicago, Milwaukee and Fargo delegations. At the airport everyone was sad to see him standing alone on the ramp and waving as they left Ciampino for their homes.

Cardinal Muench was, indeed, alone in Rome during the last period of his life. He was happy and thankful to be a cardinal but, he said, "as so often in life, it is a joy mixed with sorrow." Muench did not know the inner workings of curial life. As an American, he was a foreigner at court in his mode of operation and outlook on procedure. He found the Italians of the curial system "inscrutable," despite the fact that he had worked with them for years in his diplomatic post. Churchmen had been asking repeatedly for an internationalizing of the Roman Curia. The American bishops had hoped for years to have a representative in Rome as a cardinal and in curia. Cardinal Stritch had died in Rome before beginning his assignment by Pius XII as pro-prefect of the Congregation of the Propagation of the Faith. Now Cardinal Muench, Pope John's choice of an American cardinal-in-curia to serve at the nerve center of Catholicism was to join six other non-Italians among the thirty-two curial cardinals.

At heart, Muench lacked enthusiasm for his new position. He was not like the Frenchman, Cardinal Eugenio Tisserant, or the Armenian, Cardinal Gregorio Agagianian, thoroughly Romanized and a veteran resident in curia. He appeared to those around him to be unaware of his position and influence, oblivious of the power a cardinal has in Rome. His advice was not asked and he did not proffer it. It is a surprising fact that there is no evidence of Cardinal Muench intervening successfully for any American or German request during these final years of his life in Rome. There were three instances where he tried, failed and retreated hurt and disappointed. One concerned the request from an American bishop that Muench secure approval for a lay institute of religious in his diocese. The cardinal had a long conference with the bishop and said: "Everyone seems to think, as in so many other instances, that I have a direct line to the Holy Father and the curial offices. I can't do anything in this matter." A second case concerned a Maltese lay friend of Muench, who asked the cardinal to recommend his advancement from one position to another of higher honor in the papal court. Muench sent in a request to the Secretariat of State for this advancement and did not even receive an acknowledgment of the request. He was disheartened, but he only said quietly and sadly: "Things are done rather strangely here." The third incident concerned the appointment of a German priest to a deserved position of honor in Rome as a canon of Saint Peter's Basilica. Cardinal Muench wrote directly to Pope John recommending this appointment, as did several other German officials and ecclesiastics. The response came back to Muench from a subsecretary of a commission that the Holy Father wanted to keep the position of canon of Saint Peter's open in the eventuality that someone urgently needed to be placed there. Muench considered this to be an incomplete answer. The matter dragged on and only a week before Muench died a call came from the Secretariat of State informing him that this German priest had been given another post. The cardinal was by then too ill even to know that this much had been accomplished in a matter in which he had been deeply concerned.

Muench, unquestionably, was honored that he had been made a

cardinal. He was thoroughly devoted to the Holy See, a prime example of everything good that is implied in this particular devotion. The cardinal was willing to do anything that was asked of him and that he was physically capable of doing. But, apart from this fundamental attitude that he had developed throughout his life, he was disappointed over the appointment that had come to him with the honor of the cardinalate. He did not find any occasion in Rome to express this personal reaction. He certainly could not do so to Pope John; if Pope Pius were living he would have felt more at home in freely expressing his preferences whether they were accepted or not. He had worked so many years with Pius XII that a personal relationship existed between the two churchmen. Muench could have confided in Cardinal Cicognani, former apostolic delegate to the United States. But he was far too diffident to approach the secretary with personal concerns, once Cicognani had been advanced to secretary of state after Cardinal Tardini's death. Cicognani was no longer just a fellow cardinal who could advise him.

Cardinal Muench considered that he was still capable of administering an American diocese. He rarely and only obliquely referred to his health which those who were close to him fully understood was failing. The condition of his health was a subject which was approached most carefully. Muench did not want to face the fact that he was ill; he always had enjoyed unusually good health and he could not understand that his physical condition had changed. In conversation he would still refer to the possibility of his returning to Milwaukee or Fargo at least to live in retirement. Meanwhile German and American friends who visited him in Rome were shocked at his obvious decline. They used words such as "tragic," "sad," or "pathetic" to describe the condition and situation of a man whom they had respected so much for his past contributions. He looked melancholy, withdrawn and lost in his present situation. There was not a friend from the American or German days who did not experience this shock as they came to Salvator Mundi Hospital on the Janiculum to visit Muench. Many of them thought that he should have been allowed to return home, either to Milwaukee or Fargo, where he could have been more relaxed and apart from the tensions of an alien environment. For days at a time he would remain in his rooms at the hospital. But, interestingly, as soon as an old friend such as Cardinal-designate Joseph Ritter of Saint Louis, Cardinal Frings of Cologne, Archbishop Jaeger of Paderborn or Cardinal Doepfner of

Munich would arrive in Rome, he would become his former self. This temporary revitalization was apparent to all involved and it only made them the sadder when at the end of their visits they had to leave him alone in his final "exile."

Cardinal Muench was given curial assignments as a regular member of the Congregations of Religious, Rites and Extraordinary Affairs, three of the permanent commissions of cardinals functioning in the central administration of the Church. His responsibilities were in proportionate order to each of these assignments. The Congregation of Religious is concerned with the government of religious orders and congregations. Details concerning their rule, discipline, studies, temporal goods, rights and privileges come under the jurisdiction of this congregation. In regard to the Congregation of Religious, there was not a single meeting of that curial office that he was invited to attend during his tenure in Rome and not a single item of business was referred to him during that period. That the Congregation of Religious did not hold more frequent plenary sessions, that the cardinal members of the congregation were not consulted, was a continuous mystery to him. That the religious priests, brothers, and sisters, who compose a majority of the Church's defined religious activity, should command so little committee or collegial attention indicated to him the reality of Rome's pre-Vatican Council II procedure.

Muench's work as a cardinal-consultant of the Congregation of Rites demanded continued attention. This Congregation supervises divine worship and conducts the processes of beatification and canonization of saints. During Muench's tenure there was considerable work in breviary and missal revisions which became effective on 1 January 1961. He also had to read volume after volume of documentation relating to beatification and canonization processes. He faithfully studied and evaluated the virtuous lives and reported miraculous intercessions of holy men and women and submitted his judgments orally and in writing to the congregation. When asked by the writer in his final interview with the cardinal what he did in Rome, Muench laconically replied: "I read the lives of Italian saints."

The work connected with Cardinal Muench's activity as a member of the Congregation for Extraordinary Affairs was the most challenging of his Roman assignments. This congregation is concerned with the relations of the Church with civil governments, especially in those countries having a concordat with the Holy See. Muench found the background work connected with the naming of bishops and the establishment of dioceses in such countries engrossing and vitally important to the future of the Church. His own experience and knowledge of the German situation and persons were valuable contributions in matters under discussion.

Muench also felt competent and qualified in this area of curial affairs. He would carefully prepare his position papers and write out every statement, however short it was to be, before the plenary sessions of the congregation. Muench easily read and understood Italian, but he was hesitant in speaking the language. His vocabulary was limited and he tried to increase it by insisting that Italian be spoken by the priests at table during meals at Salvator Mundi. Day after day he worked with an Italian dictionary and, like a school boy, doggedly practiced Italian idioms. But when it came time to speak in public or at plenary sessions he would so softly and timidly read his prepared statements that he left the impression he was not at home with the language. This perhaps also explains why his advice was not sought more frequently by curial officials and why he was not brought into curial activities in a more active capacity. Those involved may well have been trying to spare him embarrassment and to protect his failing health. Actually Muench was competent in Italian but his life-long characteristic desire to be a perfectionist, now in his declining physical condition, only deepened his sense of insecurity and inadequacy.

The cardinal looked forward to the plenary sessions of the Congregation of Extraordinary Affairs and would have his secretary drive him to the Vatican in the cherished Mercedes long before time for the scheduled meetings. He was always on hand at least a half hour before the sessions in the offices of the Secretary of State and then found himself walking the corridors waiting for the meetings to get under way. Such delays annoyed and disturbed Muench. In the colder seasons of the year the doctors at Salvator Mundi tried to dissuade him from going so early, but to no avail. Muench said: "I suppose the Romans would say dozens of times 'pazienza' but I can't get used to these delays." Throughout his life he had insisted on punctuality to such a degree that those who worked with him were ever conscious that they should not be a minute late.[10]

The Congregation of Extraordinary Affairs met every two or three weeks in plenary session and whenever there was special need. Muench was genuinely pleased when his opinions were requested. He was particularly happy to be a part of discussions concerning the advancement of Bishop Julius Doepfner from Berlin to Munich. Muench's wide knowledge of the German Church enabled him to make a contribution and he came away from meetings of the Congregation of Extraordinary Affairs with a sense of accomplishment and in the buoyant good spirits he had known in earlier days in other circumstances.

Cardinal Muench was reluctant to ask for authorization to leave Rome for visits to Germany or the United States. He received a stream of invitations for special celebrations and jubilees, but he conscientiously thought he had to stay in Rome and work at his curial assignments. The German bishops asked the Secretariat of State if Muench could attend the 1960 Eucharistic Congress in Munich as their guest and when this permission came through he returned to Germany as the guest of Cardinal Wendel. At public ceremonies when the people would spot Muench in the processions they would cheer and wave in welcome. His old friends were anxious to see and talk with the cardinal, and they went out of their way to involve him in the activities of the congress. But he was unresponsive, quiet and there was lacking his former warm appreciation for all the plans that were made for him. Cardinal Wendel understood the state of Muench's health and tried sympathetically to protect him. But the former nuncio, known by everyone who passed through the cardinal's house in Munich, did not want to meet other guests even at table. He would say: "Is it necessary? It will take so long." When he had to attend sessions of the congress he would remonstrate: "Oh, they will talk for hours; why do we have all these meetings?" On one occasion he abruptly left an academic lecture in the middle of the paper, much to the consternation of all in attendance. The chairman rushed outside to ask what was wrong and Muench with no uncertainty informed him that German meetings were far too long, that the papers should be duplicated and passed out in advance and let it go at that. It was so unlike Muench to 'make a scene,' but now he was tired and aggravated at anything that kept him in public or that lasted for any length of time. Muench also thought that too much vernacular was used in the liturgical events and discussion sessions of this international congress, and the German bishops had to smile and agree with him that this was the case. His secretaries, Fathers Joseph Senger and Raymond Lessard of Fargo, were relieved when they were back in the informal and quiet environment of Salvator Mundi where the cardinal was more at ease.

Another trying experience of 1960 was Cardinal Muench's visit to Malta as papal legate for the nineteenth centenary observance of Saint Paul's shipwreck on that island. The Maltese had asked the Holy See for an English-speaking legate and had expected a ranking English or American prelate to be sent. Muench was not well-known in Malta and both he and leaders on the island expressed in private their surprise that he had been chosen as legate. A group of fundamentalist Protestants in England also caused some unpleasantness by protesting the use of the English destroyer, *The Surprise*, to bring the papal legate from Naples to Malta. After the arrival on 20 July 1960 there were five grueling days in the oppressive summer heat of pontifical functions, processions, receptions and tours which taxed the legate's strength.

There was one event, however, that the cardinal looked forward to with much anticipation. This was the observance of his twenty-fifth anniversary as a bishop to be held in Fargo during October of 1960. It would be his first return to the United States as a cardinal. After his arrival in New York on September 21 he visited old friends there, in Cincinnati and Milwaukee before landing at Hector airport in Fargo on October 1. Over 1,000 people were on hand to greet him and Cardinal Muench, deeply moved at the reception, happily said: "I am back home." On October 4 the ecclesiastical celebration was held in Saint Mary's Cathedral with forty-three close friends of the American hierarchy, the clergy of Fargo and hundreds of his former flock in attendance. Cardinal Meyer preached the sermon and Muench was in excellent spirits throughout the whole celebration, although all noted how much he had failed in health. Two days later a civic testimonial was held in the Fargo memorial auditorium with 3,000 people in attendance. Thomas Whelan of Saint Thomas, North Dakota, United States ambassador to Nicaragua and an old friend of Muench, stated in the main address:

"North Dakota, with its rugged climate, its hard-working, industrious people, its expansiveness has its own way of making honest men of us. It takes the measure of all men and strips them quickly of all sham and pretense.

"While most of our citizens spent their time cultivating the soil, you spent your time cultivating their souls. Everywhere we go in this diocese we can point to a landmark of progress as a result of your labors.

"Your work in the reconstruction of Germany was a task for which, we feel, a tried and rugged citizen from North Dakota was best qualified."

Over 1,000 messages of congratulation were received including letters from Pope John, President Heuss and Chancellor Adenauer which especially pleased Muench. On October 8 he received an honorary degree at Saint John's University, Collegeville, Minnesota, and he then moved on to Milwaukee for another civic reception for Cardinal Meyer and himself, on October 16. Through all of this he was at home and his former self with clerical and lay friends and the family in Fargo and Milwaukee. If the visits were short and he could have periods of rest, his reactions were normal and warm. But if a visitor would stay too long or interrupt him as he was watching the Milwaukee Braves on television he would become annoyed and silent. All involved in the elaborate planning for this jubilee celebration were grateful that the cardinal had enjoyed the occasion he so richly deserved.

In June of 1961 the central preparatory commission for the forthcoming ecumenical Vatican Council II began regular meetings and Muench as a cardinal in curia was an automatic member of this important body. He took his duties on the preparatory commission very seriously and entered into the pre-conciliar discussions and plans. Cardinal Muench was enthusiastic about the possibilities of the council and thought Pope John had struck upon exactly the right means of renewing and updating the procedures and outlook of the Church in the modern world. He supported Pope John in his courageous effort to assemble a council as rapidly as possible. Those curial cardinals who intransigently opposed the council as an idea and a reality received no support or sympathy from Muench. For years he had thought that the world's bishops had to be assembled in council to face the needs of a contemporary society far different from the world of 1870 and the unfinished Vatican Council I. Pius XII had thought of convoking a council, but World War II and the problems of the postwar years, as well as his own personal indecision and general approach to the papacy, had combined to delay the decision. But Pius was making remote plans for a council and in an interesting article in *Civiltà Cattolica* of 6 and 20 August 1966, Father Giovanni Caprile, S.J., described these considerations of Pius XII for a council. Among those proposed as a possible candidate for the post of secretary general of this projected council was Archbishop Muench, nuncio to Germany. Muench, of course, never knew of this possibility. But he co-operated in every way in contributing to preparations for the council that he was not to attend.

Cardinal Muench adhered to an exact daily schedule at Salvator

Mundi. He arose early and offered Mass at 7:30 A.M. at a side altar of the main chapel in the motherhouse of the Salvatorian sisters. One of the sisters would accompany him because he had to cross an outside passageway and he was nervous about stairs.[11] The cardinal liked the small private chapel where he offered Mass. It was dedicated to Mother Mary, S.D.S., foundress of the community, whose cause for beatification was in process. Breakfast followed at 8:30 and consisted of orange juice, toast, boiled egg and coffee. Meals were always brief, never more than half an hour, and his secretary and the hospital chaplain ate with him. While he would enter into their conversations, he seldom initiated the topic. The cardinal much preferred that there be no guests and certainly never wanted long table talk. He would even stand up after half an hour whether or not the others had finished eating. He seemed to be unconscious of others, which was so uncharacteristic of one who formerly enjoyed guests and lively conversation. The doctors warned everyone that Muench's creeping arteriosclerosis would result in such reactions and that they should understand his condition. They were warned that such a condition could go on for as long as ten years and the friends in Fargo, Milwaukee and Germany worried continually that the cardinal would suffer a prolonged incapacitating illness.

Muench would go to his room immediately after meals, shut the door and lie down for a short time. Mornings were invariably taken up with correspondence. Father Lessard had a room adjoining the cardinal's and he would come for dictation. As always, Muench was conscientious in answering letters. The correspondence was heavy and included documents sent from the congregations to which he was assigned as a member, letters from German and American relatives and friends, people reporting putative miraculous events, invitations and numerous letters from people of all rank who continued to write to Muench about their problems and families. Dictation usually lasted about an hour and was given to Father Lessard for Latin, Italian and English matters, and to Sister Dorothea, S.D.S., for German letters. The cardinal outlined the idea and left to the secretary the actual writing of the replies. He did not formulate his important letters by hand as was his former custom. Muench was patient and slow to criticize. However, he never lost his interest in words and would discuss with the secretaries why they had used certain words or constructions with which he did not agree.

Lunch was at 1:00 p.m. and consisted of pasta with grated cheese, boiled or grilled meat, vegetable, salad and for dessert a pudding or small cake. There was always an afternoon siesta and the cardinal would take a walk with his secretary between 3:00 and 4:30 p.m. This was the best time of day as Muench enjoyed the walk around the grounds of the hospital, the area of Rome near the Janiculum hill and through an adjoining park. On these occasions he would monopolize the conversation, talk in detail about the years in Wisconsin, North Dakota and Germany, reminisce about his old friends and evidence real concern about the problems of individual priests or acquaintances. He was relaxed and happy and would also discuss current Roman affairs. Repeatedly, however, he became annoyed at some of Rome's dirty streets and sidewalks and remarked that in Germany, despite the terrible postwar conditions, the people were never too poor to be clean.

Upon returning to the hospital the cardinal would again go to work on the afternoon's correspondence and pray and read before supper at 7:00 p.m. In the evening he liked creamed mushroom or milk soup, as the sisters at Bad Godesberg had made it, egg on toast with asparagus and cooked fruit. He would never take ice cream: "No, that is for my secretary; it is too cold for me." Toward the end he would forget what soup he had ordered and when Sister Veronica would bring him milk soup he would insist he had requested bouillon. Muench shunned every possible engagement, refused invitations to festivities, and when old friends from Germany and the United States stopped by he would not want them to stay for meals. If he could not evade meeting visitors, he would receive them in a parlor on the first floor of the hospital and make the visit as brief as possible. He did not want to be asked questions or to have problems presented to him. Those who did not understand his condition were often hurt and perplexed; it was not the Muench they had known as bishop and nuncio. His physical stamina had collapsed under the pressure of the problems and extraordinary labors in the mission to Germany.

Other cardinals in curia continued to ask Muench why he lived in two rooms at Salvator Mundi Hospital. They encouraged him to take an apartment as they did. His extremely simple personal tastes were not always understood in Rome, as they had not been in Germany. But Muench, shrewdly perhaps, realized more than he ever let on that in his present condition of health he could not manage his own household in Italy. Besides, the sisters and staff at Salvator Mundi more than generously took care of him with devotion and attention. All facilities were conveniently located there and the hospital supplied excellent modern medical care. It provided him with an American and German atmosphere in Rome. Cardinal Muench had felt very much at home there during frequent visits over the years and now it was a haven in his last illness.

The meetings of the Central Preparatory Commission for Vatican Council II proved to be an increasing burden for Cardinal Muench. He would return to Salvator Mundi from the three-hour meetings at the Vatican completely exhausted. But the pleas of the staff and community that he was not obliged to attend every meeting fell on deaf ears. As always, he was determined to do his duty. In late January of 1962 those close to him daily became more concerned at the obvious strain these sessions were causing him. On January 19 Dr. Nicholas M. Musacchio, chief physician at Salvator Mundi, advised the cardinal to slow down and not feel obliged to attend every session. The next day Muench was exhausted but insisted in the morning that he had to go to the Vatican. On Sunday, January 21, he was not able to rise from bed in the morning. He had spasms in his leg, resulting from a defective circulation symptomatic of arteriosclerosis. He could not stand alone or move from the bed or chair; it was the beginning of his final illness.[12]

Three days later, on January 24, Muench developed a chest cold but the doctors continued to find his heart beat and blood pressure normal. Cardinal Meyer missed him at the commission meetings and called to find out what was wrong. Father Lessard phoned Bishop Dworschak in Fargo and informed him of the cardinal's illness. Muench was becoming more confused and quite irritable at being confined to his room.[13] His bronchial condition was a source of worry and Doctor "Nick," who was very attached to the cardinal, called in two neurological consultants who confirmed what was already known: a normal condition for advanced arteriosclerosis with a temporary attack of influenza. The cardinal began to sleep for long hours, but on January 30 Father Lessard was able to have a barber come in to cut his hair without the usual questioning if it was necessary. Cardinal Cicognani, secretary of state, was informed and he said he would tell Pope John about the cardinal's condition.

In early February Muench became confused, especially at night, and kept asking: "Tomorrow we must go over the schemata. How did I get here? When did we cross the Danube? When are they bringing Holy Communion?" He kept insisting on having a drink of Coca Cola, which he had never drunk before, and even just before Holy Communion was brought to him. Only liquids were now being given him as nourishment. He wanted to wander around but was completely lost.

One evening he got up by himself, dressed fully and crossed the corridor from his room toward the red light of the hospital chapel. Sister Valeria, S.D.S., night nurse, found him and he said: "Open the door, what is that?" She told him it was the chapel and he entered and with all his energy tried to genuflect and for a few minutes knelt in a pew and prayed before the nurse got him back to bed. Another evening he frightened everyone by getting up and going to the bathroom. He fell on the floor and was found with a gash on his head. When he was asked if he was hurt he said: "No, no, not at all." He never complained about pain, and apart from his growing weakness and confusion this appeared to be the case. But after this scare it was determined to give him twenty-four hour nursing care.

Two nursing brothers, one German and the other Irish, were added to relieve the permanent staff. The cardinal became more and more passive and when he talked it was about Germany, then it became Fargo, next Milwaukee and finally Rome; the meetings he should be attending, processions, visitors. He withdrew more and more and seemed to be praying a great deal. When asked if he wished to receive the Sacrament of the Last Anointing he said: "Wait a while." It was obvious that his condition had become serious and when it was decided to administer the sacrament, he submitted very willingly and responded to all the prayers.

It was an extremely difficult time for Father Lessard. The cardinal was, obviously, becoming weaker and he had left no instructions in writing about what he wanted done in case of illness. Lessard kept the Secretariat of State and Fargo informed, and finally on February 1 decided to call Archbishop William E. Cousins in Milwaukee asking him to inform the Muench family. He did not wish to worry them, but he was convinced they should know the situation. Guests and visitors kept inquiring about Cardinal Muench, papers had to be signed, and the press began to ask questions. On February 5 Dr. "Nick" called in the well-known Professor Cesare Frugone, internal medicine specialist, who, after examination, saw no sign of approaching death. The cardinal was suffering from symptomatic cerebral arteriosclerosis but Frugone was optimistic. He indicated, as others had said, that Muench could live for several years. His condition was operable but not at an advanced age such as the cardinal's. A medical bulletin was released on February 6 announcing that the cardinal was ill; but this American procedure was not favorably received at the Vatican since custom proscribed that no such public statements be made.

Cardinal Gaetano Cicognani died on February 5; Cardinal Teodosio C. de Gouveia died the next day, and Lessard wondered who would be the third, according to the Roman proverb that cardinals die in threes. Cardinals and other friends in Rome came by to leave their cards, and many letters and cables of sympathy and prayers were received. On February 6 Lessard judged the family must be informed for a second time through Archbishop Cousins. Muench's sister Terry called back and said that she and her sisters, Dorothy Ott and Mary Herrick, would leave for Rome at once. They arrived on February 8 and Father Lessard went into the cardinal's room in advance to tell him that he had called his family in Milwaukee and that his sisters were in Rome. Lessard expected a strong reaction but when his sisters came into the room the cardinal, Lessard said, "just broke out in one of the most charming, and for me one of the most consoling smiles I had ever seen on his face." Muench seemed to pick up noticeably when his sisters arrived, became more alert, asked questions about the family back home and the Roman February weather.

On February 9 word came from the Vatican that Pope John would come that afternoon to visit the cardinal. This visit was not entirely unexpected and everyone was prepared for the first visit of a pope to Salvator Mundi. Cardinal Amleto Cicognani arrived in advance at 4:30 in the afternoon and visited his old friend Muench. Pope John came at 5:10 and went directly to the third floor chapel where he first knelt before the Blessed Sacrament and then crossed the corridor to Cardinal Muench's room. The cardinal had been prepared for the visit and the sisters had put his ring on his finger and placed his cross around his neck. Dr. Nick and Father Lessard accompanied the Holy Father into the room and Pope John immediately took the cardinal's hand, kissed it and said: "I come to visit you as a member of my own family." Pope John noticed a picture of Muench's father on the wall and he began to talk of his own family in Bergamo. Cardinal Muench, quite alert, told the Holy Father that he had devoted his whole life to Christ and the Church and now renewed his devotion to the Holy See. It was a cordial, joyful visit and Muench was moved to tears as Pope John expressed gratitude to the cardinal for his labors. The Holy Father also talked about heaven, imparted his blessing and kissed the cardinal's forehead in farewell.

As he passed through the cardinal's office John XXIII greeted the three Muench sisters and asked them to take his blessing with them to their families. Patients, sisters and staff lined the corridors as the Pope departed. He stopped to greet them and to joke with several of those present such as a seminarian from the Beda College for late English vocations to whom he said: "You are too young to be at the Beda." He asked a sister what her work was and she replied that she worked in the public health office of the Vatican. "Oh," replied Pope John, "in the Vatican! Then try to sanctify yourself and the Vatican." He was surprised at how many sisters there were in the community and how many nationalities were represented. Pope John said: "It would be nice to ask each sister where she comes from and what her work is, but it makes no difference because we all work for the Lord and are headed for the same country." As he was led toward the waiting car by Vatican officials the Pope saw one of the African candidates and placing his hands on her face, he said: "Keep your beautiful color and become a good sister." Then, standing in the open car, he was driven away into the night.

Everyone at Salvator Mundi was deeply moved by this papal visit and Pope John, apparently, was also touched by the welcome he received for he sent within a few hours special thanks through Archbishop Angelo Dell'Acqua, substitute secretary of state, along with three large photographs of himself for Cardinal Muench, the Muench family and the Salvatorian sisters with a handwritten inscription: "Salvator Mundi, miserere nobis." His secretary, Monsignor Louis Capovilla, also called to thank everyone for the Christian courtesy shown to the pontiff and to say that the visit was "still fresh in his eyes and heart." [14]

Father Lessard explained to Cardinal Muench what all the excitement had been about and he responded knowingly. His secretary also drafted a letter of appreciation to Pope John thanking him in the name of the cardinal, the community of Salvator Mundi and American Catholics for the paternal gesture he had extended to all of them. The next day Cardinal Muench seemed to be improving and was even placed in a chair for a time, but in the afternoon he was confused and his color was bad. He did not respond to his sisters' conversation which was a severe trial for them. There was no continuity in the few words he spoke and his memory was intermittent. Muench slept more and more and paid little attention to those around him. On February 14 he was semi-conscious with a fever and bronchial congestion. By the next day he no longer responded although he seemed at times to hear and understand.

He was in grave condition, with an irregular pulse and heartbeat along with sharp and superficial breathing. A constant vigil of prayer was maintained throughout the day. The last agony began on February 15 at nine o'clock in the evening and lasted until 10:54 p.m. The room was filled: present were the three Muench sisters from Milwaukee, the Salvatorian sisters, Father Lessard, and Father Cormac Coyne, S.D.S., hospital chaplain, who led the prayers for the dying. At the Vatican, Pope John, who had been informed, was in his chapel praying the rosary for the cardinal. It was a beautiful ending, Father Lessard said, to seventy-two years of dedicated service. His death was peaceful and without pain, "a quiet departure to God in the midst of a praying family." His breath seemed slowly to be taken from him.

A long series of preparations was now begun. Few got any sleep that night as calls were made to Milwaukee and Fargo, telegrams prepared for dignitaries, press releases written and a thousand details of a cardinal's funeral were begun. The next morning Monsignor Enrico Dante and his assistants from the office of the papal master of ceremonies came to Salvator Mundi to make plans for the Roman funeral. They wanted their undertakers, but the cardinal's family and associates insisted on their own arrangements. The body was moved to the community chapel at 11:00 a.m. on Friday, February 16, while a Vatican archivist and a lawyer coldly checked the official documents left in the cardinal's room. Visitors began to arrive and Masses were continuously offered in the chapel on Saturday and Sunday, a practice which Muench would not have approved. Cardinals, diplomats and the humblest of workers came to pay tribute. Messages of condolence and testimonials were numerous. Chancellor Adenauer expressed sympathy in the name of the Federal Republic and in his own name. Adenauer said: "Cardinal Muench has become part of the history of the Federal Republic. For his most generous, big-hearted understanding of our problems, the German people will forever hold him in grateful and honored remembrance." Bishop Kurt Scharf, chairman of the Council of the Evangelical Church in Germany, telegraphed: "The Evangelical Christians of Germany have lost a beloved advocate in the many serious problems of our partitioned fatherland, and an adviser and assistant in the interior distress of the German people." Paul Dahm wrote in *Der Feuerreiter*: "Muench's name is intimately connected with the history of the Church in Germany after World War II and to the contemporary history of the Federal Republic. The Germans bow in reverence and gratitude before our great friend." J. Anthony Panuch, special adviser to General Clay as American military governor in Germany, wrote: "If I were asked to name the four people I know who have done the most in the last fifteen years to build a firm bridge of understanding between the people of the United States and the people of Germany, I would rank them in the following order: Bishop Muench, General Clay, Conrad Adenauer and Jack McCloy."

On Sunday, February 18, the day that would have been Muench's 73rd birthday, at 4:30 p.m. the *del Rogito* ceremony was conducted by Monsignor Antonio Caretta, papal master of ceremonies. A Latin eulogy was read, the coffin sealed, and the community formed an honorary guard as the body was carried to the hearse that would take it to Saint Peter's Basilica accompanied by relatives, friends and students from the American and German pontifical colleges in Rome. Muench would never have dreamt that he would receive such an elaborate funeral. During his life he often had said that he wanted only to be buried simply in the ground at Holy Cross Cemetery in Fargo near his priests and people to await the coming of the Lord. But before that request could be fulfilled there had to be a long series of journeys with his body as tribute was paid to an international churchman who had looked upon himself in far less complicated dimensions.

Next morning, February 19, in St. Peter's Basilica, the funeral Mass was held at 10:00 a.m. in the chapel of Saints Processo and Martiniano in the crossbeam of the basilica. The pontifical high Mass was sung by Cardinal Carlo Confalonieri, secretary of the Consistorial Congregation. The Sistine choir, directed by Maestro Domenico Bartolucci, sang the seven-voiced funeral Mass the director had composed for the funeral of Pope Pius XII. Pope John and thirty-seven cardinals were in attendance, the largest number of cardinals remembered at such a funeral. This was because they were in Rome for the sessions of the preparatory commission of the council. Over 2,000 churchmen, diplomats, relatives and friends joined in paying final tribute. The cardinal's casket, according to protocol, was under a high catafalque, draped in black and surrounded with a hundred lighted candles. Cardinal Muench would not have chosen the baroque procedures of Vatican funerals for cardinals.

At 11:45 a.m. the funeral cortege left immediately with police escort for Fiumicino airport. The body was placed aboard a TWA plane that left with the Muench party at 1:15 p.m. and arrived in Chicago, after stops in Paris and New York, at 8:50 in the evening. At the airport Bishop Dworschak, Bishops Aloysius Wycislo and Cletus O'Donnell, auxiliaries of Chicago, the rest of the Muench family and a large number of people were waiting. The funeral party then proceeded by car to Milwaukee, a distance of eighty miles, where the body was to lie in state at Saint John's Cathedral to be viewed by 15,000 people in one day. The second funeral Mass was held on February 21 with Archbishop William E. Cousins as celebrant and Bishop William P. O'Connor of Madison the eulogist. That evening when the cortege left Milwaukee for Fargo it was in the midst of a blizzard.

The body was placed on a Great Northern train in Milwaukee for the last leg of the long journey to Fargo. He who had made so many trips back and forth across the ocean to Germany, across the Alps to Rome, now in death was approaching the last stop. The body was placed in his former cathedral of Saint Mary's in Fargo, and for two days his people came from the Red River Valley and the prairie to pray for the soul of their former bishop. On February 23 Cardinal Joseph Ritter of Saint Louis offered the final Mass and Archbishop Karl J. Alter of Cincinnati delivered another eulogy. So many telegrams and letters had been received from the great and the little people in Europe and America, so many tributes had been made in the press, so many words had been spoken, that it was difficult to add any more. Alter listed Muench's long record of accomplishments and stated that when the ecclesiastical history of the period was written the "immense contribution of Cardinal Muench, especially in Germany, will stand forth in the final record." Alter repeated what all knew, that Fargo was the favored place of Muench among his varied assignments on two continents. Now Fargo would be the guardian of his mortal remains "against the day of resurrection." In $+4°$ temperature on a typical February day in North Dakota, with a twenty-five mile north wind and snow throughout the day, Bishop Dworschak, with filial devotion, conducted the final graveside rites. Cardinal Muench's body was then laid to rest in the ground of Holy Cross Cemetery.

A unique chapter in the development of American Catholicism had been completed. Aloisius Muench had emerged as a first-generation descendant of nineteenth-century German immigrant parents. He was one of the proportionately few Americans of German descent who had achieved national and international stature in the first half of the twentieth century. He had grown up and acquired outlooks on the world in a

Milwaukee German national parish at the turn of the century. His major interests originally centered in this German-American parish in a lower working class section of that city. His cultural milieu was folk orientated. His education was obtained primarily in parochial and church schools, from primary grades through doctoral studies in the United States and Europe. Theologically he was a traditionalist and firmly papal in conviction. His main interest was in Catholic societies and organizations.

Muench taught in the closed world of a major seminary, administered that same seminary as rector and was appointed a bishop of a diaspora diocese on the American prairie embracing a vast area with a struggling minority of rural Catholic immigrants and their descendants. He was sent to Germany to assist in restoring the Church at a time when Catholics in that nation had experienced their most traumatic and bitter persecution. He advanced to the post of nuncio there and carried out a diplomatic assignment of guarding the interests of the Church. Finally, he lived as the first American cardinal in curia in the centralized Roman administrative complex of the Church.

His spiritual emphasis was pietistic, moralistic and based on simple virtues. Bishop Fulton J. Sheen told him, after a visit to Bad Godesberg on 20 June 1951: "I found the same beautiful spiritual simplicity that first I saw in you years ago when we were fellow students at Louvain." Muench indicated to Archbishop Leo Binz of Dubuque, on 14 September 1957, what he considered to be the spiritual qualities of a bishop:

"A bishop should always be guided by the exalted ideals of his office, and in carrying out his office be directed by what he considers to be right and proper. He does not love the spectacular. His undertakings do not bear the marks of haughtiness, conceit or pride. He is a simple, modest and humble apostle of the Lord. He always has a kindly smile, a cheerful word, and when needed, a helping hand."

Muench was a classical product of the American Catholic ghetto with its characteristic thrusts. His writings and speeches were filled with phrases and ideas that indicated thought patterns of a linear culture. On 3 May 1956, for example, he told his friend James A. Farley: "We must make breeches in the strong ramparts that secularism has thrown up against Christian traditions." He was not a modern man nor a secular city man. Throughout his life he repeatedly found himself in positions for which he had not been trained and that he would have preferred not holding. The paradox of human achievement has few better examples than the life of Aloisius Muench.

How did he develop into a relevant instrument for good? How did he cope so successfully with the environmental involvements coherent to human experience in the post-Christian world? People from the highest to the lowest levels of life in Europe and the United States found his personal commitment a witness which was welcomed and esteemed. He was involved more deeply than the vast majority of his contemporaries in the so-called secularistic structure confrontation. "In the years to come," Archbishop Gerald P. O'Hara told him on 28 March 1954, "historians will record that in the building up of a new Germany it was a bishop from the Midwest who played a major role." German authorities in interviews confirmed this opinion without qualification. They placed Muench on the same plateau with Adenauer as a charismatic instrument for social reconstruction in postwar Germany. Whatever he did was carried out with scholarly precision. As one of the few American bishops of his generation who had received authentic academic training in a real university atmosphere, he brought a solid tradition of scholarship to his writings and work. An American Catholicism, still lacking in appreciation for scholarship, especially among its Church leaders, had a competent student in Muench.

Aloisius Muench, personally, would not have considered it necessary to analyze the influences and motivation of his life. He simply would have replied, as he did in life, that he only did his duty. Commitment was not a complicated phenomenon for Muench. He believed firmly in tradition and the proved values of human relations. At every stage of his life he saw that better understanding, tolerance and respect among men were needed. Minority groups, of which he was a conspicuous member, deserved acceptance without condescension. His parents had not wanted assistance; they only asked for the opportunity to work in freedom and dignity. Muench tried to create similar situations where all men could do likewise. He acquired an intense interest in and dedication to the social problems of human beings in the German-American fraternal organizations and rural life societies which he never failed to support. He believed equally in the overriding providence of God in every human experience. He did not judge that any advance in human relations could be achieved without an understanding and respect for the spiritual experience of the past. It was an uncomplicated and rather pedestrian conviction. There were no secrets about the success of Aloisius Muench. He moved out from where he was into environments he had never experienced with a calm assurance that, without faithful attachment to his spiritual roots, a modern man could not relate. He considered his whole life to be simply a part of the providence of God.

On his eightieth birthday, 17 January 1956, Chancellor Adenauer receives the
Papal honor of the Golden Spur, at the Nunciature. With Cardinal Frings and the
Nuncio are Adenauer's four sons.

A Fargo private audience with Pope John XXIII, 6 October 1959: l to r: Genevieve
Murray, Larry Boyle (Archbishop Muench's secretary in Fargo), Father
Joseph Senger, Archbishop Muench, Pope John XXIII, Bishop Dworschak,
Mrs. Leona Naylor and Monica Canning. On this day Pope John told Archbishop
Muench he was being considered for an appointment to the college of cardinals.

Christmas, 1959, at the Nunciature in Bad Godesberg. The Sisters, l to r: Sisters Martina, Fridburga, Anna Maria, Berthilla, Ilga, Ruth and Regulinde.

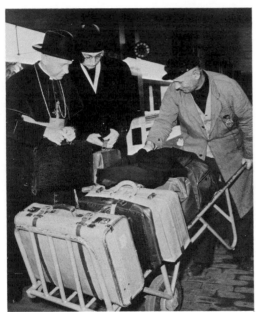

Cardinal-designate Muench and Father Senger arrive in Rome for the consistory, 9 December 1959.

Cardinal-designate Muench is welcomed to Villa Salvator Mundi on 9 December 1959: l to r: Dr. Nick Mussachio, Dr. Victorio DeStefano, Father Cormac Coyne, chaplain, Mother M. Olympia Heuel, S.D.S., superior general, Sister Henriella, S.D.S., and Dr. George Randegger.

With the delegation from Diocese of Fargo, Rome, 15 December 1959.

Seven of the eight new cardinals pictured with Cardinal Tardini at the consistory held 17 December 1959: l to r: Cardinals Meyer, Muench, Testa, Tardini, Larraona, Morano, Heard, and Bea.

New Cardinals are led into St. Peter's Basilica, where the red hats are conferred by Pope John, 17 December 1959.

During Consistory in St. Peter's Basilica, the new cardinals await reception of the red hat: l to r: Cardinals Morano, Larraona, Meyer, Muench, Testa. Father Joseph Senger is the trainbearer for Cardinal Muench.

Cardinal Muench greets Pope John at the throne during ceremonies of the consistory.

*Cardinal Muench visits with members of his family who
came to Rome for the consistory: l to r: Cardinal Muench,
Dorothy Ott, Bishop Dworschak, Philip Ott, Teresa
Muench, David Ott, Mrs. Dorothy Ott, Barbara Ott.*

*Cardinal Muench assumes title to his church, San Bernardo in Rome,
18 December 1959: l to r: Msgr. F. J. Nestor of Fargo, Cardinal Muench,
and Msgr. L. J. Arrell of Fargo.*

*Pope John greets Cardinal Muench after delivering Christmas
message to cardinals, 24 December 1959.*

*Cardinal Muench, Papal Legate to
Malta, moves through the city of
Valletta, 20 July 1960.*

*Procession leaves St. Mary's Cathedral, Fargo, following Pontifical Mass
in honor of silver jubilee of consecration as a bishop, 4 October 1960.*

Civic reception in Fargo Memorial Auditorium: l to r: Bishop Dworschak,
Norman D. Black, Cardinal Muench, and the Hon. Thomas Whelan,
Ambassador to Nicaragua.

Goodbye Fargo, 8 October 1960.

Cardinal Muench, at home, October, 1960:
l to r: Frank Herrick; sister, Mary (Mrs. Frank
Herrick); and sister Teresa.

Last photo of Cardinal Muench, taken on 12 January 1962 as he signed the
Papal Bull, "Humanae Salutis," whereby Pope John XXIII convoked
the Second Vatican Council: l to r: Msgr. Francesco Tinello, regent of the
Apostolic Chancellery; Father Raymond W. Lessard, the Cardinal's secretary;
and Father D. Rino Marsiglio, staff member of the Apostolic Chancellery.

Pope John visited Cardinal Muench at Salvator Mundi Hospital six days
before his death, 9 February 1962. In foreground, Msgr. Louis Capovilla,
Pope's secretary; Dr. George Randegger, director of hospital, stands at
entrance; behind Pope is Bishop Salvatore Ballo Guercio, a retired Italian
bishop living at Salvator Mundi, and the Pope's valet.

*Body of Cardinal Muench lies
in state in chapel of Salvator Mundi
Hospital, Rome, 16–18 February 1962.*

*Pope John XXIII officiates at absolution, assisted by Msgr. Enrico Dante,
papal master of ceremonies, in St. Peter's Basilica, 19 February 1962.
Following behind are Cardinals Ottaviani and DiJorio and Msgr. Oddone
Tacoli, private chamberlain.*

Funeral of Cardinal Muench in St. Peter's Basilica, Rome, 19 February 1962.

Procession in St. Mary's Cathedral, Fargo, for Pontifical Requiem Mass, 23 February 1962. At center is Bishop Dworschak, Archbishop Karl J. Alter, homilist, in the right foreground, and Cardinal Joseph Ritter, celebrant.

Burial in Holy Cross Cemetery, Fargo, 23 February 1962.

Final resting place of Cardinal Muench. His grave is at the right, in front of the central monument which he planned in 1940.

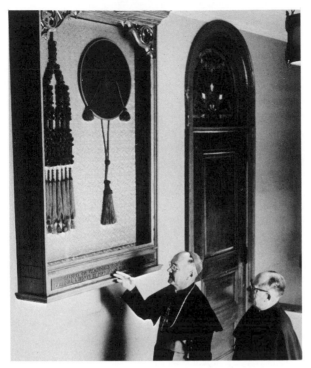

Bishop Dworschak and Msgr. L. J. Arrell, Cathedral pastor, view the "red hat" or galero of Cardinal Muench mounted in a glass case in the vestibule of St. Mary's Cathedral, Fargo.

Air view of Cardinal Muench Seminary in Fargo, named in his memory in 1966.

APPENDICES

APPENDIX I

PUBLICATIONS OF ALOISIUS J. MUENCH

ANNUAL LENTEN PASTORALS

Pastoral Letter, 1936

The Christian Home, 1937

The Priest and His People, 1938

A Catholic and His Church, 1939

Matrimony, A Great Sacrament, 1940

The New Social Order, 1941

Youth, A Chosen Generation, 1942

New Men for a Better World, 1943

Give Us Peace, 1944

Pitfalls For Peace, 1945

One World in Charity, 1946

The Times Challenge Us, 1947

For Christ's Sake, A New Social Order, 1948

Contributions of the Catholic Church to the State, 1949

The Year of Great Return, 1950

The Catholic Church, Our Champion of Freedom, 1951

The Catholic in the World, 1952

The Call of the Lord, 1953

Thou Art All Fair, Mary Immaculate, 1954

Religion in Education, 1955

The Lay Apostolate in the Church, 1956

The Catholic Way of Life, 1957

Security for the Soul, 1958

Blessed is the Catholic, 1959

BOOKS

Muench, Aloisius J. and Ryan, Vincent J., *The Church, Fascism and Peace*, Our Sunday Visitor Press, Huntington, Indiana, 1944, 88 pp.

Muench, Aloisius J., Ryan, Vincent J., and Mulloy, William T., *Manifesto on Rural Life*, Bruce Publishing Co., Milwaukee, 1939, 222 pp.

Synodus Dioecesana Fargensis Prima, Bruce Publishing Co., Milwaukee, 1941. 303 pp.

PAMPHLETS

Sterilization by Law, Central Bureau of the Central Verein, Saint Louis, 1929, 44 pp.

The Outstretched Hand of Communism, Central Bureau Press, Saint Louis, 1938, 24 pp.

Partnership With God, National Catholic Rural Life Conference, Des Moines, 1941, 8 pp.

Parish Religious Discussion Clubs, Confraternity of Christian Doctrine, Washington, D.C., 1941, 10 pp.

Credit Unions in Parishes, Central Bureau Publications, Saint Louis, 1936, 8 pp.

ARTICLES

"Nationalization in France," *America*, 22, 9 (December 20, 1919), 174–177.

"That France May Live," *America*, 22, 10 (December 27, 1919), 98–101.

"Life and Death in Germany," *America*, 22, 19 (February 28, 1920), 417–418.

"Industrial Democracy Through Law," *America*, 22, 24 (April 13, 1920), 539–541.

"The First Peace Conference," *America*, 22, 25 (April 10, 1920), 565–567.

"Switzerland and the League of Nations," *America*, 23, 1 (April 24, 1920), 9–11.

"The Swiss and the League," *America*, 23, 9 (June 26, 1920), 224–226.

"Europe's Spiritual Distress," *America*, 23, 10 (July 3, 1920), 245–246.

"The Allies and Catholic Missions," *America*, 23, 15 (July 31, 1920), 346–348.

"International Labor Legislation," *America*, 23, 19 (August 28, 1920), 442–444.

"Catholic Total Abstinence League of Switzerland," *America*, 23, 21 (September 18, 1920), 510–512.

"Europe and the League of Nations," *America*, 24, 5 (November 20, 1920), 102–104.

"The League of Nations at Geneva," *America*, 24, 10 (December 25, 1920), 225–226.

"The Swiss Referendum on a Labor Law," *America*, 24, 12 (January 8, 1921), 279–281.

"The Presidents of Three Republics," *America*, 24, 21 (March 12, 1921), 493–494.

"Socialism in France," *America*, 24, 26 (April 16, 1921), 616–618.

"Tenth International Cooperative Congress," *America*, 25, 23 (September 24, 1921), 537–539.

"The Swiss Health Insurance Law," *America*, 25, 25 (October 8, 1921), 588–590.

"International Labor Legislation," *America*, 26, 5 (November 19, 1921), 105–107.

"First International Democratic Congress," *America*, 26, 14 (January 21, 1922), 317–318.

"Housing and Coal Miners in Holland," *America*, 27, 16 (August 5, 1922), 366–368.

"The State and the Worker," *America*, 45, 4 (May 2, 1931), 85–86.

"Industrial Unionism in the United States, I," *Social Justice Review*, 17, 1 (April, 1924), 5–7.

"Industrial Unionism in the United States, II," *Social Justice Review*, 17, 2 (May, 1924), 40–43.

"A Parliament of Industry," *Social Justice Review*, 17, 5 (August, 1924), 150–151.

"A Parliament of Industry," *Social Justice Review*, 17, 6 (September, 1924), 186–187.

"Cooperation Among the Lithuanians," *Social Justice Review*, 17, 7 (October, 1924), 223–224.

"The Catholic Rural Life Conference," *Social Justice Review*, 17, 8 (November, 1924), 258–259.

"Governmental Price Fixing," *Social Justice Review*, 17, 9 (December, 1924), 295–296.

"Land as Property," *Social Justice Review*, 17, 12 (March, 1925), 400–401.

"Farm Tenancy, I," *Social Justice Review*, 18, 1 (April, 1925), 4–5.

"Farm Tenancy, II," *Social Justice Review*, 18, 2 (May, 1925), 40–42.

"Long-Term Land Tenancy, I," *Social Justice Review*, 18, 3 (June, 1925), 76–78.

"Long-Term Land Tenancy, II," *Social Justice Review*, 18, 4 (July, 1925), 112–114.

"The Farmer and His Work," *Social Justice Review*, 18, 5 (August, 1925), 148–150.

"The Endowment of the Family, I," *Social Justice Review*, 18, 7 (October, 1925), 221–222.

"The Endowment of the Family, II," *Social Justice Review*, 18, 8 (November, 1925), 257–258.

"The Endowment of the Family, III," *Social Justice Review*, 18, 9 (December, 1925), 293–294.

"The Endowment of the Family, IV," *Social Justice Review*, 18, 10 (June, 1926), 329–331.

"The Endowment of the Family, V," *Social Justice Review*, 18, 11 (February, 1926), 366–367.

"The Endowment of the Family, VI," *Social Justice Review*, 18, 12 (March, 1926), 402–404.

"Appraisal of the British Unemployment Insurance System," *Social Justice Review*, 19, 5 (August, 1926), 148–149.

"Unemployment Insurance in Great Britain," *Social Justice Review*, 19, 6 (September, 1926), 186–188.

"The State and Charity," *Social Justice Review*, 19, 7 (October, 1926), 222–223.

"Juvenile Delinquency, I," *Social Justice Review*, 19, 8 (November, 1926), 257–258.

"Juvenile Delinquency, II," *Social Justice Review*, 19, 9 (December, 1926), 292–294.

"Juvenile Delinquency, III," *Social Justice Review*, 19, 10 (January, 1927), 328–330.

"Fundamentals of Christian Charity, I," *Social Justice Review*, 19, 11 (February, 1927), 365–367.

"Fundamentals of Christian Charity, II," *Social Justice Review*, 19, 12 (March, 1927), 400–403.

"Fundamentals of Christian Charity, III," *Social Justice Review*, 20, 1 (April, 1927), 4–7.

"Fundamentals of Christian Charity, IV," *Social Justice Review*, 20, 2 (May, 1927), 41–43.

"Fundamentals of Christian Charity, V," *Social Justice Review*, 20, 3 (June, 1927), 76–79.

"Sterilization by Law, I," *Social Justice Review*, 20, 4–5 (July–August, 1927), 113–114.

"Sterilization by Law, II," *Social Justice Review*, 20, 6 (September, 1927), 163–165.

"Sterilization by Law, III," *Social Justice Review*, 20, 7 (October, 1927), 200–202.

"Sterilization by Law, IV," *Social Justice Review*, 20, 8 (November, 1927), 237–239.

"Sterilization by Law, IV (2)," *Social Justice Review*, 20, 9 (December, 1927), 276.

"Sterilization by Law, V," *Social Justice Review*, 20, 10 (January, 1928), 309–310.

"Sterilization by Law, VI," *Social Justice Review*, 20, 11 (February, 1928), 344–346.

"Church and State, I," *Social Justice Review*, 21, 1 (April, 1928), 3–4.

"Church and State, II," *Social Justice Review*, 21, 2 (May, 1928), 39–41.

"Church and State, III," *Social Justice Review*, 21, 3 (June, 1928), 75–77.

"Church and State, IV," *Social Justice Review*, 21, 4–5 (July–August, 1928), 112–113.

"Church and State, V," *Social Justice Review*, 21, 6 (September, 1928), 166–168.

"Church and State, V (2)," *Social Justice Review*, 21, 7 (October, 1928), 201–203.

"Church and State, VI," *Social Justice Review*, 21, 8 (November, 1928), 237–239.

"Church and State, VII," *Social Justice Review*, 21, 9 (December, 1928), 273–274.

"Church and State, VIII," *Social Justice Review*, 21, 10 (January, 1929), 309–310.

"Catholic Action and Parish Societies," *Social Justice Review*, 21, 12 (March, 1929), 382–384.

"Well Advised Caution Regarding 'Farm Relief'," *Social Justice Review*, 22, 6 (September, 1929), 169–170.

"The Downfall of Capitalism," *Social Justice Review*, 22, 8 (November, 1929), 237–239.

"The Prevention of Destitution and Credit Unions," *Social Justice Review*, 22, 11 (February, 1930), 345–346.

"The Bishop Writes," monthly essays in *Catholic Action News*, 1936 through 1959.

"Das Salesianum in Milwaukee," *Jahrbuch des Reichsverbandes fuer die Katholischen Auslanddeutschen*, 1935, 293–298.

"Die Soziale Liebe," *Die Neue Ordung in Kirche, Staat, Gesellschaft, Kultur*, VII, (1953), 11–18.

"Friede durch Gerechtigkeit," *Sudetendeutsche Ackermann-Gemeinde*, IV (August, 1952), 29–38.

Der Arbeiter und das Socialprogramm der paepste. Address on the Anniversary of Pope Pius XII, Cologne, 22 June 1947.

Theologische Grunddanken zur katholischen Landvolkbewegung. Address on receiving an honorary doctorate from the University of Muenster, 5 July 1948, Regensburg-Muenster, 1948.

Annual Final Address at the *Katholikentage*, published in the volumes of the *Katholikentage*, 1948–1959.

Address of Bishop Aloisius Muench to the German Bishops' Conference, Fulda, 20–22 August 1946.

My first word to you, Most Reverend Confrères, is a cordial greeting from the Holy Father.

When I was granted an audience by the Holy Father a few weeks ago, he spoke with moving words of his high appreciation of the German episcopate, and he gave me the specific order to tell you of his esteem and cordial love with which he feels united with you.

In dark, anxious days, so he told me, the German episcopate remained at his side in fidelity and determination. This was for him a great consolation and a source of new strength. History will one day recount with golden script the high merits that the German bishops acquired in leading their flock through most difficult times.

In touching words the Holy Father described the deep life of faith and the loyalty of the priests and the laity in Germany with which they carried on their Catholic work. I do not have to explain to you in detail with what kind of paternal love he cares for the destiny of the German people.

Germany will recover, and it will rise out of the ruins of war to new prestige among the peace-loving nations of Europe.

It is also an honor and joy for me to convey to you, most esteemed confrères in Christ, the greetings of the American episcopate. With growing admiration we have watched from America how the bishops of Germany protected and cared for their flock, entrusted to them by God, before the outbreak of World War II and during the war. Be assured that the American hierarchy knows about the bitter need of the Catholic Church in Germany, and that the Catholics of North America are eager to give as much help as they can.

In the coming month of November an extensive collection will be held again in all the Catholic churches of the United States. I, on my part, shall not fail to send a detailed report on the needs of the German bishops to the chairman of the episcopal committee, His Eminence Cardinal Stritch, archbishop of Chicago.

Furthermore, in order to assist the Catholic people in Germany I have already written to the above-mentioned cardinal, asking for a substantial sum for this purpose.

Most Reverend Confrères, I have come to Germany as apostolic visitator. Being fairly well informed about the heroic spirit of confession of faith of the German bishops, I must admit that I have come to you in humble acknowledgment of an apostle-like courage, proved in so much sorrow and suffering. It will always be my earnest and firm endeavor to safeguard and protect the interests of the Catholic Church in collaboration with you, most esteemed brethren.

My tasks as apostolic visitator are not those of a nuncio or apostolic delegate, although I was entrusted with the faculties of the former nuncio. It is the wish of the Holy Father that I visit the Most Reverend Ordinaries, that I let myself be informed on religious life in its various forms, on ecclesiastical establishments and organizations in individual dioceses, that I take cognizance of your intentions, worries, needs, and then report about these things to the Holy See. I have in mind to start a trip of inspection after the middle of September.

In order to obtain a survey as precise as possible it would be most useful to me if you, most esteemed Confrères, had your referees and experts prepare reports on their specific fields of work. It would be physically impossible for me, and it would also not be advisable were I to fritter away my energy and time by having to listen to individual reports presented to me by priests and lay people. In order to be able to cope with this I lack the necessary number of collaborators, having only a very small staff at my disposal. Above all, I would be prevented from concentrating on the more important and urgent questions of Catholic life. Therefore permit me to request that you give me your kind assistance in this regard to enable me to do justice to the more important tasks of my mission, as much as is in my strength.

The providence of God has ordained that I was requested by President Truman via the Defense Department in Washington to accept the position of a liaison consultant for religious matters in order to render possible a better contact between the German hierarchy and the military government. This position provides for access to higher officers. Thus it was possible for me in Berlin to discuss various important matters with General Clay and his political adviser, Ambassador Murphy. Also in Frankfurt several meetings with high officials of the occupation authorities could be arranged. It gave me much satisfaction not only to have been received with great courtesy but also to have been assured again and again of their willingness to co-operate with the Catholic Church.

Ambassador Murphy expressed his deep regret that in some cases subordinate officers gave occasion for disagreeable happenings and misunderstandings. He asked not to conclude from this that American Military authorities have no real appreciation of the interests of the Church. On the contrary they have a firm intention to promote the work of the Church.

Just to show you an example of this good will that I found in Berlin, I can inform you, Most Reverend Confrères, that General Clay gave his consent to free, censorless communication service between the Holy See and the German bishops. When I asked him for this according to Article 4 of the Reich Concordat, he at once gave his agreement and, beyond this, he even suggested that he arrange for a code communication. At present, work is in process on the technical possibilities for this development.

Furthermore, General Clay informed me that the occupation authorities aim at designating all ecclesiastical matters directly to Church authorities. The importance of this is obvious, especially with regard to the question of school and education, welfare work for young people, and lay organizations. I consider it my special obligation as liaison consultant to foster good relations between the episcopacy and military government, to strengthen the already existing good will of military officers toward the Church, to protect the holy rights of the

Church, and, above all, to smooth the way for the German Church to a freedom, intended for it by God, and to a prosperous co-operation between Church and State.

It would be a great help to me if you, Most Reverend Confrères, would consider the question of how to establish lasting and practical relations between the hierarchy and the occupation authorities. I will be most grateful for any suggestions in this matter.

As you will have noticed, in my capacity as consultant to military government, I am only competent in religious matters in the American zone of occupation in Germany. The division of your country into zones did not allow another solution. This may seem to be a disadvantage, but this is somewhat counter-balanced by the following two facts: first, my position with General Clay also opens the way for me to the representatives of the other powers of occupation in Berlin so that there is hope for me to be able to work to the advantage of the Church also in the other zones. And, secondly, in my capacity as apostolic visitor, that is in the purely ecclesiastical field, I have been sent to the whole of Germany.

Before I conclude, it is my sincere desire to thank you for your trust and the truly brotherly love shown me. I respond to this, your love, with the love of a confrère in the same office of Christ's apostles, and with a deep love for the German people, a love that I have always felt for them and which I witnessed again in the words and the mind of our mutual father, Pope Pius XII. It was not easy for me to leave my diocese — even though it is only temporarily — and you, as bishops, will understand my feelings. But in order to serve the Church in Germany I willingly accepted this office, and it will be the most gratifying satisfaction for me if I can help you with the dedication of all my energy and might. I beg you, my Most Reverend Confrères, to assist me in this my mission with your counsel and co-operation.

And now, Most Reverend Bishops, I wish for your conferences on the well-being of your faithful, good people, on the alleviation of the spiritual and physical suffering and needs of so many people thrust into poverty, and on the spreading of the Kingdom of God the light and the strength of the Holy Spirit who, as the spirit of the love of God, alone can overcome the hatred of the world and bring true peace.

APPENDIX III

Letter of Murray D. Van Wagoner to General Lucius D. Clay, 22 May 1948.

As I have not been able to confer with you for some weeks, I am taking this means of inviting your attention to the activities of Bishop Muench, Catholic liaison representative and apostolic visitor in the American zone. His representations here and his dealings with certain Bavarian ministers, Catholic bishops and Cardinal Faulhaber have not been any help to Military Government. On the contrary, he has obstructively interfered with the very delicate negotiations we have been conducting for the attainment of school reform.

In the statement of functions and status of the liaison representatives from U. S. Churches, it is to be noted that the liaison representatives shall not 'become special pleaders to Military Government for the Churches of Germany,' nor shall they assume responsibilities in the functional fields of operation now directed and supervised by religious affairs officers of Military Government. It is also stated that these representatives shall serve 'between the churches of their respective faiths in Germany and in the U. S. in the field of purely religious and clerical functions of the Churches.'

In my opinion Bishop Muench has acted outside his functions and has gone beyond them in that he has interfered with Military Government in a field in which he himself admitted that Churches had only an indirect responsibility. He has created friction in this area and has tried to strengthen the opposition of certain Germans to Military Government.

In January Cardinal Faulhaber wrote Bishop Muench stating his concern with a number of provisions of the school reform plan as proposed by Military Government. Copies of the cardinal's letter were in the hands of the press and radio correspondents on January 19; they were not received by Military Government until January 22. The ordinariate at Munich declared that the release was issued at Frankfurt, Bishop Muench's headquarters, and not at Munich. We infer that Bishop Muench wished to arouse as much public opinion as possible before Military Government had the opportunity to answer the questions raised by Cardinal Faulhaber.

Immediately thereafter I invited Bishop Muench to confer with my staff on the questions raised by Cardinal Faulhaber for the purpose of giving the bishop a clear interpretation of the points at issue. This conference was held on February 3 in my office although I was not present. It was the purpose of the conference to explain thoroughly to Bishop Muench the details of the school reform plan in order to show that our proposals were reasonable and in order to obtain (as was his suggestion) his assistance in explaining these points to the Bavarian bishops. In the conference it developed that Bishop Muench was more determined in his opposition to several specific essential points of the whole reform program than were or are the members of the hierarchy in Bavaria.

On January 31 prior to the conference, as I wrote you, the chief of our religious affairs branch discussed the entire school reform program with Cardinal Faulhaber. The latter had agreed that he could see no reason for further opposition. Prelate Meixner, CSU chairman of the Landtag committee on the school reform plan, had made the same statement to representatives of this office on January 30.

In the conference, however, Bishop Muench disregarded the agreements which had been reached with the Cardinal and Praelat Meixner and continued his opposition. He was opposed to closing confessional kindergartens, he insisted that the *gymnasium* must remain, he insisted that the six-year *grundschule* did not fulfill democratic aims, and he insisted that the financial burden of the school reform was too great. He was corrected on every point but continued to maintain his opposition not only in our conference but in his private conference on February 3 and 4 with Bavarian officials and church heads.

For example, in the late afternoon of February 3 he telephoned from the cardinal's office and accused Military Government officials of misstating the case and hiding from him the 1 December 1947 letter from educational and religious affairs branch, OMGUS, on implementation of control council directive no. 54 with particular reference to the confessional teacher training schools. In the earlier conference this subject had been discussed and he had been informed that the confessional teacher training schools which were to be closed because they were not on a university level, could reopen if they met the requirements of Military Government regulations. He also questioned the members of the ordinariate on their relationships with officials of Military Government and declared that school reform would be impossible if the Bavarian bishops took the issue to the people.

Immediately after a conference in a conversation with one member of my staff he argued for the course of action taken by Dr. Hundhammer, the Bavarian minister of education. He declared that Dr. Hundhammer was correct in saying that kindergartens would be closed, that the *gymnasiums* would be forbidden and that convent teacher training institutions were permanently forbidden. It was pointed out to him that these points had been clarified in the conferences with Dr. Hundhammer over a period of one year.

In discussion with Bishop Neuhaeusler, Bishop Muench argued that the American system of double expense for confessional schools was inequitable (this was a point never raised by anyone of the Catholic or Evangelical bishops).

The fact that Dr. Hundhammer continually raises religious issues in connection with the school reform plan and the fact that points raised by him parallel comments and observations of Bishop Muench lead us to believe that Bishop Muench aids and abets Dr. Hundhammer, instigates fears, and endeavors to create difficulties for Military Government in connection with school reform. We have reason to believe, as evidenced by his many expressions on the subject, that Cardinal Faulhaber is in full accord with our school reform proposals. Of how many of the Bavarian bishops of either the Catholic or Evangelical faith this is also true, I do not know. I am convinced, however, that Bishop Muench is in active opposition to our plan.

As this is a delicate matter which cannot be settled at my level I am referring it to you.

General Lucius Clay's letter to Mr. Murray D. Van Wagoner:

I have had a long talk with Bishop Muench. While he advises me he has expressed his views to Military Government at Military Government request, he has not at any time opposed Military Government policies with or before the Germans.

He thinks that Military Government has misjudged him because he has expressed to us views other than those we sponsor. Sometimes all of us are disposed to find that those who express themselves against our views are concurrently trying to defeat our efforts with the Germans.

I am glad I discussed the question with Bishop Muench. Of course, I do not and I cannot question the honesty of his declaration.

I trust that we will find sufficient progress soon so that this problem no longer continues to be our number one irritation.

Sincerely yours,
L. D. C.

APPENDIX IV

Comments of Bishop A. J. Muench to General Lucius D. Clay on the Bavarian School Reform Plan, 21 June 1948.

1. Herewith I respectfully submit my comments on proceedings in the matter of the School Reform Plan for Land Bavaria.

2. On 7 January 1948, Cardinal Faulhaber of Munich wrote me a letter on behalf of the Bavarian bishops expressing concern about certain developments regarding the proposed School Reform Plan, which he requested me to transmit to the competent authorities of Military Government.

3. Pursuant to this request I wrote the Land Director, Mr. Murray D. Van Wagoner, on 17 January 1948.

4. Neither the cardinal's letter nor my letter to Mr. Murray D. Van Wagoner, was released by me, directly or indirectly, to the press, American or German. In fact when reports of the cardinal's letter appeared in the newspapers I expressed both my concern and indignation to the personnel of our house. Much was at stake to achieve an amicable and satisfactory settlement of a difficult problem between Military Government and the Bavarian authorities of Church and State. I feared that premature newspaper announcements imperiled such a settlement.

5. In reply to my letter Mr. Van Wagoner and his special assistant, Mr. Edward Kennedy, called on me at Kronberg in the early forenoon of 29 January 1948. Before leaving, the Land Director handed me his letter of 27 January 1948.

The discussion throughout was most friendly. I called attention to the seriousness of the growing tension in Bavaria over the proposed school reform plan. The Rev. Dr. Stanley J. Bertke, assistant liaison consultant, had gone to Munich about the middle of December and brought back to me a report on the gravity of the situation. He had been invited by Dr. James M. Eagan to attend a conference between education section, OMGUS, and the minister of education, Dr. Hundhammer, 16 December 1947.

In our discussion of the problem with the Land director and Mr. Kennedy I pointed out that the cardinal was in full agreement with the policy of Military Government for achieving democracy, peace, demilitarization, and equal opportunity in education, granting, too, that reform was needed in many sectors of German schooling and education.

There were serious points of disagreement, however, which the cardinal noted in his letter. I expressed the conviction that, since many of them rested on misunderstandings and misapprehensions, a settlement could be reached through conferences between the several parties concerned. Mr. Murray D. Van Wagoner agreed with me as to the effectiveness of the give-and-take method of conferences, and said that he was preparing a question and answer statement with a view to allaying fears and removing misapprehensions. This program was released on 29 January 1948. It did much subsequently to relieve the tensions that had arisen.

In our conversation I urged that serious consideration be given to the cardinal's contention that the people, through their constitutionally elected representatives, should assume the responsibility for achieving school reform. Education, he maintained, is an internal cultural matter which lies beyond the competence of occupying powers.

At this point I observed that the history of the Roman Empire as well as that of the British Commonwealth proves clearly that a conquering power serves its interests best if it does not enter into the cultural realm of a conquered people, unless necessary beyond all question or doubt. England, I added, violated this policy in the instance of Ireland and experienced centuries of trouble because of it.

Furthermore, knowing the temperament and character of Bavarians quite well, I proffered the suggestion that Bavarians be not driven. In this they are like the Swiss, lovers of freedom and independence; they can be led but not driven.

Mr. Murray D. Van Wagoner thanked me for my interest in this highly controversial question, and invited me to see him about it when I came to Munich again. Before leaving he handed me his reply to my letter of 17 January 1948. It should be noted that in the closing paragraph he thanked me for the interest that I had shown in achieving the common aims of the Catholic Church and Military Government.

6. Late that forenoon I went to see Mr. Robert D. Murphy in Frankfurt, who had just returned with General Clay from the United States to Germany. I gave Mr. Murphy a verbal report of my conference with Mr. Murray D. Van Wagoner. With General Clay I was privileged to have but a brief chat as I met him by chance in the corridor just as he came out of his room. There was no occasion to discuss the school reform plan with him. He had other more serious problems at the moment — the Semmler affair.

7. An opportunity to see the Land director, Mr. Murray D. Van Wagoner, came within a week. I had gone to a Latvian D. P. Camp near Nuremberg for religious services on Sunday, 1 February 1948. In the afternoon of that day I left for Munich.

8. Cardinal Faulhaber invited me to stay at his house, and at dinner that evening he discussed with me some of the points in the school reform plan that were to him and the Bavarian bishops a cause of great anxiety. These points he had mentioned in his letter of 7 January 1948. A great step forward toward a

solution of these controverted issues had been made, he said, in the twenty-eight point question-and-answer statement of the Land director. He had studied this statement with much satisfaction.

9. The next day, 2 February 1948, I had an appointment with Mr. Edward Kennedy, special assistant to the Land director. I met him in his office for a chat on the issues involved in the school reform plan about 3 p.m.

At the noonday lunch Cardinal Faulhaber had as guests Bishop Johann Neuhaeusler, his auxiliary bishop, and Msgr. Dr. Zinkl, diocesan director of education. They took up one by one the controverted issues, explained them in detail, and presented their anxieties and misgivings regarding a number of points in the proposed school reform plan. Having heard in full their side of the question I left for my appointment with Mr. Kennedy.

In this private meeting I reviewed what I had heard from the Cardinal, Bishop Neuhaeusler, and Msgr. Zinkl. There had been no discussion with any one else.

In the course of our chat Mr. Kennedy brought to my attention a report that he had just received about Mr. Karsen (Berlin) who had founded and directed the Karl Marx School of Social Reform in Berlin before he left Germany for the United States, and who had returned to Germany after the war. In what capacity I do not know; nor do I know whether or not he had become a naturalized American. Mr. Karsen and a Herr Hylla (a Socialist, it was alleged) were blamed by Bavarian Catholics for influencing the drafting of the school reform plan along lines that coincided in a number of important points with the school plan of the SPD. This was a factor of distrust and suspicion in Bavaria, I was told.

Mr. Kennedy proposed that we see the Land director. Knowing that he was much occupied with many problems, I touched as briefly as I knew how on the important controverted points. I told him with what satisfaction the cardinal had received his twenty-eight point statement.

The land director proposed to Mr. Kennedy that a conference be held the next day at which some of the key men of the education section would be present to hear and discuss my report of what I had learned about the school reform plan in Bavaria. Anxious to help settle this vexing problem, I accepted the invitation to attend. The purpose of the conference was not to enlighten me, as has been erroneously reported. For this no special conference was needed. I was well acquainted with both sides of the issues involved.

10. The conference was held in the Land director's office, although he himself was not present. Mr. Edward Kennedy presided. Present were Mr: Al D. Simms, Dr. James M. Eagan, Dr. Mays, and Mr. Bradford. Mr. Lord was called in later to discuss some of the financial aspects of the school reform plan.

In my opening remarks I emphasized two points, first, that I was attending the conference at the request of the land director, Mr. Murray D. Van Wagoner, for, strictly speaking, the matter was not a religious issue, excepting in so far as some points in the school reform plan had implications and consequences for the Church and her institutions; and, secondly, that I came merely to present the doubts, anxieties, misgivings, and objections as I had heard them in my conversation with the Cardinal, Bishop Neuhaeusler, and Msgr. Zinkl.

Mr. Kennedy first remarked that he knew little about the issues involved, and had come to learn. He then asked me to present the various controverted points one by one.

a) In starting the discussion I said that the change from a four-year to a six-year elementary school was still meeting with considerable opposition. The grounds for objection were an intermixture of pedagogical, economic, and financial reasons. The teacher load would be increased especially in rural schools and rural towns throughout Bavaria; teachers are not trained for an additional two years of schooling, especially where the teaching of foreign languages is involved; more class rooms and, in some areas, additional school buildings would be required; economic uncertainties make such a change at this time a questionable venture; the governmental budget is already topheavy in view of the impoverished German economy not to say anything about reparation claims and occupation costs that still remain to be paid.

To this latter point Dr. Eagan replied that we should not be too concerned about that if we recall what a heavy load of reparations the Germans put on the French after the War of 1870. I answered that, granting the truth of what he said, the point was not germane to the issue under discussion. As Americans who are carrying a heavy load of dollar payments to prevent the economic collapse of Germany our questions should be: Is the load too heavy to carry? Is it economically and financially wise to press such a change at this time, particularly in view of the fact that precisely for fiscal reasons in our own country, not demolished and not impoverished, needed educational reforms are postponed?

In the discussion that ensued Dr. Simms replied that the reforms are envisioned for a long range period, possibly a period of from ten to twenty years, and therefore the burden would be bearable.

Another objection to the change had been urged by the cardinal in his letter of 7 January, namely, that it was of small consequence to the program of re-educating German youth to democracy whether children are educated four years or six years in the elementary school. I elucidated the point, and called attention in this connection to comments made by a group of professors of the University of Chicago regarding this and other features of the school reform plan. In their memorandum they remarked that other countries of Europe, such as Great Britain, France, Holland, Denmark, Norway, and Sweden had a system of education similar to that of Germany, and no one questions their democracy.

Dr. Eagan interjected saying that these professors were formerly Germans. 'Should their observations, therefore, not receive respectful consideration,' I countered, 'since they know from personal experience how to evaluate both the German and American systems of education? After all we can not lightly brush aside the contention of Bavarians that the proposed change is not essential to democracy.' It seemed to me that we ought to be as objective as possible in appraising the situation.

Mr. Kennedy now entered the discussion, saying: 'I am now a Bavarian. Really, what difference will it make for the future democracy of Germany if a child goes to an elementary school six instead of four years?' In answer it was contended that a child knows its mind better at the age of twelve than at ten, and that a sense of social solidarity is fostered by keeping the children at this early age together for as many years as possible in a common school.

b) The discussion raised a second point of concern, namely, the demand of Military Government that the double or even triple track system of education be eliminated after elementary schooling. It touched the question of the *gymnasium*.

Fears were allayed on this point, I commented, because of the assurances given by Mr. Murray D. Van Wagoner.

Misgivings were still expressed, however, because the raising of the elementary school level from four to six years would shorten the course of studies of the *gymnasium* by two years. In other words, instead of having a four-eight year plan, the plan would now be a six-six year plan.

Full justice could not be done in a *gymnasium*, the cardinal feared, with regard to the study especially of the ancient languages of Latin and Greek, and the modern languages of French or English, usually required in the curriculum of the *gymnasium*. Dr. Eagan remarked here that the men whom he had met and who had attended a *gymnasium* had no speaking knowledge of a foreign language. Specifically he named Dr. Hundhammer.

At no time was the question raised of a permanent abolition of the *gymnasium*. The cardinal had not mentioned that in my talks with him.

A further misgiving was raised in my talk with the cardinal with regard to the demand that the *gymnasium* become a part of the general middle or secondary school. This would necessitate large central high schools which only larger urban centers could afford, and would undermine the educational and cultural morale of the students of the division called the *gymnasium*.

Dr. Mays explained that after all only about 8% to 10% of youth of high school age entered the *gymnasium*, and that according to point five of the land director's question-answer statement no requirements were demanded by Military Government as to how these middle or secondary schools are to be set up; this is a matter for the educator to fit to the will and desire of the Bavarian people.

Upon Mr. Kennedy's request, Mr. Lord, who had now arrived, explained that the additional estimated costs of the entire School Reform Plan would be only about 3% of the entire budget of the Bavarian government. They would be almost 25%, however, of the entire educational budget.

This is quite an additional burden, which, I observed, most states at home, especially in the west and south, would not be willing to assume. I recalled the . debates of more than twenty years in Congress with respect to federal aid to schools legislation.

Dr. Eagan expressed the opinion that the burden could be carried because Germany would be spared costs of rearmament.

While this is true, I observed, Germany will have other costs — reparations, occupation, reconstruction, and ultimately some costs, too, for policing and security, as every nation must provide. For these reasons I counseled that, granting the need of school reform, we go slow in achieving it. I was assured that such was the intention. Mr. Murray D. Van Wagoner had expressed himself similarly in my private chat with him the day before.

c) Another matter of concern to the cardinal was that of teacher training, specifically, so far as it concerned convent teacher training schools.

On this point there had been some misapprehensions, Dr. Eagan observed, inasmuch as it was believed that sisters would now have to attend universities for their training. He explained that teacher training on a university level could still be given in convent schools. Of course, it would be difficult for some religious orders to readjust themselves to this new requirement, and therefore he had requested that steps be taken at once to set up adequate teacher training courses. Furthermore, sufficient time would be given to effect the change.

In the course of his remarks Dr. Eagan said that Dr. Hundhammer, in his address in the *Landtag* of just a few days before (28 January 1948), had declared that the directives of Military Government would force the closing of all convent schools. Upon my question whether he had a copy of this address he replied that he had none with him.

After I returned to the cardinal's residence, his secretary, Dr. Joseph Thalhammer, gave me a copy of the address.

Thereupon, in the afternoon of that day, I called Mr. Kennedy, and told him that in the interest of an amicable settlement it was important that further misunderstandings be not injected into the controversy. I gave him in translation over the telephone what Dr. Hundhammer had actually said. This is the pertinent paragraph: 'We have expressed misgivings regarding the extension of compulsory training on a university level (to teachers in vocational schools, domestic science, trade, and craft departments, and even kindergartens). I should like to say something about the consequences of such directives: If they are to be implemented in their entirety, then most of the kindergartens conducted by religious will have to be closed.' Dr. Hundhammer elucidated these remarks by saying that both Catholic and Evangelical sisters conduct their kindergartens as social welfare institutions, in consequence of which some religious orders, such as the Mallersdorfer sisters (Catholic) and the sisters from Neuendettelsau (Evangelical), not being in educational but only in charity and social welfare work, and not having training facilities such as the new directives require, would have to close their kindergartens.

Mr. Kennedy thereupon put me on the wire with Dr. Eagan. I gave him Dr. Hundhammer's statement, together with the reasons advanced for it. Dr. Eagan's reply was that Dr. Hundhammer could not be trusted, relating three or four incidents out of past relations with him to substantiate his charge. Not acquainted with the facts in these cases I could not discuss them, I answered, nor were they directly relevant to the matter on which I had called.

d) In our conference of the forenoon the matter of kindergartens was but briefly discussed, and that only in connection with teacher training on a university level.

At Kronberg, near Frankfurt, I remarked, Catholic sisters have a kindergarten which they would have to close if the directives applied to them because they are not teaching-sisters but charity work-sisters, who conduct their kindergartens as social welfare institutions and not as schools. Other sisterhoods would be confronted with the same difficulties.

On this point assurance was given, however, that private kindergartens would be allowed to exist; however, the state would have to offer opportunities which parents may use or not as they prefer.

Discussing this matter with the cardinal in the evening of that day I learned that not only Bavarian Catholics but also the Evangelicals would continue to look with suspicion upon the provision of making kindergartens a part of the school system. They retained memories of a similar move on the part of the Hitler government. Furthermore, the socialists are also advocates of such a change. They feared state control of the pre-school child. The cardinal did not share the optimism of some of the personnel of Military Government that ideological elements, favoring wide powers of state control over youth, would be kept out of the school system. The experiences of more than one generation in Germany give no promise of that.

e) In the course of the discussion in the conference the question of equal opportunity in education was raised.

In his letter to me Cardinal Faulhaber expressed his confidence in the Bavarian government and in the minister of education that they would so shape the school system that equal opportunity of education would be given children regardless of the economic and social status of the parents.

In conversation with me he deplored misrepresentations and distortion of facts on this issue, and mentioned a number of leading men in Germany who, though of humble origin, had not been denied the advantages of a university training. He himself, I learned from his secretary, was the son of a small-town baker.

His secretary gave me a copy of a letter which deprecated the misinformation that was abroad in regard to the lack of equal opportunity in the schools of Bavaria. I was assured that the case mentioned was not at all singular, but could be multiplied many times over in Bavaria.

With such information given me I urged in the conference that a further study be given to the implementation of the accepted principle of equality of opportunity. Undue haste would complicate matters.

In illustration I commented that we were still far from solving that problem in our own country in the elementary schools of the west and south, and in the high schools in certain urban areas, and in colleges and universities. Surveys had revealed shocking results.

f) This led to a spirited discussion on allied questions, such as teachers in the States leaving rural country schools for town and city schools, or for positions in industry, resulting in the closing of thousands of schools in rural areas, ill-prepared teachers in no wise trained on a university level, stratification of social classes in urban centers so that the children of working-men and the lower middle class hardly ever met the children of the upper middle class, and certainly not the children of the so-called 'gold coast' areas of a city.

This last observation caused Dr. Eagan to inject the irrelevant comment that it was the first time that he had heard a Catholic bishop talk like a Communist. I merely replied that we have to face the facts as they are. Furthermore, I added, Communists do not accept a society composed of various classes, inevitably arising out of a free enterprise system such as ours, but that they advocated rather a one-class society, the proletarian class, down to whose level all other classes would have to be reduced.

g) In view of the grave problems still unsolved that a rich and resourceful country such as ours faced in the field of education, I thought it wise and prudent if we did not press a hasty solution of problems in Germany in cultural fields. We shall live to regret it, I said.

h) From what I had learned from the survey of the situation made in December by the Rev. Dr. Stanley Bertke, and made by me the first days of February, I expressed the opinion that the members of the *Landtag*, under pressure of public opinion of Catholics and Protestants alike, might not vote for the proposed school reform. Mr. Bradford allowed that there would be difficulties but that with further patient negotiations the remaining obstacles could be overcome.

11. That evening I gave the cardinal a report on the proceedings of the conference. He expressed his deep appreciation of my mediation, and declared himself more hopeful of a favorable issue of a difficult and complicated problem. He concurred in my opinion that willingness to see each other's difficulties as well as patience in negotiations would lead to a satisfactory settlement.

At all times I have collaborated in full accord with Cardinal Faulhaber. All statements to the contrary are absolutely without foundation. It is stupid and absurd to charge that I worked at cross purposes with the cardinal. The cardinal would be the first one to bear testimony to the fact that I collaborated fully and whole-heartedly with him to settle the differences of opinions and viewpoints that had arisen over the school reform plan.

In fact he did so in the spring conference of the Bavarian bishops held at Freising, 16 March 1948, the first session of which I attended. He reviewed with appreciation the efforts I had made to find an accord with the Church authorities and Military Government regarding the school reform plan.

This was the first time that I saw the other Bavarian bishops in connection with the issues it raised. At no time had I seen them before, either individually or collectively, to discuss with them any phases of the school reform. It is, therefore, not true that there were representations and dealings with the Catholic bishops of Bavaria. Even at the March conference there was no discussion with them. The cardinal gave a brief report, and asked me then to relate what I knew about the subject. There was no further discussion of the matter.

12. Nor did I at any time discuss the matter with any of the ministers of the Bavarian government.

About fifteen to twenty minutes before I left Munich for Kronberg, the morning of February 4, Dr. Hundhammer brought me a copy of the school reform plan submitted on 1 February 1948, to Military Government. Dr. Joseph Thalhammer, secretary to the cardinal, and Father Ivo Zeiger, S.J., my companion on the trip, were present at this brief interview.

I questioned Dr. Hundhammer on what he said in his *Landtag* address, and asked him whether he had not received assurances from responsible officials of Military Government that some of the projected policies in respect to teacher training on a university level for religious orders and in respect to kindergartens conducted by sisters would be reasonably enforced, with due regard for the peculiar circumstances of the Catholic and Evangelical sisterhoods involved. He replied in the affirmative, but said that he had received only verbal assurances. Nothing had ever been given him in writing, and as an official of the government he could be guided only by the written directives of Military Government. These directives were orders, he said, as is plainly stated in the letter of Military Government under date of 14 January 1948.

In response to a question on the change from a four year to a six year elementary school he said that a compromise had been found in a five year common school.

Upon my question whether or not the *Landtag* would accept the school reform plan which he had submitted to Military Government, 1 February 1948, he replied that he was not sure that it would do so. Some of the controversial issues left that in doubt.

Having faith in the conference method to iron out difficulties I urged him to do his utmost in this regard because the land director's twenty-eight-point question-and-answer assurances paved the way for resolving the issues still under controversy. That ended the interview.

At no time did I talk to or in any other way communicate with ministers of the Bavarian Government in the matter of school reform plan. Any statements to the contrary are absolutely false.

13. Subsequent to the conference of 3 February 1948, there was some further correspondence between Mr. Murray D. Van Wagoner and me.

In my letter to him of 10 February 1948, I expressed appreciation to him of the efforts that he had made to eliminate misunderstandings, and the progress that had been achieved. In this letter I took occasion to say: 'My interests in the matter are those of all Americans in the Occupation Government who are anxious to contribute toward the reconstruction of Germany with as little friction as possible. If, then, through my contacts with the leaders of the Church I can be of further assistance to you, I should deem it an honor and a pleasure to have you call on me.'

His reply in his letter of March 3 was friendly in his expression of appreciation of my interest in the matter and of my collaboration in seeking to remove suspicion and misunderstanding. Certainly, the Land director gave no indication whatsoever that I was encroaching on fields beyond my competence.

14. On 10 March 1948, I wrote him with regard to two points that still gave concern: kindergartens and teacher training on university level. I gave the reasons, but expressed the confidence that through further conferences, especially with the sisterhoods involved, the problems could be adjusted.

These two points I discussed briefly with Mr. Edward Kennedy on March 17, having gone to Munich for the St. Patrick's Day celebration.

When I told him that the directives of Dr. Richard Alexander, OMGUS, would prove to be a stumbling block for solving the problems, he said: 'You can throw Dr. Alexander out of the window.'

On this occasion I handed Mr. Kennedy a sheet containing excerpts from a survey made by the New York *Times* on the school situation in the United States, adding the remark: 'This is not an argument for a bad school situation in Germany, but the ugly picture which the survey presents ought to make us humble in pressing plans for the re-education of youth of Germany.' I gave a similar sheet to Dr. Eagan with the same remark.

That same day 17 March 1948, the Land director sent me a letter in which he expressed the assurance that the December, 1947, letter of Dr. Alexander was not retroactive.

In this same letter Mr. Murray D. Van Wagoner, contrary to indicating any displeasure over my interest in school reform, declared himself happy to note that I was continuing my interest in the progress of school reform.

15. On Sunday, 9 May 1948, I arrived in Munich to go to Eichstaett the next morning with His Eminence for the funeral of the late Bishop Rackl.

Bishop Neuhaeusler came to me much disturbed over the suspicions and misjudgments of Dr. James Eagan relative to Dr. Hundhammer, and particularly with regard to a recent incident that caused Dr. Eagan to charge that Dr. Hundhammer was influencing the bishop unduly in the matter of the school reform plan in Bavaria. The bishop declared this to be absolutely without foundation, and handed me a copy of the letter that he had written Dr. Eagan to explain the facts in the case.

Bishop Neuhaeusler questioned me about our school system in the United States, specifically relative to our private, parochial school system, free schooling, and free textbooks. I told him that the situation varied from state to state, but told him of the situation in the diocese of Fargo, where in 116 parishes and sixty-nine missions we had but twenty-three parochial elementary schools, and thirteen high schools. The financial problems arising largely from competition with a free public school system, toward which Catholic parents pay school taxes but which for reasons of conscience they cannot use for their children, are not small. I added that practically all the small dioceses of the south and the west faced similar problems. I envied Bavarian Catholics, I continued, their confessional schools.

16. As late as 21 May 1948, Mr. Murray D. Van Wagoner wrote me to express his satisfaction over our mutual interest not to allow the educational position of the churches to be endangered because of politicians who wish to use the churches as a screen for their own political ends.

17. In view of the friendly attitude of Mr. Murray D. Van Wagoner in all my conversations and communications with him it is inexplicable that he should address a letter of complaint to General Clay at about the same time of his writing his letter of 21 May 1948. Furthermore, that the charges were made four months after the conference of 3 February 1948, creates fresh wonderment.

The charges that he makes are unwarranted, unfounded, and unjust. They are best refuted by his own communications to me.

I assume full responsibility for what I said or wrote, but not for constructions based on falsehoods, suspicions, misjudgments, distortions of statements, and half-truths. The latter are especially vicious because they lend a semblance of truth to allegations preferred.

That the charges were maliciously made I refuse to believe, but certainly they should not have been made without giving me an opportunity to present my side of the case. And certainly they should not have been made under cover of a confidential communication. Attacks of this kind are despicable from every viewpoint.

For the fair and honorable treatment that General Clay gave me by bringing the communication with its charges to my attention I express my sincere and heartfelt gratitude.

APPENDIX V

Memorandum of the Bishops of the American Occupied Zone of Germany in accordance with the chairman of the Fulda Bishops' Conference, Cardinal Josef Frings, submitted to the Chief of American Military Government in Germany, General Lucius D. Clay, July–August, 1947

Subject: Effects of de-nazification:

1. It has been known in an increased measure in the world's public opinion to what degree the Catholic Church in Germany has opposed the Nazi dictatorship and that in subsequence this Church has suffered terror and persecution. Therefore, it is obvious that the Church not only welcomed the final collapse of this dictatorship of the Third Reich and longed for the re-establishment of a genuine democracy, but that the Church also considers the liberation of our people from all that is connected with National Socialism and militarism as an urgent demand.

2. In order to achieve this goal, the German people have to be seriously turned away from the detestable and even criminal principles of Nazi doctrine about the totalitarian state and an understanding of freedom and the dignity of man has to be awakened, the re-establishment of the order of a constitutional or legal state has to be guaranteed.

3. The value of the de-nazification law depends on its effectiveness to realize these three goals. But in this first year of its implementation the hopes cherished in this direction have vanished. Now if the bishops are compelled to make such a statement, it has to be considered that the Catholic clergy is living in a very realistic and even close connection with the people and therefore is in a position to have a true judgment of how dangerous and alarming the situation caused by this law is in reality.

4. But the worst consequences of the law, i.e., its implementation, are the following:

a. The law violates important principles of justice and legal order: retroactive punishment for formerly not illegal actions; long detention without judicial hearings; neglecting a just proportion between guilt and measure of penalty; arbitrary violation of the validity by law of the sentences — so that the Germans unfortunately have begun to lose confidence in the Americans' sense of justice.

b. The law does not proceed from the reality of living conditions in the Third Reich and does not consider the limits of the capacity of judgment of men who were compelled to live under total coercion and terror by the state. Therefore, not only the confidence of the German people in American justice but also in the formerly much praised tolerance and objectiveness of the Americans is fading.

c. The bitterness and even despair of persons concerned and their relatives who see themselves treated unjustly is being consciously taken advantage of by radical political individuals. Communists systematically endeavor to aggravate de-nazification by all means, they denounce and incite denunciation in order to increase thereby dissatisfaction and inner unrest. Through this, resentment toward the Americans is deepened.

d. The application of the law leads to the punishment of a large number of people who are not guilty of anything other than having belonged to the Party or one of its organizations whereas at least as many Nazi-minded persons of the worst kind go free as they are by chance 'not concerned' according to the regulations of the law.

e. The drawn out implementation of the law delays economical reconstruction in a disastrous way as far too many slightly incriminated persons who are needed everywhere as skilled laborers are compelled to remain away from work.

f. De-nazification is being misused again and again by radical political groups, especially by Communists to remove inner-political adversaries and leaders of economics because the wording of the law and its regulation makes it possible to attach an 'incrimination' to nearly everybody.

g. The law is misused as a 'legal' foundation for coercion and terror against a very great part of the people. Thus it helps essentially to bring about conditions in the public life of Germany which hardly differ from those of the former totalitarian regime. A caricature of democracy is produced which prevents the intentions of the occupation forces relating to the political re-education of the German people.

Summarizing we state:

De-nazification has driven the political situation into a nearly hopeless condition, the re-education of the German people to true democracy has been made nearly impossible and has withdrawn the ground for all attempts to achieve legal security and legal order.

5. With these statements we do not intend to identify ourselves with the criticism of those circles who would like to present the failure of de-nazification as a proof of the bad attitude of the Allies toward the German people. On the contrary we draw the attention of Military Government to the effects of the law so they may find ways and means to secure the results of their efforts, for this we also hope with all our heart: liberation from force, suppression and fear; re-establishment of freedom, justice and order.

6. We fully recognize the difficulties which present themselves in trying to improve the methods of de-nazification and we do in no wise want to stop at theo-

retical criticism but would like to make practical propositions. Therefore, we beg you to examine the following suggestions:

a. To issue a new amnesty for all party members and members of all Nazi organizations without higher rank in as far as they have not developed any special activity or taken part in any criminal acts.

b. In case such an amnesty is not possible, to proclaim a period of probation effective immediately for persons named under 'a' above.

c. Establishment of the principle that a classification in the groups 1–3 can only take place when personal guilt in the sense of articles 7–9 has been proved.

d. Discharge of all internees where no real danger for the security or no danger of concealment is evident, but especially (as far as this has not been done yet) of women with minor children, of persons over sixty years of age, of those seriously ill and invalids.

e. In case the entire de-nazification as cited under 'c' above cannot be placed under the principle that a criminal prosecution is exclusively applied to offenses and crimes but that a graduated fine without further legal disadvantages is imposed on all other persons concerned, the law should be amended in some important points which are drawn up in the following appendix.

Munich, 27 July 1947. Also in the name of the bishops of Bamberg (Josef Otto Kolb), Wuerzburg (Matthias Ehrenfried), Regensburg (Michael Buchberger), Augsburg (Johann Kumpfmueller), Eichstaett (Michael Rackl), and Passau (Simon Conrad Landersdorfer, O.S.B.)

Cardinal Michael Faulhaber
Archbishop of Munich

Freiburg, 30 July 1947, Conrad (Groeber), Archbishop of Freiburg; Rottenburg, 31 July 1947, Johann Baptist (Sproll), Bishop of Rottenburg; Fulda, 1 August 1947, Johann (Dietz), Bishop of Fulda; Limburg, 3 August 1947, Jakob (Rauch), Vicar of the Chapter, Limburg.

Proposals for amendments re paragraph 6 'e' of the memorandum.

1. Repeal of the ordinance dated 3 June 1946, by which on principle certain categories (party officials, leaders and subleaders of organizations) are not to be classified as followers. — This ordinance is untenable as it is in contradiction to the most important principle of the law in article 2 and likewise contradicts the principle of refutableness of the supposition of guilt. Its maintenance would sanction the principle of collective responsibility.

2. Remove the 'affiliated,' 'supervised' and 'other' organizations from the supplement to the law since these organizations existed before 1933. They were not attached in a legal-organizational way to the party or its organizations. The members were not previously individually asked before being made members of the party.

3. Guarantee of genuine legality of the decisions of the tribunals and immediate withdrawal of all repeals of legally effective decisions which were repealed pursuant to the above cited ordinance dated 3 June 1946.

4. A more just wording of the exoneration article thirteen, especially the re-

Appendix V   311

moval of the requested interdependency of cause and effect between resistance and damage.

5. Modification of the prohibition of activity according to article fifty-eight and the blocking of property according to article sixty-one and law number fifty-two, especially as far as the property of women and children not concerned by the law is affected.

6. Clearance of the question of the internees of other zones.

APPENDIX VI

Memorandum written by Bishop Muench after his interview with President Harry S Truman, Washington, D.C., 8 February 1949:

President Truman greeted me very graciously, and I told him that I was highly honored in having been granted an interview.

With a friendly smile he replied that it was a pleasure to see me, and added at once that undoubtedly I had most interesting experiences in Germany in connection with my work there.

In reply I said to him that I was very grateful for the invitation which he had extended to me in the spring of 1946 to go to Germany as liaison consultant for the American Military Government in affairs touching the Catholic Church in Germany.

I also expressed appreciation and gratitude for his warm, human interest in the sad lot of displaced persons.

The President gave me his assurance that he would continue his interest because he felt that it was necessary that something be done quickly to get these unfortunate, homeless people out of Germany. He expressed his disappointment with respect to the Law that was passed in 1948. He said that he signed the bill with great reluctance, because he felt that the law would not be workable. He added that the recent report of the Displaced Persons Commission corroborated his predictions. Instead of bringing 100,000 displaced persons into the United States during the current year, hardly 40,000 to 50,000 will be brought in.

I told him that only the evening before I had read S. Bill 311 introduced by Mr. McGrath and Mr. Neely, and, while it is an improvement over the Law of 1948, it still contained too many bottlenecks to make it workable. I suggested that a strong red-tape cutter would be needed if displaced persons were to be moved in larger numbers to the United States than has been the case up to now. There are prejudices, I observed, with regard to displaced persons which have no foundation in fact. Instead of being a liability to our country they would really prove to be an asset. For the greatest part, they are good people. We must not judge them by the few bad people that are to be found among them. We would not want to have our American people judged by the small minority whose conduct is not in accord with our ideals and principles of a good life.

In my further comments I added the thought that a large population seems to be required in our country in view of the increased capacity of production in industry and agriculture. Our present production capacity quickly saturates our domestic markets. The foreign market is impoverished, and therefore has not the dollars necessary to buy what we produce unless we first give them the dollars through Lend-Lease, Postwar Loans, and now, the Marshall Plan. This method of giving dollars to other nations is much like a merchant on Fifth Avenue, New York, who, having no business, would stand outside the doors of his shop, handing out dollar bills to passers-by on condition that they go into his store to buy and, later on, pay back the loan. The President added wryly: 'The result would be that, in the end, the merchant would have neither goods nor money.'

In my further comments I observed that if we had a better balanced population so large that we would have to buy from other nations they, getting our dollars for our purchases, would in turn buy what we produced in industry and agriculture. We would enlarge and strengthen both our home and foreign markets.

The President then commented that he had tried also to interest other countries to take displaced persons, but with small success.

This gave me the opportunity to say that concerted action on the part of the nations of the world, similar to what was done under the Marshall Plan, would seem to be required to relieve European countries from their congested populations. I cited Italy in illustration of this problem. Despite all efforts to revive industry Italy still has about 1,500,000 unemployed. We shall help Italy little with our dollars unless, at the same time, we also help her to recover at least some of her former colonies, or succeed in lowering immigration barriers in both our country and other countries of the earth. This large number of unemployed provides fuel for communistic fires. We have the Marshall Plan for financial and economic assistance. This is good, but we need another plan, let us call it the X-Plan, under which the nations would get together and assume quotas of immigrants.

The President interjected to say that, after all, only a small quota would have to be taken by the nations concerned if such a plan were to be devised. He seemed to be interested in the idea.

In further observation on the bill now before Congress I said that little seems to be done for Germans of ethnic origin, that is, Germans from countries behind the Iron Curtain. No provisions are made at all for German-Russians. I explained that they were Germans who had left Germany in the eighteenth century upon the invitation of Catherine the Great to come to Russia to develop the production of wheat. They were given special privileges, exemption from military duty, certain tax exemptions, retention of their language, the establishment of their own churches and schools. These Germans settled in the Valley of the Volga and in the fertile areas around the Black Sea. Then in the last century when revolutions started in Russia and the Bolsheviki came into power, large numbers emigrated to the United States. The President said he knew about them in the State of Kansas, and added that they are good farmers and good citizens.

Many of these German-Russians, now in Germany, would like to come to the United States, but there is a prejudice against them because many of them fought with Hitler's armies. These good people really fought our battles against Communism long before we did. I said that they should not be judged too harshly because they linked arms with one devil (Hitler), whom they did not know, to destroy another devil (Stalin), whom they knew. We did the same thing in reverse, I said, because we marched with one devil (Stalin) to destroy the other devil (Hitler), which we accomplished. With a smile, the President remarked, 'And now we are having a difficult time to handle him.'

Thereupon, I turned to another subject, namely, the Church in Germany. I told him that in preparing the draft of the new constitution for Germany, the Socialists had combined forces with the Communists and liberals to deny parents the primary right to the education of their children.

The President exclaimed, 'Why, that is totalitarian!'

'Mr. President, you took the words out of my mouth,' I said, and told him of one of the Socialist leaders who had stated that the child belongs not to the parents but to the State. This is totalitarianism, indeed National Socialism all over again, even though under another name.

These same forces showed their hand also with regard to the Concordat of 1933. And, briefly, I explained that the Holy See entered into this agreement with the German Reich for the protection of the rights of the Church. It was foreseen that these rights would be in great peril under National Socialism. The combine of Socialists, Communists, and Liberals refused to recognize this international engagement in the new Constitution except in a very dubious way. Our Military Government has taken the position during the entire occupation that the concordat is still technically binding. But this group is not willing even to allow this. I made the point that if they do not respect this international agreement we can put little trust in any agreements that they may make with us. I remarked that the Socialists in Europe are not to be trusted. All too quickly they jump on the Communistic bandwagon when the going is good, as they did in Poland, Czechslovakia, Hungary, Romania, Bulgaria, Yugoslavia, and also in the Russian zone and Berlin. If they do not honor the concordat as an international pact, neither will they honor agreements and pacts that we may make with them. Our own interests are jeopardized by their action.

Thereupon the President remarked that the great difficulty in our times is that pacts are not observed. He said that Russia has broken more than forty agreements in recent years. Unless pacts are honored, he said, it is impossible to have peace prevail.

Respectfully I requested the President to give sympathetic understanding to the opposition of the Catholics to the new draft should knowledge of that be brought to his attention.

In closing I expressed my profound satisfaction over the co-operation that I had received from General Clay, his advisers, and his personnel on top levels. I did not have this same co-operation, though, with personnel on lower administrative levels.

Having been a captain in World War I, the President remarked with a laugh, the lower one gets down into the ranks of an army the greater become the difficulties. One has more trouble, he said, with a second lieutenant than with a colonel or general.

In taking my leave from him I told him that I was not unaware of the great load of responsibility that rested on his shoulders in these difficult times, and, wishing him God's blessing, I promised him my prayers. He was visibly moved at these words.

Rev. Stanley A. Bertke, *"Report on Displaced Priests,"* September, 1947.

General Observations:

The first remark to be made about displaced priests is that they are *displaced.* They are not adventurers. Through no fault of their own they are not able to exercise their priestly ministry in places for which they were ordained and to which they had given their lives. They are not elsewhere of their own choice.

Time after time the priests have told me their dominant hope is to return to the country of their origin. But they cannot. By order of their ecclesiastical superiors who forbid them to return home to face further exile or death, they remain displaced priests, priests in exile.

What manner of men are these priests in exile? Many of them were pastors of large parishes in their native lands, others were caught up in the maelstrom of history and flung into concentration camps soon after their ordination, still others were seminary professors or officials in the diocesan curia. They are men who have suffered years of degrading indignities and worse simply for being and remaining what they are — priests of God. It is difficult to realize what they have gone through; the uprooting from their native place, the disdain of their captors, the constant fear and uncertainty, the concentration camp with its subhuman treatment and years of dashed hopes and endless waiting. Then the liberation; an opportunity to breathe free air again; the expectancy of seeing their homes once more! Then, again, the slow giving up of hope, the crowded, wretched, squalid conditions of the DP camps, unsympathetic officials, and finally the sad realization that return is impossible, exile their lot. And through it all there was the backbreaking labor of keeping the faith alive among the people of their camps. Now there is the belief of many of the displaced priests that, of all the displaced persons, they are the forgotten regiment.

What sort of impression do they make on an American priest who has no ties with them save the priesthood? Were we to take the priests of a typical American diocese, deposit them in a foreign land, clothe them in makeshifts, and work them long and hard on poor food for three or four years, I imagine they would make the same general impression as these priests in exile. They have offered Mass for their people, they have preached, they have administered the sacraments, they have kept the faith, they have remained, in spite of severe trials, priests.

The health of the displaced priests is, generally speaking, amazingly good. It would be almost miraculous were there not among them those who are nervous and run down. And there are such. But there is another aspect to be considered. It is that perhaps only the strong survived the years of grueling physical demands of concentration and DP camps. In round numbers one out of every four priests in Dachau did not live to tell the story. The ones who survived are usually strong men.

The problem of displaced priests has to do almost exclusively with diocesan priests. Almost all of the religious priests have already found refuge with their respective institutes in some part of the world. The religious, with edifying brotherly charity, have taken care of their own. But the diocesan priest is in a difficult position because he cannot return to the diocese for which he was ordained.

The above are general impressions gathered in two months by a 7,000 mile tour of Germany, Austria, and Italy. The report now discusses the situation of the displaced priests in those countries.

Germany:

There are some 448 displaced priests in Germany. There is at the same time a great lack of German priests due to the influence of Nazism, the war, and the tremendous influx of refugee Germans from the East. For example, in two parishes in the city of Hannover there are only three active priests to care for 18,000 souls.

Obviously, even if all the displaced lay persons in Germany were to emigrate, there would still be work enough for all the priests presently in the country. The solution, however, of the displaced priests is not that simple. The strong emotions of hate and fear engendered by Nazism and Communism have created psychological factors which make it almost impossible for a great number of displaced priests to work in the ordinary German *seelsorge*. I spoke with many otherwise exemplary priests who are simply blind on the subject of Germany and Germans. One can understand their attitude. They have suffered much at German hands. It would be much better for such priests and for the Church in Germany, were they to emigrate.

The DP camps in Germany will probably close in June, 1950. By that time the IRO officials hope to have solved by emigration the greater part of the DP problem. There is no doubt, however, that many displaced persons will have to accept permanent residence in Germany. These persons constitute the so-called "hard core." It is estimated that 100,000 people of all nationalities will be in this group. It is thought that these people will be dispersed all over Germany. They will not live in special quarters or camps as at present.

This situation will affect of course the ministrations of DP priests who remain in Germany after the close of the IRO program. The peoples of their respective nationalities will be too scattered to make up separate parishes. Two courses would then be open to the priests. They could become itinerant priests, traveling all over Germany to minister to small groups of their people, or they could form part of the German diocesan clergy, receiving an appointed post in a German parish. The ultimate decision concerning the DP priests who remain in Germany depends of course upon the authorities.

Several of the German bishops expressed willingness to accept DP priests for parish work. The priests, however, must be willing to study the language and to accept the present hardships of the priests' life in Germany. The bishops also stated frankly that they would need assistance in order to pay the salaries of the priests they accept.

A plan has been submitted to the American bishops to help support during the transition period the DP priests who are not able to emigrate.

The above is written under the assumption that not more than half of the 448 displaced priests in Germany will be able to emigrate.

We shall now consider the problem of displaced priests in Germany in the light of the various nationalities.

Polish Priests:

The 140 Polish priests in Germany wish, almost to a man, to emigrate. Most of these priests withstood the horrors of Dachau and all of them did a magnificent piece of work in caring for their people after the liberation. Their authorities have designated forty-two of them for emigration to the United States, provided the American bishops will find refuge for them. The rest will be sent, if possible, to areas where they are needed, such as Canada, Australia, and South America.

It must be stated in all frankness that it would be very difficult for the Polish priests to adapt themselves to life in a German diocese. Some of them know little German after eight years in the country, and only a few have attained sufficient fluency to hear confessions and preach in that language.

Lithuanian Priests:

Other than the Ukrainians, the next largest group of displaced priests in Germany are the Lithuanians. There are 128 of them. Unlike the Poles, they came to Germany in a certain sense of their own free will. They fled before the Russian advance and now cannot return home. They do not have the strong antipathy to the Germans possessed by the Poles. Many of them have learned to speak German fluently. They could be assimilated much more easily into the Catholic life of Germany. Their desire to emigrate is, however, just as strong as that of the Polish priests. This desire is prompted by the wretched conditions of the camps in which they have lived in Germany, mostly by a very real and ever present fear of Communism. In the event of a Communist advance, they know they would be marked men.

The authorities of the Lithuanian priests have given forty-eight of them permission to apply for emigration to the United States.

Another psychological factor affecting the emigration of Lithuanian priests is their fear of a hot climate.

I am confident that, with sufficient good will on both sides, at least half of the Lithuanian priests could be absorbed by the German dioceses.

Latvian Priests:

The observations concerning the Lithuanian priests apply in a general way to the ten Latvian priests in Germany, though the process of assimilation would be slightly more difficult because the Latvians do not know German as well as the Lithuanians.

Hungarian Priests:

Most of the seventeen Hungarian priests now in Germany fled to that country before the Russian advance. Some few are there as a result of postwar persecution. Most of them speak German quite well. Three or four are already working in German parishes. Prompted by fear of Communism, their desire to emigrate is also very strong. Perhaps half of them could be absorbed by the German dioceses.

Czech Priests:

The eight Czech priests now in Germany are there now as the result of postwar persecution. There is a strong antipathy to German things among them. The process of assimilation in Germany would be very difficult, due to obvious and recent historical reasons.

There are only one or two priest representatives of the other nationalities in Germany.

It would seem that, if bishops outside of Germany would accept 200 of the DP priests, the problem would be well on the way to solution.

Austria:

The problem of the displaced priests in Austria is not nearly so severe as in Germany. Due to many psychological factors, among them the cultural heritage of the old Austrian empire, assimilation of foreign priests into the Austrian *seelsorge* is not so difficult as in Germany.

Many of the displaced priests are already acting as pastors, chaplains, and assistants in Austrian parishes and are paid directly by the Austrian bishops. Two Austrian vicar generals assured me that places could be found for practically all the displaced priests in Austria, provided the priests themselves were willing to accept such posts.

Notwithstanding the possibility of entering Austrian diocesan life, some fifty displaced priests in Austria wish to emigrate. The reason is quite simple — their fear of Communism. For example, the Slovenes who escaped the clutches of Tito Communism after the war know Communism by personal experience and are deathly afraid that Communism will conquer Austria. In that event they know their lives are forfeit. They could be considered traitors and spies. Many of these priests told me that they were registering for emigration merely to keep open for the future a way of security.

Italy:

The Pontifical Commission of Assistance has precise information concerning all the displaced priests in Italy. Of the 191 priests receiving assistance from IRO in Italy, only thirty-five evinced a desire to emigrate to the United States. Most of these are now completing studies at the Roman universities. They are studying canon law, sacred scripture and church history. They should not have too much difficulty in finding an *episcopus benevolens.*

I am informed that the other displaced priests in Italy are here either on permanent assignment or have no desire to emigrate.

Ukrainian Catholic Priests of the Oriental Rite:

There are in Germany and Austria approximately 150 Ukrainian priests of the Oriental rite. About one-third of these priests are married.

Of all the displaced priests theirs is perhaps the most tragic lot. There is, for obvious reasons, apparently little disposition on the part of bishops outside of Germany and Austria to give them refuge and they cannot be assimilated into the ordinary Catholic life of the countries in which they now reside. Their present standard of living is quite low and, with the disbandment of the displaced persons camps, will become much lower unless steps are undertaken to give them assistance. I did not interview many of them because their cases were beyond my competence, but I did talk with those who came to me. One can understand, if not excuse, the attitude of some of them who say the Church has forgotten them.

Statistics

Number of Displaced Priests in:

Germany

Poles	140	
Lithuanians	128	
Czechs	8	
Hungarians	17	
Latvians	10	
Ukrainians	140	
Croatians	1	
Slovenes	1	
Slovaks	2	
Romanians	1	
Total	448	448

Austria

Total priests of various nationalities ...about	100	100

Italy

Lithuanians	42	
Poles	48	
Croatians	44	
Slovenes	27	
Romanians	2	
Hungarians	16	
Czechs	5	
Slovaks	1	
Russians	1	
Albanians	3	
Bulgarians	2	
Total	191	191
Total		739

N.B.

1. The figures for Italy include only those priests receiving assistance from IRO.
2. The above statistics make no claim to absolute accuracy. They are indicative only.

1. When the Kraus family left Kemnath in 1882, Johann gathered the children under a linden tree on the outskirts of the village where they all prayed together and the father nailed a crucifix, which was a cherished family heirloom, to the tree. When Bishop Muench first visited Kemnath he went in search of the crucifix, found it, and sent a picture to his mother in Milwaukee. On his second visit after he was nuncio in Germany the tree had blown down and Muench went in search of the crucifix again. A Frau Braun had it in a place of honor on the landing of her stairs and she would not give it up, even to the nuncio. He promised to get her a similar one from Konnersreuth and she finally agreed to part with the crucifix which, by this time had become a well-known object in the area. Muench sent the crucifix, which had an eighteenth century corpus on the cross, to his brother Frank who hung it in the garden. Their mother was still living and was deeply grateful to have it back again in the family. The father died 23 July 1936.

2. Mary Muench, the second oldest child, married Frank Herrick who worked for the Wisconsin Telephone Company in Milwaukee for forty-five years; Dorothy Ann died of spinal meningitis at the age of two and a half years; Joseph T. owned and operated bowling lanes in Neenah, Wisconsin; Frank J. also worked for the Wisconsin Telephone Company for forty years; Albert drowned at the age of ten years in the Milwaukee River while catching crabs. Aloisius, a first theologian at the time, was rowing in a boat with his father looking for the body when it surfaced after three days. Teresa E. became a stenographer for the Owens Illinois Company in Milwaukee and lived with their mother until she died; Dorothy T. was a registered nurse and married Ray Ott.

3. Interview with the Muench family, Milwaukee, 26 June 1962: Mary Muench Herrick, Frank Herrick, Mrs. Frank (Doris) Muench, Frank Muench, Teresa Muench, Dorothy Muench Ott, Barbara Ott.

The brothers and sisters recalled that they called each other "Muench-Minnefish" because they were all small of stature. Allie liked baseball, was a good fisherman and hunter, and retained these interests throughout his life.

4. In grateful memory of Sister Vitalia, Bishop Muench established the Sister Vitalia Scholarship for priesthood students of Fargo. He kept building it up with gifts that came to him until the invested fund totaled the desired $5,000 by August of 1957. In thanking Joseph A. Dockendorff of Skokie, Illinois, on 22 De-

cember 1956, for a contribution toward the fund Muench said: "I owe Sister Vitalia a lot. But for her I might not be what I am today. Conditions at home were not easy, the family was dependent on a weekly paycheck that was not very large, there was a mortgage on the home. I was the oldest among eight children so that I could have helped add to the family income if, instead of creating outlays for my seminary studies, I would have sought a job after I graduated. In those days, as you know, very few children went on for high school studies."

Thomas Schmitz and Allie Muench remained close friends through all of their seminary training and both taught at Saint Francis Seminary until the early death of Father Schmitz from leukemia on 6 January 1930. Muench was so depressed by this loss that his friends, worried that he might suffer a nervous breakdown, encouraged him to take treatments at Sacred Heart Sanitarium in Milwaukee.

5. Interview with Cardinal Aloisius Muench, Fargo, Summer 1961.

6. Cf. Appendix I for a bibliography of the main writings of Aloisius Joseph Muench.

7. Interview with Aloysius Croft, Milwaukee, 20 June 1962. Cf. also David J. Boyle, "From Shore to Shore — Lake Michigan to Red River," *Catholic Action News*, XXIII (October, 1960), 2.

8. Cf. Aloisius J. Muench, "Father Coughlin's Money Program," *The Salesianum*, XXX, 2 (April, 1935), 8–21. Cf. also "Internationalization of Money, *The Salesianum*, XXX, 3 (July, 1935), 1–10.

9. Chicago *Tribune*, 7 May 1935.

10. Gleason recommended that Bishop Muench deal directly with individuals who held overdue notes on several parishes in the Diocese of Fargo. In previous years parishes had floated bonds for expansion through the Thomas McDonald and John J. Schmidt Companies of Chicago. Now these people were pressing for payment from such parishes as Langdon where a school had been built, from Rugby, Page and Lisbon where churches had been built. Bishop O'Reilly had always taken the attitude that these were parochial debts and never troubled himself with them. But Bishop Muench realized that no diocesan progress could be made until existing debts were resolved. Following Gleason's direction, Muench offered individual creditors a settlement which would include payment of the principal and 2% interest. The creditors accepted this offer as a just and realistic settlement since it was obvious that the people of North Dakota, in their distressed circumstances at that time, would not be able to settle these obligations in the foreseeable future.

11. Cf. Elwyn B. Robinson, *History of North Dakota* (Lincoln: University of Nebraska Press, 1966), pp. 399–401.

12. Muench became a member of the Knights of Columbus chaplains' bowling team and learned to hunt pheasants on the Dakota plains. His favorite recreation remained fishing. Priest friends in Milwaukee had given him a fishing rod embossed with his coat of arms at the time of his consecration, and Muench would regularly say to the chancery office staff: "Let us go fishing." They were

not fishermen and Muench would chide them that they were not like the apostle Matthew. He said: "The world with its problems vanishes on the waters of a lake with the flinging of lures at the fish."

Shortly after Muench was called to Germany, Bishop Dworschak spent a vacation with their mutual friend Charles M. Muench, president of Allen Silk Mills, New York, at his summer home on Murray Bay, Canada. Muench wrote Dworschak on 27 August 1947: "It borders on a sin that cannot be forgiven in this world to have been in one of the best fishing grounds of North America and not even to have put a hook into the water. What an awful shame. A successor of the fishermen of the Lord can hardly justify this in conscience."

During the first years in Germany it was not difficult for the staff of NCWC War Relief Services personnel to lure Muench off to fish in the Rhine. He liked the speckled trout (*Forellen*) of Germany but enjoyed arguing with Germans that American lake and brook trout were superior.

13. Cf. Appendix I for a complete listing of the Muench pastorals and other writings. *The Wanderer* Printing Company, St. Paul, issued German translations of these pastorals for the German-Russian parishes of the Diocese of Fargo.

14. A diocesan publication, *Confraternity News*, was started in 1937 as a diocesan paper which in January of 1939 developed into *Catholic Action News*. There had been no paper in the diocese since Bishop O'Reilly discontinued *The Bulletin* in February 1911, the year after he came to Fargo.

15. The correspondence with Frederick P. Kenkel, as well as with Joseph Matt, senior, editor of *Der Wanderer*, Saint Paul Catholic weekly, would make an interesting separate study in the development of German-American social and religious thought in the 1920's through the 1940's.

16. *Catholic Action News*, XVIII (October, 1955), 2–3. At the annual conventions of the Central Verein during the years of World War II Bishop Muench repeatedly recommended that Pope Pius XII be invited to the peace negotiations at the end of the conflict. Muench received a national flood of letters, many in protest, as a result of this suggestion.

17. Muench to Victor T. Suren, Bad Godesberg, 20 June 1955. Cf. Philip Gleason, *The Conservative Reformers* (Notre Dame University Press, 1968) for an excellent study of the German-American Catholic community of this period.

NOTES TO CHAPTER TWO

1. Interview with Monsignor Alberto Giovannetti, Rome, 19 November 1963. Monsignor Giovannetti is currently serving as Permanent Observer for the Holy See at the United Nations, New York.

2. Interview with Archbishop Joseph Gawlina, Rome, 20 November 1963. Archbishop Gawlina died on 21 September 1964.

3. Father Ivo Zeiger, S.J., was born in 1898 at Moembris, Diocese of Wuerzburg. He was wounded twice during World War I, studied law after the war and became a Jesuit in 1921. He completed studies in Rome, Innsbruck and Berlin and was ordained in 1928. After teaching assignments at Valkenburg, Holland, the diocesan seminary in Aachen, and at Saint Georgen, Frankfurt am Main, he was appointed professor of canon law at the Gregorian University, Rome, in 1935. There and as rector of the German college in Rome after 1939, he trained several generations of young German clerics, including the present archbishop of Munich, Cardinal Julius Doepfner. He served in the Vatican missions to Germany from 1946–51 until poor health forced him to retire to Berchmanskolleg, Pullach near Munich, where he was a member of the staff of the journal *Stimmen der Zeit*. Zeiger died there on 24 December 1952.

For a summary of Zeiger's attitude toward the rebuilding of the Church in Germany following World War II, cf. his article "Um die Zukunft der katholischen Kirche in Deutschland," *Stimmen der Zeit*, 141, 4 (April, 1947), 241–252.

4. Cf. Appendix II: "Address of Bishop Aloisius Muench to the German Bishops' Conference, Fulda, 20–22 August 1946.

5. Interview with Cardinal Josef Frings, Rome, 25 November 1963; Interview with Monsignor Bernhard Hack, Rome, 21 November 1963.

6. Bishop Michael Keller of Muenster explicitly expressed his gratitude to Pope Pius XII, on his first visit in 1948 to Rome following the war, for having sent Muench to Germany. Keller was convinced that Muench was the best possible representative for those times, and that he showed more understanding for German problems than a representative coming from Rome could have done. Keller died on 7 November 1961.

7. Interview with Cardinal Josef Frings, Rome, 25 November 1963. In an interview, Rome, 23 November 1963, Archbishop (later Cardinal) Lorenz Jaeger of Paderborn stated: "Muench met us with heartwarming, convincing openness. He was very conscious of propriety, discreet, modest, and careful in avoiding anything that might look like intrusion. He never, never allowed himself to get involved in matters he felt were not his business. I am thinking here of certain difficulties that exist in other countries concerning apostolic delegates and nuncios. Although Muench could have decided simply to copy the position of the apostolic delegate in the United States, he never did."

Dr. Heinrich Koeppler, former secretary general of the Central Committee of German Catholics, currently state secretary of the Federal Minister of the Interior, commented in an interview, Bad Godesberg, 13 October 1963: "Bishop Muench was extraordinary in the sense that he was not the usual type of diplomat in general, and of an ecclesiastical diplomat in particular. It was obvious that he was not one of those men who had gone through diplomatic training; he was a man who looked at things without bias. Above all, for us Catholics in Germany, he was a man who in all he said and did left us with the impression that he was a true bishop and pastor of souls. He was not a diplomatic functionary who had been promoted to the rank of bishop."

Father Robert Leiber, S.J., in an interview, Rome, 18 November 1963, declared: "Muench was for Germany Providence personified. He understood the plight and misery existing throughout the country and he helped as much as he could. I would like to stress, secondly, what I heard from German bishops during Vatican Council II on the subject of apostolic nuncios and delegates. Nuncios are not only diplomatic representatives of the Holy See at the respective governments, but, like apostolic delegates, also informants on the Catholic religious and ecclesiastical situation in a country. The German bishops unanimously stated that Muench as visitator and nuncio avoided with utmost care everything that would look like supervision even in the remotest way. He always maintained — how shall I express it — perfect relations between himself, as visitator and nuncio, and the bishops. He never interfered in the least with their episcopal administration. This fact was emphasized very strongly and persistently. Just recently Cardinal Doepfner of Munich mentioned this topic again as did others."

8. "The statement really gets down to facts and is written with much brotherly love. Who is this Bishop Muench?" Cf. *Berliner Tagesspiegel*, 24 April 1947.

9. Interview with Monsignor Bernhard Hack, Rome, 23 November 1963.

Monsignor Octavian Barlea, representative for Romanian Displaced Persons in the Vatican missions to Germany, stated in an interview at Munich on 7 December 1963: "Muench was also accused by Military Government officials of having too much affection for the German people. As Muench and Zeiger traveled across Germany for the first time contacting the German bishops Muench always made a point of calling upon the local Allied Command in each area. These officials reported him to Berlin as preparing a too favorable report on the Germans, and when Muench arrived in Berlin he had to defend himself again before the central administration of the International Control Commission."

10. Muench to Smith, Kronberg, 4 March 1947.

11. During the Weimar Republic, Monsignor Ludwig Kaas was the leader of the Catholic Center Party in Germany. He acted as liaison between Pacelli, the bishops and the government in the first discussions of a possible concordat. When Hitler came to power, Kaas was forced to leave Germany for Rome where he was named econome of the Reverenda Fabbrica di San Pietro, 1937–52 (plant manager of the Vatican). During Kaas' tenure the excavations under Saint Peter's Basilica were undertaken.

12. Ivo Zeiger, S.J., "Report on the Papal Representation," Rome, February, 1947.

13. An official Vatican photographer of the Felici Studio took pictures of the Pope and Muench in the warehouse but none of the photographs turned out. The next day the Pope willingly came to the warehouse again with Muench for a re-take of the photographs which came out this time. Muench, with his typical German prudence, had brought along a New York *Times* photographer who took shots at the same time as the Roman photographer. While the photographs

were being taken, Bishop Muench turned to Pope Pius and said: "St. Peter did not have to do things of this kind," and the Pope laughed heartily.

14. Muench to Dworschak, Kronberg, 14 April 1947; Muench to Smith, Kronberg, 14 April 1947. Father Howard Smith told Muench on April 15: "The news release of the appointment of Bishop Leo as your auxiliary was received with great joy in Fargo and other parts of the diocese. It is as welcome — almost — as if the news told that you yourself were on the way home. Naturally, there is a lot of speculation as to what will happen to you. Rumors around here have you as nuncio, archbishop, cardinal, or even the next pope. I wonder which it will be." To which Muench replied on April 24: "Well, why just be a cardinal since friends want me to be nothing less than the pope!"

NOTES TO CHAPTER THREE

1. Robert Deubel came to Kronberg in March, 1947. He had been drafted at the age of seventeen and at the end of the war was a prisoner in England. When he returned to Germany he wanted to resume his study of dentistry but found it impossible due to adverse conditions. Friends of Father Zeiger introduced Deubel to the Vatican mission. He was interviewed by Muench and was hired as a secretary for English correspondence. Up to that time Muench had written the bulk of his English correspondence by hand. Mr. Deubel, presently a staff member of the Overseas Service Corporation, Frankfurt, supplied invaluable background material on details of the daily operation at the Vatican mission in Kronberg. He also generously accompanied the author in the fall of 1963 on trips throughout Germany to interview persons who had associations with Bishop Muench.

2. Sister Ilga Braun, O.S.B., member of the community of Benedictine Sisters of St. Lioba, did advanced studies in London and joined the community at Freiburg im Breisgau in 1941. Sister Ilga began secretarial service at the nunciature in Bad Godesberg in 1951 where she continues at present. At the invitation of Bishop Leo F. Dworschak, bishop of Fargo, and with the permission of her superior and of Archbishop Corrado Bafile, successor to Cardinal Muench as nuncio to Germany, Sister Ilga spent a year in Fargo during 1962 and 1963 arranging the Muench Papers in the chancery archives. She supplied invaluable assistance in the preparation of the cardinal's biography especially in translating over fifty interviews with representatives of Church and State who had worked with Cardinal Muench during his years in Germany, organizing and translating when necessary his extensive speeches and writings, and supplying information on his procedures in Germany.

3. Interview with Robert Deubel, Frankfurt, 20 October 1963.

4. Interview with Cardinal Aloisius Muench, Fargo, 15 July 1961.

5. Eileen Egan and Elizabeth Clark Reiss, *Transfigured Night. The CRALOG Experience* (Philadelphia and New York: Livingston Publishing Company, 1964), p. 37. This primary source outlines the significant contribution of eleven voluntary American welfare organizations who formed themselves into the Council of Relief Agencies Licensed for Operation in Germany, or CRALOG. Among the founding members were the American Friends Service Committee, Brethren Service Committee, Committee of Christian Science Wartime Activities of the Mother Church, Church Committee on Overseas Relief and Reconstruction of the Federal Council of Churches of Christ (Church World Service), International Rescue and Relief Committee, Incorporated, Labor League for Human Rights of the American Federation of Labor, Lutheran World Relief, Incorporated, Mennonite Central Committee, Community Service Committee of the Congress of Industrial Organizations, Unitarian Service Committee, Catholic Relief Services of the National Catholic Welfare Conference.

In March of 1949, three years after beginning relief work in Germany, CRALOG reported that the organization had helped over twenty million Germans. One person among three of the defeated nation had felt the newly-forged bonds of fraternity and compassion. A million children were the recipients of regular food. In all, CRALOG supplied 67,325,279 pounds of clothing, a quarter million pounds of medicine and helped build 30,000 homes.

6. Interview with Bishop Edward E. Swanstrom, Auxilary Bishop of New York, and James J. Norris, Rome, 2 November 1963.

7. The litany of German Americans who asked Bishop Muench to be their almoner included such individuals as Mary E. Becking, Marty, South Dakota; Monsignor Albert Rung, Saint Joseph's Church, Buffalo, New York; Mrs. Luise Faschingbauer, Saint Paul; Miss Josephine Fox, Milwaukee; Father A. H. Wietharn, Sacred Heart Church, Paxico, Kansas; Mrs. Mary Meyers, Hinsdale, Illinois; Father John Haeusler, Saint Mary's Church, Pewaukee, Wisconsin; Mrs. George Volta, Washington, D. C.; Sister Pacifica, O.S.F., Saint Francis Home, Buffalo, New York; Miss Mary Schroth, West Allis, Wisconsin; Fred Tuke, Cincinnati, Ohio; Monsignor E. L. McEvoy, Corpus Christi Church, Fort Dodge, Iowa; Charles M. Muench, Sr., New York City; Monsignor Edward Stehling, Holy Angels Parish, West Bend, Wisconsin.

8. Fred P. Hansen of the D. B. Hansen and Sons Church Goods House, Chicago, sent cloth, cassock material and silk for altars. In one shipment he sent enough material for 200 suits, and wrote: "Your Excellency is assisting us in doing a little charity."

9. Cf. Ivo Zeiger, S.J., "Die religioes-sittliche Lage und die Aufgabe der deutschen Katholiken," *Der Christ in der Not der Zeit. Mainz 72 Deutscher Katholikentag 1948* (Paderborn: Verlag Bonifatius Druckerei, 1949), pp. 24–39.

10. *Idem*, p. 37.

11. Otto B. Roegele, "German Catholicism Amidst the Ruins," *Blackfriars,*

XXX (November, 1949), 504–20. Roegele, editor of the strongly Catholic and independent *Rheinischer Merkur*, later professor of journalism in the University of Munich, was a close friend of some of the staff members of the nunciature at Bad Godesberg.

12. Karl Josef Hahn, "The Church in Germany Today," Lectures on the Religious Problems of Germany Delivered at the Summer School of the University of Fribourg, Switzerland, September, 1949.

NOTES TO CHAPTER FOUR

1. Interview with Monsignor Alberto Giovannetti, Rome, 19 November 1963.

2. Interview with Bishops John Pohlschneider, Aachen; Joseph Stangl, Wuerzburg; Adolph Bolte, Fulda; Edward Schick, auxiliary of Fulda; Rome, 1 December 1963.

3. Interview with Monsignor Bernhard Hack, Rome, 23 November 1963.

4. Lucius D. Clay, *Decision in Germany* (New York: Doubleday and Company, 1950), p. 305.

5. Letter from Bishop Muench to Archbishop McNicholas, 23 December 1947: "All Bavarian children without exception attend the four year *Grundschule* or basic school. Attendance at this school begins at the age of six and terminates at the age of ten.

"At the age of ten the Bavarian child enters secondary education. There are four types of secondary schools in Bavaria, the *Humanistische Gymnasium*, in which emphasis is placed upon the study of Latin and Greek; the *Realschule*, whose curriculum emphasizes positive science, mathematics, and modern languages; the *Mittelschule*, which prepares students for business and civil service careers; and the *Volksschule* which is simply the prolongation of the *Grundschule* in the same building and which prepares students for work in the skilled trades. The *Humanistiche Gymnasium* and the *Realschule* prepare students for university work. Students in both schools become eligible to take university entrance examinations at the age of nineteen. Students of the *Mittelschule* terminate their studies at the age of seventeen. Graduation from the *Mittelschule* does not entitle the student to enter the university. Students of the *Volksschule* complete their course at the age of fifteen. They are not eligible to enter the university.

"The above is a simplified explanation of German secondary schools as they obtain in Bavaria.

"The Education Branch of American Military Government operates under the basic thesis that the German people including Bavarians need to be re-educated if they are to take their place in a democratic and peaceful world. Now, if the Germans are to be re-educated, it seems logical to Military Government that the point or beginning should be the German school system. In the view of Military Government the school system of Germany has been, is, and will be responsible for the type of people Germans have been, are, and will be. Military Government wants to change that type and thinks the way to do it is to change the system that produces the type.

"One of the reasons for the rise of Hitler and Nazism in Germany was, according to Military Government, the stratified form of German society in which subordinates were always ready to obey blindly the commands of superiors. This stratification of German society appeared in all forms of German life: the school was authoritarian, the family was authoritarian, the Church (according to some — Cf. Warburg's *Germany — Bridge or Battleground*) was authoritarian. The German student at the age of ten is confronted with four possibilities of secondary education. American educators in Germany call this 'the double track system.' In their view, students of the *Volksschule* are condemned at the age of ten to a subordinate position for the rest of their lives. Having entered upon this track students do not believe themselves capable of critical political judgments and remain obedient, plodding Germans, ever at the mercy, because of their innate discipline, of demagogues and dictators.

"Our educators here believe that the child at the age of ten is too immature to decide his life's vocation. They believe further that the progress of the German people toward democracy will be helped considerably by the elimination of the 'double track system.' In other words they would lengthen the basic school course from four to six years and eliminate the sharp distinction between *Humanistische Gymnasium, Realschule, Mittelschule,* and *Volksschule.* Ideally, they would have all Germans in the same secondary school, believing thus to eliminate the stratification of the German society. It is the opinion of our educators that as a general rule only the children of the rich and titled families have the opportunity to attend the *Humanistische Gymnasium* or the *Realschule* and thus prepare themselves for university work. Sons of poor parents could finally reach the university only under the greatest of difficulties.

"In Bavaria the urgings of our educators have not met with much success. The Bavarian school system, under Dr. Hundhammer, minister of Education, remains basically the same as it was in 1933. According to most recent directives American education officials in Bavaria do not have, nor do they desire to have, direct power to change the organization of Bavarian schools. They are, however, able to bring considerable pressure to bear on Bavarian officials and this pressure has been increased recently. General Clay, military governor for the American zone, has written Dr. Hundhammer, Bavarian minister of education, demanding that he submit in early February a plan for a sweeping school reform.

"Dr. Hundhammer, a bearded, vivacious, intelligent Bavarian, who, as American officials have come to know, can also be quite stubborn, describes the American attempt at school reform as a demontage of Bavarian culture. Cardinal Faulhaber doubts that any victor nation has the right to impose its own culture upon the vanquished, and most certainly considers the American plan to reform the Bavarian school system as such an imposition. The Bavarian answer to the American attack upon the so called 'double track system,' in which the child decides at the age of ten its future life's work, is that precisely the age of ten is the best age psychologically to begin secondary education. Dr. Hundhammer, who is himself the son of a poor farmer and had a brilliant university career, claims that Bavarian children are afforded the opportunity to attend the *Humanistische Gymnasium* and the *Realschule* on the basis of talent, not of rank or economic status. He maintains that there is no lack of equal opportunity in the Bavarian system, for, if in its subsequent development the child demonstrates that he is capable of university work, he may transfer from the *Volksschule* to the *Mittelschule* or to either of the other secondary schools. Furthermore, the Bavarians do not propose to accede to the American attack upon the teaching of the classical languages in the *Gymnasium*. They consider the teaching of Latin and Greek to be an integral part of their culture and force will have to be applied to eliminate them from the curriculum.

"With regard to the American plan to lengthen the basic school from four to six years, Bavarians reply that such a lengthening process would mean a loss of two years in the child's life. They cannot afford to lose these two years if they are to rebuild their cities and their culture. In reply to the allegation that Bavarian society is stratified, Bavarians answer that democracy does not mean sameness nor still less an equal level of mediocrity. They want very frankly to develop an intellectual elite and think that respect for the human rights of all is consonant with such development.

"Bavarians would rather concentrate upon the development in all classes of society of a universal respect for the basic rights of others. In the development of the people toward democracy they would depend more upon the awakening and realization of the concepts of human dignity and right than upon a structural reorganization of the German school system. In other words they consider their school system a part of Bavaria's culture, and think they have a perfect right to retain that culture.

"The above paragraphs are a rather sketchy exposition of the Bavarian educational problem. Dr. Hundhammer along with his other qualities is an astute politician. In spite of numerous attacks in the American sponsored press and public reprimands by General Clay, his position in Bavaria's political life is stronger than ever. If General Clay and our educators here decide to resolve the Bavarian educational problem by the removal of Dr. Hundhammer, it is quite possible that they would have a mild revolution on their hands. At present Dr. Hundhammer is also the leader of the Christian Democratic Party in the Bavarian *Landtag*.

"It should also be noted that Cardinal Faulhaber is convinced that Dr. Hundhammer is acting in the best interests of the Catholic Church in Bavaria and will not hesitate to defend his policy if he thinks it is unjustly attacked. In a word, the Bavarian educational situation is potential dynamite."

6. Letter from Cardinal Michael Faulhaber to Murray D. Van Wagoner, 19 July 1948: "The Office of Military Government for Bavaria informed me by letter of 10 May 1948 (signed Eagan and Miniclier) that for Catholic nuns a high-school

training was not required for superintending kindergartens. I expressed my thanks to the Governor for this kind information by letter of 12 May 1948. In this letter I did not allude to other questions in the sphere of the school reform, not seeing any reason in this connection for doing so. Therefore I am highly surprised to learn that it is said in a letter of 21 May 1948 from the Military Government to His Excellency, Bishop Muench (and probably also in a letter to Cardinal Spellman): 'The high school training of kindergarten superintendents was the last objection raised by Cardinal Faulhaber in matters of the school reform. This matter was settled satisfactorily and His Eminence raised no further objections in matters of the school reform.'

"Thus from the reason in the above-mentioned letter of 12 May 1948 to Governor Van Wagoner other questions except the training of conventual kindergarten superintendents were not referred to, the conclusion was drawn that I had given my assent to the requests of Military Government in all questions concerning the school reform. My letter of 12 May 1948 gives no reason for such a supposition. To this supposition I must plainly oppose what I wrote on behalf of and according to the order of the Bavarian bishops in my letter of 7 January 1948 to His Excellency, Bishop Muench against the school reform ordered by Military Government. These objections were reported to Military Government and have not been taken back in any point by me since then. In order to remove any doubt, I shall put them down again in the following lines:

"Against the school reform ordered by Military Government, I then declared on principle, from the standpoint of moral and right as it is the duty and task of the bishops: The public instruction and educational matters belong to the innermost concerns of a people. Therefore it is an imprescriptible right of every people to arrange this decisively important matter independently, on their own responsibility and in accordance with the rights of all persons concerned with educational matters, in the first line, the parents. It would be against the natural right and outside the legitimate claims of an occupation government if they were to force a school-system on a vanquished people and a vanquished country. Such an interference, though explained with the intention of democratizing the educational system, would entirely contradict the spirit of true democracy and annihilate the belief in democracy, therefore bring about the very contrary of what is really wanted.

"I feel myself obliged to repeat this warning, but also the assurance that the Bavarian people are willing to arrange their public instruction and the whole of the education of youth in family, school and church in such a way as to assure to the coming generations the life-values of Christendom and therewith its blessings for personal and social life — the blessings of peace, justice and true humanity.

"I need not enter into particular items of the school reform all the less as this is the task of the State-government constitutionally appointed and confirmed by Military Government. The Bavarian secretary of state for educational and cultural matters, Dr. Hundhammer, submitted in fulfillment of this task to Military Government a program of principles on 31 March 1947 and a detailed program on 30 September 1947. These not only contained his personal conceptions, but also the resolutions formed in this question by the competent *Landtag*-committees.

Both these school programs were rejected by Military Government and that in the gruffest way. This rejection aroused with the majority of the people the bitter impression that school reform was to be withdrawn from the autonomy of the Bavarian people, whereas a school tyranny was to replace it. This impression was still enhanced since Military Government joined to the rejection the formal order, the secretary for education and culture should submit within the shortest time a new plan meeting with the requests of Military Government. The secretary did as he was told. He had a plan drawn up 'according to the instructions of Military Government,' submitting it to Military Government on 31 January 1948. The prefatory note leaves no room for doubt, that the secretary is unable to bear the responsibility for such a plan, and the final note expressly points out that the *Landtag* is not expected to give its assent to this plan in essential details.

"In the face of this state of affairs it is difficult to understand that the secretary of state, Dr. Hundhammer, is reproached for intermingling religious concerns with questions of the school reform with the aim of assuring to him the support of the Church for his political ends.

"The heavy, entirely unfounded reproach against the secretary of state comprises in its reverse just as heavy and unfounded a reproach against the Church. The Bavarian bishops cannot put up with this reproach in silence. Therefore I declare that the Bavarian bishops look upon Dr. Hundhammer with complete confidence, being ready to stand up for his cause. It is perhaps not known that the conceptions of the secretary in the questions of the school reform are shared by the great majority of the people, particularly by the parents to whom in our constitution the supreme decisions in all matters of education are granted. Therefore, I may request Military Government to take into account this state of affairs.

"I send a copy of this letter to His Excellency, Bishop Muench as answer to his letter of 9 June 1948 and likewise to His Holiness Pope Pius XII, since upon a letter from Cardinal Spellman I was asked by the Vatican on June 21 if the assertion stands that Cardinal Faulhaber is to raise no further objections against the school reform.

"I may ask the honorable gentlemen of Military Government kindly to explain on occasion the misunderstanding about my position in regard to the school reform."

Van Wagoner replied to Faulhaber on 9 August 1948:

"I have received your letter of 19 July 1948 correcting my understanding of your position on school reform. It is most unfortunate that this misunderstanding has arisen. I regret any embarrassment you may have been caused as a result.

"You will recall that in May 1948 you expressed appreciation to me personally for having clarified Military Government's position in respect to the educational requirements for kindergarten teachers, particularly Catholic sisters. I then asked if Your Eminence had any further complaints or questions with respect to school reform. Both Dr. Eagan and myself took this to mean that you had no opposition to school reform.

"In previous discussion with Your Eminence, Dr. Eagan had the impression that you had no other complaints. The purpose in asking these questions was finally to remove any misunderstandings between the Churches and Military Government on the question. When the reply was received twice that there were no further objections, it was but natural to assume that Your Eminence meant that literally. It did not occur to me to look for implications other than the thought directly expressed by Your Eminence.

"In your letter, Your Eminence refers to the May 21 letter from this headquarters having been sent to His Eminence, Cardinal Spellman. No letter was sent by this headquarters to Cardinal Spellman, my letter having been directed solely to His Excellency, Bishop Muench.

"Inasmuch as your letter of July 19 was sent to His Holiness, Pope Pius XII, His Eminence Cardinal Spellman, and His Excellency, Bishop Muench, I am enclosing extra copies of my reply so that you may forward each a copy.

"I regret that there should have been any misunderstanding and I deeply appreciate your having invited my attention to this matter."

7. Muench wrote Bertke of his opinions in the matter on 29 August 1948:
"The enclosures will acquaint you with new developments in the Bavarian school reform. I felt that I should send them to you not only because of your interest in the controversy, but also because Archbishop McNicholas may talk to you about the matter.

"While we have no direct proof that Dr. James Eagan is responsible for the mess that developed, it would seem that he must be charged with it. He was the one who saw Cardinal Faulhaber on a number of occasions regarding the controversy; the recent letters of Murray Van Wagoner would indicate that Dr. James Eagan gave him the information; and more important, Dr. James Eagan has held the view that owing to his efforts the Cardinal of Munich is now fully satisfied with the school reform plan for Bavaria.

"I want to be charitable toward him, and continue to believe that his inadequate knowledge of German is responsible for what Cardinal Faulhaber is willing to call a 'misunderstanding.' The cardinal is still the 'grand old man' of the German hierarchy.

"Who gave Cardinal Spellman the information? Father Klaus 'perhaps' has written him, it is now reported in Munich [Father Ermin Klaus, O.F.M., New York, formerly with NCWC War Relief Services — Munich]. At least the investigation, sent down from Berlin, brought back this information. Dr. Carl Friedrich, Harvard University, was asked by General Clay to come to Germany to assist him during the summer months. I had quite a chat with him before he went to Munich. Having received his education in Germany, he is dismayed over the demands that have been made in Bavaria. He helped write the memorandum issued last October by the thirteen Chicago University professors in criticism of the school reform plan.

"Well, I too, may have written Cardinal Spellman, it is said. I would not do so stupid a thing because I know the mind of Cardinal Faulhaber on the issues of the school reform . . .

"Cardinal Faulhaber does not want to fight, but it is clear from what he said to me as well as from his letters that he and the Bavarian bishops may have to take a public stand relative to the controverted issues. If they do, they will have not only the Bavarian people behind them, but also Germans quite generally, except the SPD who more or less favor the plan. But even they are dismayed that new tax burdens arising from the ordered reform are placed on the German people now after the hardships of the currency reform.

"Murray Van Wagoner has the reputation in Bavaria of being 'just dumb.' Clay, Murphy, Panuch, etc., do not like him. He is going to Rome. Think of it, he asked Cardinal Faulhaber to request the Holy Father to write him a testimonial letter which he wants to use at a Knights of Columbus celebration to be held presumably on October 12 in Michigan. Of course, the Cardinal had to tell him that the Holy Father does not write letters of that kind."

"On 11 August 1948 Faulhaber replied to Van Wagoner and stated unequivocally his unchanged position and determination to oppose the school reform plan:

"Acknowledging your letter of August 9 I regret for my part that misunderstandings have arisen with regard to my position in the question of school reform. You informed me in your letter as follows: Catholic Sisters acting as kindergarten teachers are no longer required to acquire education on the university level in order to qualify as kindergarten teachers. In my letter of May, 1948, I politely thanked you for your kind letter, and again, repeated my expression of gratitude on the occasion of our interview on July 18. The subject discussed in both letters concerns only kindergarten teachers. Our three-minute interview offered no occasion to touch on other points of the school reform, which are indicated in the Bavarian bishops' letter of 7 January 1948.

"My dear Land Director, I am absolutely unable to remember that anyone asked me, either you or Mr. Eagan, whether I had further complaints with regard to school reform. I am also unable to recall that I answered that there are no more points of difference of opinion. Also Msgr. Thalhammer, who was present at this interview from the beginning to the end, declares that he does not recall having heard such a question. Moreover, the record that was written immediately after the interview by my secretary does not show any points regarding the school reform problem other than that of the kindergarten teachers. So there is a misunderstanding, although both parties are in *bona fide*, as it may happen in life.

"I should like to suggest: Let us forget this question, since through mutual declarations the divergence of opinion was discovered as a misunderstanding.

"I give attention to your desire that a copy of your letter of August 9 be forwarded to His Holiness, Pope Pius XII, to Cardinal Spellman, and to Bishop Muench. Naturally, I shall enclose with this copy also a copy of this letter.

"I thank you for the information that no notice was given from your office to Cardinal Spellman saying that there is full accord with regard to school reform.

"I consider the above misunderstanding as existing no longer. However, I deem it a duty to declare openly that by reason of the directives concerning free tuition and free textbooks beginning 4 August 1948, a severe crisis has arisen in the development of democratic ideas in the Bavarian school system. I foresee the hour when the Bavarian bishops will be forced to safeguard publicly the natural rights of the Bavarian people and the traditions of the Bavarian school system relative to other points of differences that have arisen in the school reform plan."

The lines were now clearly drawn as a result of the whole comedy of errors. Muench wrote on 26 July 1948, in protest, to his friend J. Anthony Panuch, political adviser to General Clay:

"Through tactlessness on the part of someone in Munich the school reform controversy has brought His Eminence, Cardinal Faulhaber, into it with both feet.

"How serious the affair has become may be gauged from the fact that the cardinal will have the bishops, the clergy, and the people on his side against Military Government.

"Whoever wrote Cardinal Spellman created a serious blunder. And why was he drawn into it? Why did the cardinal write Pius XII? What are the contents of the letter? A copy of it would reveal much. I am sure that OMGUS has a copy."

Muench was so agitated that he sent another letter to Panuch the same day:

"I have my own surmises as to why a letter was sent to Cardinal Spellman. I hope that I am wrong. It does not benefit our interests in Germany by attempting to get Cardinal Spellman as a helper to grind personal axes in matters as important as school reform.

"I'm learning a lot in a world that is totally different from the one in which I was accustomed in dealing with honorable gentlemen.

"Mr. Van Wagoner has some awfully bad advisers. That he does not see how bad the advice is causes me to share your opinion of him.

"In my talks with Military Government in Munich I warned against making a martyr of Dr. Hundhammer. I knew that he had the confidence of the cardinal and of the Bavarian bishops. It is evident that I was not believed. The whole affair is ominous in this that the cardinal asserts that the Bavarian bishops stand behind Dr. Hundhammer 'with fullest confidence — *mit vollstem Vertrauen.*' "

8. Letter from Bishop Muench to J. Anthony Panuch 3 July 1948: "I tried to keep the statement as factual and restrained as possible, although I was at the boiling point at several places and was tempted to use a vitriolic pen. Never in all my life have I seen such an unfair and perverse report. Every line contains fabrications, distortions of fact, unfounded suspicions, or false judgments.

"Reports of this kind certainly are not a help to General Clay. They give him a distorted picture of what is happening in the American zone.

"As a clergyman I come out of a world where there are no such snakes in the grass. All my life I have dealt with honorable men.

"Now I know that I have come into another world, in which one must tread carefully. Believe me your 'million dollar advice' to look ahead, to prevent such happenings as much as possible, to be a good many steps in advance of possible adversaries, and, therefore, to demand minutes of conferences with the right to sign them, is advice that I shall never forget . . .

"As long as I live I shall remember with gratitude the confidence General Clay showed me in bringing the letter to my attention. Nor shall I ever forget the fair deal that he gave me in allowing me to present my side of the affair.

"Since the letter of Mr. Murray D. Van Wagoner, Land Director for Bavaria, will go into the official files of Military Government, I should be deeply grateful if my statement should be attached to the Land Director's letter and filed with it. Self-respect and pride in my work urge me to make this request."

Seldom in his career did Muench write such a strong letter.

9. Muench informed Archbishop McNicholas on 28 August 1948:

"Excitement is running high. Comments such as 'democracy through dictatorship' are heard on all sides. Sentiment in favor of democracy has not been at so low an ebb as now.

"The bishops are aroused over the whole affair. They fear for their private schools. The currency reform has made parents poor and, unable to send their children to private schools that must charge tuition to maintain themselves, they will send them to tuition-free public schools. Moreover, there is no tradition in Germany to have a system of private schools charging tuition side by side with a system of public schools that charge no tuition.

"Military Government has no objection if the Bavarian Government pays subsidies to private schools. The bishops fear subsidies because of possible control by some future government none too friendly or even hostile to the Church. They cite recent precedents in France and Belgium.

"The order was issued in the interests of democracy. This was tactless. A well-informed German told me if tuition-free schools and free text books are an essential of democracy, then most democratic countries in Western Europe are not democratic. Furthermore, your own country, he said, had no tuition-free school system until late in the last century, and even now some States have no free text-book school laws. Apparently he had read up on our educational history, and not having at hand an educational library I have not been able to check the correctness of the assertions.

"The Bavarians are very bitter about it all, because similar orders were not issued for Land Hesse and Nord Baden-Wuerttemberg, both in the American zone. They talk of 'deliberate persecution.'

"The situation is so grave as to cause a report to be spread about that General Clay has ordered a special conference for the middle of September to review the whole school reform plan. We Americans anxious about our interests in Germany hope that this is true. Secularistic American educators, supported by 'liberal,' antireligious groups of Germans, are riding high because they can impose their reforms without responsibility to a legislature or to taxpayers.

"The financial burden imposed all of a sudden on an impoverished people by the ordered school reforms is especially a matter of grave concern to responsible officials of the Bavarian Government."

10. Interview with Dr. Alois Hundhammer, Bavarian Minister of State, Munich, 10 December 1963. Hundhammer recalled an interesting episode in connection with the school controversy: "While Van Wagoner was still in office, the ministers of cult and education in the American zone of occupation, that was Bavaria, Wuerttemberg (part of it; some of Wuerttemberg belonged to the French zone of occupation), Hesse and Bremen received invitations to come to Washington. As minister of cult and education in Bavaria I had been invited and had accepted. The evening before our departure the Bavarian prime min-

ister gave a reception. I was among the guests, also Van Wagoner. When I mentioned in conversation with him, 'so, tomorrow we'll start our trip to the United States,' he answered, 'you will not go.' Astonished, I asked 'why not? I have the papers already.' He replied, 'you will find out tomorrow.'

"Next morning when I was about to leave, I received a message that my invitation had been withdrawn. This decision was effective as long as Van Wagoner was in office. After he was informed of his demotion as Land commissioner, I received a special invitation a half year later to come first to Hunter College where Professor Shuster was president. I made the trip to the United States, met Professor Shuster, talked with him about our school question and traveled around in the United States."

Muench informed Archbishop McNicholas on 8 January 1948:

"Dr. Hundhammer is credited with having told General Clay: 'In Nuremberg men are being judged and punished for not having followed their convictions against the dictates of their government. Am I now to give up my convictions because of dictations from above?'

"The German Socialists are supporting the American school plan. They dislike, if not hate, Dr. Hundhammer as an ultramontane, and would like to see him dismissed by the Americans from his position."

11. Hundhammer explained:

"Our Bavarian system of education was entirely contrary to American educational personnel who entertained more liberal views. We Catholics presuppose this attitude toward religion in our brothers in the faith. I do not mean to accuse Van Wagoner or his educational advisers of ill will; they just did not have an appreciation of our fundamental ideas.

"We had the impression that the policy Americans were pushing was a general policy directive from above, but we had a much stronger suspicion that forces in our own country were at work, that opponents of confessional schools made use of the Americans for their own aims. This group was the liberal party, the Free Democrats, consisting for the most part of people who belong to no denomination. The liberal wing of this party goes back 150 years. They formed in 1848 with an Enlightenment and French Revolution background. Their aim is to abolish all religion from school and education. 'Religion a private matter' is their famous maxim. These people were confident they would at last succeed with the help of the Occupation Forces, having failed to reach their goal in the democratic proceedings of our parliament in Bavaria, and even in the *Landtag* before 1933.

"The negotiations of these liberals, supported by certain circles of the Social Democratic Party, were accepted as serious considerations in the school question. In retrospect, our extraordinary stubbornness has proved right. I was told once that it was only we in Bavaria who were so obstinate, while Wuerttemberg, Hesse and Bremen had given consent. This is easily understood because Bremen is a land with a strong social democratic foundation, and Hesse is also strongly influenced and ruled by Social Democrats.

"The whole school system would have been changed if we had not resisted. It is not easy to re-establish a system once it has been changed; it would have involved questions of organizations and teacher training. We needed confessionally trained teachers for our confessional schools.

"Parents decide what type of school the child will attend: Catholic, Protestant or interconfessional. We said: this is freedom, this is the true right of man. The person who has the right to decide on the education of minors decides on the type of school the child should attend."

12. Muench wrote Monsignor James H. Griffiths on 8 February 1949:

"Before Dr. John Henley comes over he ought to be briefed as to the real situation in Bavaria because he will get a good deal of one-sided if not prejudiced briefing when he lands here. I have found that there are two sides to the question, and that Catholic Bavaria is not as 'reactionary' as some of our Americans make it out to be.

"The situation there is tense regarding the School Reform Plan which was dictated by Dr. Richard Thomas Alexander from Berlin. In conferences with the Land director Murray D. Van Wagoner and Mr. Edward Kennedy I have tried to find a compromise solution.

"Some of our American educators are trying to impose a pattern of education in Germany which they would never succeed in imposing on the people back home.

"Apparently, they have forgotten the dismal facts of the American educational system as revealed last year by the national survey of the New York *Times*. Of course, the survey is not an argument for a bad educational system anywhere, also not in Germany, but it is an argument for being humble in not taking the pharisaical attitude that we have an educational system without serious flaws in the United States.

"Some of the reforms proposed have really nothing to do with re-education for democracy because countries in Europe that have the same pattern of education as Germany have never been questioned as to their democracy, for instance Switzerland."

13. Muench wrote Dr. George N. Shuster on 2 March 1950:

"In a conversation with Mr. McCloy I learned to my delight that he talked to you about taking over the post of Land Commissioner in Bavaria, and that you were willing to take it.

"The reasons that he gave are decisive: you are a Catholic, know the German people, speak the language, and would approach the problems in Bavaria with tact and prudence.

"The school problem has again caused a flareup, mainly because of a tactless offensive on the part of some of the personnel in the Bavarian HICOG. We think that, if the problem is properly handled, it is easy of solution. There are good men in Bavaria who listen to reason . . . There have been misunderstandings and misconceptions on both sides regarding the issues involved. Regrettably some American newspapermen have stated that the Church in Bavaria is opposed to a change in matters of education. This is one of those half-truths that does much harm. I know definitely that the Church authorities are in favor of changes that will improve the educational system, but they are not willing to go along with some of the methods proposed . . .

"A man like you is really needed over here. You would render a service to your country at a critical point in the affairs of Germany such as few others could render. Let us then leave nothing undone to have you come over soon."

14. Because the Murray Van Wagoner, Clay, Muench documents of May, 1948, detail the seriousness of the charges made against the Catholic liaison consultant, the only such charges brought against Muench from any side during his long years in Germany; and because these documents reveal clearly the intensity of the Bavarian school reform controversy, the exchange of reports is included in Appendix III.

15. On the same day, 10 May 1949, Muench also wrote J. Anthony Panuch, special adviser to Clay, a further exegesis of his tribute to the Military Governor:

"Herewith I send you a copy of my recent letter to General Clay. Since you know my sentiments of regard for him, I need not emphasize that what I wrote came from a sincere and grateful heart. Nor need I instruct you what to read between the lines of my letter.

"When the archives are opened some day to historians on General Clay's administration, the world will learn what a magnificent job of reconstruction he did.

"Few men faced problems of such grave importance and vast proportions as he did. The wonder is that he did not make more mistakes than he did. He took over a shattered, impoverished, distrustful Germany. There were recalcitrant allies, dishonorable foes across the ocean, sabotaging personnel in lower levels of administration in military government, second-rate and self-seeking carpet-baggers, inefficient and ignorant of the history, customs, and traditions of the country they set out to rule.

"In the midst of all this General Clay held to a steadfast course of conciliation and peace. His policy is best characterized, I think, as that of Lincoln, 'with malice toward none, and charity toward all.'

"History will some day record the anxious hours he suffered in consequence of vindictiveness in de-nazification and war-crimes trials. But history will record, too, with pride the courageous step he took, in the face of a 'hard peace' advocates, to give the Germany of the American zone self-government at the earliest possible date as well as constitutions for its *Laender*. History will justify his stand on the Ruhr question and on that of federalism for a new Germany.

"The socialists of England's labor government betrayed him by underhandedly divulging information to the socialists of Germany in order to win for them a centralized government as against one built on federalism.

"In our recent conversation I told you of my reasons why I distrusted the socialists. After all they are the twin brother of Communism, with whom they are now fighting over a position of power. Schumacher's demagoguery to arouse his red rabble following against the allies in a critical moment for Germany is despicable beyond all words of description. The ingratitude of the socialists, to say the least, is contemptible.

"In his administration General Clay had to work against the heavy odds of wartime propaganda. France played the game to a finish, yet France could hardly come to conference tables with clean hands in the matter of aggression.

"Successfully it played up the propaganda that Germany committed acts of aggression three times since 1870.

"Well, history plainly records the fact that Napoleon III, who had a bad record as an aggressor, especially against Austria and Russia, declared war in 1870. The London *Times* denounced the aggression, declaring plainly that the sympathies of the world were on the side of Germany. Nor is France so innocent regarding the war of 1914 if the documents of historical archives have any meaning at all. But that is a long story.

"The point is that General Clay had to work out his policies of reconstruction against the heavy odds laid against him through a distortion of historical facts.

"His victory over the Russians in conference and especially through the most stupendous achievement of his entire administration, the Berlin airlift, is history so close to us that nothing more need be said about it.

"To me it is a matter of poignant regret that General Clay is being sacrificed to the ambitions of politicians who are playing a dubious role in world affairs of today."

16. The complete text of the "Memorandum of the Bishops of the American Occupation Zone to General Lucius D. Clay, 27 July 1947," is included in Appendix V.

17. On Christmas day 1955, Muench informed John Foster Dulles, Secretary of State, as follows:

"This morning's papers reported that Mr. Timothy J. Murphy, commander of the Veterans of Foreign Wars, demanded the removal of Mr. Edwin A. Plitt, American member of the International Board which reviews cases of convicted war criminals, for having approved paroles for prisoners detained in Landsberg in connection with the Malmédy case.

"Having discussed this case on a number of occasions with Mr. Plitt, allow me to say that I have learned to admire him for his moral integrity and for his conscientious grasp of the issues involved.

"Mr. Plitt is an American of upright character, much concerned that the voice of conscience of our nation be heard and respected, and that our ideals of justice be blest by rendering deeds of mercy now that we speak words of peace to nations everywhere in the world.

"I trust sincerely that pressure groups will not prevail in their demands. It is obvious from statements made by their leaders that they do not know *all* the facts of the Malmédy case. They might read with profit the briefs of Mr. (Col.) Willis M. Everett, Jr., Atlanta, Georgia, and learn that they should not do to former enemy soldiers what under similar circumstances we would not want to have done to ours.

"After much study of the documents pertinent to the Malmédy case during the more than nine years that I am now in Germany, I may be permitted to say that I put full trust in Americans such as Col. Willis M. Everett, General T. T. Handy,

General Clarence Huebner, Lt. Col. Hal D. McCown, et al., who gave thorough conscientious attention to a fair and just settlement of the Malmédy case, rather than in that handful of naturalized Americans who, not imbued with the spirit of Anglo-Saxon traditions of jurisprudence, unwittingly, I am sure, dishonored due process of law in essential points.

"In writing you in this matter I do so with the sole thought that injustice be not done to a red-blooded American such as I know Mr. Plitt to be."

By that time Robert Murphy was back in Washington as deputy under-secretary of state. He informed Muench that there was much appreciation in the Department of State over his letter, but since Plitt was in the foreign service it was judged best to give him a Washington assignment as a foreign service inspector, and appoint the former senator, Robert W. Upton, as American member of the board so there would be no misunderstanding of the independent position of the Mixed Board and its members.

NOTES TO CHAPTER FIVE

1. Cf. Carl Amery, *Capitulation, The Lesson of German Catholicism* (New York: Herder and Herder, 1967), p. 51.

2. Monsignor Bernhard Hack summarized the scope of this activity in an interview in Rome 23 November 1963:
"Gradually the German civil government began to take shape. First the *Laender* were created, elections held, governments installed, constitutions given, legislation passed. Cultivation of relations between the Holy See and the newly created *Laender* by Bishop Muench, the representative of the Holy See, became more and more important. For Muench that called for quite an adjustment. He came from a country where such relations were unknown, where an absolute separation existed between church and state. Muench adjusted well to this unfamiliar situation and set about to take his first steps on diplomatic grounds. This, too, was providential. His simple, human and cordial way procured his first successes in the field. In the form of a series of official state visits in 1948 he met the new governments in their respective state capitals: at Stuttgart, Freiburg, Tuebingen, Munich, Wiesbaden, Duesseldorf, Hannover, Hamburg, and Bremen. A formal address of greeting was delivered to each premier and discussions with state political leaders were held. A truly extraordinary achievement. The representative of the Holy Father was the first to pay an official visit to these states; the first representative of a spiritual power that did not belong to the group of victors . . .

"It should not be a secret that many sacrifices were part of Muench's life from this time forward. As an American, it was easy for him to understand the administration of American dioceses, the American political system, and American society. However, even an experienced European had difficulty in comprehending the political and social situation of European countries other than his own. So much the more for Muench, even though he wasn't a stranger to Germany. His German forefathers, his travels and studies in Europe, and other factors facilitated his orientation and information. But the bishop of Fargo had never encountered such kind of chains, if I may use this comparison, as he did here again and again, and that impeded the accomplishment of certain ecclesiastical aims.

"In his country he was free to act and decide as a bishop in accordance with his duties as pastor of his flock. He did not have to take into consideration so many aspects of tradition, historical heritage, and manifold ties of a legal nature. In Germany many a step of a bishop or nuncio leads into a thicket of long-established rights and customs often touching on church and state alike. Historical development has created intricate relations between church and state in the different cultural centers of Germany. It is a science proper which is hard to absorb even for an expert. There are so many political partners. Formerly there were fourteen, now there were twelve distinct *Laender* with their own parliaments and governments; fourteen prime ministers, fourteen ministers for cult and education — and added to this the coming Federal Government. In West Germany alone there were fifteen, now thirteen constitutions in existence.

"During this period these constitutions and the Basic Law were drawn up and put into effect. What an enormous amount of work that entailed! And Muench studied this formidable material, so alien to him, to the last detail, not without an occasional sigh.

"A number of contacts were still in existence between the Holy See and Germany; I mention particularly the Reich Concordat (1933). The proposed federal legislation in Germany had to take into account, and to keep in conformity with, the existing agreements. The Holy See as well as Muench and the German bishops anxiously watched over this. Muench gained and retained thorough evaluation of the whole matter. A truly amazing accomplishment. He took great pains to make himself familiar with these strange problems, to work on them, and to manage them with great skill. There wasn't a day that he wasn't confronted with questions of this kind."

3. An example of Bavarian independence and regionalism was evidenced when Cardinal Faulhaber was offered, as the first Catholic, the Cross of Merit by President Heuss and Chancellor Adenauer of the new Federal Republic. The award was offered at the same time to Albert Schweitzer. While Faulhaber and Schweitzer were professors at Strassbourg in Alsace they had open disagreements regarding conservative and liberal theological positions. Faulhaber decided not to accept the honor because he considered the new Federal Republic not to be a German state. It was to him a political concept of the Rhineland faction and nothing more. In terms of his life over five generations he had witnessed the death of the Kaiser Reich, of the Bavarian dynasty of Wittelsbach kings, of the Weimar Republic which he considered to be Freemason, and of the immoral

Hitler regime. Faulhaber personally favored a restoration of the monarchial Wittelsbach family in Bavaria because the principle of order in a monarchy is different from that of even the best democracy. The Bavarians called Faulhaber himself the "uncrowned king of Bavaria." (The above information was supplied by a person close to Cardinal Faulhaber who asked to remain unnamed.)

4. Bishop Leo F. Dworschak of Fargo learned at first hand of the attitude of the German bishops toward Bishop Muench during his visit in Germany in the autumn of 1949. At breakfast with Cardinal Frings of Cologne, the chairman of the German Bishops' Conference was profuse in praise of Bishop Muench's accomplishments in Germany. Bishop Dworschak replied: "We have recognized from the beginning that Bishop Muench is a great man. That is why we are so anxious to have him come back to us in Fargo very soon." Cardinal Frings looked up in shocked surprise: "What! Back to Fargo? That is utterly unthinkable. Germany needs him."

Two days later Dworschak visited Faulhaber in the company of Muench. As the bishops were leaving for Rome, Faulhaber took Dworschak aside and spoke to him with deep feeling of Germany's debt to the apostolic visitator. Bishop Dworschak repeated what he had said to Cardinal Frings. The reaction of the elderly Faulhaber was even more emphatic: "No, no! Not back to Fargo, ever. We have already made our wishes known to Rome that if and when Germany can re-establish diplomatic relations, Bishop Muench will be appointed nuncio without delay."

5. Monsignor Dr. Octavian Barlea, Romanian priest who cared with devotion for the Romanian refugees throughout the whole period, described this search and aid effort in an interview in Munich, 7 December 1963:

"In the first years I left Kronberg every month to spend two to three weeks with groups of refugees. These were extensive trips in search of our countrymen. We brought gift packages which Bishop Muench had collected and prepared at Kronberg. I went to Heidelberg, Mannheim, Karlsruhe, Stuttgart and suburbs, Augsburg, Donauwoerth, Munich, Freising, Moosburg, Kempten and Nuremberg.

"With regard to ecclesiastical jurisdiction, the refugees in Germany were under the autonomous control of their national delegates. The delegates had episcopal authority, they had their own baptismal and marriage records, and they were not obliged to report to the German bishops or German ecclesiastical administration.

"For the most part I distributed gifts from charity and welfare organizations. Often I intervened for the refugees at American, English and French military quarters and was accorded many a relief for them. I tried hard to better their condition. In some cases I was successful, in others not. For example, those who lived in prison camps during the war were still treated as prisoners of war after release but they should not have been treated this way. Because they were found wearing uniforms at war's end, the only clothes they had, they were locked up again in these camps.

"In the beginning there were about twenty to thirty thousand Romanians. They had come to Germany during the war and now they wanted to go home. They definitely hoped that the Soviet occupation would only last a few months, or at the most, a year, and that the Americans and the English and all the Allies would then drive out the Russians. The situation in Romania was particularly intricate because the king was still tolerated there in the first years. The Russians did not change the situation radically but gradually, and that was a cause of bewilderment and a heavy load for many . . .

"I was deeply impressed by Bishop Muench's kindness. It is hard to imagine greater kindness and understanding than he had, especially in those years of need and misery, his heroic years. And then also his equilibrium, particularly during those difficult years. He was in the very best of health. He considered a situation carefully and calmly, and then helped whenever and wherever it was possible for him." Barlea left the impression of an eremite with all who met him. One curial official in Rome whom he asked for 60,000 lire for his beloved Romanian refugees immediately recommended that he be given 120,000. Archbishop McNicholas gave him $10,000 in the years 1948 to 1950; the NCWC supplied $10,000; Pope Pius XII, 8,000 DM; Father Giorgio Babutiu of the Romanian Catholic Relief Company, Cleveland, $2,250; Father John Trutia of the American Romanian Relief, Inc., $1,125.

During the year 1948 there were ninety-four Romanian DP students who came to him for tutoring in their studies and in Romanian culture. He not only worked tirelessly for the material aid of the sick and needy; his main interest, throughout the whole period which attracted Bishop Muench to him, was in the cultural and religious heritage of his people. Barlea stands out for his special interest in the intellectual displaced person, and his advancement of Romanian prayer books and books of art.

6. As Monsignor Aloysius J. Wycislo of the NCWC's Catholic War Relief Services wrote in "Haven Provided," *Catholic Action*, XXIV, (April, 1952), 12–13:

"It took several years for these governments to demonstrate to the world that the mark of a civilized country is the attitude of its government towards men as men. Where justice did not compel to restitution for such violations of the rights of the displaced persons, charity, at last, prevailed in the opening of doors to these victims of war.

"In our own United States, highly selective permissions, based on our immigration laws, were set aside in emergency legislation that demonstrated our ability to give hospitality to the unhappy victims of 'man's inhumanity to man.'

"The Presidential Directive of 22 December 1945 marked the first frustrating attempt to introduce some solution to the problem of the refugee and displaced person and provided some example of American leadership towards its solution. The government of the United States had really committed itself to the making of effective plans for the resettlement of displaced persons. It had contributed the largest part of the costs of maintaining them in camps and had taken active part in international planning for the movement of these people to other countries; yet, we could not in good conscience, keep asking other countries to provide a haven for the displaced persons without opening our own doors to a substantial number."

7. Interview with President Harry S. Truman, Washington, D. C., 8 February 1949. Cf. Appendix VI.

8. Wycislo, *op. cit.*, 13.

9. Frings wrote to John J. McCloy, U. S. high commissioner in Germany, on 6 July 1949:

"As chairman of the Fulda Conference of the Catholic Bishops of Germany allow me to bring to your attention a matter that is of urgent importance to our German nation, and may be of no small interest to you in your present high office with its difficult tasks.

"In his special message to Congress, 24 June 1949, on aid to economically underdeveloped countries, President Truman mentions as first aid in his plan the need of persons who have medical, educational, and technical knowledge in such basic fields as sanitation, communications, road building, agriculture, and industry.

"It is not unknown to you, I am sure, that Germany, and with it the occupying powers, carry a heavy burden of millions of unassimilated refugees who will be a drain on their resources for many years to come. Among them are doctors, agricultural scientists, chemists, industrial managers and other able-bodied workers, of which Germany has a surplus, and who could be of invaluable help for the furtherance of President Truman's plan.

"May I respectfully propose, then, that skilled surplus help be allowed to emigrate to underdeveloped countries for implementing the plan. The Church through its pastors and organizations would be glad to assist in screening and selecting persons of good character, trustworthy and responsible, and endowed with the skills and knowledge required. Many would seize the opportunity of leaving Germany if only for a temporary period until their help is no longer required.

"We of the Catholic Church would like to give every possible assistance to the plan not only in order to help these unfortunate refugees and expellees in distress, as is our duty as churchmen, but also in order to express our gratitude to the American people for their magnanimous help given to Germany on a scale unprecedented in the history of nations. Germany, therefore, would be given an opportunity to repair at least to some extent the great damage that was caused to peoples the world over by the infamous and execrable Hitler regime.

"While I can speak only for our Catholic people, I am confident that our Protestant brethren share with us the same sentiments.

"May I, then, respectfully request that favorable consideration be given to my proposal if circumstances at all warrant doing so?

"By relieving, at least to some extent, Germany's distress of overpopulation, made very critical by a shortage of housing and lack of work in important fields of industry and agriculture, we shall help not only Germany but also the United States. We realize only too well what a heavy burden your people are carrying in the interest of establishing a good and enduring peace."

10. During Vatican Council II Bishop Edward E. Swanstrom and James J. Norris of Catholic Relief Services commented in an interview in Rome, 25 November 1963, on Muench's activity:

Bishop Swanstrom: Muench was a very quiet, kindly man. I remember particularly the cautious way in which he began his dealings with the very serious problems that faced the Church in Germany after the war. He was concerned about the lack of food and clothing and necessities of life first among the Germans, and then among the expellees and refugees in the 1950's. I think he played a big part in influencing us in our efforts to re-establish a stable Germany and to bring as much relief as possible to the people who had been forced into Germany. One thing that stands out very much in my mind is how much he did to bring about an excellent resettlement program of displaced persons throughout the world. I remember also his continual concern about refugees and expellees who remained in Germany. He constantly contacted me about the necessity of having the Catholic nationality groups in the United States continue their interest in refugees and to do whatever they possibly could to help them. Many times he said to me: 'Don't allow the interest of the people in the United States to grow cold in regard to the problems of the displaced persons and the refugees, particularly those who have to remain behind.'

James Norris: I went into Germany in 1946 shortly after Bishop Muench came there as apostolic visitator. Throughout the years I had very close contact with him. Germany was devastated and Bishop Muench was given the task of trying to help the Church in Germany get back on its feet. He day by day worked very closely with the bishops of Germany, and also at the same time with the refugee priests who were faced with the tremendous problem of helping their displaced and refugee people.

"The German bishops, clergy and people welcomed the material assistance that Catholic Relief Services brought them.

Bishop Swanstrom: We moved directly to assist, but there was a varied attitude on the part of the German bishops. I know some who said to me: 'Well, you helped to destroy our country, certainly you ought to help build it back.' We couldn't build it up again. You couldn't be sure whether they were being facetious about it or not. I think maybe a few didn't understand our motives entirely. There was that general question about the Americans. I think they were most surprised that their conquerors were so ready to help put them back on their feet.

"Catholic Relief Services had started with refugees in Spain and Portugal. Then as countries opened up we moved into Italy, France, Belgium and Holland. Everyone knew there was a tremendous problem in Germany. So as soon as the war ended we had men who went into Germany and tried to meet these problems. I was there myself in the fall of 1945, and Father James H. Hoban, now Monsignor Hoban out in Cincinnati, was in charge of our programs in France. Monsignor Aloysius J. Wycislo, now Bishop Wycislo of Green Bay, came up from the Middle East. Then we brought four laymen over and we began to operate out of Frankfurt; Father Hoban and I went back and forth to Berlin. I remember going to Berlin in November and December of 1945 and the situation was really tragic. The people of Berlin were hungry and cold, and all of the expellees were coming in from the former German states. They had been expelled by the agreement made at Potsdam. Incidentally, that deportation had been going on for a few years before 1945, and the American bishops, I often say this, were the first ones to speak out against it. In their statement of 1946 they said: 'Something has been happening in Europe which is new in the annals of recorded history. By agreement among the victors, millions of Germans who for centuries lived in Eastern Europe, are being forced from their homes without resources, into the heart of Germany. We boast of our democracy, but in this transplantation of peoples we have perhaps unwittingly allowed ourselves to be influenced by the hard theory of heartless totalitarian philosophy.' I remember making a statement when I came back to the United States that I actually saw people dying in the *Bahnhof* in Berlin, and some congressmen cited it in the House. I saw people with my own eyes die in the station when I was there.

"That brings back to mind Bishop Muench's concern for the ethnic German priests and sisters who frequently were in the carloads that came into the various cities in Germany. Frankly, it was a dreadful sight. The bridges were destroyed and frequently they had to get off a train on one side of a river and walk across to the other side, and there would be hundreds of them coming along. Overnight they would be in the *Bahnhofs*. We used to go down and pick out the priests and sisters and try to help them if we could.

James Norris: Usually private agencies in Germany were not even permitted to help anybody of German origin and it wasn't until 1946 that private agencies were permitted to operate. The German Catholics give us credit for restoring their normal operations through the money furnished via the American hierarchy from the American people. And it should be recorded that it was Bishop John M. Gannon of Erie, treasurer of the NCWC executive board, who, after a trip to Germany and a visit with Bishop Muench, convinced the American bishops to allocate $300,000 to the Holy Father for the construction of churches for the expellees and refugees in Germany.

"England, Canada, Belgium, Australia, New Zealand and South American countries took a number of displaced persons along with the United States which took the largest number. Groups of Catholics in Switzerland, Denmark, France and Ireland brought help to Germany, but from the viewpoint of an organized hierarchy, the Americans were the only ones helping on a large scale. The American bishops developed this broad program for anyone who was suffering, to help bring relief to the victims of war, to help re-establish the agencies of mercy in the Church so they could carry on the job themselves. We've always operated on that basis.

"I think one of the main things that Bishop Muench was able to do for the Church in Germany was to interpret the problems to the military authorities. He did it in such a nice way, without any belligerency, that slowly they did come around to realize that the Church had these problems and they were willing to try to be of as much assistance as possible. I think this is one of the great things he did. He was able to make some very fine personal contacts and get the voice of the Church heard where otherwise it would not have been heard in high places."

11. Interview with Monsignor Dr. Gerhard Fittkau, Rome, 26 November 1963.

12. *Ibid.* Fittkau traveled across the United States soliciting funds for German expellees and refugees during 1949–50. On 6 May 1950 Fittkau wrote Muench from New York in a different vein: "I felt obliged very often to write and thank you during the past first year of my work in this country. Almost every important step I could take in my mission over here reminded me of my debts of gratitude to the priceless introduction you had given me. Not only in your home town Milwaukee, but all over the States, I found open hearts and hands, whenever I could show your letter. His Excellency, Most Rev. Archbishop Moses E. Kiley, gave me a plastic cover even, so as not to spoil this precious document. It is a very great help to feel backed in this urgent work of ours here, by the representative of the Holy Father, who himself held the same position as Your Excellency after the first World War in Germany and who helped to establish the American Branch of the St. Boniface Society by a wonderful letter to the Apostolic Delegation in Washington. . .

"The good response resulting from our own efforts here have enabled us to forward for the diaspora missions close to 400,000 Western German Marks and more than 30,000 lbs. of valuable materials. . .

"I was happy also often to have the occasion to enforce the personal appeals of Your Excellency who are so much concerned and successful in the same work of the rehabilitation of the Church in Germany."

13. Karl Josef Hahn, "The Church in Germany Today," *Foreign Affairs*, XXVI, 14.

14. Otto B. Roegele, "German Catholicism Amidst the Ruins," *Blackfriars*, XXX (November, 1949), 511–14. "Catholics in the country have not shown up well under the strain which the refugees have placed upon them. For over a century the people in the cities have been consciously taking their stand for or against Christianity, and the urgency of the decision has led to more whole-hearted Christianity, but the villages are only just beginning to face up to it. The trimmings to the pretty picture of village religion have been shown for what they are worth and all essentially Christian inspiration is seen to be missing. Even in the cities the sense of urgency is weak enough, but in the villages it simply does not exist. The strict external order based upon traditional customs and conventions has been shattered. Now we can see what genuine feeling there was behind it all, which was little enough in all conscience.

"The villages had a duty toward the refugees of doing everything they could to build new homes for them; they have almost entirely failed to do so. Although it goes against the grain, we must also admit that an alarming number of presbytery doors have remained shut whenever the needy have knocked on them. If the village clergy had taken in refugees and offered shelter to priests from the East they would have proved themselves witnesses of our Lord's message to the world; they might have softened the bitterness of many hearts both by word and example and have repeated with Christ, 'Let the little ones come to me.' Throughout almost all German dioceses the reports make it obvious how infrequently this has been the case.

"Naturally there have been shining examples of self-sacrifice and brotherly love to set against this dereliction of duty. But a terrible lot of dust has in fact been stirred up. And the ecclesiastical authorities have not been anything like energetic enough in bringing home to their clergy their duties as good shepherds. There would have been a great deal more noise if Christians occupying important public positions had not stifled it, and if they had not been ready to humiliate themselves to do so . . . Special difficulties have arisen out of the position of the refugee priests and one cannot overstress the injustice which would be inflicted upon them if they were to be treated strictly according to their official status in terms of canon law. Most of these priests are old and they have been driven hither and thither for years; frequently they are at the beck and call of dependents, and whatever positions they have won for themselves have only come as a result of hard toil. It is sheer nonsense that they should give up these positions and begin all over again in subordinate positions in the diaspora where the material resources available are so inadequate and while all the time no arrangements are being made for the younger German clergy from the Western Zones to do some years of 'front line' service in the diaspora. A just solution to this problem is not easy to find because there are many of the younger clergy whose attitude on this matter is entirely praiseworthy and who would regard such 'front line' service as a grace rather than a burden.

"In this context also it needs to be made clear that the refugee problem cannot be solved merely through charity and love of our neighbors. Much more will have to be done by the German nation and its Christian communities and this is a question which involves all of us. It is simply not true, for instance, as we had every right to hope, that those regions where nominally Christian parties are predominant have given better and speedier aid to the refugees. Often the opposite is true. Christians seem to have forgotten (and not only on this issue) that the will of the Father is not fulfilled simply by almsgiving, but by seeing that justice is realized in political decisions and political action.

"In many places the coming of the refugees has resulted in outbursts of hatred and violence between the refugees on the one hand and the securely-established country folk on the other. Perhaps there is no general solution but this does not alter the fact that many individuals have failed to make the sacrifices which have been demanded of them personally. In more than one place the police have had to be called in to commandeer shelter and the barest essentials of life for the refugees. And it is no answer to say that other nations would have behaved the same in similar circumstances. We have reason to doubt the basis of this argument. In any case it is certain that large sections of the German people have not behaved honorably. All of which is most relevant when we hear so much about that inner 'conversion' and that 'penitence' which gave rise to such high hopes."

15. *Ibid.*, 515–16.

16. *Ibid.*, 517–19. Roegele concluded: "Above all German Catholics place their hopes in those of the laity who are awake to the fact that it is God who has brought them to the age of discernment. The limitless tasks of the German diaspora cannot be carried out in any other way than through the lay apostolate. This refers both to the territorial and to the spiritual diaspora. It expresses a notion which is not easily arrived at, but which is much less rare in Germany than it used to be and is penetrating even into official German circles. The lay movement in Germany has not found the struggle for recognition against traditional forms and regulations easy. But it has its allies, including some who are influential besides being well-disposed. It is full of admiration for lay movements abroad and finds them a great encouragement, particularly that in France because the French movement has recently received some degree of approval from the bishops. Its greatest weakness is due to the fact that no one knows precisely what the movement is, and what it is supposed to be doing. So far its aims have been too narrowly conceived and it has been too much restricted to the bourgeois-academic class. Nevertheless the Eastern Zone is the great testing ground of Christianity and it is there also that the Christian laity have a chance to prove their zeal.

"To be worthy of the occasion German Catholicism must first of all develop a thoroughly missionary spirit. It must get rid of its defensive and apologetic attitude, it must burst the bonds of that ghetto into which it was once forced and where it has since remained of its own free will. This ghetto is that of the 'purely religious sphere' (which is nothing but an idea of the devil). Apostolic work from now on must be functional, which means it must take risks and improvise methods, get on with its job and forget the *a priori* necessity of material conditions.

"German Catholicism must carry on with its work in spite of its own disappointments or of current widespread disillusionment. It must be convinced that even a great political landslide would not alter the essential tasks of either the territorial or the spiritual diaspora and it must spread this conviction. Furthermore it must try to assimilate the refugees as smoothly as possible, protecting them from the fate which threatens them at present, which would turn them into a featureless proletariat. If this means that we have to overthrow certain thoroughly respectable traditions and if it offends the sensibilities of both priests and laymen belonging to the settled communities, then that is unfortunate, but it must still be done. The outstanding need is for able-bodied priests to be sent where they can be most useful without worrying about diocesan boundaries.

"We must not be frightened of acknowledging the truth, and we must stop trying to water it down, which does not mean to say that we need be gloomy and only see the difficulties. Primarily the diaspora is a great opportunity and it will only become a menace if the opportunity is not taken with both hands. That is the decisive issue: whether Germany can give birth to a genuine lay movement and a form of Catholic Action which will be wide enough in scope and spiritual enough in inspiration to meet this situation. We believe that the fate of Europe depends upon it, and that in it the destiny of Europe is equally at stake." *Ibid.*, 517–19.

17. Fittkau, *op. cit.*

18. Archbishop Conrad Groeber of Freiburg im Breisgau, for example, wrote Muench on 21 January 1948, twenty-four days before his death, in a way that typified the attitude of another generation of German churchmen who considered the existential and ideological world which they were leaving as threatening the Church with new cycles of disintegration:

". . . The manner of my administration of my diocese puts me in contrast with most of the Prussian bishops and with Altenberg [Interdiocesan Center of German Catholic Youth Organizations now at the Jugendhaus in Duesseldorf]. Lately this matter has been on my mind to an extraordinary degree, especially in the past days in connection with the ever growing laicistic movement.

"Large organizations have been seized by it; Altenberg with its directives for youth is leading. We discovered that all that is being praised now as a cure-all — in France this was attempted in the 'Sillon' — was condemned by Pope Pius X. If the laity seize the leadership by pushing the clergy into the background, they hurt Catholic Action and walk down a road that will end in religious shallowness.

"But, alas, I am a caller in the desert, because the new leading Catholic magazines in particular take an opposite stand and large publishing houses swim along in the current. The Herder publishers, the owner, Herder-Dorneich, I hold in high esteem, are being weakened and under suspicion by Dr. Knecht's publishing houses that sprout up like meadow saffrons. *Caritas* unreservedly sails along in the modern stream.

"The West German Bishops' Conference at Fulda does not care at all about the southern German bishops. The conference contents itself with informing us about its resolutions as if there existed something like a predominant power in Germany. However, when it comes to paying, for that we are good enough. So I have to contribute 30,000 DM per year for Koenigstein [Seminary to train priests for the East zone and Eastern countries] whose works do not appeal to me at all. The executive board was established without the knowledge of the southern German bishops.

"Because of these and of other things there is a danger of a division among the German bishops, rendering the Fulda Conference unnecessary. For some time now I, personally, have found it hard to participate in this conference for reasons already shared by other bishops. Two of the three days of this conference pass in idle conversation, and on the third day the points on the agenda are either not dealt with at all, or in such a hurry that their treatment is absolutely insufficient. I was given exactly ten minutes for my own talk on *Caritas*! Another talk on the Catholic viewpoint on modern art and literature was not delivered at all.

"What do we know of each other, we German bishops? The separating [River] Main border has certainly been established, and this at a time when unbelief is sprouting up and Protestantism is gaining strength. We are spending our efforts on the 'Una Sancta,' holding meetings and delivering imposing talks, and we forget that in the end the debts have to be paid by a weakening Catholic conviction. Luther is a saint, and it is the Roman Pope first and foremost who is to be blamed for the schism.

"As soon as I am well enough to be able to get around, I am going to collect material on the present situation and forward it to you. Poverty cries up to heaven. Moral standards are lower than ever before. Christianity is declared abolished in public, especially under American influence. The German political attitude is outdoing the behavior of the former ill-reputed German miniature states, and general world politics are such that they will finally lead toward a third world war which in turn will finally destroy the rest of European culture.

"Foreign countries, including the Holy Father, admittedly make every effort to reduce German misery, but the occupying powers — with whom I get along well in general — rob us of the last necessities so that only scanty crumbs are left and hunger in some cases leads to death.

"There is enough paper available for publication of foreign literature and for certain political parties, but we do not even have enough to be able to put a catechism and a bible into the hands of children. The history texts introduced in higher schools evoke the loud protests of the students because of their hostile contents toward things German and their indiscriminate caricature of militarism and other matters that are just as bad and brightly flourishing among the Allies.

"The courts and the blood tribunal at Nuremberg do their best to keep alive the memory of the Hitler regime, adopting the Italian motto: *'Quando stava peggio, stava meglio'* [when things are worst, they are best].

"Considering all this, and knowing what a heavy load of worries weighs down the Holy Father, the fact that we are old and will soon have to make room for someone else does not upset us. Dear confrere, I have unburdened my heart to you; but still I cannot say that I am discouraged. On the contrary, I am anxiously awaiting the hour when, delivered from the chains that keep me in bed, I can dedicate myself anew to the public even more than I could before, God willing."

19. Interview with Monsignor Albert Buettner, Bonn/Beuel, 18 October 1963. Buettner explained what then happened:

"In search of a suitable place for such a seminary I took any train I could get, mostly freight trains, to travel around the country. Koenigstein was mentioned as a possible site. There the French troops had built large barracks for their own use during the First World War. Later these barracks were turned into an army hospital, then a Nazi organization, the *Arbeitsfront*, took over the buildings and, finally, during the Second World War they were used again as an army hospital. Now they were for sale.

"When I saw the main buildings with their attached houses I decided they would be ideal as a seminary for theologians and as a high school/college for boys. I negotiated with the government of Land Hesse, met there with understanding and good will, and finally was offered the large buildings including fairly extensive grounds for a reasonable amount.

"I hesitated before completing the deal for fear of not being able to meet the payments. It was on a Saturday before Pentecost, 1947, that I went to Kronberg.

Bishop Muench was not at home but I talked with Father Zeiger. There was no one with a better knowledge of German conditions or better suited to advise me. After listening to my story Zeiger drove with me the short distance to Koenigstein to look at the buildings. These were difficult times. I had to act fast, so I could not apply for the German bishops' consent, and I could not call because the telephones did not yet work. I had to decide on my own responsibility.

"The following conversation — it would not be quite fitting in better society — led to my final decision. Father Zeiger and I talked in our Frankfurt/Hessian dialect because we both came from that part of the country and we were not too particular about our vocabulary. I said: 'Well, Father Zeiger, what shall I do now? If I acquire this building complex from the Hessian State and the thing doesn't work, not even a dog will water it.' To which Zeiger retorted: 'The main thing is to have the pig; the meat inspector can stamp its back side later on.' That was decisive talk: I was determined to buy.

"I successfully concluded the negotiations with officials of the Hessian government, bought beds, tables, chairs, etc., which were in the buildings, organized work such as plastering and painting, and transported necessities in a little old car I had acquired.

"Bishop Muench helped a great deal with money. A special collection was taken up among the poor expellees and refugees who gave so generously when they had so little themselves. A number of German dioceses gave grants, benefactors in the United States, Belgium, Holland and Switzerland donated, and a loan was made. I also had managed to save quite an amount of money from my former work in the *Reichs-Union* and I was able, even during the war, to transfer this money from Berlin, a transaction not without danger.

"The house was opened on 15 November 1947 with sixty students from the dioceses of the east, Silesia, Sudeten, Breslau, Ermland, Prague. On the recommendation of Bishop Muench and Father Zeiger I wrote to Rome and informed them of developments. To our great joy two large trucks arrived from the Vatican just as we were opening the seminary, filled with gifts which I could distribute. I named this undertaking: *Opus Confraternitatis*. The priests and seminarians received suits, shoes and basic necessities they had not seen in years. The first group that started studies there had to finish a half-year course first in order to pass examinations required by the state before beginning university studies. On Easter, 1948, the first class passed final examinations and received its matriculation. An agreement had been signed, through the help of Father Zeiger, with the large Jesuit philosophical-theological Saint Georgen University nearby in Frankfurt to accept Koenigstein students for theological studies, and the rector of Saint Georgen inter-diocesan seminary was also named rector of the theology department at Koenigstein until we could open our own philosophical and theological school.

"In the fall of 1947 Monsignor Dr. Adolph Kindermann came as rector. He had been professor of theology in Prague and he asked to come to Koenigstein. At the request of Bishop Maximilian Kaller, Monsignor Dr. Paul Ramatschi was nominated regent of the seminary. I asked several of my friends to teach there. That was not so easy in those years because many professors, good and religious men, had first to be cleared of former Nazi party attachment. The Hessian head of the department for cult and education, a Catholic, was most obliging and co-operative and finally we were able to obtain the necessary faculty for Koenigstein."

20. Muench stated in his formal address to President Heuss at the colorful ceremony on 4 April 1951:

"Just as the German people after 1945 found themselves placed in an unprecedented situation in the history of contemporary political and international law, so are today's events unique in the practices of diplomacy. This unique quality, however, contains a significant hope for your people, and an honorable and joyful satisfaction for the representatives of the Catholic Church.

"For today that has come to pass what everyone who has a genuine love of the German people has long wished. That indispensable measure of sovereign authority has been restored to the state bodies of the German Federal government, without which it is impossible to conceive either an exchange of diplomatic representatives or the maintenance of interstate relations under conditions of mutual respect and dignity.

"The fact that this turning point in postwar politics manifests itself for the first time at this moment is not without deep-lying reasons.

"Was it not my high sovereign, His Holiness Pope Pius XII, who only a few weeks after the capitulation of the German Reich, in the midst of the rising flood of hate and defamation of the German name, openly espoused the cause of the German people in a broadcast to the world on 2 June 1945. By this action he was the first, in all public statements, to draw, not merely in words, a clear line of distinction between your people and that political system, which, in the years from 1933 to 1945, persecuted, not the Catholic Church alone, not alone every genuine expression of Christianity, not only the freedom and dignity of other nations, but first and foremost what was best in the nature of the German people themselves. In the address referred to above, Pope Pius XII appealed to the mass of people sunk in the prevailing depression to find new courage and confidence, by saying that he was firmly convinced that your people, thanks to their great and strong qualities, would once again recover.

"As Apostolic Visitator in Germany I have been able from 1946 onwards to observe this persevering recovery. I know, too, from experience what love and anxiety my esteemed pastor has devoted to your bitter distress, as a mother tends the slow and hesitating convalescence of a child which has lain at death's door.

"However, in the joy over what has been achieved, the pain of the wound which rends the heart of your people remains doubly acute. The duty, which the supreme authority of the Catholic Church recognizes as binding her to her sons and daughters both in the east and west of the German territory, rests first and foremost upon the foundation of an all-embracing pastoral care, which, by Our Lord's command, must be extended to all who bear the seal of Christ, irrespective of the frontiers behind which they live. It is, moreover, and to a particular degree, an outcome of the solemn special undertaking, to which the Apostolic See has pledged itself in the various concordats concluded with German governments, which concordats it considers still validly binding for the entire German territory.

"In fulfillment of this sacred obligation to foster friendly relations which fortunately exist between the temporal and spiritual powers in your land, I have the distinguished honor, Mr. President, of now handing to you, as the head of the German Federal Republic, the document in which His Holiness accredits me as Apostolic Nuncio for the German people.

"During the all but five years of my activity on German soil I have always honestly striven to maintain and safeguard a peaceable understanding between Church and State, and to aid the German people to the best of my ability on its thorny path to recovery. I shall continue in the future to consider it my royal mission to foster internal peace, mutual respect and understanding co-operation and to be a 'nuntius,' a messenger of that peace which rests on the love of God and of one's neighbor.

"May I express the respectful request that my efforts in this respect may be encouraged through Your Excellency's wisdom, and by the support of all competent government organs.

"Finally, it is my agreeable duty to express my sincere and heartfelt wishes to the honorable person of Your Excellency, to the government and the representatives of the people, and to the entire German nation, that the path of recovery, begun in such suffering, may lead upwards to the light of peace, well-being, unity and freedom."

President Heuss accepted the nuncio's credentials and then replied:

"I have been deeply moved by the words which Your Excellency has had the kindness to address to me. I, too, am conscious of the importance of this hour in which you are able to hand me the document by which your high sovereign, His Holiness Pope Pius XII accredits Your Excellency as apostolic nuncio in Germany. This extremely welcome event is indeed a notable one on the path of the Federal Republic towards its return to the community of free people. The path of affliction to which God committed our people, bleeding from its many wounds and torn apart by outside force, was a thorny one, and helping hands and hearts were lacking in the dark years which followed the war. With all the more gratitude, therefore, do I think of His Holiness the Pope who was the first to acknowledge from his elevated station, the natural right to existence of the German people; and who by means of charitable works remedied the terrible misery which prevailed in Germany in many different forms; and whose manifold efforts to achieve true and righteous peace, and freedom, have brought comfort and encouragement to the German people on both sides of the artificial boundary which at present divides them.

"As visible surety of sentiments inspired by an all-embracing Christian charity, your high sovereign, some years ago, sent you as his representative to Germany. I recollect with satisfaction the visit that Your Excellency had the goodness to pay me and the Federal Government a year ago. Your Excellency is, therefore, now that you take up your high office as official representative of His Holiness the Pope, no stranger to us. I welcome this solemn opportunity of conveying to you my genuine thanks, as well as that of the German people, for the energetic work of welfare, and the sympathetic interest which German misery and worries have always met with on your part.

"I therefore welcome Your Excellency most heartily in our midst as a cherished and trusted friend. The assurance of Your Excellency that it is your wish to further the friendly relations which fortunately exist between the temporal and spiritual powers in the Federal Republic, and to assist the German people in continuing its heavy task of reconstruction, has filled me with particular satisfaction. In fulfilling the mission which awaits you, Your Excellency may be assured of every attention and support on the part of myself and of the Federal Government, mindful of the contractual agreements which have been concluded by former governments with the Holy See, to the continued validity of which the Federal Republic also adheres for the whole of Germany's territory.

"In the name of the Federal Government, of the *Bundestag* and of the entire German people, I thank Your Excellency sincerely and heartily for the good wishes which you have been kind enough to express. I have every hope that Your Excellency will continue to find conditions here amenable to your work, and for my part I wish Your Excellency personal well-being and God's blessing on your activities."

Rudolph Ernst, editor of the weekly survey of German affairs issued by the Press and Information Office of the Federal government, stated: "Thus the man who today is the dean of the Diplomatic Corps in Bonn did not come to Germany as a career diplomat but for work of a pastoral and religious nature. During the two years following his arrival 10,000 CARE parcels were brought in on his initiative alone. This was a great deal more important at the time than diplomatic routine." *Bulletin Des Presse und Informationsamtes Der Bundesregierung*, VII (24 February 1959), 6.

21. Hack, *op. cit.*

22. Father Robert Leiber, S. J., in an interview on 18 November 1963, stated: "At the time when the archbishopric of Milwaukee was open in 1953 I said to Pius XII: 'Holiness, that would be the right position for Muench.' As archbishop he could not return to Fargo from the Bonn nunciature. Muench wanted to go back to Fargo but the Pope could not have allowed that because it would have looked to the world like a disqualification. It would have to be an archbishopric. And I told the Pope that Milwaukee would be the seat for Muench. He answered: 'If I had a successor for him in Germany, but right now I do not have one.' Bonn was not an easy place. The Bonn nunciature is considered among the difficult ones. And the Pope could not have sent just anybody as successor to Muench. I was sorry for Muench that this opportunity to return to his country passed him by. I am convinced that Muench would have been very happy and satisfied."

23. There was a castle on the site of the *Turmhof* during Roman times according to the historian, Geistlicher Rat Dr. Dr. Groeteken. The oldest picture of the *Turmhof* dates back to 1569 when it was a knight's manor of Kurkoeln. From 1577–96 the Metternich family owned the castle. In 1690 Johann Friedrich Karrich, canon of Saint Gangolf's Church, Bamberg, and abbot of Saint Michael's

in Normandy, purchased the building and grounds. When Emperor Leopold made him a count of the Reich, his name was changed to von Karg. This Johann Friedrich Karg bought the *Turmhof* in Bad Godesberg-Plittersdorf in his new capacity as chancellor and first minister of Archbishop Josef Clemens of Cologne who was a prince elector or *kurfuerst* of the emperor. Toward the end of the eighteenth century the building, with its two corner turrets that gave it the name *Turmhof*, burned and was replaced by a stone structure. Another fire destroyed the mansion in 1838. When reconstructed without alteration, the *Turmhof* has not been changed since that time. It was the home of a succession of burghers including Johann Maria Farina, the maker of the famous Cologne water, which fact was a source of constant joking in the nunciature family. *Turmhof* also served as a Freemasons' lodge and their cult room became the sisters' chapel. When the Nazis confiscated the building they used it as a school of the *Bund Deutscher Maedchen*, a party organization for girls. The size of the original property was sixty-three acres, reduced at present to 5.3 acres. Cf. Alfred Wiedemann, *Geschichte Godesbergs und seiner Umgebung* (Godesberg: Verein fuer Heimatpflege, 1920).

NOTES TO CHAPTER SIX

1. Interview with Monsignor Bernhard Hack, Rome, 25 November 1963. Hack continued:

"A number of contracts were still in existence between the Holy See and Germany. I only mention the *Reichskonkordat* in particular. New legislation in Germany had to take into account and be in conformity with existing agreements. The Holy See as well as the nuncio and the German bishops anxiously watched over this. Muench gained and retained thorough evaluation of the whole matter. A truly amazing accomplishment. He was interested in every little detail. This achievement deserves special recognition. Muench took great pains to make himself familiar with those strange problems, to work on them and to manage them with great skill. There wasn't a week that he wasn't confronted with questions of this kind.

"Take for example just one case: the famous legal proceedings concerning the *Reichskonkordat* at the Federal Court of Justice in Karlsruhe. The issue was the validity of the concordat. Many persons of high rank and groups of experts worked on this subject. But it was the sole responsibility of the nuncio to evaluate the proceedings and to report to Rome. Inquiries, obtaining all documents, and many other things were his responsibility, as well as numerous discussions, meetings, negotiations with the Federal Government and with the bishops. Imagine the extensive correspondence with these authorities, the exchange of notes with the foreign office and with the *Laender*. For a note of the Apostolic Nunciature the nuncio has to take full responsibility. The preliminary work consists of painstaking reports to and check-backs with the Holy See; renewed orientations, repeated consultations with jurists. Before such a note can be expedited, it has consumed much work on the part of all concerned. Muench was familiar with the entire background of this case. This is just one small chapter of his work.

"Someone might interject that this is really routine work for a nuncio. However, that was not the case with Muench; much depends on the spirit, the principles according to which one accomplishes one's work. Here again is something very typical of Muench. He was a resident bishop, he knew very well by his own familiarity with the administration of a diocese, a bishop's reactions and feelings. His knowledge of the episcopal office and the resulting responsibility was not gathered from books on these subjects. It would really be desirable that every nuncio be given the opportunity to have the personal experience of running a diocese. So the reports of Nuncio Muench to the Holy See, his suggestions, his decisions and provisions were inspired by his personal experience, and also his handing on of instructions from authority to the bishops was done accordingly. If he deemed it necessary, he would submit to the Holy See in all humility new pertinent points to consider and he continued to ask for renewed consideration and study.

"He had an unlimited fidelity and filial devotion to the Holy Father and the Holy See. His unassuming, simple manner, his formation and experience as a residential bishop did not hurt his mission as nuncio. On the contrary, it proved to be an advantage for the Holy See to have made use of the services and abilities of this man, sent by Providence. The Catholic people of Germany, loving the representative of the Holy Father, were most grateful to Pius XII for leaving Muench with them."

2. Interview with Father Eberhard Welty, O.P., Walberberg bei Koeln, 18 October 1963. Muench was interested in the social science institute conducted by the Dominicans at Walberberg, visited there, had conversations with Welty, and wrote the introduction to Welty's volume *Social Catechism* which was used widely in German Catholic circles.

3. Monsignor Alberto Giovannetti, his first Italian assistant in Germany, faced this fact realistically in an article on Muench in *L'Osservatore Romano* of 15 February 1963:

"Muench's thoughts about his lack of preparation for tasks reaching far beyond the administration of a diocese did not grow in him from lack of courage. He always accepted his responsibilities with apostolic zeal. These thoughts arose from a deep humility, from a rigid sense of duty, from an awareness he always possessed that some day he must give an account to God. But it was just this spiritual depth which enabled him to accept the wishes of the Holy See. He had chosen as a maxim of his life; *factus obediens et paratus semper doceri.*

"The diffidence of Muench originated from his humble opinion of himself . . . In his new service he decided to learn. From the very beginning he requested that his collaborators teach him at once and on a large scale how to communicate with the curia and later, as nuncio, the diplomatic protocol, the history of the Church under the Nazi regime, the implications and meanings of the *Reichskonkordat* and the concordats with the *Laender*, the duties and limitations of the nunciature in Germany. As he did not consider it fitting for himself to be only the signer of the reports written in Italian, he started requesting that the originals be made in one of the languages he knew. But that was not enough for him. Although he knew perfectly English and German, and had a good mastery of French, at the age of fifty-seven he started studying Italian. He obtained two books: one large English-Italian grammar Manzoni's classic, *I Promessi Sposi*. In the grammar the reading exercises told of a trip which led to the discovery of *Bel Paese* by an imaginative group of American tourists led by a not less imaginative but polite Miss Fontana. How many times did he, Father Zeiger and the author run up and down and across the sunny peninsula with the tourists as we sat by the fireplace while a cold wind was blowing down the Taunus during the long winter evenings. We would have preferred to be somewhere else but the bishop used to ask with such a gracious delicacy that we always stayed until he bid us 'good night' and went to the chapel for an examination of conscience. Miss Fontana became more and more a symbol of perseverance among us, she spoke at the table as an exercise in Italian, German and English for all of us, and sometimes in Polish for our young servant."

4. Interview with Father Robert Leiber, S.J., Rome, 18 November 1963.

5. Interview with Cardinal Josef Frings, Rome, 21 November 1963. Frings also commented on Rolf Hochhut's play *Der Stellvertreter*: "It really is a phenomenon that this play should find such wide interest and that it is still of such interest despite the contradictions and publications against it. The play does have weak passages. It is by no means a masterpiece. It is a hit play, without doubt, but it does not have any psychological development. Whoever knew Pius XII also realizes that great injustice is done to his personality by picturing him as he is in this play. And it is a terrible ingratitude of the Germans toward him. But that attracts attention. Young people do not know those years from their own experience; they did not know Hitler. The people in their twenties have no memory of Hitler. The past is forgotten already; eighteen years have gone by.

"In this connection I know a good joke. The rumor spread that the German bishops would no longer insist on the use of the German language in the liturgy for if they went ahead with the vernacular they would be forced to say 'Hochhut' for *mitra* and "Stellvertreter' for *pileolus*."

Heinrich Koeppler, secretary general of the Central Committee of German Catholics, and Dr. Maria A. Lueckers of the Central Committee said in an interview at Bad Godesberg, 13 October 1963: "After the war the Catholic and Evangelical Churches met with an overwhelming amount of trust because they were the only institutions for all Germans to see which survived National Socialism in some measure and which kept spiritual sanity. The fact that after the war this confidence in the churches was never shaken when all other influential sources and institutions, all of them in some way or other involved with National Socialism, completely broke down, now shows some negative results. Nowadays young historians discover that even the Church did not stand up unflinchingly like a marble block against National Socialism, but that the Church, too, especially during the first years of National Socialism here and there tried to evade martyrdom, to find some basis for coexistence with it. Of course, not all that is said in this new historical literature is historically correct. However, it is true that some bishops in 1933 did not at once recognize the full scope of criminality inherent in National Socialism. They judged that this new movement was rather unbalanced but still a political movement, and that it could surely be brought under control and develop a sense of responsibility once it was entrusted with the government. This interpretation was rather widespread, and it explains why in some instances efforts were made to establish a legal situation with the help of some kind of Catholic treaty or concordat, in particular since the National Socialists emphasized their recognition of what they called a 'positive Christianity'.

"But this holds true only for the first years. After two or three years there was no more uncertainty about the true nature of National Socialism. All German Catholics who lived through the years after 1935–36 will always remember the definite unyielding stand the Catholic Church took, and from these later years the rightful reputation of the churches as a bulwark against National Socialism can be understood. The churches were the only public institution in Germany that withstood National Socialism. I would say that it is wrong to judge the attitude of the Church toward National Socialism solely from her position of uncertainty and bewilderment in 1933–34.

"There were bishops, and in particular leaders of Catholic lay organizations, who, from the very start, insisted that it was impossible to co-operate with National Socialism. But there were others who believed that the risk could and should be taken to find some *modus vivendi* with them. After 1935 discussions on this point had completely ceased.

"The Catholic Church did not openly confess having been guilty as the Protestant Church did after the war. The formulation of the Protestant Church certainly could not have been accepted by the Catholic Church. Instead the Church tried to make the lesson fruitful for a future which had been learned with so much suffering during the time of National Socialism. I do think that honest efforts have been made to draw the right consequences of the past experience, and that the accusation, heard sometimes in our days, does not have any justification."

6. During the negotiations for the establishment of the new diocese of Essen the nuncio kept in contact with the three bishops involved, informed them of each step and asked for their consent or recommendations. Muench told the bishops that the division of a diocese was not always done this way in the United States. He said that a bishop, especially of a small diocese, could wake up in the morning and find a letter informing him that part of his diocese had been taken away and given to a new bishop. With a laugh he added that small people have to take it as it comes.

When Muench first came to Germany there was prolonged discussion among the occupying powers concerning French demands that the Saar be detached either politically or economically from Germany and internationalized or attached to France. One of the first problems he faced in 1947–48 was to study the relationship of the Saar territory to the Diocese of Trier. If the *Saargebiet* was separated from the Diocese of Trier a new diocese would have to be erected in the Saar territory. Members of the apostolic mission made their own investigations on the scene while Muench asked the advice of the German bishops. He also paid the first of many visits to Maria Laach Abbey to consult with Abbot Basilius Ebel, O.S.B., concerning the question. Ebel informed him that it would be, in his judgment, a political and ecclesiastical regression if the Saar were detached from Germany. Since the large majority of the people were German, the new ordinary of a separate diocese in the Saar would have to be German. Since the question of what would happen to the Saar was an open one, it would be harmful to make a move at that time. Besides, the diocese of Trier depended upon the Saar territory for the majority of its vocations to the priesthood and religious life. After all the information was in, Muench recommended to the Vatican that no new diocese be established in the Saar because of the indefinite political situation and because of the Saar's integral part in Trier's development. The matter was dropped as was the demand for separation of the Saar from Germany when Chancellor Adenauer successfully negotiated concessions to France and the return of the Saar to Germany on 1 January 1956. Cf. Interview with Abbot Basilius Ebel, O.S.B., Abtei Maria Laach, 10 October 1963.

7. Koeppler, *op. cit.*

8. Interview with Ambassador Frants Hvass, Bonn, 18 October 1963.

9. Interview with Mrs. Erika Pappritz, Bad Godesberg, 17 October 1963.
Monsignor Hack commented: "Only with horror, truly with horror, would Muench go to those festive diplomatic dinners. He went because it was his duty. Once a year each ambassador gave a reception and a dinner to which the nuncio was obliged to go. As more and more states sent ambassadors to Germany this became quite a burden. It really is a good sign that the representatives of other nations value so much the presence of the papal representative on their festive days. It was always noted whether the nuncio was present, which of the federal ministers took part, etc. These were obligations he could not forego in the interest of the Holy See, but they were strenuous and they fatigued him. Naturally, these festivities, according to protocol, consumed much of his time, month after month. But these occasions also offered him many opportunities to meet important people." Cf. Hack, *op. cit.*

10. "After these receptions the archbishop saw to it that all who had in any way been engaged in the preparation and execution behind the scenes received gifts from him. He came down after the receptions and visited with the men of the police force who had been directing the incoming and departing traffic. He insisted that these men have dinner at the nunciature and the nuncio would sit with them, ask them about their families and offer them cigars. He showed

genuine kindness and friendliness to the workers in the kitchen. One of the older cooks from a large hotel in Bonn who helped on these occasions remarked: 'We are always eager to help cook at the nunciature because here we are not treated as servants but as human beings'." Interview with Sister Berthilla Pertzborn, O.S.B., cook, and the community of sisters at the nunciature, Bad Godesberg, 10 March 1964.

Heinz Reuter, editor of Deutschland-Union-Dienst (DUD), stated in an interview on 12 October 1963: "As often as we were with Muench we never had the impression that he was a diplomat of the classical school, neither in his behavior nor in his whole being, let alone a papal diplomat. Papal diplomats have the reputation of being particularly reserved and inaccessible. I have met papal diplomats who were inaccessible but who were not cold or indifferent once the other person had penetrated the barrier, but that usually was very difficult. Surely there are good reasons for this behavior; great discretion is needed in such a position. Without doubt, Muench observed this discretion as much as any other high papal diplomat, and even more. But he understood how to combine this with an informal, friendly sociability, always disposed to good humor and witty remarks."

11. The nuncio in preparing these addresses first sketched his own ideas in English and then had the whole translated into German by one of the staff. He regularly consulted with German experts about background material for his formal papers. Muench placed confidence in the Catholic journalist, Max Jordan, foreign correspondent of N.B.C. and N.C.W.C., whom he consulted often. One of the memorable occasions for the archbishop in Germany was when he ordained Jordan to the priesthood for the diocese of Fargo in 1951, when Dr. Jordan was fifty-seven years old. Later Father Jordan joined the Archabbey of Beuron as Father Placid and continued to write on German Catholic developments. His book, *Beyond All Fronts* (Milwaukee: Bruce Publishing Company, 1944), provides a chronicle of German developments during the first and second world wars.

Nuncio Muench's articles and addresses were clear and detailed but generally not strikingly original. The Germans noticed his use of a nineteenth-century vocabulary and phrasing and that his statements lost something in translation. Nor was the nuncio a distinguished orator. When he delivered a sermon with a clear idea he was most successful. He found it difficult, as do most diplomats, to deliver an address before other diplomats. He always read from a manuscript. The gift of words was not his; the source of his contacts, success and strength was his personal warmth.

Journalists, particularly, found that they could talk with him at any time and that only a telephone call was needed to arrange an appointment. Heinz Reuter stated: "The atmosphere was always relaxed and did not even change when, as is bound to happen with journalists, indiscreet or delicate questions were asked. I suppose he had learned in the United States how to remain unperturbed by this. He either gave some hint that for this or that reason it was not opportune to discuss the subject, or else he would talk about it openly and then appeal to our sense of honor and responsibility not to publish anything about the discussion. As far as I know, the journalists never let him down; the agreement was always kept. Not once did I witness a break of confidence. It was obvious that Muench had trusted his partners in the discussion, and that he took for granted that the same trust was given in return."

12. The German people were attracted to the nuncio because of his love of children. During the first years he used to stand at the entrance gate of the nunciature and watch the St. Martin's parade of children on the evening of November 11. Carrying lanterns the children passed from house to house singing the story of St. Martin. Archbishop Muench at the gate questioned them about St. Martin and his giving of half his clothes to the needy. He would say: 'Look at me. I, too, am a bishop.' Then he would fill their pockets with candies and cakes. On Low Sunday, the traditional first communion day in Germany, he would stand on his balcony at the *Turmhof* and watch the procession of the children with their pastor, parents, flags, banners and bands pass by. He would wave to them and bless them. The children all waited for the nuncio to greet them and distribute presents to them. Muench in later years withdrew more and more from these contacts as his health began to fail.

The nuncio regularly took walks along the Rhine in the earlier years and talked with people as he passed. He would check his opinions with those of the people he met on these walks, joke with them and try to find out what they were thinking. He enjoyed especially these relaxed conversations. The Germans of Bad Godesberg still talk about the pious, unassuming, humble priest and bishop who was warmhearted and interested in the well-being of all he met. In 1953 one of the poor old men who regularly received meals at the nunciature met the nuncio on the road near the Rhine and, not recognizing him because he was dressed unassumingly in black street clothes said: "Gruess Gott, Herr Pfarrer." Muench thanked him and lifted his hat. Later the man came to the nunciature and excitedly apologized because he had not recognized the nuncio. Muench laughed and answered: "But I am really a pastor."

13. At one of the major celebrations in Saint Peter's Basilica, Rome, during the Holy Year of 1950 Bishop Muench commented to Monsignor Montini: "I see the honorary seats filled with deserving and eminent people. May I ask where the honorary seats are for the working people, for our Catholic workers' unions, for our good people who keep and defend the faith and the Holy See in most difficult circumstances?" Montini was impressed with this question and jotted it down. Later this suggestion was heeded on several occasions and put into practice.

14. The assistants sent by the Secretariat of State included Monsignor Ottavio De Liva, 1950–54, who went on to Holland; Monsignor Guido Del Mestri, 1953–59, who was appointed apostolic delegate at Nairobi, Kenya, on 5 October 1959, presently stationed in Mexico; Monsignor Bruno B. Heim, 1954–1961, presently apostolic delegate to the Scandinavian countries at Copenhagen; Monsignor Opilio Rossi, 1948–53, who became nuncio to Ecuador, Chile and presently Austria.

Archbishop Muench consecrated Rossi a titular archbishop at Piacenza on 27 December 1953 and delivered his first Italian sermon on that occasion. Monsignor Paolo Mosconi, presently apostolic nuncio in Madagascar, came to the nunciature in 1959.

15. On Ascension Thursday, 14 May 1953, Archbishop Muench prepared a letter to his mother which he placed in his files to be sent if he preceded her in death. He wrote:

Dear Mother,

In his abundant clemency God has deigned to call me to his eternal home. Together with me you will give thanks to him for this merciful favor. For, by death he opens up the gates to his eternal kingdom that we may take in possession the promised heritage with its unfading joys. We Christians have the firm, unshakable conviction that death itself, by Christ's redemptive work, became for us a gift of God's love. Filled with such thoughts, you will not mourn and shed tears for me.

With a loving heart I thank you, my Mother, who gave life to me, for all the good you showered on me with loving care and dedication. With many sacrifices you saw to it that I, your first-born, would get a good education, first in our Catholic home, then in St. Boniface's school, and finally, in St. Francis Seminary. For this I once again offer you a 'Vergelt's Gott', for by this education I became what I am now: a priest forever according to the Order of Melchisedec.

In particular I want to thank you for the good example you gave me as a truly pious mother. On all my ways it always served me as incentive to dedicate myself totally to the service of God. May God reward you abundantly for the support of your daily prayers and sacrifices that you gave me as priest, bishop, and, last but not least, as representative of the Holy Father in Germany.

In my last will I have made provision to send you an adequate sum every month for your support. Your wealth are your children; you have always loved them, and they will always love you.

As you did throughout my life, so also now do at my death: give me your prayers, dear Mother. Lord, be merciful to me, a poor sinner.

I take my longing with me to eternity to meet you there again in the community of saints.

And I send you my blessing from eternity, asking the dear Lord to grant you much joy among your children and grandchildren throughout the years that he will keep you on this earth.

God the Father and God the Son and God the Holy Spirit bless you now and in all eternity. Amen.

Your ever grateful son,

† ALOIS

16. Father David J. Boyle, chancellor, wrote cheerful letters full of news about the household, local happenings, the weather and the crops. The archbishop looked forward to Boyle's letters since he was an alumnus of Saint Francis Seminary, Milwaukee, who had come to Fargo under Muench and who always buoyed him up by his good spirits. Boyle and Smith exchanged letters in which they en-

couraged each other with light talk. Smith told Boyle that he should come to dinner with them at the nunciature: "Knoedel, sauerkraut, apfelstrudel und Rheinwein; I'd rather have a good fried pork chop and strawberry shortcake with whipped cream oozing all over the dish."

17. Archbishop Muench strongly supported the drive during 1949–50 for a new Shanley High School in Fargo. When the pledges exceeded $400,000, he sent a grateful message of congratulations to all who worked and donated to the cause. He personally pledged $5,000 to the drive over a three-year period. This was a major sacrifice for him since he received a monthly salary as nuncio of $109. He tried during all the years in Germany to pay his own way through donations and gifts of friends and in this way not be in any way a burden on the Holy See. Food, clothing and cars as well as spending money were donated by friends from Fargo.

When Bishops Muench and Dworschak made the *ad limina* visit to Rome in November of 1949 it was the auxiliary's first report to Pius XII. Muench had been with the Pope for an hour and a half discussing German affairs and then Dworschak came in for a review of the Fargo report. Pius noticed at once that two parishes in Fargo had contributed $400,000 for the first unit of Shanley High School. His eyes lit up and he said: "The American people are very generous. Is the high school for boys and girls?" When Bishop Dworschak answered that it was a shadow fell over the Pope's features. He was strongly opposed to coeducation beyond the primary grades. Dworschak tried to explain that it was a choice of one high school or none, that two parishes were building it at great sacrifice. Pius said nothing and changed the subject. Afterwards Muench said to Dworschak: "You were putting your foot in and I couldn't interfere. The Pope effusively congratulates those bishops who build separate schools."

NOTES TO CHAPTER SEVEN

1. Cf. Igino Cardinale, *Le Saint-Siège et La Diplomatie* (Brussels: Desclée et Cie, 1962).

2. Muench to E. J. O'Donnell, S.J., Bad Godesberg, 28 June 1956.

3. Muench also suggested to his Milwaukee friends that Adenauer, like many Germans who avidly read Karl May and James Fenimore Cooper, was most interested in the American Indians. During a public reception for the chancellor a group of Indians from the Consolidated Tribes of American Indians burst in upon the formal gathering with a dance and a ten minute ceremony making Adenauer a chief under the title of "Layadaholu" or "wise leader of many."

Adenauer was genuinely pleased, enthusiastically donned his headdress and smoked the peace pipe although he was not a smoker.

4. Koeppler, *op. cit.*

5. Hack, *op. cit.*

6. The other six cardinals-designate were Augustin Bea, German Jesuit confessor of Pius XII and biblical scholar; William Heard, Scottish dean of the Roman Rota Tribunal; Arcadio Larraona, Spanish secretary of the Congregation of Religious; Gustavo Testa, Italian nuncio to Switzerland; Paolo Marella, Italian nuncio to France; Francesco Morano, Italian secretary to the Ecclesiastical Tribunal.

7. Reuter, *op. cit.*

8. Muench wrote a moving letter to the German bishops on 5 December 1959 in which he thanked them for the fraternal charity they had shown him from the beginning of his mission among them. Their warm and ready support, their loyalty and devotion to the Holy See, the strong proclamation of the faith he had come to admire in German dioceses — were memories he would live with for the rest of his life. He would never forget the beleaguered clergy and people of East Germany before the Lord. He was so sorry to have to leave and wanted them to know how much his heart longed to express adequately how much he admired them before he placed them back in the hands of the Vicar of Christ.

9. Thirteen years earlier, at the 1946 ceremonies elevating thirty-two cardinals, which Muench had attended in the party of Cardinal Stritch, Clement Cardinal von Galen, bishop of Muenster was assigned San Bernardo alle Terme as his titular church. When the bishop of Fargo learned that Cardinal von Galen did not have funds to pay for the *cappa magna* part of a cardinal's wardrobe, Muench asked that the bill be sent to him. He had never met von Galen, but he wanted to express his admiration for that noble cardinal's opposition to Hitler. Little did he realize at the time that he would soon be in Germany as papal representative, or that he would himself be assigned the same Roman church as a cardinal that von Galen held. It was a moment of many memories for Muench.

10. Sister Veronica, S.D.S., cook at Salvator Mundi Hospital, Rome, stated in an interview on 18 November 1963: "Cardinal Muench said to me: 'Did you ever get used to people not being punctual here?' I told him I had to in the course of the twelve years I have been here since I left Germany. In the beginning I sometimes thought I couldn't take it anymore. When I ordered sausages one day they would ask how many, and then the day after tomorrow they would finally bring the sausages. But I had no sausages for lunch on the previous day. The cardinal laughed and said: 'That is even worse than are my hour and a half of waiting for the rest of the cardinals.' He said his mother had taught him always to be on time and he brought this habit from his home in the United States to Germany. Adenauer, too, was always on time, he said. I replied: 'Well, he had to or the others would have taken his job.' He had a good laugh at that."

11. On inclement days Muench would go to the chapel through a corridor which led past the kitchen. He always stopped and looked to see who was around

so he could talk and joke with them. The cardinal enjoyed small talk with the workers that involved no decisions. He would ask Sister Veronica, who was busy preparing the patients' breakfasts, if she had taken a cup of coffee yet. "Have a cup of coffee and all will be easier for you," he would repeatedly say, but she would reply that she could not until he returned. Muench especially enjoyed this jovial and kind nun whose humor reminded him so much of his days in Germany.

He always wanted to talk about Germany. Sister Veronica continued to encourage him to eat more and he would assure her that he would eat a big breakfast. In Germany he observed that Adenauer ate very little, even less than he did, of all the delicacies that were served at an evening banquet. "Why do you think Adenauer ate so little," he asked? Sister Veronica replied: "Well, Eminence, in the morning. . . ." "Oh yes," he immediately said, "I know what you are going to say. The Germans eat in the morning like an emperor, at noon like a king, and in the evening like a beggar. That is what Adenauer did and that is what I am going to do in the future: a good breakfast, half the amount for lunch, and a small supper."

On another occasion he brought with him a beautifully hand painted and bound book of devotions given him by the Benedictine community of nuns at Eichstaett. "Can you make something like that for me, Sister Veronica?" he joked. "No, Eminence," she retorted, "I can only cook and serve your meals. More I did not learn." Then he answered gently and with a laugh: "But I think you have learned the best. I even prefer it to this beautiful book because you keep me alive." And he would disappear down the corridor in good spirits. The hospital personnel soon learned that Muench would always respond to simple and uncomplicated conversation.

12. Details of Cardinal Muench's last illness were supplied through interviews with Father Raymond Lessard, Rome, 1–5 December 1963; and with Sister Valeria, S.D.S., Rome, 18 November 1963. Father Lessard was the cardinal's secretary in Rome and Sister Valeria his special nurse.

13. During the slow progress over the years of arteriosclerosis, Cardinal Muench was often irritated but seldom showed it. He would just abruptly break off a conversation or leave the room. It was obvious that he was trying to control himself. Father Lessard stated that only once in the two years he served him in Rome did Muench lose his patience with his secretary. This incident occurred when Lessard answered a personal phone call in Muench's room and talked for some time in a loud voice. After the conversation was over Muench said: "Is it necessary for you to talk so loudly?" But almost immediately the cardinal regretted his correction of the young priest and asked his pardon. Noise of any kind particularly bothered him and he unconsciously reacted to it.

14. "Salvator Mundi Informationes," Special Edition No. 23, *Salvator Mundi Quarterly*, IX (April, 1962), 7–10.

INDEX

German Catholicism, postwar, 66

German churchmen, de-nazification program, 141

German churches, liaison with Military Government, 133

German conflicts, 4, 10

German Council of Christians and Jews, 120

German, diaspora statistics, 184, 185

Germans, 1952 emigration, 181

German Jewish refugees, 121

German liturgical movement, 219, 220, 222

German parties, support "Basic Law", 156

German people, American justice among, 148

German people, prejudice toward, 121

German population, increased by expellees, 171

German Protestants, generosity of, 175

German religious bodies, secular functions of, 132

Germans, Muench's first impressions upon, 113

Germany,
    aid organizations, 94, 95, 96, 98, 99
    American policies, 120
    Catholicism in postwar, 185, 186
    census, (1950), 181, 182
    Church position re-evaluated, 103
    Church and State, 130
    currency reform, 103
    de-nazification consequences, 142
    Department of State, 66
    depression, 102, 206
    devaluation of mark, 101
    devastation of dwellings, 171
    diaspora, 106–107
    dioceses of, 68
    displaced Jews, 160
    displaced persons (statistics), 160, 161, 167, 168
    displaced priests, 168
    ecclesiastical-legal situation, 201
    economic revival, 103
    educational system, 14
    emigrants to U.S., 3
    expellees and refugees, 160
    first apostolic mission, 53
    free elections, 141
    freedom of worship, 120
    growth of interfaith work, 139, 140
    independent church in free society, 139
    internal affairs, 120
    lasting reform, 120
    man in modern, 107
    mission land, 108
    new position of religion, 104
    partitions, 68
    pioneer in ecumenical movement, 223
    postwar church-state relations, 227
    postwar issues, 109, 170
    refugee problem, 176
    relief work, 55
    restoration motivation, 98
    school reform, 123
    school systems, 129, 210, 211
    terroristic pressures, 228
    theological seminaries, 120
    trials of war criminals, 145
    war states, 93

Gillen, John Lewis, 15

Gilligan, Msgr. Francis J., 28

Giovanetti, Msgr. Alberto, 55, 56, 59, 64, 66, 90, 91, 114, 209, 267

Gleason, Neal, 33

Gleichschaltung, churches' resistance to, 138

Glennon, Cardinal John J., 51

Globke, Dr. Hans, 212

Gockeln, Josef, 238

Good Samaritan Guild, 22

Góral, Dr. Boleslaus, 11

Grand Rapids, diocese of, 23

Great Falls, diocese of, 43

Green Bay, diocese of, 10, 36, 44

Gregorian University, 54

Grellinger, Bishop John B, 243

Griffin, Bishop Wm. R., 31

Griffiths, Msgr. James H., 61, 131

Muench, (cont.)

Muench, (cont.)

The biography of Cardinal Aloisius Muench has been designed by Frank Kacmarcik and is set in Linotype Granjon. The paper is Warrens Olde Style bound in Bancroft Kennett. The book was composed, printed, and bound by North Central Publishing Company of Saint Paul, Minnesota and completed on the twenty-third day of April in the year of the Lord one thousand nine hundred and sixty-nine.

Berlin.
Sonntag, Aug 4. 1946.

Liebe Mutter!

Die zwei Briefe von Terry, July 11 u. 18
haben mir grosse Freude gebracht. Gott sei Dank,
dass Dr. K. die Ursache deiner Krankheit gefunden
hat und dass er mit den neuen Pillen dir helfen
kann. Der Goiter ist sicherlich der Grund deiner
Nervösität gewesen, und auch der Ursache deiner
Sorgengedanken. Ich bin sicher, dass du jetzt
besser werden wirst. Gott wird dir sicherlich dazu
seinen Segen geben.

Seit gestern sind B. Bertke und ich in Berlin.
Wir sprachen eine Stunde lang mit Gen. Clay,
amerikanischen Militär-Kommandanten
amerikanischen Zone über verschiedene kirchli-
legenheiten, die das Interesse der
ffen. Wir kommen zu guten Er-
gut, dass ich nach Deutschland
einem amerikanischen Bischof
Tochen, und die Aussprache
Zweifel werde ich den
esenheit viel helfen
de ich in Fulda